Krishna Bista, *Founding Editor*
Morgan State University, USA

Chris R. Glass, *Editor-In-Chief*
Boston College, USA

Vol. **12** No **2** Nov **2022**

JOURNAL OF INTERNATIONAL STUDENTS

A Quarterly Publication on International Education

Access this journal online at http://ojed.org/jis

Learn about the 12(2) cover art, *Knowledge Structure* by Marco Cianfanelli (South Africa), an exploration of human progress in relation to our planet. Drawing a parallel between tree and the human brain, *Knowledge Structure* explores the systems and structures of nature's organic forms. As our viewpoint changes, the tree morphs into a human brain, the trunk becoming vertical conduits to the ground.

Disclaimer

Facts and opinions published in *Journal of International Students* (JIS) express solely the opinions of the respective authors. Authors are responsible for their citing of sources and the accuracy of their references and bibliographies. The editors cannot be held responsible for any lacks or possible violations of third parties' rights.

Special Issues

Special Issue | English
Internationalization for an Uncertain Future:
Emerging Conversations in Critical Internationalization Studies (2021)
Special Issue Co-Editors:
Sharon Stein, University of British Columbia, Canada
Dale M. McCartney, University of the Fraser Valley, Canada

Special Issue | English
Reflection and Reflective Thinking (2020)
Special Issue Co-Editors:
Georgina Barton, University of Southern Queensland, Australia
Mary Ryan, Macquarie University, Australia

Special Issue | *Bahasa Indonesia*
International Students and COVID-19 (2020)
Special Issue Co-Editors:
Handoyo Puji Widodo, King Abdulaziz University, Saudi Arabia
Sandi Ferdiansyah, Institut Agama Islam Negeri, Indonesia and
Lara Fridani, Universitas Negeri Jakarta, Indonesia

Special Issue | *Chinese*
International Students in China (2020)
Special Issue Co-Editors:
Mei Tian and Genshu Lu
Xi'an Jiaotong University, China

Special Issue | English
Fostering Successful Integration and Engagement
Between Domestic and International Students (2018)
Special Issue Co-Editors:
CindyAnn Rose-Redwood and Reuben Rose-Redwood
University of Victoria, Canada

Special Issue | English
Role of Student Affairs in International Student
Transition and Success (2017)
Special Issue Co-Editors:
Christina W Yao, University of Nebraska-Lincoln, US
Chrystal A. George Mwangi, University of Massachusetts Amherst, US

Special Issue | English
International Student Success (2016)
Special Issue Editor: *Rahul Choudaha, DrEducation, US*

Emerson is a campus without borders.

We believe producing inspired work requires a global perspective, which is why the Emerson experience isn't limited to one city or even one country. As a global hub of arts and communication in higher education, we strive to provide our students, faculty, and staff with opportunities to connect and collaborate across countries and cultures. From our Global Pathways Programs to our castle in the Netherlands and beyond, we offer more than opportunities for students to study abroad—we provide access to enriching cultural experiences that will guide you on the path to becoming a global citizen.

Our newest global degree programs:

- **Global BA in Business of Creative Enterprises: Australia**
  Our accelerated Global BA in Business of Creative Enterprises (BCE) is powered by a rich management-focused curriculum; immerses students in the life of companies and organizations across two continents through intensive internship programs; and spans venues in **Sydney**, **Boston**, and **Los Angeles**.

- **Global BFA in Film Art**
  Our intercontinental joint Global BFA in Film Art spans venues in **Paris**, **the Netherlands**, and **Boston**. In this one-of-a-kind degree program, students will not only study visual and media arts in the City of Light itself, but will also receive a foundation in the liberal arts and French language.

Learn more at **emerson.edu/global**.

Academic Book Series

Call for Book Proposals

The STAR Scholars Book Series seeks to explore new ideas and best practices related to international student mobility, study abroad, exchange programs, student affairs from the US and around the world, and from a wide range of academic fields, including student affairs, international education, and cultural studies. STAR Scholars publishes some titles in collaboration with Routledge (Taylor & Francis), Springer, Palgrave Macmillan, Open Journals in Education (OJED), Journal of International Students, and other university presses. Scholars interested in contributing a book to our current and future book series are invited to submit a brief proposal directly via this form. All chapters will go through the standard review process before a decision is made. https://www.ojed.org/index.php/gsm/Series

Series Editors
Dr. Chris R. Glass & Dr. Krishna Bista

For questions and submission, email at Krishna.bista@morgan.edu

---

Recently Published Books

1. *Chinese Students and the Experience of International Doctoral Study in STEM*
2. *Developing Intercultural Competence in Higher Education*
3. *International Student Mobility to and from the Middle East*
4. *Inequalities in Study Abroad and Student Mobility*
5. *The Experiences of International Faculty in Institutions of Higher Education*
6. *International Students at US Community Colleges*
7. *Critical Perspectives on Equity and Social Mobility in Study Abroad*
8. *Online Teaching, Learning and Virtual Experiences in Global Higher Education*
9. *International Student Support and Engagement in Higher Education*
10. *Impact of COVID-19 on Global Student Mobility and Higher Education*
11. *Global Higher Education During COVID-19: Policy, Society, and Technology*
12. *COVID-19 and Higher Education in the Global Context*
13. *Reimagining Mobility in Higher Education*
14. *Cross-Cultural Narratives: Stories and Experiences of International Students*
15. *Reimagining Internationalization and International Initiatives at HBCUs*
16. *Delinking, Relinking, and Linking Writing and Rhetorics*
17. *Global Footprints in Higher Education*

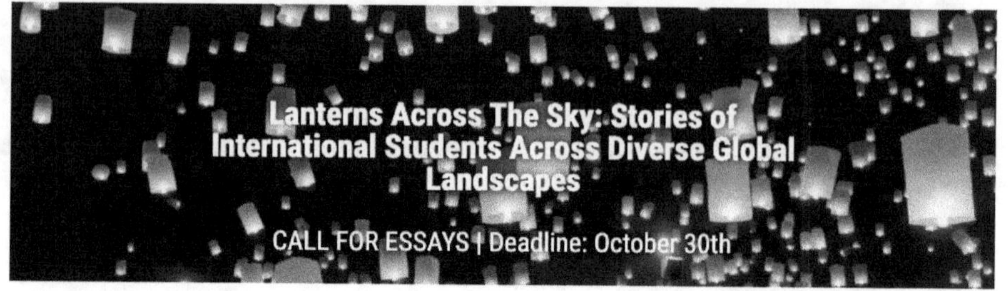

Call for Essays

Everyone has a memorable story of studying or working outside the country of birth. What is your story about studying overseas? What are your cross-cultural experiences from exchange programs or study abroad? Are you a current or former international student? Tell your stories of exploring the words, the world, and the wonders.

Essay Categories

International Student Experience (long-term/degree seeking programs/experiences)
Study Abroad / Exchange Program Experience (short-term/program experience)
Faculty/Staff Experience (International faculty, study abroad mentors, Fulbright scholars)

Languages

You can write your story/essay in any of the following eight languages: Arabic, Chinese, English, French, German, Hindi, Russian, Spanish

Essay Writing Suggestions

Share a story: Focus on moments, encounters, and experiences that shaped your journey as an international student. Tell a story that no one else could tell. Your story can be about friendship, service, freedom, discrimination, injustice, activism, belonging, family, courage, resilience, citizenship, academics, spirituality, parenthood, discovery, inclusion, self-discovery, growth, etc.

Tell your challenges and lessons. Flavor your writing with idioms and figures of speech from your language. Paint the picture. Be concrete about what you have seen in your travels, academic encounters, woes, and wows!

Format Requirements

A story or essay of 1000-1,500 words; Typed in 12-pt size, Times Roman font; double-spaced; 1-inch margins on all sides; includes page numbers. We accept Microsoft Word files only.

More guidelines and sample essays:

https://starscholars.org/lanterns-across-the-sky/

ISSN: 2162-3104 Print/ ISSN: 2166-3750 Online
© *Journal of International Students*
http://ojed.org/jis

Editorial Team

Founder/Executive Editor
Krishna Bista, Morgan State University, USA

Editor-in-Chief
Chris R. Glass, Boston College, USA

Senior Editor
Stephanie K. Kim, Georgetown University, USA

Special Issues Editor
Nelson Brunsting, Wake Forest University

Digital Production Team
Senior Copy Editor: *Joy Bancroft, Emporia State University*
Digital Production Editor, Xi *Lin, East Carolina University*
Editorial Assistant (Digital Production): *Sonali Kathuria, Boston College*

Digital Storytelling Team
Editor, Global Connections, *Györgyi Mihályi, Kent State University*
Director, Social Media: *Sarah Schiffecker, Texas Tech University*
Producer, Global Scholar Stories, *Asuka Ichikawa, Boston College*
Producer, Critical Conversations in International Education, *Mary Ann Bodine Al-Sharif, University of Alabama at Birmingham*

Asma Bashir, Beaconhouse National University (PK)
Sushma Basnet, Brunel University (UK)
Amir-Hossein Bayat, Saveh University of Medical Sciences (IR)
Bradley K Beecher, New Mexico State University (US)
Ibrahim Bicak, University of Texas at Austin (US) ◊
Galicia Blackman, University of Calgary (CA) ★
Mary Ann Bodine Al-Sharif, University of Alabama at Birmingham (US) ◊
Shihua Brazill, Montana State University (US)
Mandy Brunson, University of Delaware (US)
Janina Brutt-Griffler, University at Buffalo, The State University of New York (US)
Tram-Anh Bui, Brock University and Ho Chi Minh City University (VN)
Elif Cankaya, Oakwood University at Huntsville (US)
Heather Carmack, University of Alabama (US)
Loredana Carson, California Lutheran University (US)
Shanton Chang, University of Melbourne, Australia (AU)
Bo Chang, Ball State University (US)
Jun Mian Chen, Conestoga College (CA)
Kenneth Chen, University at Albany-SUNY (US)
Baoyan Cheng, University of Hawaii at Manoa (US) ◊
Prashanti Chennamsetti, Texas A&M University (US)
Porshe Chiles, Wake Forest University (US)
Hyun Jin Cho, Purdue University (US)
Courtney Collins, University of Nebraska-Lincoln (US)
John Connolly, University of Texas at Arlington (US)
Shasha Cui, University of Rochester (US)
Kim Dianne Curtin, University of Alberta (CA)
Kimberley Daly, George Mason University (US)
Benjamin Denga, University of Alberta (CA) ★
David Di Maria, University of Maryland - Baltimore County (US)
Dan Dickman, Ivy Tech Community College (US)
Trang Dinh, Rice University(US)
Dely Lazarte Elliot, University of Glasgow (UK)
Omolabake Fakunle, University of Edinburgh (UK)
Mehrdad Falavarjani, University of Saskatchewan (CA) ◊
Xumei Fan, University of South Carolina (US)
Rai Farrelly, University of Colorado - Boulder (US)
Barry Fass-Holmes, University California San Diego (US)
Sarah Fehrman, Purdue University (US)
Amy Fenning, Maryville University (US)
Cesar Augusto Ferrari Martinez, Universidade Federal de Pelotas (BR)
Christine Fiorite, University of Chicago (US) ◊
Steven Fraiberg, Purdue University (US)
Keri Freeman, Queensland University of Technology (AU)
Ann Frkovich, Concordia University Chicago (US)
Yan Gao, University of Victoria (CA)
Jaime Garcia, University of Queensland (AU)
Tiberio Garza, University of Nevada, Las Vegas (US)
Charles Gbollie, Central China Normal University (CN)
Lin Ge, University of Regina (CA)
Danielle Geary, Georgia Tech (US)
Chrystal A. George Mwangi, University of Massachusetts Amherst (US) ◊

Peggy Gesing, Eastern Virginia Medical School (US) ◊
Peter G. Ghazarian, Ashland University (US)
Bianca Gomez, York University (CA)
Ricardo Gonzalez-Carriedo, University of North Texas (US)
Adam Grimm, Michigan State University (US) ◊
Sarah Grosik, University of Pennsylvania (US)
Ning Guo, Saint Louis University (US)
Clarisse Halpern, Florida Gulf Coast University (US)
Karleah Harris, University of Arkansas at Pine Bluff (US)
Catherine Hartman, University of South Carolina (US) ★
Nigel Harwood, University of Sheffield (UK)
Ahdi Hassan,International Association for Technology (TR)
Xuewei He, The George Washington University (US) ◊
Niall Hegarty, St. John's University, United States (US)
Tang Tang Heng, National Institute of Education--Singapore (SG)
Elizabeth Margarita Hernández López, University of Guadalajara (MX)
Andrew Scott Herridge, The University of Southern Mississippi (US)
Sara Hosseini-Nezhad, Eötvös Loránd University (CA)
Ning Hou, St. Cloud State University (US)
Jennifer Hoyte, Florida Southern College (US)
Jing Hua, Troy University (US)
Rong Huang, University of Plymouth (US)
Graham Robert Huether, University of North Texas (US)
Ireena Nasiha Ibnu, Universiti Teknologi MARA(UiTM) (MY) ★
Irene Irudayam, Anna Maria College (US)
Polina Ivanova, Ritsumeikan University (JP)
Laura Jacobi, Minnesota State University at Mankato (US)
Xiushan Jiang, College of Charleston (US)
Shuiping Jiang, Clemson University (IE) ★
Li Jin, DePaul University (US)
Karin Johnson, Texas A&M University (US)
Christopher Johnstone, University of Minnesota (US)
Jae-Eun Jon, Hankuk University of Foreign Studies Seoul Campus (KR)
Alexander Jones, Wheaton College (US)
Jessika Jones, University of Houston (US)
Cebrail Karayigit, Pittsburg State University (US)
Sonali Kathuria, Wake Forest University (US)
Jacob Kelley, Auburn University (US)
Jamshed Khalid, Universiti Sains Malaysia (MY)
David Killick, Leeds Beckett University (UK)
Regine Lambrech, International Education Consulting (US)
Jiva Nath Lamsal, The University of Sydney (AU)
Marleny Leasa, Pattimura University (ID) ★
Sherrie Lee, Tertiary Education Commission (NZ)
Injung Lee, Purdue University Northwest (US)
Anke Li, The Pennsylvania State University (US)
Dan Li, University of North Texas (US)
Jason Li, Wichita State University (US)
Ching-Ching Lin, Touro College (US)
Yang Liu, Beijing Foreign Studies University (CN)
Charles Liu, Michigan State University (US)

Lin Ma, University of Bristol (UK) ★
Kyunghee Ma, University of South Carolina (College of Social Work) (US)
Yingyi Ma, syracuse university (US)
Marc Malone, The University of Kansas (US)
Catia Margarida da Cunha Marques, University of Minho (PT)
Nara M. Martirosyan, Sam Houston State University (US)
Blair Matthews, University of St Andrews (UK)
Elena Maydell, Massey University (NZ)
Dorothy Mayne, University of Illinois Urbana Champaign (US)
Abhijit Mazumdar, Mt. Enterprise High School (US)
Rachel McGee, Nagase/Speaking Partners (US)
Jon L. McNaughtan, Texas Tech University (US)
Megan Mischinski, Wake Forest University (US)
Chi Yun Moon, Texas A&M University (US)
Darlinda Pacheco Moreira, Universidade Aberta (PT)
Heba Mostafa, Saint Louis University (US)
Michael Mu, Queensland University of Technology (AU)
Amirul Mukminin, Jambi University (ID)
Doreen N. Myrie, Jackson State University (US)
Jasvir Kaur Nachatar Singh, La Trobe University (AU)
Atsushi Nagai, Hiroshima University (JP)
Nina Namaste, Elon University (US)
Steve Nerlich, Australian National University (AU)
Bao Trang Thi Nguyen, University of Foreign Languages, Hue University (VN)
Huong Thi Lan Nguyen, Swinburne University of Technology (AU)
Pii-Tuulia Nikula, Eastern Institute of Technology (NZ) ★
Per A. Nilsson, Umeå University (SE)
Yuanlu Niu, University of Arkansas (US)
Conor Nolan, National College of Ireland (IE) ★
Sarah Nutter, University of Victoria (CA) ★
Robert M O'Connell, University of Missouri (US)
Adesola Ogundimu, John Hopkins University (US)
Yakup Öz, Karamanoğlu Mehmetbey University (TR)
Emily-Marie Pacheco, University of Glasgow (UK)
Yolanda Palmer-Clarke, University of Saskatchewan (CA)
Pengfei Pan, Queensland University of Technology (AU) ★
Moses Glorino Rumambo Pandin, Universitas Airlangga (ID)
Astadi Pangarso, Brawijaya University, Telkom University (ID)
Melania Pantelich, Federation University (AU)
Satyanarayana Parayitam, University of Massachusetts Dartmouth (US)
Eunjeong Park, Sunchon National University (KR)
Jerry Parker, Southeastern Louisiana University (US) ◊
Reshma Parveen, University of Queensland (AU)
Kelly A. Pengelly, American University (US)
Bethany Peters, University of Minnesota (US)
Lien Pham, University of Technology Sydney (AU)
Thanh Pham, Monash University (AU)
Huong Le Thanh Phan, Deakin University (AU)
Gareth Phillips, University of Technology, Jamaica (JM)
Bright Phiri, Lovely Professional University (ZM)
Nattavud Pimpa, Mahidol University (TH)

Josef Ploner, University of Hull (UK)
India Plough, Michigan State University (US)
Surendra Pokhrel, Daito Bunka University (NP)
Senel Poyrazli, The Pennsylvania State University - Harrisburg (US)
Bambang Pratolo, Universitas Ahmad Dahlan (ID) ★
Maria Prikhodko, DePaul University (US)
Dana Rad, Aurel Vlaicu University of Arad (RO)
Sophia Glenyse Rahming, Florida State University (US) ◊
Namrata Rao, Liverpool Hope UNiversity (UK) ★
Andres F. Restrepo, Valdosta State University (SK)
Alexandra Reynolds, Université de Bordeaux (FR)
Maureen Rhoden, Independent Researcher (UK) ★
L. Erika Saito, National University (US)
Laura Schaffer Metcalfe, Mesa Community College (US)
Nathaniel H Schierman, Penn State University (US)
Jason Schneider, DePaul University (US)
Lleij Samuel Schwartz, Southern New Hampshire University (US)
Charles J Schwartz, University of Cincinnati (US)
Mary Ann Seow, Past National President of ISANA International Education Association (AU)
Noel L Shadowen, La Salle University (US)
SuYeong Shin, University of Iowa (US)
SuYeong Shin, University of Iowa/University of Utah (US)
Prabin Shrestha, Tri Chandra Multiple Campus (NP)
Anupma Singh, University of Wyoming (US)
Janice Smith, Morgan State Universityt (US)
Adem Soruc, The University of Bath (UK)
Garth Stahl, University of Queensland (AU)
David Starr-Glass, SUNY Empire State College (US) ◊
William Stewart, Hankuk University of Foreign Studies (KR)
Jennifer A. Strangfeld, California State University, Stanislaus (US)
Mengwei Su, Ohio University (US)
Yi Sun, University of Massachusetts Amherst (US)
Manca Sustarsic, University of Hawaii at Manoa (US) ★
Elena K. Taborda, University of Massachusetts Boston (US) ◊
Fujuan Tan, Morehead State University (US)
Bettina Teegen, University of Surrey in England (DE) ★
Eric Terzuolo, American University (US)
Carrie Anne Thomas, The Ohio State University (US) ◊
Mei Tian, Jiaotong University (CN)
Lu Tian, University of Northern Colorado (US)
Ethan Trinh, Georgia State University (US)
Linda Tsevi, University of Ghana (GH)
Siqi Tu, New York University Shanghai (CN)
Haijing Tu, Indiana State University (CA)
Mengwei Tu, East China University of Science and Technology (CN)
Mei-Ling Tung, Saint Louis University (US)
Kandy K. Turner, Widener University (US)
Lisa Unangst, Ohio University (US)
Faith Valencia-Forrester, Griffith University (AU)

Nicole D Vaux, Lindenwood University (US)
Jeanne-Marie Viljoen, University of South Australia (AU)
Louise Michelle Vital, Lesley University (US) ◊
Rong Wang, University of North Carolina at Charlotte (CN) ★
Xingchen Wang, Illinois State University (US)
Xin Wang, Baylor University (US)
Xinxin Wang, University of North Carolina at Chapel Hill (US)
Caroline Wekullo, Texas A&M University (US)
Zhenjie Weng, The Ohio State University (US) ★
Tsung-han Weng, University of Kansas (US)
Nancy Will, University of Washington Seattle (US)
Gloria Wong, Hong Kong University (HK) ★
Jon Woodend, James Cook University (AU) ★
Congcong Xing, Queensland University of Technology (AU) ★
Weiyan Xiong, Lingnan University Hong Kong (HK) ★
Yiying Xiong, Johns Hopkins University (US)
Xing Xu, Sichuan International Studies University (CN)
Jiayi Xu, University of Florida (US)
Fikri Yanda, Universitas Pendidikan Indonesia (ID)
Lili Yang, University of Oxford (UK)
Ruijin Yang, School of International Studies (CN) ◊
HyeJin Tina Yeo, University of Illinois Urbana Champaign (US)
Hyejin Yoon, University of Wisconsin-Milwaukee (US)
Jingran Yu, University of Manchester (CN)
Xi Yu, University of Minnesota-Twin Cities (US)
Roseline Jindori Yunusa Vakkai, De Rose Community Bridge and Holistic Health (US)
Fanyi Zeng, Wake Forest University (US)
Jie Zhang, Guangdong University of Finance (CN)
Xiaoqiao Zhang, Harvard University (US)
Ying Shan Doris Zhang, University of Alberta (CA)
Lin Zheng, University of Portsmouth (UK)

Recent Publications

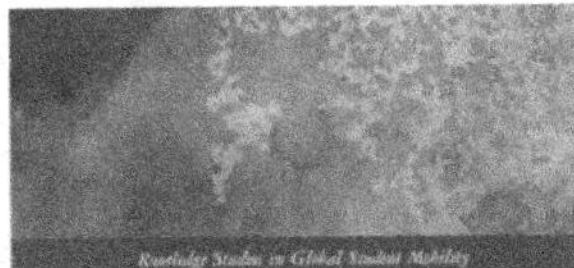

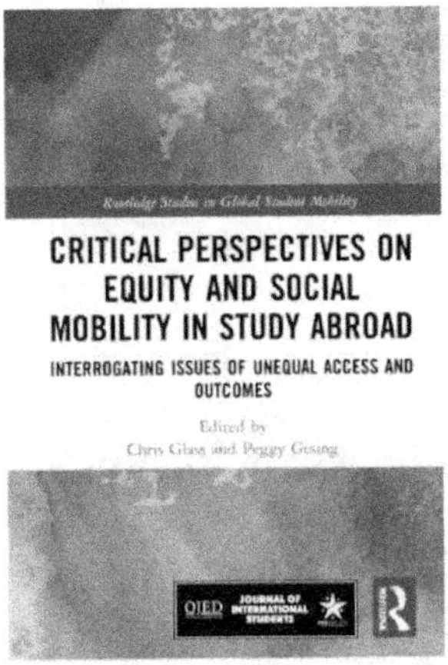
Routledge Studies in Global Student Mobility
CRITICAL PERSPECTIVES ON EQUITY AND SOCIAL MOBILITY IN STUDY ABROAD
INTERROGATING ISSUES OF UNEQUAL ACCESS AND OUTCOMES
Edited by
Chris Glass and Peggy Gesing

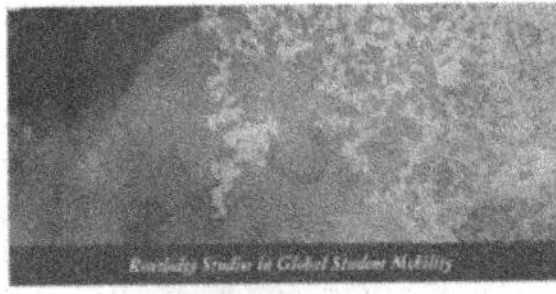

Routledge Studies in Global Student Mobility
INEQUALITIES IN STUDY ABROAD AND STUDENT MOBILITY
NAVIGATING CHALLENGES AND FUTURE DIRECTIONS
Edited by
Suzan Kommers and Krishna Bista

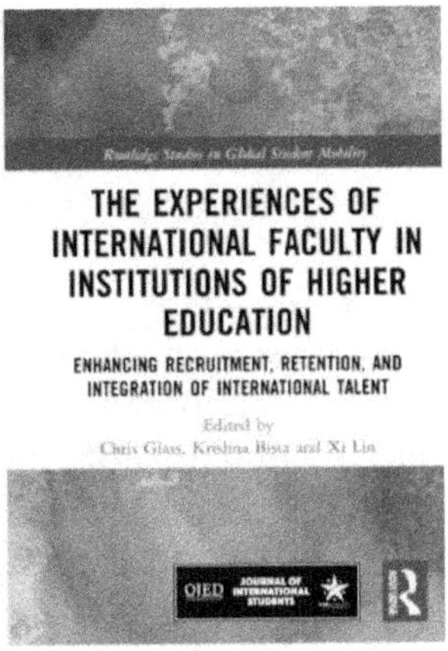

Routledge Studies in Global Student Mobility
THE EXPERIENCES OF INTERNATIONAL FACULTY IN INSTITUTIONS OF HIGHER EDUCATION
ENHANCING RECRUITMENT, RETENTION, AND INTEGRATION OF INTERNATIONAL TALENT
Edited by
Chris Glass, Krishna Bista and Xi Lin

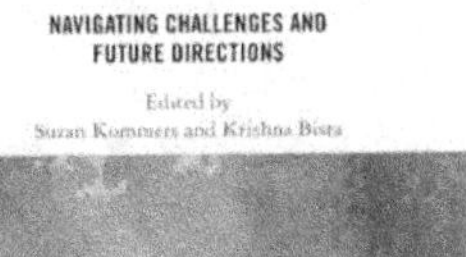

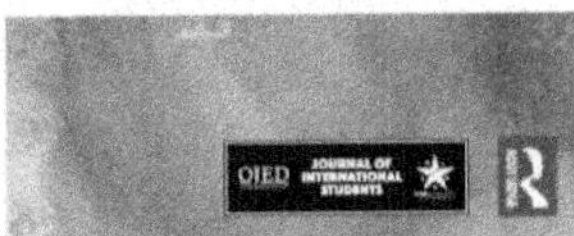

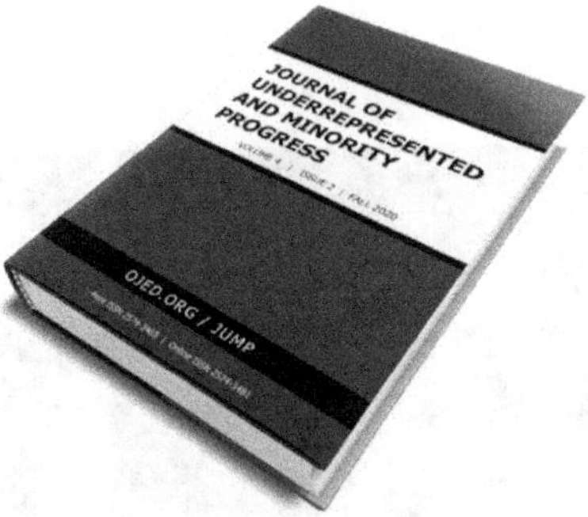
JOURNAL OF UNDERREPRESENTED AND MINORITY PROGRESS
OJED.ORG / JUMP

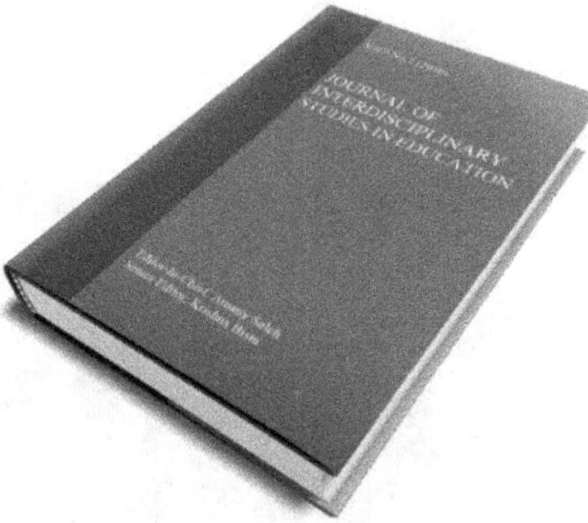
JOURNAL OF INTERDISCIPLINARY STUDIES IN EDUCATION

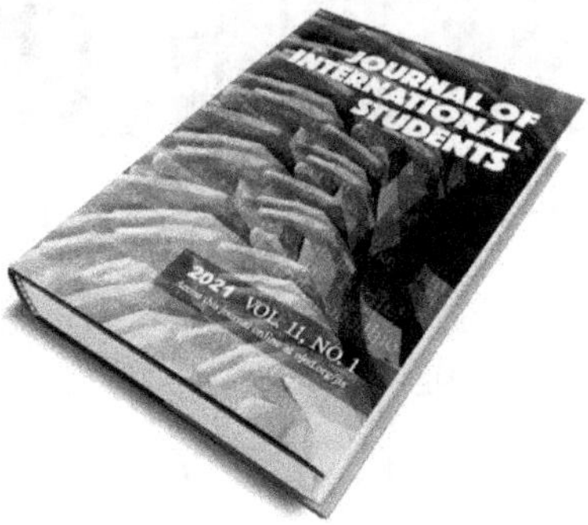
JOURNAL OF INTERNATIONAL STUDENTS
2021 VOL 11, NO.1

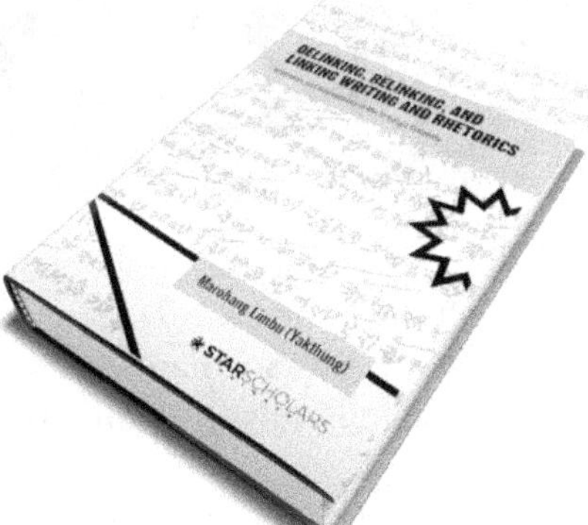
DELINKING, RELINKING, AND LINKING WRITING AND RHETORICS
Marohang Limbu (Yakthung)
STAR SCHOLARS

Open Journals in Education (OJED) publishes high quality peer reviewed, open access journals based at research universities. OJED uses the Open Journal System (OJS) platform, where readers can browse by subject, drill down to journal level to find the aims, scope, and editorial board for each individual title, as well as search back issues. OJED journals are required to be indexed in major academic databases to ensure quality and maximize article discoverability and citation. Journals follow best practices on publication ethics outlined in the COPE Code of Conduct. Explore our OJED Journals at www.ojed.org

***

A. Noam Chomsky Global Connections Awards celebrate the power of human connections. The awards recognize distinguished service to the global mission of the STAR Scholars Network. Several individuals with a deep impact on advancing global, social mobility are recognized every year.

For more information, visit https://starscholars.org/global-connections-award/

Indexing

ISSN: 2162-3104 Print/ ISSN: 2166-3750 Online
Journal of International Students
http://ojed.org/jis

SUBJECT: Education- Higher Education/ DEWEY #378

Directory of Open Access Journals, 2011-
EBSCOhost, Education Source, 03/01/2012-
Gale
- o   Academic OneFile, 09/01/2011-
- o   Contemporary Women's Issues, 09/01/2011-
- o   Educator's Reference Complete, 09/01/2011-
- o   Expanded Academic ASAP, 09/01/2011-
- o   InfoTrac Custom, 09/01/2011-

ProQuest
- o   Education Collection, 10/01/2011-
- o   Education Database, 10/01/2011-
- o   Education Database (Alumni Edition), 10/01/2011-
- o   ProQuest Central, 10/01/2011-
- o   ProQuest Central - UK Customers, 10/01/2011-
- o   ProQuest Central (Alumni Edition), 10/01/2011-
- o   ProQuest Central (Corporate), 10/01/2011-
- o   ProQuest Central (US Academic Subscription), 10/01/2011-
- o   ProQuest Central China, 10/01/2011-
- o   ProQuest Central Essentials, 10/01/2011-
- o   ProQuest Central Korea, 10/01/2011-
- o   ProQuest Central Student, 10/01/2011-
- o   ProQuest Research Library, 10/01/2011-
- o   ProQuest Research Library (Corporate), 10/01/2011-
- o   ProQuest Social Sciences Premium Collection, 10/01/2011-
- o   Research Library (Alumni Edition), 10/01/2011-
- o   Social Science Premium Collection, 10/01/2011-

Clarivate Analytics
- o   Web of Science
- o   Emering Sciences Citation Index
- o   Higher Education Abstracts

Source: Ulrichsweb Global Serials Directory

You may access the print and/or digital copies of the Journal of International Students from **686 libraries worldwide** (as of July, 2022).

The Journal of International Students (Print ISSN 2162-3104 & Online ISSN 2166-3750) is a member of the STAR Scholars Network Open Journals in Education (OJED), a OJS 3 platform for high-quality, peer-reviewed academic journals in education.

Upon publication articles are immediately and freely available to the public. The final version of articles can immediately be posted to an institutional repository or to the author's own website as long as the article includes a link back to the original article posted on OJED.

None of the OJED journals charge fees to individual authors thanks to the generous support of our institutional sponsors.

For further information

Editorial Office
Journal of International Students
URL: http://ojed.org/jis
E-mail: contact@jistudents.org

ISSN: 2162-3104 Print/ ISSN: 2166-3750 Online
2022 Volume 12, Number 2
© *Journal of International Students*
http://ojed.org/jis

CONTENTS

Editorial

Research Articles

Cross-Border Narratives

Book Reviews

To order online, visit
www.ojed.org/jis

Paperback and e-books
available.

available at

The *Journal of International Students* is a Gold Open Access publication thanks to the generous institutional sponsorship of Old Dominion University and publication partnership of Emerson College and American Council on Education.

Editorial

© *Journal of International Students*
Volume 12, Issue 2 (2022), pp. i-iv
ISSN: 2162-3104 (Print), 2166-3750 (Online)
doi: 10.32674/jis.v12i2.4898
ojed.org/jis

Further Understanding on International Student Mobilities in Asia is Needed

Hiep-Hung Pham
*EdLab Asia Education Research and Development Centre
and Phu Xuan University*

Traditionally, Asia was regarded as one of the most prominent sources of international students (ISs) for developed countries in the Western world, including North America, Europe, Australia, and New Zealand. Nevertheless, the first decade of the 21st century observed a shifting pattern of international student mobilities (ISM) in Asia (Chan, 2012). From being sole exporters or deficit exporters (i.e., number of inflow students are smaller than number of outflow students) of international students as observed in 2010 backward, Asian countries, notably China, Japan, Korea, and Singapore have been increasingly identified as the new hubs of international students, especially those coming from the neighboring countries within the region. In the second decade of the 21st century, the shifting pattern of ISM in Asia as observed between 2000 and 2010 appeared to intensify. On the one hand, new competitors entering the race of international student attraction include Hong Kong, Taiwan, and Malaysia (Vuong et al., 2021). On the other hand, increasing non-Asian students (ISs from other contingents) select Asia as destinations for education purpose (see Belyavina, 2013; Tran & Vu, 2018). By 2019, there was 746,983 international students in Asia, which accounted for 12.3% of total ISM across the globe (UNESCO Institute for Statistics, n.d.). The figures are significantly higher than the respective data in 2010 (442,938 students, 11.7%) and 2000 (176,912 students, 8.4%)

Despite becoming a growing hub of international students, Asia appears to receive insufficient attention from researchers in the field of international education and student mobilities. The trajectory of newly published research on ISM in Asia does not appear to keep pace with the growing inflow of international students in Asia. In a review of studies on ISM in Asia between 1984 and 2019 (Pham et al., 2021), my colleagues and I computed the two set of ratios for comparison, these are: (i) the number of studies on ISM in Asia/the number of studies on ISM in general; and (ii) the number of ISs in Asia/the number of ISs in the world. Our analysis reveals that the former ratio ranges approximately between 2 to 4% in the period of 2000 and 2017; meanwhile the respective range for the latter is approximately between 12 to 14%. These figures show that there is stillroom for further investigation of ISM in Asia.

International students have brought a range of socio-cultural, intellectual, and economic benefits for Asian countries such as "human capital investment, knowledge transfer, and national capacity building" (see Chan, 2012, p.221). Therefore, I would like to call for attention from colleagues in international education community to prioritize ISM in Asia in their research agenda, including comparative research across countries and regions. I recommend some implications for stakeholders and potential avenues for future studies on ISM in Asia:

First, closer linkage between government authorities and international education scholars is crucial. Over previous decades, although several national strategies on higher education internationalization among Asian countries have been released with targets on international students being placed at the center, few government-funded projects have been allocated to international education scholars to develop nuanced understandings of ISM in Asia, including their motivations, well-being, educational experiences and outcomes, engagement, lifestyles, expectations, plans and impacts. Most extant literature on ISM in Asia are bottom-up and in many cases, these studies reflect the personal interests of the authors but not the views of policymakers, students, and other key stakeholders. Thus, it is crucial to have more strengthened liaison between government and researchers for enhancing our understandings of ISM in Asia and for supporting the internationalization of higher education in Asian countries.

Second, current and future scholars on ISM in Asia should consider overlooked or under-researched areas, including : (i) horizontal perspective (i.e., geography), the extant studies mainly focus on Malaysia, China, Hong Kong, Singapore, or South Korea as studied samples. Thus, the under-represented destination countries of international students to be considered in future studies may include Taiwan, Thailand, Indonesia, or Vietnam. (ii) vertical dimension (i.e., level of education), since the current literature on ISM in Asia mainly focus on undergraduate levels, future research may pay more attention ton under-researched education sectors such as postgraduate studies, school and vocational education and training sectors. (iii) Another potential avenue is the research of ISM in Asia and COVID-19. Over the past two years, there have been several initiatives on ISM stemming under the conditions and impact of the COVID-19 pandemic. For instance, some universities have implemented virtual mobility programs in which physical presence of international students in an Asian university is not necessary. Instead, an exchange student is able to participate in host university virtually (e.g., see ITS Global Engagement, 2021).

Third, ISM studies, indeed, are interdisciplinary by nature. It is critical to research ISM from different perspectives: education, psychology, culture, language, behavior, or management to name a few. This possibility is highly illuminated in our bibliometrics work on ISM in Asia between 1984 and 2019 (Pham et al., 2021). In this study, we identified the key citation sources from previous studies on ISM in Asia, which come from different disciplines. For instance, among "culture" category, International Journal of Intercultural Relations is identified as one of the main major citation sources. Other high-profile sources include Foreign Language Annals (Language), Higher Education (Education) or Tourism Management (Tourism). Subsequently, previous documents on ISM in Asia were also published in various journals focusing on different disciplines such as International Journal of Educational Development (category "education"), Business Process Management Journal (category "management") or Journal of Behavioral Addictions (category "behavior").

In conclusion, it is apparent that ISM in Asia has become an essential component of the current ISM across the globe. Nevertheless, extant research on ISM in Asia seems to play only a peripheral role in the overall literature on ISM. It is therefore a critical time for scholars in the international education community to pay more attention to this under-researched topic.

REFERENCES

Belyavina, R. (2013). *US students in China: Meeting the goals of the 100,000 strong initiative.* Institute of International Education. https://www.iie.org/Research-and-Insights/Publications/US-Students-in-China#:~:text=The study finds that American,2014 will likely be met.

Chan, S.-J. (2012). Shifting Patterns of Student Mobility in Asia. *Higher Education Policy, 25*(2), 207–224. https://doi.org/10.1057/hep.2012.3

ITS Global Engagement. (2021). *Virtual Exchange Program at Asia University Intake Fall 2021.* ITS Global Engagement. https://www.its.ac.id/international/2021/07/07/virtual-exchange-program-at-asia-university-intake-fall-2021/

Pham, H.-H., Dong, T.-K.-T., Vuong, Q.-H., Luong, D.-H., Nguyen, T.-T., Dinh, V.-H., & Ho, M.-T. (2021). A bibliometric review of research on international student mobilities in Asia with Scopus dataset between 1984 and 2019. *Scientometrics, 126*(6), 5201–5224. https://doi.org/10.1007/s11192-021-03965-4

Tran, L. T., & Vu, T. T. P. (2018). Beyond the 'normal' to the 'new possibles': Australian students' experiences in Asia and their roles in making connections with the region via the New Colombo Plan. *Higher Education Quarterly, 72*(3), 194–207. https://doi.org/10.1111/hequ.12166

UNESCO Institute for Statistics. (n.d.). *Global Flow of Tertiary-Level Students.* UNESCO Institute for Statistics. http://uis.unesco.org/en/uis-student-flow

Vuong, Q.-H., Pham, H.-H., Dong, T.-K.-T., Ho, M.-T., & Dinh, V.-H. (2021). Current Trends and Realities of International Students in East and Southeast Asia: The Cases of China, Hong Kong, Taiwan, and Malaysia. *International Journal of Education and Practice, 9*(3), 532–549. https://doi.org/10.18488/journal.61.2021.93.532.549

HIEP-HUNG PHAM, PhD, is the director of Center for Research and Practice on Education at Phu Xuan University. Dr Pham also affiliates with Center for Educational Research and Development EdLab Asia as director of research. Email: phamhunghiep@pxu.edu.vn

This research is funded by the Vietnam National Foundation for Science and Technology Development (NAFOSTED) under the National Research Grant No. 502.02-2019.22.

Research Article

© *Journal of International Students*
Volume 12, Issue 2 (2022), pp. 283-301
ISSN: 2162-3104 (Print), 2166-3750 (Online)
doi: 10.32674/jis.v12i2.1986
ojed.org/jis

A Leap of Academic Faith and Resilience: Nontraditional International Students Pursuing Higher Education in the United States

Yvonne Hunter-Johnson
*Department of Workforce Education and Development at
Southern Illinois University (Carbondale)*

ABSTRACT

International students pursuing higher education in the United States are faced with a multiplicity of challenges such as relocating to a new country, navigating an unfamiliar educational system, overcoming negative stereotypes associated with being an international student, and, in some instances, learning a foreign language. Despite such challenges, international students remain motivated to pursue higher education in the United States. This qualitative study, utilizing Schlossberg's adult transition model as a theoretical framework, explores the lived experiences of 16 international students pursuing higher education in the United States. Emphasis is placed on their transitional experiences in relation to their learning. The major theme that emerged is "major adjustment." Subthemes that emerged regarding these students' adjustments includes (a) diversity and cultural differences in the learning environment, (b) comparative differences in the learning environment, (c) language barriers, and (d) combatting stereotypes. Implications for theory and practice are also discussed.

Keywords: adult learners, higher education, international students, non-traditional students

A leap of academic faith and resilience are terms that describe the relocation endeavor of a nontraditional adult learner moving to a foreign country to pursue higher education. Many underlying factors motivate international adult learners to seek higher education in the United States, including, but not limited to, pursuing academic and professional growth; garnering experience in intercultural contexts; improving future career opportunities; obtaining enhanced social status, economic benefits, and greater political freedom or stability; and bridging the gap between educational supply and demand of the country of origin (Chiswick & Miller, 2010; Kahanec & Králiková, 2011; Khadria, 2011; Kim et al., 2011; Li & Bray, 2007; Valdez, 2015; Zhou, 2015). Despite differing reasons for obtaining higher education in the United States, a common thread of resilience tightly links international adult learners. Conversely, another common stereotype linking international adult learners portrays them as beneficiaries of U.S. higher education. Specifically, the view that only international students receive this benefit is pervasive. However, the benefits extend to the faculty, the overall student population, the institution of higher education, the local community, and the U.S. economy (Hunter-Johnson, 2016).

The migration of international students to the United States for the purpose of receiving higher education contributes greatly to the U.S. economy and has a positive impact on academia. According to the *Open Doors* report (Institute of International Education [IIE], 2017a), more than 1 million international students are presently studying in the United States. As a result, $35.8 billion was contributed to the U.S. economy during the 2016–2017 academic year alone. As to academia, the inclusion of international students within the college or university community greatly enhances the learning experiences of all enrolled students, exposes domestic students to international perspectives in the learning environment and in research initiatives, and affords networking opportunities and the development of long-term business relationships. Moreover, such exposure and interaction prepare students to be global citizens. Additionally, the American Council on Education has emphasized the value of preparing graduates to "operate effectively in other cultures and settings" (as cited in Center for Internationalization and Global Engagement [CIGE], 2012, p. 3). From an educator's perspective, the inclusion of international students prompts educators to modify their teaching strategies to create a learning climate that benefits multiple and different groups, resulting in the promotion of learning environments that are more culturally aware and sensitive (Halx, 2010).

Despite the presence of academic faith and resilience in international adult learners, their experiences in higher education differ greatly from those of domestic adult learners. As a result, this study was conducted to explore the lived experiences of international adult learners and how their cultural transitions influence their experiences in the learning environment. Given the academic and economic impact of international students in higher education in the United States, this study offers valuable insights. It contributes to the academic literature by highlighting the perspective of international students regarding their experiences of cultural transition and how such experiences influence learning. Additionally, the study addressed a gap in the literature by providing recommendations for how adult educators can improve the learning experience of international students in higher education settings and proposes a foundational platform upon which to modify the U.S. system of higher education to instill greater cultural competency. Further, it supplements the literature on international students from the non-traditional student perspective, a unique student population regarding international student literature.

GUIDING RESEARCH QUESTIONS

Given the impact of and on international students pursuing higher education in the United States, the guiding research questions for this study are as follows:

1. What are the lived experiences of international students as adult learners while pursuing higher education in the United States?

2. How do international students perceive the impact of their transitional experiences on their learning?

THEORETICAL FRAMEWORK

Schlossberg's (1981, 1984) adult transition model served as an underpinning that explains the transitional process of adults in higher education. According to Schlossberg et al. (1995), a transition is "any event, or nonevent, that results in changed relationships, routines, assumptions, and roles" (p. 27). Specifically, Schlossberg's transition theory emphasizes individual perspectives on transitions, including anticipated and unanticipated transitions (Anderson et al., 2011). Individuals may adapt to a transition with different resources at various times (Goodman et al., 2006; Schlossberg, 1981). According to Schlossberg et al. (1995), four factors influence adult transitions: (a) situation (e.g., the characteristics of the event or nonevent); (b) self (e.g., personal characteristics and psychological resources); (c) support (e.g., social support systems); and (d) strategy (e.g., coping responses).

Schlossberg's adult transition model was the most appropriate theoretical framework for this study because the nontraditional adult international student population experiences both academic and social transitions which are anticipated, unanticipated, and nonevents. Therefore, this theory mirrors the characteristics of the population and situation of international non-traditional students in higher education. In addition, nontraditional adult international students manage the transitions they undergo differently based on their abilities, backgrounds, experiences, personalities, resources, and the timing of their studying abroad. Regarding anticipated transitions, international students have more time to prepare psychologically and physically for the adjustment and, therefore, possess greater capacity to achieve success (Anderson et al., 2011). However, as to unanticipated transitions and nonevents, individuals may experience greater challenges due to a lack of preparation and the need, in some instances, to transition with their immediate family (i.e., spouses and children). Hence, they are forced to address these unanticipated events not only for themselves but also for the transitional challenges experienced by their family members entering and living in a foreign country.

LITERATURE REVIEW

The International Adult Learner and Motivation

Following the desire to pursue higher education as a working adult, balancing work and family after years removed from being in any formalized learning environment is a complex decision. However, this decision can be persuaded and/or influenced by an individual's level of motivation (intrinsic or extrinsic). For an international adult learner, the factors to consider when deciding to pursue international education are much more in-depth, and the motivational factors often differ from those of the domestic adult learner.

No distinct definition of a nontraditional adult learner has become universally accepted, but there are distinguishing characteristics. For example, characteristics include age (Metzner & Bean, 1987); risk factors for dropping out (U.S. Department of Education [U.S. DE], 2002, 2005); and ethnicity, lower socio-economic status, first-generation college student status, and employment status (Rendon et al., 2000). However, the U.S. Department of Education (2002, 2005) classified nontraditional adult learners as students who possess one or more of the following characteristics: delayed enrollment, part-time student status, full-time employment, financial independence, responsibility for dependents, and enrollment after their 25th birthday.

Given the increasing focus on such learners, the literature regarding the motivation of nontraditional adult learners for pursuing higher education has blossomed (Chu et al., 2007; Hunter-Johnson, 2017; Jinkens, 2009) and expanded to include, to a lesser degree, nontraditional international learners. A review of the literature found the following themes emerge as motivational factors influencing the decisions of nontraditional international learners to pursue higher education in the United States: opportunity to improve English-language skills; financial assistance from the country of origin; pursuit of academic and professional growth; experience in intercultural contexts; enhancement of future career opportunities; and augmentation of social status, economic benefits, and political freedom or stability (Bista & Dagley, 2015; Chiswick and Miller, 2010; Kahanec & Králiková, 2011; Khadria, 2011; Kim et al., 2011; Li & Bray, 2007; Sato & Hodge, 2009; Summers & Volet, 2008; Verbik & Lasanowski, 2007; Zhou, 2015). Such factors often serve as a foundational platform that assists international students with remaining focused while fueling their drive to pursue academic excellence. Compared with the domestic students, international student motivation would differ because their backgrounds, experiences (personal and professional), and quality of life vary depending upon their country of origin.

Challenges of the International Nontraditional Adult Learner

The international nontraditional adult learner, like any domestic nontraditional learner, encounters numerous challenges in the pursuit of higher education. However, there are added layers of challenge for the international nontraditional adult learner that the domestic student does not encounter, such as acclimation to a new country, a different culture, an unfamiliar educational system, and the social isolation related to national origin. As a result, many studies have focused on the challenges international students encounter from a social or societal perspective. Some studies have specifically highlighted language issues and first-time awareness of having an accent, differences in classroom and instructional culture, and awareness of skin color (Graham & Donaldson, 1999; Mwaura, 2008); disconnection and confusion at encountering a different social value system, unusual food, gender-role adjustments, separation from family and friends, and loss of social status and power (Lacina, 2002); and identity issues due to reclassification as a minority and the associated stigmas that often impact employability (Constantine et al., 2005).

The international nontraditional adult learner is expected to function in a learning environment where (a) unfamiliar teaching and learning styles prevail; (b) a generational gap between the nontraditional student and traditional-age students exists; (c) the perception that others deem one to be inferior arises; and (d) a general sense that one does not fit in exists within and beyond the classroom (Graham & Donaldson, 1999; Kasworm, 2003). Additionally, international students are challenged with financial hardship due to the exorbitant costs associated with being an international student, including increased tuition and related institutional fees, visa expenses, continuously paying cash because of limited or no credit history in the host country, and having to reestablish themselves financially within a new country with minimal financial support. While these factors can impact the international nontraditional adult learner socially and emotionally, they also play a crucial role in whether the international nontraditional adult learner will complete his or her program of study.

In addition, overall stress also contributes significantly to the success or failure of international adult learners by impacting their performance ability and giving rise to feelings of incompetence and a fear of failure (Eccles & Wigfield, 2002; Gardner, 2009; Golde, 2000, 2005; Gonzalez, 2006; Lovitts, 2008; Wigfield & Eccles, 2000). Overall, international adult learners are burdened with heightened stress at all stages of their educational experience—from passing qualifying exams to obtaining relevant academic experiences, from identifying the right mentor to gaining entry to networking opportunities, and from transitioning into independent researchers to finding employment upon graduation (Gardner, 2009; Golde, 2005; Gonzalez, 2006; Lovitts, 2008). The perils and stresses associated with these stages can threaten persistence and, ultimately, successful completion. Moreover, the pressure is magnified for international nontraditional adult learners due to the impending implications, such as employment upon graduation in a foreign country, job security, and the ability to apply the knowledge gained in their studies to their respective work environment. And, in the event the international student returns to their home country, the ability to reacclimatize to both their home country and to its different work environment create anxiety.

International Student Adjustments and Differences in the Learning Environment

A few contributions to the literature regarding international student adjustments to the United States while pursuing higher education. Yi et al. (2003) indicated that international students experience adjustments in five arenas: academic systems, financial situations, physical health, vocational environments, and personal/social issues. Gebhard (2012) identified three major areas in which international students might have trouble in adjusting: academic, social interactions, and emotional reaction to the new environment. Mesidor and Sly (2014) summarized four types of adjustments for international students: cultural adjustment, social adoption, academic adjustment, and psychological adjustments. According to Trifonovitch (1977), there are four stages of cultural adjustment: the honeymoon stage, the hostility stage, the humor stage, and the home stage. In their new academic environment, international students must adapt their learning style and adjust to different methods of evaluation (Mesidor & Sly, 2014). Studies have shown that international students experience homesickness, loneliness, depression, and anxiety during the adjustment process (Nilsson et al., 2004; Yakushko et al., 2008; Yi et al., 2003). This adjustment period escalates for nontraditional students compared with traditional international and domestic students because of the vast difference in their social roles, level of responsibility, common requirement to relocate with spouse and children, and, in most instances, the role of "bread winner" of their immediate family.

METHODS

Study Design and Data Collection

A qualitative phenomenological approach was selected for this study. According to Fischer (2009), this approach allows in-depth understanding of the participants' perspectives on the same phenomenon while minimizing researcher prejudices and allowing the purity of participants' perspectives to emerge.

Participants

This study consisted of 16 participants ($n = 16$). The participants represented diversity in their discipline of study and country of origin. Both genders ($n = 11$ females, and $n = 5$ males) were included in the study, and there was also variation in age. Eight ($n = 8$) universities throughout the United States were represented. The inclusion criteria for this study were that the participant had to be (a) born in a country outside the United States, (b) studying in the United States for at least two years, planning to return to their country of origin within five years of degree completion, and over the age of 25 while receiving a higher education degree. The demographic profiles of the participants are in Table 1.

Data Collection and Analysis

Boeije (2010) described purposeful sampling as "intentionally selecting participants according to the needs of the study. These participants can teach us a lot about the issues that are of importance to the research" (p. 35). Additionally, this method was selected because it provides a platform for a diverse range of cases relevant to a particular phenomenon or event—in this instance, international nontraditional students who study abroad in the United States.

Table 1: Participants' Demographic Profile

Variable	N	%
Gender		
Male	5	31
Female	11	69
Age Range		
21–30	3	19
31–40	9	56
41–50	4	25
Educational Program Level		
Masters	6	37.5
Doctorate	10	62
Program of Study		
Education	8	50
Business	4	25
Psychology	1	6
Science	3	19
Home Origin		
Africa	2	13
Asia	4	25
Caribbean	9	56
Middle East	1	6

Note: *n = 16.*

The purpose of this kind of sample design is to provide as much insight as possible into the event or phenomenon under examination. Study participants were solicited via emails and telephone calls utilizing a script provided by the Office of Sponsored Research. Once the potential participants indicated interest in joining the study, they were advised to contact the study's primary researcher. After contacting the primary researcher, the potential participants were given detailed information about the overall study objective, study criteria, study procedures, and proposed benefits of the study. After agreeing to participate, subjects were scheduled for interviews. All participants and prospective participants were also given the option to "opt out" of future emails or telephone calls.

Semi-structured interviews were utilized for data collection. Questions were crafted to reflect the study's objective and guiding research question. The interviews lasted between 45 and 60 mins and were audio recorded. Notes were also taken by the researchers during each session to ensure accuracy. Once each interview was completed, it was transcribed immediately. Member checking was conducted by sending a copy of the completed transcript to each participant to review for accuracy. As validity and reliability are of utmost importance, an independent peer reviewer, "someone who is familiar with the research or phenomenon explored" (Creswell & Miller, 2000, p. 9), assisted by reading the transcripts to confirm themes and categories corresponding with the research question. Data were then analyzed using open coding, a method of qualitative analysis used to establish themes and main concepts (Miles & Huberman, 1994; Corbin & Strauss, 2008). Themes and subthemes linked to the research question were identified from the transcripts and contributed to a greater understanding and explanation of the issues being studied.

FINDINGS

This study explored the lived experiences of international nontraditional students pursuing higher education in the United States and how their transitional experiences influenced learning. Data were collected through semi-structured interviews, administered to 16 participants representing five geographical regions. After careful analysis of interviewee responses, the major theme that emerged regarding the most influential factors impacting their experiences in the U.S. learning environment was "major adjustment." As defined by the participants, *adjustment* encompassed adaptation to the new learning environment. Subthemes that emerged regarding the adjustment of these students included (a) diversity and cultural differences in the learning environment, (b) comparative differences in the learning environment, (c) language barriers, and (d) combatting stereotypes. Despite the need for major adjustment, there was an overarching sense of positivity among the participants regarding their experiences while in the United States. Some key descriptive phrases representing the optimism of these participants about their experiences while studying in the United States were "enjoying my experience," "good experience," "relatively good," "new experience," "positive experience," and "exciting but overwhelming."

Diversity and Cultural Differences in the Learning Environment

From an American perspective, academic inclusion of study participants—and international nontraditional students, in general—contributes to a diversified learning environment. However, with such diversity and cultural differences come added layers of emotional and psychological challenge that can manifest in the learning environment and impede the learning process. In addition, international non-traditional students are required to make major adjustments to assimilate to a new culture that often has an unfamiliar demographic profile. As a result of these major transitional adjustments, many international students question themselves at some point during their pursuit of higher education in the United States, asking "Am I doing it right?," "Am I saying it right?," "How do I sound in comparison with others?," "How am I being perceived by others in the learning environment?," "Is it okay that my religious beliefs are different?" A married female and mother of three who participated in the study indicated, "It was an eyeopener for me being in a classroom with a diverse student population and different cultures where we had to respect each other and learn about different cultures and religions. That was a new experience for me." She further explained, "Learning to have an open mind … was something I had to adjust to. This was kind of foreign to me coming from my culture." While some international nontraditional students acclimated rather quickly, challenges still existed and, in some instances, persist. A single male study participant stated, "I was trying to understand the atmosphere and understand how to get along with other individuals. My first classes were with more white students than students of color. It's just … I guess, communicating with them." This adjustment to the change in student demographics created an adjustment challenge. In addition, there was great concern about accents and language differences. A female from the Caribbean who was taught British English versus American English explained her linguistic challenges while in higher education. The issue she experienced revolved around the "enunciation of words that Americans may think is correct. I am constantly corrected [on how] I enunciate a word because I said it the British way, and [Americans] would say: 'No, that is not correct.'"

Comparative Differences in the Learning Environment

The participants in this study unanimously agreed (100%, $n = 16/16$) that there was a vast difference between the U.S. educational system and that of their home country. Such differences, as defined by the participants, extended to curriculum, instructional methods and techniques, learning processes, and overall educational expectations. A single male indicated that "it was a new experience for me. It was different from what I was used to regarding the standard of education, the curriculum, and the organization." While most participants echoed this sentiment, there were many students who eluded to the fact that the U.S. educational system, while different, is easier than the one in their home country (43%, $n = 7$). Further probing of what contributed to the U.S. educational system being perceived as easier revealed that the testing procedures and frequency of testing make it easier to focus on one aspect of learning at a time. A single male participant explained, "In the USA, you have a first, second, [and] third test, and then the final exam. This set up is very different [from my home country] and makes you more focused, and your learning ability is better." He further explained, "When you are writing your exam based on four weeks [of class material], ... you would not easily forget. But if you are studying ... 16 weeks [of class material], you may forget in a year." The giving of a single exam at the end of the semester is a common practice in his country of origin. Another participant indicated that, in the U.S. educational system, there is more support provided by the faculty compared with his home country. However, despite the limited support systems in his country, the expectations of students are higher there. He explained that it is more difficult to matriculate through the education system in his country. He added that resources such as continuous internet service, textbooks, well-equipped libraries, and access to faculty are not as common in his country and are viewed as luxuries there, whereas they are commonplace in the United States.

The instructional methods and approaches utilized by the instructors in higher education pose adjustment challenges for international students as well. In U.S. higher education, guided by andragogy, instructor-facilitated discussion is a common practice. However, this common U.S. instructional method often presents a challenge for international students, who are more accustomed to the pedagogical approach often practiced in institutions of higher education in their countries of origin (Baba & Hosoda, 2014; Jackson et al., 2013; Kim, 2012; Kuo, 2011; Sherry et al., 2010; Sue & Rawlings, 2013; Telbis et al., 2013; Young, 2011). A married mother of one stated, "Normally, [U.S. instructors] ask the students for discussion, and this is a tough time for me because, in my country, we don't have discussion between students and professor." This challenge was echoed by another participant, who stated,

> You just listen to the professor [in my home country]. Even for homework, we need to write an essay paper here in the USA. But, in my country, we don't have homework like this. Our homework is more focused on memorization.

Language Barriers

Study participants expressed concerns about language barriers and adjustments resulting from this barrier. Such concerns were not only identified by English-as-a-second-language (ESL) participants but also shared by native English speakers. All the ESL participants explained the challenges they encountered. Some ESL participants (25%, $n = 4$) indicated they had taken six or more months of English classes prior to beginning their graduate program. In some instances, this was not necessarily at the school where they pursued their graduate degree or even in the same state. A female mother of one indicated she had to take a year of English to prepare herself prior to beginning her graduate degree. A married male participant stated, "I went to Boston to attend a language school for nine months to improve my language and improve all my application material[s], ... then I attended a summer program for two months at Harvard." Another participant, a married female, stated she had taken "eight months of language classes prior to beginning her graduate degree." A married male participant stated that although English is the only language he speaks, Americans perceive him to be speaking with an accent, which is a negative perception that creates a language barrier. He explained that he was assigned as a graduate teaching assistant and was reported by one of the students who failed the course, complaining that she could not understand what he was saying as his accent was a barrier for her. On another occasion, a male graduate teaching assistant indicated that although he spoke only English, when he began to teach his class, two white males got up and left the classroom, stating that they could not learn from him as they could not understand his accent. Another single male participant echoed this theme regarding his accent. "When I first moved here, and even now, the [questions] come [in]to my head: … am I saying the right thing, and am I saying it clearly? The one thing associated with me is my accent." It was also noted by some of the native-English-speaking participants that there was a significant difference between American English and British English. This became evident during class discussions as some words are pronounced differently, and, in written assignments, it was necessary to maintain constant vigilance as to the differences between British and American spelling.

In addition, some participants (19%, $n = 3$) indicated that it takes them twice as long to complete assignments for class, twice as long to complete the assigned readings, and twice as long to comprehend the discussions that are taking place in the learning environment. One participant indicated that she must complete assignments in her native language first and then translate them into English. Upon completion, she also must go to the university's writing center to ensure that her assignments are written in proper English. Another participant expanded on this point, stating that she must process her thoughts, what is being said, and what she reads in her native language prior to speaking or comprehending in English. This makes it extremely difficult to participate in class discussion and to read materials in the classroom environment in a set timeframe.

Combatting Stereotypes

Numerous participants explained that, as international students, they were often perceived as being different—frequently in a negative, condescending manner—by American students and, in some instances, by instructors. A male participant described a constant need to demonstrate proof of excellence. He explained,

> The thing with … proof of excellence is I have done more work than traditional White students to show I am capable or have the capacity. The downside of that is that a single mistake will dash it. The view anyone would have of me would be being looked down upon.

He further explained that this includes both students and faculty. He added, "What is interesting is this is not something I found with White professors but something I have found with scholars of color." He justified this statement by saying,

> Just taking on the mainstream thought that a person of color has to work twice or three times as hard as the typical White person in this country,

> I feel they [view] a person of color making a mistake … poorly. I think, because [scholars of color] have to work really hard to get where they are, there is a mismatch when they see persons of color making a mistake.

Study participants also indicated they must confront and overcome many—often negative—stereotypes associated with being an international student. A single, male participant of color reported, "I had people make comments [like] 'what planet are you from.'" He explained this statement arose in reaction to an incident when he found himself well-versed on a topic the instructor was teaching and began answering questions posed by the instructor to the class, while the other "predominately White" students did not know the answers. In this situation, what should have been an opportunity to shine academically became a negative experience due to the condescension from his domestic classmates. This participant indicated that students would seek assistance from him in private regarding course material; however, in the classroom environment, these same students refused to acknowledge him. He said, "They would wait until all the students leave [class] so they would not be seen with me in the class for other students to know we communicate."

> Another male participant echoed the sentiments of negative stereotypes. He stated,

> When you come from a third-world country, people do not take you serious[ly,] or [they] think you are dumb or don't know what you are about. [But, when] you do better than everyone else, and it is hard for them to meet your standards, they … respect you.

Such stereotypes go beyond the classroom and extend to prevalent U.S. stereotypes against people of color. A male participant explained that although he is in a graduate program, he is afraid of being shot by the police because of negative stereotypes associated with "Black males." He stated that he was pulled over by the police on one or two occasions, and, in those instances, he was genuinely concerned about being shot by the police. Hence, the psychological and emotional transitions stem from the community itself and pose a ripple effect for some international students that carries over to learning.

DISCUSSION AND IMPLICATIONS FOR PRACTICE

This research contributes to the field of adult education and adult learning in many ways. Specifically, the study illuminates the adult education literature regarding challenges in pursuing higher education as a nontraditional learner from an international learner's perspective (Baba & Hosoda, 2014; Campbell, 2015; Hechanova-Alampay et al., 2002; Hunter-Johnson, 2016; Rajapaksa & Dundes, 2002; Sullivan & Kashubeck-West, 2015; Zhao et al., 2005). Additionally, this study highlights the defining the roles of adult educators and institutions of higher education in promoting globally friendly learning environments. The findings from this study revealed that international nontraditional students pursuing higher education in the United States experience tremendous transitional adjustments in both the educational and social arenas. Some challenges associated with the adjustment process include (a) diversity and cultural differences in the learning environment, (b) comparative differences in the learning environments, (c) language barriers, and (d) combatting stereotypes.

Although the findings related to the experiences of international adult learners while pursing higher education were neither new nor surprising, specifically regarding transitioning to the United States from a societal perspective (Graham & Donaldson, 1999; Kasworm, 2003; Lacina, 2002; Mwaura, 2008); adjustments to the learning environment (Mesidor & Sly, 2014); and adjustments regarding loneliness, anxiety, and depression during adjustment (Nilsson et al., 2004; Yakushko et al., 2008; Yi et al., 2003), the study's findings augmented the current literature by including transitional experiences in relation to the learning environment. Additionally, the study provides recommendations and considerations for adult educators and institutions of higher education, as well as for current and potential international learners pursuing higher education in the United States.

The findings regarding diversity and cultural differences in the learning environment can have a major impact on the international student emotionally and societally and can present as learning barriers. The resulting impacts could negatively impact retention and success rates for international students. Therefore, institutions of higher education should promote an institutional culture that welcomes and supports international students, especially nontraditional students with unique needs. Specifically, the implementation of an international student mentoring program to assist with acclimatization to methods of instruction and learning environments that are likely unfamiliar to such students are recommended. These programs can include domestic and international students. International students can be paired with two peer mentors—one a domestic student and the other an international student, preferably from the same country—who has already experienced the transitional adjustments. The domestic student would assist with social and cultural transitions and associated barriers such as familiarization with local transportation options and the general locality, identification of local supermarkets and similar resources, exposure to social events and entertainment, and orientation to the American educational system. The experienced international student peer mentor would aid the new international student with adjusting from a cultural perspective. Together, these peer mentors would create an automatic support system for the arriving international student and help ease the transitions. To be effective, peer mentors must be able to relate to and empathize with the new international nontraditional student and be vested in the mentoring process. In addition, training would be required for the student peer mentors, including instruction in the areas of cultural competency, diversity and inclusion, and effective mentoring techniques. Such peer-mentoring programs could become a key part of the greater set of resources for international students provided by institutions of higher education.

Regarding academic challenges faced by international nontraditional students such as writing assignments, classroom dynamics, or classroom discussions, institutions of higher education should offer an international student learning support program as an extension of the university's international student office or in conjunction with library services. Such programs should include foci on writing assignments, linguistic challenges, classroom dynamics, and the educational culture in American universities. These offerings differ from student support programs designed for the general student body. Like the recommended peer mentoring program, this international student support program could be staffed by trained international and domestic student volunteers, nontraditional students who can empathize and sympathize with being a nontraditional adult learner. Program offerings could include one-on-one instruction, workshops, seminars, online training, and conferences. At the beginning of the semester, an orientation specifically for international students could be hosted to assist with the academic transitions.

To the adjustment challenges within the classroom environment, it is paramount that institutions of higher learning institute training opportunities for adult educators that enable them to better serve the international nontraditional student population. Such training could mimic cultural sensitivity training and could provide best practices for ensuring that the classroom environment is one that is sensitive to the cultural experiences of international learners and respects cultural differences. Furthermore, where relevant, adult educators must actively include the experiences of international students to enhance the learning experience for international and domestic students alike by valuing global perspectives. Such efforts and modeling establish a foundation for networking opportunities between and among students and faculty that can extend beyond the educational environment and the duration of the academic program.

LIMITATIONS OF THE STUDY

The primary limitation of this study is that it relied on the experiences and perspectives of a small number of international students ($n = 16$), which cannot accurately or fully capture the experiences of all international students pursuing higher education in the United States. As a result, the countries of origin and backgrounds of this small number of participants limit the ability to extrapolate the findings to unrepresented international student populations.

RECOMMENDATION FOR FUTURE RESEARCH

As noted in the findings, there are often significant differences between the learning environments of international students' home countries and U.S. learning environments. International nontraditional students are required to adjust socially, psychologically, emotionally, linguistically, academically, and physically while they undertake higher education pursuits. While much of the literature regarding international students echo such adjustments (Mesidor & Sly, 2014; Nilsson et al., 2004; Yakashko et al., 2008; Yi et al., 2003), there is limited emphasis on adjustment strategies for international nontraditional adult learners pursuing higher education in the United States. Further research is needed on the role of academic institutions in the acclimation process of international students in higher education and on the institutional support systems needed to promote the retention and success rate of international students. Such research would establish best practices in this arena.

REFERENCES

Anderson, M. L., Goodman, J., & Schlossberg, N. K. (2011). *Counseling adults in transition: Linking Schlossberg's theory with practice in a diverse world.* Springer Publishing Company.

Baba, Y., & Hosoda, M. (2014). Home away from home: Better understanding of the role of social support in predicting cross-cultural adjustment among international students. *College Student Journal, 48*(1), 1–15.

Bista, K., & Dagley, A. (2015). Higher education preparation and decision-making trends among international students. *College and University, 90*(3), 2–11.

Boeije, H. 2010. *Analysis in Qualitative Research.* Sage Publications Ltd.

Campbell, T. (2015). A phenomenological study on international doctoral students' acculturation experiences at a U.S. university. *Journal of International Students, 5*(3), 2166–3750.

Center for Internationalization and Global Engagement. (2012). *Mapping internationalization on U.S. campuses: 2012 edition.* American Council on Education.

Chiswick, B., & Miller, P. (2010). Educational mismatch: Are high-skilled immigrants really working in high-skilled jobs, and what price do they pay if they are not? In B. Chiswick (ed.), *High-skilled immigration in a global labor market* (pp. 111–154). American Enterprise Institute.

Chu, H. C., Hsieh, M. C., & Chang, S. C. (2007, February). *A study of career development, learning motivation, and learning satisfaction of adult learners in unconventional scheduling graduate programs.* Paper presented at the Academy of Human Resource Development International Research Conference in the Americas, Indianapolis, IN.

Constantine, M. G., Anderson, G. M., Berkel, L. A., Caldwell, L. D., & Utsey, S. O. (2005). Examining the cultural adjustment experiences of African international college students: A qualitative analysis. *Journal of Counseling Psychology, 52*(1), 57–66. https://doi.org/10.1037/0022-0167.52.1.57

Corbin, J., & Strauss, A. (2008). *Basics of Qualitative Research: Techniques and Procedures for Developing Grounded Theory.* Thousand Oaks, CA: Sage Publications.

Creswell, J. & Miller, D. (2000). Determining Validity in Qualitative Inquiry. *Theory into Practice, 39*, 1–130. 10.1207/s15430421tip39032

Eccles, J. S., & Wigfield, A. (2002). Motivational beliefs, values, and goals. *Annual Review of Psychology, 53*, 109–132. https://doi.org/10.1146/annurev.psych.53.100901.135153

Fischer, C. (2009). Bracketing in qualitative research: Conceptual and practical matters. Psychotherapy research. *Journal of the Society for Psychotherapy Research, 19*, 583–90. 10.1080/1050330090279837

Jackson, M., Ray, S., & Bybell, D. (2013). International students in the U.S.: Social and psychological adjustment. *Journal of International Students, 3*(1), 17–28. https://doi.org/10.32674/jis.v3i1.515

Gardner, S. K. (2009). The development of doctoral students: Phases of challenge and support. *ASHE Higher Education Report.* Jossey-Bass.

Gebhard, J. G. (2012). International students' adjustment problems and behaviors. *Journal of International Students, 2*(2), 184–193. https://doi.org/10.32674/jis.v2i2.529

Golde, C. M. (2000). Should I stay, or should I go? Student descriptions of the doctoral attrition process. *Review of Higher Education, 23*, 199–227. https://doi.org/10.1353/rhe.2000.0004

Golde, C. M. (2005). The role of the department and discipline in doctoral student attrition: Lessons from four departments. *Journal of Higher Education, 76*, 670–700. https://doi.org/10.1080/00221546.2005.11772304

Gonzalez, J. C. (2006). Academic socialization experiences of Latina doctoral students: A qualitative understanding of support systems that aid and challenges that hinder the process. *Journal of Hispanic Higher Education, 5*, 347–365. https://doi.org/10.1177/1538192706291141

Goodman, J., Schlossberg, N. K., & Anderson, M. L. (2006). *Counseling adults in transition: Linking practice with theory.* Springer Publishing Company.

Graham, S., & Donaldson, J.F. (1999). Adult students' academic and intellectual development in college. *Adult Education Quarterly, 49*(3), 147–162. https://doi.org/10.1177/074171369904900302

Halx, M. D. (2010). Re-conceptualizing college and university teaching through the lens of adult education: Regarding undergraduates as adults. *Teaching in Higher Education, 15*(5), 519–530. https://doi.org/10.1080/13562517.2010.491909

Hechanova-Alampay, R., Beehr, T. A., Christiansen, N. D., & Van Horn, R. K. (2002). Adjustment and strain among domestic and international student sojourners: A longitudinal study. *School Psychology International, 23*(4), 458–474. https://doi.org/10.1177/0143034302234007

Hunter-Johnson, Y. (2016). *Against all odds: Socio-cultural influence on non-traditional international learners pursuing higher education in the United States.* Proceedings of Commission for International Adult Education Conference, Albuquerque, New Mexico.

Hunter-Johnson, Y. (2017). Demystifying educational resilience: Barriers of Bahamian nontraditional adult learners in higher education. *The Journal of Continuing Higher Education, 65*(3), 175–186. https://doi.org/10.1080/07377363.2017.1275230

Institute of International Education (2017a). International students. *Open Doors Data.* http://www.iie.org/

Jinkens, R. C. (2009). Nontraditional students: Who are they? *College Student Journal, 43*(4), 979–987. https://eric.ed.gov/?id=EJ872313

Kahanec, M., & Králiková, R. (2011). *Pulls of international student mobility.* (IZA Discussion Paper No. 6233).

Kasworm, C. E. (2003). Setting the stage: Adults in higher education. *New Directions for Student Services, 102*, 3–10. https://doi.org/10.1002/ss.83

Khadria, B. (2011). India amidst a global competition for its talent: A critical perspective on policy for higher and university education. In S. Marginson, S. Kaur, & E. Sawir (Eds.), *Higher education in the Asia-Pacific: Strategic Responses to Globalization.* Springer Science & Business Media. https://doi.org/10.1007/978-94-007-1500-4_21

Kim, D., Bankart, C. A. S., & Isdell, L. (2011). International doctorates: Trends analysis on their decision to stay in US. *Higher Education, 62*, 141–161. https://doi.org/10.1007/s10734-010-9371-1

Kim, E. (2012). An alternative theoretical model: Examining psychological identity development of international students in the United States. *College Student Journal, 46*(1), 99–113.

Kuo, Y. H. (2011). Language challenges faced by international graduate students in the United States. *Journal of International Students, 1*(2), 38–42. https://doi.org/10.32674/jis.v1i2.551

Lacina, J. G. (2002). Preparing international students for a successful social experience in higher education. *New Directions for Higher Education, 117*, 21–27. https://doi.org/10.1002/he.43

Li, M., & Bray, M. (2007). Cross-border flows of students for higher education: Push–pull factors and motivations of mainland Chinese students in Hong Kong and Macau. *Higher Education, 53*, 791–818. https://doi.org/10.1007/s10734-005-5423-3

Lovitts, B. E. (2008). The transition to independent research: Who makes it, who doesn't, and why. *Journal of Higher Education, 79*, 296–325. https://doi.org/10.1080/00221546.2008.11772100

Mesidor, J. K., & Sly, K. F. (2014). Mental health help-seeking intentions among international and African American college students: An application of the theory of planned behavior. *Journal of International Students, 4*(2), 137–149. https://files.eric.ed.gov/fulltext/EJ1054822.pdf

Metzner, B., & Bean, J. (1987). The estimation of a conceptual model of nontraditional undergraduate student attrition. *Research in Higher Education, 27*(1), 15–38. https://doi.org/10.1007/bf00992303

Miles, M. B., & Huberman, A. M. (1994). *Qualitative data analysis: An expanded sourcebook.* Sage.

Mwaura, J. N. (2008). Non-traditional age black African international students' experiences: Phenomenological heuristic inquiry. *Adult Education Research Conference.* http://newprairiepress.org/aerc/2008/papers/44

Nilsson, J. E., Berkel, L. A., Flores, L. Y., & Lucas, M. S. (2004). Utilization rate and presenting concerns of international students at a university counseling center: Implications for outreach programming. *Journal of College Student Psychotherapy, 19*, 49–59. https://doi.org/10.1300/J035v19n02_05

Rajapaksa, S., & Dundes, L. (2002). It's a long way home: International student adjustment to living in the United States. *College Student Journal, 35*(1), 52–62. https://doi.org/10.2190/5HCY-U2Q9-KVGL-8M3K

Rendon, L. I., Jalomo, R. E., & Nora, A. (2000). Theoretical considerations in the study of minority student retention in higher education. In J. M. Braxton (Ed.), *Reworking the student departure puzzle* (pp. 127–156). Vanderbilt University Press.

Sato, T., & Hodge, S. R. (2009). Asian international doctoral students' experiences at two American universities: Assimilation, accommodation, and resistance. *Journal of Diversity in Higher Education, 2*(3), 136–148. https://doi.org/10.1037/a0015912

Schlossberg, N. K. (1981). A model for analyzing human adaptation to transition. *The Counseling Psychologist, 9*(2), 2–18. https://doi.org/10.1177/001100008100900202

Schlossberg, N. K. (1984). *Counseling adults in transition: Linking practice with theory* (1st ed.). Springer Publishing Company.

Schlossberg, N. K., Waters, E. B., & Goodman, J. (1995). *Counseling adults in transition: Linking practice with theory* (2nd ed.). Springer Publishing Company.

Sherry, M., Thomas, P., & Wing-Hong, C. (2010). International students: A vulnerable student population. *Higher Education, 60*(1), 33–46. https://doi.org/10.1007/s10734-009-9284-z

Sue, E., & Rawlings, M. (2013). Preparedness of Chinese students for American culture and communicating in English. *Journal of International Students, 3*(1), 330–341.

Sullivan, C., & Kashubeck-West, S. (2015). The interplay of international students' acculturative stress, social support, and acculturation modes. *Journal of International Students, 5*(1), 1–11.

Summers, M., & Volet, S. (2008). Students' attitudes towards culturally mixed groups on international campuses: Impact of participation in diverse and non-diverse groups. *Studies in Higher Education, 33*(4), 357–370. https://doi.org/10.1080/03075070802211430

Telbis, N. M., Helgeson, L., & Kingsbury, C., (2013). International students' confidence and academic success. *Journal of International Students, 1*(2), 43–49.

Trifonovitch, G. J. (1977). Culture learning/culture teaching. *Educational Perspectives, 16*(4), 18–22.

U. S. Department of Education (2002). Nontraditional undergraduates. *National Center for Education Statistics.* https://nces.ed.gov/pubs2002/2002012.pdf

U. S. Department of Education (2005). Digest of education statistics. *National Center for Educational Statistics.* U. S. Department of Education.

Valdez, G. (2015). US higher education classroom experiences of undergraduate Chinese international students. *Journal of International Students, 5*(2), 188–200. https://files.eric.ed.gov/fulltext/EJ1060060.pdf

Verbik, L., & Lasanowski, V. (2007). International student mobility: Patterns and trends. *World Education News and Reviews, 20*(10), 1–16.

Wigfield, A., & Eccles, J. S. (2000). Expectancy-value theory of motivation. *Contemporary Educational Psychology, 25*, 68–81. https://doi.org/10.1006/ceps.1999.1015

Yakushko, O., Davidson, M., & Sanford-Martens, T. C. (2008). Seeking help in a foreign land: International students' use patterns for a U.S. university counseling center. *Journal of College Counseling, 11*(1), 6–18. https://doi.org/10.1002/j.2161-1882.2008.tb00020.x

Yi, J. K., Lin, J. C. G., & Kishimoto, Y. (2003). Utilization of counseling services by international students. *Journal of Instructional Psychology, 30*(4), 333–342.

Young, A. (2011). First time international college students' level of anxiety in relationship to awareness of their learning-style preferences. *Journal of International Students, 1*(2), 43–49. https://doi.org/10.32674/jis.v1i2.552

Zhao, C. M., Kuh, G. D., & Carini, R. M. (2005). A comparison of international students and American student engagement in effective educational practices. *Journal of Higher Education, 76*(2), 209–231. https://doi.org/10.1080/00221546.2005.11778911

Zhou, J. (2015). International students' motivation to pursue and complete a Ph.D. in the US. *Higher Education, 69*(5), 719–733. https://doi.org/10.1007/s10734-014-9802-5

YVONNE HUNTER-JOHNSON holds a PhD in Adult Education with an emphasis on Human Resource Development and Research and Evaluation from University of South Florida. She also holds a Master of Art in Professional Management with an emphasis on Human Resource Management. She is a certified business teacher (K-12). Currently, she is an Associate Professor at Southern Illinois University (Carbondale) in the department of Workforce Education and Development. As a faculty at SIU, she teaches in the fields of workforce education, human resource development, human resource management, and adult education. As a scholar and educator, she has presented research-based papers in over 10 states and internationally. She has also published a multiplicity of articles in peer-reviewed journals and book chapters. Dr Hunter-Johnson's research interests include: (a) Adult learners and learning, (veterans and international students), (b) Career Transition (veteran and international students), (c) Transfer of Training, (d) Learning Organizations, (e) Motivation to Learn, and (f) Employability and Support Systems in Higher Education. Dr Hunter-Johnson is actively involved in the field of Adult Education, Workforce Education, and Human Resource Development and serves on editorial boards for numerous journals in the field of Adult Education, Teacher Education, Workforce Education, Higher Education, and Criminal Justice. She also serves in a leadership capacity on numerous academic conference committees. As service to the community is essential, Dr Hunter-Johnson is actively involved in committees at the university, college, and departmental levels. Email: yvonne.hunter-johnson@siu.edu

Research Article

© *Journal of International Students*
Volume 12, Issue 2 (2022), pp. 302-323
ISSN: 2162-3104 (Print), 2166-3750 (Online)
doi: 10.32674/jis.v12i2.3594
ojed.org/jis

Adaptation Challenges of Domestic and International Students in a Russian English-Medium Instruction University

Natalia V. Volkova
HSE University, Russia

Anatolii A. Kolesov
Teesside University, UK

ABSTRACT

With the increasing focus on the internationalization of higher education, universities are developing student mobility. This paper examines the challenges experienced by domestic and international students who adapt to a Russian English-medium instruction university. A mixed-method approach with interviews and surveys was utilized to specify, evaluate, and discuss the students' internationalization experiences in these educational settings. The results indicated that both groups of students mentioned different aspects of language barriers, friendship networks, and university social life as critical areas for adjustment. Domestic students avoid taking part in university social life, instead focusing on their academic performance, this fact probably rooted in the Russian approach to secondary education. The specific finding of the Russian educational landscape is a lack of differences between domestic and international students concerning academic integration. All of this suggests institutions to adopt more student-oriented adaptation mechanisms, informed by the concept of inclusion in education; these implications are discussed.

Keywords: international education, international students, Russia, student adjustment, student diversity

---

INTRODUCTION

The internationalization of higher education (HE) has become an ongoing trend for many universities worldwide. This tendency brought together students with different socio-cultural, linguistic, and ethnic backgrounds (Ivanova et al., 2018; Yuan et al., 2019). As a result, research established that sojourners arriving to study at foreign universities experienced numerous challenges that play a critical role in their academic and socio-cultural adaptation to host institutions. Globally and in Russia, these hindrances include, but are not limited to, language barriers (Akanwa, 2015; Arefyev & Sheregi, 2014; Beregovaya & Kudashov, 2019; Li et al., 2018), institutional support (Ivanova et al., 2018; Smith & Khawaja, 2011), social isolation (Bittencourt et al., 2021; Markina, 2018), and difficulty in developing friendships with local students (Golubkina et al., 2018; Guo & Guo, 2017). Moreover, domestic students have their own issues with internationalization. Russians expected that their international classmates would have a general knowledge of the host country's history and cultural aspects (Novgorodtseva & Belyaeva, 2020). Yuan and colleagues (2019) established that studying under an internationalized curriculum led Chinese students to confusions concerning individual, academic, and cultural identities. Anglophone students expressed resentment at the education quality because of the lower entry requirements for their international peers and their negative effects on the grade for teamwork (Marangell et al., 2018). Not surprisingly, the literature has been centered on understanding students' real experiences and mechanisms of adaptation to an internationalized environment (Bittencourt et al., 2021; Rienties et al., 2012; Zhou et al., 2008).

Following the internationalization trend, Russian universities have started introducing English-medium instruction (EMI) programs over the past decade (Block & Khvatova, 2017; Plakhotnik & Volkova, 2020). To provide an excellent learning experience, it is paramount for educators to examine what is necessary for both domestic and international students to adapt to such universities successfully. However, little is known about EMI students' experiences with adapting socially and academically to Russian institutional settings. Prior research mostly considered international students' adaptation to Russian-medium instruction universities (Beregovaya & Kudashov, 2019; Golubkina et al., 2018; Novgorodtseva & Belyaeva, 2020). This study aims to address a gap in cross-cultural adaptation literature by investigating international and domestic students' experiences in a Russian EMI university. These findings can have meaningful implications for international partners of Russian and other post-Soviet countries' universities, professional associations, students, scholars, and teachers preparing to study at or collaborate with HE institutions in these regions.

INTERNATIONALIZATION IN RUSSIAN HIGHER EDUCATION: PROGRESS SO FAR

The general definition of internationalization encompasses "the process of integrating an international, intercultural, or global dimension into the purpose, functions, or delivery of postsecondary education" (Knight, 2004, p. 11). Depending on the needs and expectations, internationalization initiatives vary from country to country (Hill et al., 2019; Uzhegova & Baik, 2020). While universities in Western countries were gradually advancing in their internationalization, post-Soviet HE institutions experienced several challenges in becoming competitive globally, due to a number of structural and economic differences (Dobbins & Kwiek, 2017; Yudkevich, 2014). Before joining the Bologna Process in 2003, Russia was isolated from the main developments in the internationalization of higher education, which led to a lack of English proficiency overall and in the education sphere, in particular (Frumina & West, 2012). In a 2013 OECD report, Russia was marked as a country that had "no or nearly no programs offered in English" (Organisation for Economic Co-operation and Development [OECD], 2013). Most international students coming to Russia before that time were from post-Soviet countries, accounting for 76% of all international students in 2010/2011 (Rosstat, 2020). Such sojourners experienced a relatively small cross-cultural transition due to the absence of language barriers and having general knowledge about the host culture. Besides, they thought more highly the Russian education market, in general (Arefyev & Sheregi, 2014).

Over the last decade, several reforms have been launched to transform Russian higher education and lift national HE institutions in global rankings. In 2012, the Russian government implemented the federal program '5–100-Project,' to advance at least five HE institutions into the top 100 universities worldwide by 2020. Altogether, 21 national universities were gradually selected for this program—15 in 2013, and other 6 HE institutions were added to this group in 2015. The result was an increase in the share of international students in Russia, from 2.2% in 2010/2011, to 7.3% in 2019/2020 (Rosstat, 2020). In this measurement, international or mobile students were defined as individuals "who have moved from their country of origin with the purpose of studying" (OECD, 2013, p. 305). Moreover, according to the Russian Ministry of Science and Higher Education, there are separate indicators for international students from CIS, the Baltic States, and Georgia (all being in the same group), and other countries, as presented in Table 1 from 2010 to 2020.

Table 1: Number of International Students in Russia 2010–2020

Indicators	2010/2011	2016/2017	2017/2018	2018/2019	2019/2020
International students, thou. persons By region:	**153.8**	**244.0**	**260.1**	**278.0**	**298.0**
the CIS, Baltic, and Georgia	116.7	186.8	191.6	198.7	205.9
Europe	1.3	2.5	2.7	3.1	2.8
Asia	28.1	37.5	47.4	55.5	65.4
Central and South America	0.9	1.8	2.0	2.4	2.8
North America (the United States and Canada)	0.1	0.4	0.2	0.3	0.2
Africa	6.7	12.6	15.0	16.7	20.7
Share of international students in total number of students, percent	**2.2**	**5.5**	**6.1**	**6.7**	**7.3**

Additionally, in 2017, to involve the remaining Russian public universities into internationalization, another state project called 'The Development of the Export Potential of the Russian Education System' (Presidium of the Presidential Council for Strategic Development and Priority Projects [PPCSDPR], 2017) was developed. According to this document, attracting international students, running advertising campaigns, and encouraging domestic student mobility are supported by legislation from the Russian government. All these measures are aimed at stimulating all Russian public universities to include internationalization in their strategic development programs before 2022 and increase the number of international students threefold by 2025. This project is a part of non-energy non-commodity export promotion policies aimed to diversify Russian exports with more technologically advanced goods and services. In 2018, the Russian government included non-energy non-commodity export promotion in the National Development Goals (World Bank [WB], 2020).

To summarize, all these educational reform initiatives lead university leaders to develop various internationalization activities, in part by attracting international students (and faculty) through EMI programs. However, foreign and domestic students are different in their adjustment to the university experience (Marangell et al., 2018; Merola et al., 2019). This fact indicates a necessity to examine and develop appropriate mechanisms for the adaptation of learners to international/intercultural environment, internationalized curricula, and teaching practices (Jones & Killick, 2013; Knight, 2004; Ryan, 2011).

CONCEPTUAL FRAMEWORK OF STUDENT ADAPTATION TO EMI UNIVERSITIES

Commonly, adaptation refers to the relatively stable changes in an individual or group, in response to external requirements (Berry, 1997). Cross-cultural adaptation has two fundamental dimensions—psychological (e.g., sense of well-being) and socio-cultural (e.g., social skills for a daily intercultural living) (Ward & Kennedy, 1993). The former is predicted by one's personality, life change events, coping styles, and social support; the latter is connected to behavioral competence, such as knowledge about the host culture, language ability, degree of contact, and intergroup attitudes (Berry, 1997; Ward & Kennedy, 1999). All these factors affecting an individual's cross-cultural adaptation were combined in an acculturation framework developed by Berry (1997), updated in 2005 (Berry, 1997, 2005). Berry (2005) defined acculturation under this model as "a process of cultural and psychological changes that involve various forms of mutual accommodation, leading to some longer-term psychological and socio-cultural adaptations between both groups" (p. 699). Researchers have applied this model as a conceptual lens to make sense of how international students can function in dominant cultures (Li et al., 2018).

In the context of the current study, Berry's framework (1997, 2005) provides one perspective on student adaptation to an institution where they engage in intercultural relations or, in our case, to EMI university settings. However, this model has not been used in its entirety. The literature review showed widespread consensus on the importance of language competence and social support via friendship networks and institutional assistance in adapting to host-university life (Glass et al., 2014; Smith & Khawaja, 2011). According to Berry's framework (1997, 2005), all these challenging issues are associated with acculturative stress. The following sections review studies on student friendship networks, institutional support through integration practices, and language competence in internationalized university environments.

Language Competence

The linguistic ability remains a central index for student adaptation (Ivanova et al., 2018; Smith & Khawaja, 2011; Ward & Kennedy, 1993). Language proficiency is acknowledged to accelerate academic and social integration into university systems (Akanwa, 2015; Beregovaya & Kudashov, 2019; Li et al., 2018), as well as socio-economic, behavioral, and emotional outcomes (Piller, 2016). Language difficulties and subjective cultural differences constrain international students' leisure participation more than the study loads (Glass et al., 2014). It is worth keeping in mind that language differences are associated with disruptive effects on communication due to a lack of vocabulary or a difference in accents (Pudelko & Tenzer, 2019). Not surprisingly, language skills among students and the staff were identified as the decisive obstacle to internationalization in emerging countries (Hill et al., 2019). Hence, the literature on mobility and scholar careers has associated language barriers with a low proficiency in organizational language (or, in the current case, English for university staff members) and/or in the country language of the university (Russian for the international students in this study) (Arefyev & Sheregi, 2014; Pudelko & Tenzer, 2019).

Studies conducted in Russian-medium instruction HE institutions have shown that, for international students, language barriers are the most challenging issue (Arefyev & Sheregi, 2014; Beregovaya & Kudashov, 2019), coupled with weather conditions (Golubkina et al., 2018). However, little is known about student experiences in Russian EMI universities, as learning in English is a new approach in this country.

Institutional Integration Practices

According to Berry's framework (1997, 2005), positive cross-cultural adaptation is usually characterized by striving for an integration acculturation strategy, which requires mutual accommodation between international and domestic students. Integration takes many forms (Merola et al., 2019); research specifically suggested that social and academic integration, which together form institutional integration (French & Oakes, 2004), bolster students' persistence to graduate (Glass et al., 2014; Tinto, 1997). According to a student retention model of Tinto (1975), updated in 2012, individuals' integration is based on their adjusting to HE institutions' academic and social systems (Rienties et al., 2012; Tinto, 1975, 1997). Academic integration refers to grade performance, skill development, and knowledge acquisition. Social integration, however, is connected to participation in university life and can be related or unrelated to one's studies (Rienties et al., 2012). Such adjustment can take the form of developing friendships, participating in formal and informal social activities on campus, doing sports, and team-based projects (Merola et al., 2019). This results in developing communicative and linguistic skills, higher awareness of cultural differences, and greater tolerance (Golubkina et al., 2018; Novgorodtseva & Belyaeva, 2020). Besides, participation in social events on campus, such as volunteer services and cross-cultural events, can help students experience university culture (Akanwa, 2015).

The greater social context is undoubtedly vital for internationalization (Marangell et al., 2018). To this end, it is essential for university staff to develop innovative ways for institutional support, involving all learners in university life. In essence, it leads to the process of inclusion in education. This concept is concerned with identifying and removing barriers for students who may be at risk of marginalization, exclusion, or underachievement (Ainscow, 2005, p. 119). Hence, the design, selection, and use of particular adaptation mechanisms should arise from perceptions about all students' needs.

Student Friendship Networks

Several studies highlighted the critical role of supportive, social, and friendship networks (Smith & Khawaja, 2011; Zhou et al., 2008) for student adaptation. These types of relationships provide much-needed social support (Furnham, 2004; Hendrickson et al., 2011), reflect the degree of contact, and eliminate social isolation (Rose-Redwood & Rose-Redwood, 2013). In the seminal study of Bochner and colleagues (1977), foreign student social networks were classified under three categories: (a) *a co-national network* with compatriots in the host and home countries, established to maintain the original cultural values and behavior (Golubkina et al., 2018; Zhou et al., 2008) and to accelerate understanding of a new culture through conversations and intellectual exchange with those who experience similar attitudes (Bittencourt et al., 2021; Woolf, 2007); (b) *a network with host nationals*, such as home-based students, faculty, and counsellors, established to facilitate academic and professional success; (c) *a multi-national network* with non-compatriot international students, established to boost engagement in recreational activities or get advice. Although international students initially prefer interactions with co-nationals (Glass et al., 2014; Guo & Guo, 2017; Zhou et al., 2008), previous studies demonstrated that friendships with people from the host country are universally more valuable to adapting students (Akanwa, 2015; Golubkina et al., 2018; Novgorodtseva & Belyaeva, 2020; Ward & Kennedy, 1993).

Accordingly, to gain insight into learner experiences, four specific research areas were developed to explore student adaptation to such settings: internationalization experiences, language use, friendship networks, and institutional support via academic and social integration practices.

RESEARCH QUESTIONS

This research delves into how internationalization experiences, language use, student friendship networks, and academic and social integration practices were interpreted and experienced by domestic and international students. In line with these points, two overarching research questions (RQ) are as follows:

RQ1: What internationalization experiences are important for domestic and international students of a Russian EMI university?

RQ2: What challenges do domestic and international students face in terms of friendship networks, language use, and academic and social integration?

Drawing on the concept of inclusion in education (Ainscow, 2005), university adaptation should establish a congruence between perceptions and initial expectations of all learners and university offers (Deil-Amen, 2011; Glass et al., 2014). Therefore, the third research question focuses on comparisons between domestic and international students regarding their social and academic integration.

RQ3: How are academic and social integration different for domestic and international students in a Russian EMI university?

Assuming that local and international students will have different wants and needs, this question goes beyond merely expecting such variations. The particular point is to identify the discrepancies between social and academic integration inside each group of learners.

METHODOLOGY

Data Collection and Context

The data were collected from students studying at one of the Russian research-intensive universities specializing in management and social science, located in the metropolis of the North-West region in 2019–2020. Since 2013, this university has been actively involved in the internationalization process, being a member of the federal program '5–100-Project.' Since then, three bachelor's and seven master's programs, conducted entirely in English, have been opened on this campus to attract international students. The admission requirements include, alongside professional knowledge, evidence of English proficiency—either in the form of passing the Unified State Exam (USE, EGE) in English or an international certificate such as IELTS or TOEFL. A key target indicator of the university development program is increasing the percentage of international undergraduates and postgraduates in full-time student enrolment to 20% by 2030. Overall, 315 international undergraduate and postgraduate students were studying on this campus during the research, which accounted for 5.3% of the total student enrolment there. The five countries from which the most significant number of international students came were, in descending order, Uzbekistan, Kazakhstan, China, Belarus, and Moldova.

Given this study's exploratory nature, a mixed-method research design involving qualitative and quantitative methods was applied (Zachariadis et al., 2013). This approach enabled us to show more valid results by finding agreement across different research strategies (Turner et al., 2017). First, interviews with students were conducted to capture their respective experiences in an internationalized context. Next, an online survey was performed to identify the participants' opinions about their academic and social integration. In this study, all non-Russian citizens who moved to the country with the purpose of studying were considered to be international students.

Qualitative Method

Semi-structured interviews were conducted to grasp students' attitudes during their university adaptation. This method allowed us to gain deeper insights into the entirety of students' integration experience and hidden aspects of university life (Qu & Dumay, 2011). The interview questions centered on students' previous academic backgrounds, internationalization experiences, and drivers of and obstacles to adaptation. The questions were mostly open-ended, to learn participants' perceptions and interpretations, and their order and specifying details varied for each interview, depending on the interviewees' responses. The interviews were recorded and transcribed verbatim, their duration varied from 30 to 60 mins.

The interview transcripts were analyzed via the thematic content analysis method (Burnard, 1991). First, reflective notes summarizing the main ideas and topics raised by the respondent were made after each interview. Second, the interviews were transcribed, and all themes relevant to students' adaptation and internationalization experiences were open-coded and listed. This list was reread to exclude irrelevant themes and merge similar topics in order to develop a unified list of codes. Lastly, the transcripts were coded again according to this unified list, and the pieces of interviews relevant to each particular theme were grouped and given an appropriate title.

Overall, 21 interviews with both domestic and international students from undergraduate (81%) and postgraduate (19%) levels were conducted. The interviewees were recruited through international students' societies, other relevant communities at the university, and the snowball method. The interviewees came from Russia (11), ex-USSR countries (4), Africa (3), Middle East (2), and Asia (1). This classification of countries by region is used intentionally to highlight the number of Russian-speaking students from ex-USSR countries. Out of all the interviewees, 11 were female and 10 were male. The interviewees' average age was 22.4 (SD = 2.55) and 19.7 (SD = 0.91) for international and Russian learners, respectively. The length of stay in Russia ranged from 1 to 4 years (M = 2.70, SD = 0.82) for student sojourners.

Quantitative Method

An anonymous questionnaire was disseminated among 280 students studying in programs conducted in English. The students were contacted online with the help of the heads of two international student associations at the university. All participants completed the survey voluntarily and were informed about the goal of the study. Overall, 102 surveys were returned, an acceptable response rate for organizational studies (36%) (Baruch & Holtom, 2008). Of the total, international and domestic students constituted 51% and 49%, respectively. The sojourners came from 24 countries of the following regions: ex-Soviet Union (42%), Europe (23%), Asia (11%), Middle East (10%), Africa (10%), and Latin America and the Caribbean (4%). Regarding gender, 55% were females, and 45% were males. The average age of international and domestic students was 22.7 ($SD = 4.00$) and 20.0 ($SD = 1.16$), respectively.

The questionnaire included two sections: demographic and university-related characteristics (age, gender, country of origin, study year, and mode) and assessment of academic and social integration, measured on a seven-point disagree–agree scale. Two single-item measurements for academic and social integration were developed on the basis of the literature review and then discussed by three subject matter experts. Each expert evaluated to what extent this single item captures critical aspects of the construct measured and its utility for practitioners (Fisher et al., 2016). According to the feedback, the items for academic and social integration were 'In your opinion, how well are you integrated into the university's academic life (classes, exams, studies, in general)?' and 'In your opinion, how well are you integrated into the university's social life (students' clubs, career days, public lectures, parties, etc.)?'

Statistical analysis was performed via SPSS 20.0 for Windows. First, descriptive statistics were calculated for age, academic, and social integration. Then, independent-samples *t*-test was used to analyze the discrepancy between domestic and international students regarding integration forms. Finally, the paired-sample *t*-test was run to compare social and academic integration for each group of learners.

Limitations

This research has several limitations. First, it explored students studying at only one English-medium instruction institution located in a Russian metropolis. The findings might differ if the sample included individuals from other Russian universities. However, the region of origin makeup of international students mirrors that which is common for other Russian HE institutions (Rosstat, 2020). Second, non-Russian-speaking students used English to answer the interview questions, while other participants communicated through their mother tongue. Thus, the former could not express their opinion in greater detail; however, all interviewees had opportunities to revise interview transcripts. Third, previous studies established other challenges influencing university adaptation, such as ethnicity, socio-economic status, and gender (Deil-Amen, 2011; Guo & Guo, 2017; Jones & Killick, 2013; Markina, 2018; Rienties et al., 2012), all of which went beyond the scope of this inquiry. A final caveat is that doing the survey was voluntary, and the results may have been impacted by what types of students chose to respond.

FINDINGS

The qualitative analysis examined internationalization challenges and opportunities that students reported during university adaptation. Themes and ideas were often similar between domestic and international participants. Many of the interviewees shared identical views and opinions, suggesting homogeneity in this university's student population.

At the beginning of the interview, participants were asked about their internationalized university life experiences to answer the first research question. Most participants (18 out of 21) expressed positive attitudes toward internationalization, which brought a new educational form—EMI programs. Furthermore, as in other countries (Guo & Guo, 2017), the enrolment of international students increased.

> I like it [internationalization]; I think that it is an opportunity to see a different perspective, and it develops you as a person. (Russian student, Political science)

Most students (eight international, six domestic students) noted socio-cultural aspects of internationalization, namely having an opportunity to meet new people, develop intercultural understanding, and get used to a multicultural environment, as illustrated by the following comment:

> I think it's good because a person coming to a different country will talk about their culture, learn something about other cultures. He or she will understand people from different countries — it will help bridging the gap a lot. (International student, Tajikistan, Management)

In the interview, nobody mentioned the competitive advantages of the internationalization experience for future employment. This point keeps the institution relevant to the needs of the society by providing a global workforce (Agnew, 2012; Marangell et al., 2018).

No Russian students perceived classmates from post-Soviet countries as 'international' peers, mostly due to the latter's host language fluency. Such sojourners, in turn, did not have any difficulty in host-university adaptation and mentioned that it was very easy for them to adapt compared with the non-Russian-speaking students.

The key interview themes related to adaptation were (1) lack of English-language information and the low level of English proficiency of the university staff, (2) involvement in social activities, and (3) direct support of student friendship networks. In the following sections and Table 2, these themes are shown, ordered by the frequency of responses and the potential impact that each experience has on adaptation.

Table 2: Adaptation Challenges and Drivers

Theme	International students	Russian students	Both groups
Language barrier	Lack of information in English in online university sources. Lack of Russian language proficiency.	–	Lack of English vocabulary and differences in accents among faculty, students, and staff.
University social life	Lack of social events in English.	Lack of motivation to participate in university social life.	–
Student friendship networks	Contacts with students from ex-USSR countries provide extra support.	–	Main adaptation driver providing support for academic and social integration.

Language Barrier

The participants (18 out of 21) reported that the language barrier was the main problem for university adaptation and their studies. For example, all international students spoke about the current lack of English-language information in different university sources. Here is how one interviewee explained it:

> Sometimes, on the same information platform, they do not provide the same information in English that they provide in Russian; it makes it challenging, because you need to have a Russian in your group to translate the information that was not provided in English. (International student, Ghana, Management Master's)

English-speaking participants stated that administrative staff often failed to understand them, and students would then communicate with their peers, as illustrated by this comment:

> Sometimes, dealing with a certain department at the university, where no staff members speak English nor understand, it was quite difficult. (International student, Nigeria, Political Science)

Russian students (9 out of 11) mostly expressed resentment at the English proficiency of the faculty, as stated below:

> I would say that [the level of English proficiency] varies greatly. There are professors with great English and those whose English is quite primitive. There is a contrast — professors with excellent English and those with mediocre English. (Russian student, Political science)

These comments suggest that developing administrative services for international audiences and monitoring English proficiency among staff members should be included in campus-wide goals. Such results are not unexpected; studies on internationalization in non-Anglophone emerging economies highlighted the lack of English language skills and of professional development of staff as a weakness in these countries (Hill et al., 2019).

Student Friendship Networks

The topic of friendship networks was raised many times (16 out of 21), in response to different interview questions. At this university, students seek assistance from their peers first and only then consult with professors or administrative staff. The following comment illustrates this approach:

> All of my friends are activists, curators, or something like that, so if I don't like something [related to university], I go and tell them, and we think of a solution together. (Russian student, Sociology)

The university provides several peer-mentoring programs and encourages students to participate in these activities. The examples below illustrate such support:

> I think that the most useful and great guys overall were the curators. [...] They are always online, always ready to help. (Russian student, Philology)

> Among the things that helped me the most are the curators. I would often ask them different questions [...] I could find the information the hard way, but if there are curators — they are there for us to ask questions — I always used this opportunity, and they always replied to me. (International student, Kazakhstan, Sociology)

However, information about these programs is scattered among different sources. This fact makes it hard for students to learn about these opportunities, clearly understand their purpose, or find out where they can get the necessary help. Such issues are not new, as universities in developed countries faced similar problems (Akanwa, 2015). In this respect, Russian-speaking students from post-Soviet countries have a unique role in supporting international students from other countries. They assist the latter when there is a lack of information in English, as described below:

> When I have any problem in general, I get in touch with my friends from Russia or the CIS countries, like Ukraine. When it comes to studies, I always write to the study office, but before that… I'd ask my colleagues, especially those who are international students [speaking Russian], because sometimes we get an email in Russian and there is nothing in English. (International student, Pakistan, Management)

Therefore, a subcategory can be added to Bochner et al.'s (1977) model of noninstitutional social networks, to distinguish between non-resident Russian-speaking students and other international sojourners. This category plays a significant role in shaping international students' recreational and educational experiences in Russian education settings. In reference to Berry's (1997, 2005) framework, home-based and international students strived for integration acculturation strategies, negotiating actively with others to seek information.

University Social Life

Most participants (17 out of 21) reported that they were generally satisfied with their academic integration despite occasional minor issues. However, non-Russian speaking students' social integration remains a challenge for most Russian institutions (Markina, 2018). One reason for this fact is that Russian learners did not actively participate in social events because of their heavy study load or interests. Only 3 out of 11 domestic interviewees spoke about being actively involved in the university's social life. Statements made by two participants capture this finding:

> I would not say that I participate a lot in [social events]. I am just not interested. (Russian student, Sociology)

> I did not really have any time for [social events] — especially during the 1st and 2nd year; we had many classes on the same day, and I did not want to go to the university at the weekends. (Russian student, Logistics)

The participants went on to say that most social events were in Russian, which fact became an 'informal' communication barrier for international students, as reported below:

> Some events were organized well, but I had difficulty with the first one. Some presentations were in Russian, so I was lost. Some were in English. Individual students doing specific activities at particular stations spoke English, so it was easy to communicate with them. But at the main event, the main speakers spoke in Russian. (International student, Ghana, Management Master's)

While the language barrier was the main obstacle for participation in social life for the international students, many locals simply did not see sufficient value in the university extracurricular activities. The view of participants emphasized the importance of the linkage between participation in social activities and their motivation. However, social connections acquired at these events "serve as a vehicle through which academic involvement is engaged" (Tinto, 1997, p. 615). Therefore, any mechanisms enhancing engagement, such as listening to students' voices, sharing learning experiences, or delegating managerial issues in organizing these activities, coupled with external impetus, may enhance students' social and academic integration.

Comparative Analysis of Social and Academic Integration

A statistical analysis was performed to establish the difference between domestic and international students in terms of social and academic integration. Table 3 reports means and standard deviations for age, as well as for social and academic integration for each group of participants. To start with, an examination of student differences, via the independent-samples t-test, showed a non-significant result between domestic and international students for both academic (t (100) = 0.994, p = 0.323) and social (t (100) = -1.926, p = 0.057) forms of integration. These results suggest that all learners are almost equally adapted to university life academically and socially.

An examination of the dissimilarity in social and academic integration, via a paired-sample t-test, indicated that these two variables differ significantly for domestic (t (49) = 7.344, p < 0.001) and international (t (51) = 4.041, p < 0.001) students. However, the latter demonstrated a lower discrepancy between these integration forms with paired mean differences, equaling 1.17, compared with 2.14 for locals. Since all participants scored significantly higher academic integration, it leads us to conclude that international and domestic students seem to be more adapted to studies than university social life within this educational context.

Table 3: Means and Standard Deviations for Age and Institutional Integration

Variables	Domestic students $N = 50$		International students $N = 52$		Total $N = 102$	
	Mean	SD	Mean	SD	Mean	SD
Age	20.04	1.16	22.67	4.00	21.38	3.24
Academic integration	5.70	1.31	5.44	1.30	5.57	1.31
Social integration	3.56	1.93	4.27	1.78	3.92	1.88

Note: SD—standard deviation.

DISCUSSION AND CONCLUSIONS

The findings contribute to the existing cross-cultural adaptation literature on the student experience in an internationalized university environment, establishing the stages for further research in this area and suggesting certain implications for university management. *First*, home-based and international students are almost similarly adapted to academic life in this educational landscape, which contradicts some studies conducted in Western countries. For instance, in the Netherlands, international students with a (mixed) Western ethnic background performed better on academic and social integration than domestic peers (Rienties et al., 2012). Given the qualitative and quantitative results, this Russian EMI university rather successfully integrates all learners into academic life. This might be derived from the local education system, focusing more on academic success than developing social competencies (Froumin et al., 2018). This feature is likely to be so prevalent that once students are placed in this educational environment, it provides relatively high academic integration for everyone regardless of their country of origin. Thus, this result supports the notion that academic and social integration is multi-faceted, depending greatly on contextual factors.

Second, this study suggests that Russian students are less actively involved in university social life than their international peers. This discrepancy is likely to be rooted in the local high school system, focusing mostly on academic success (Kuzminov et al., 2011). For instance, research established that high school students with high academic achievement focus less on communicative interaction and emotional components in their motivation than their less academically successful classmates (Nikolaeva, 2018). In view of this, socio-academic interactions advocated by Deil-Amen (2011) could be used to enhance student involvement in social life. Personalized procedural help from administrative staff, coupled with mentoring by trusted teachers, can change students' minds regarding social activities. These techniques reflect the ideas of inclusion in education, which focus on supporting and welcoming diversity amongst all learners and responding to their needs (Ainscow, 2005), alternatively to traditional student integration practices that concentrate on university adjustments (Bittencourt et al., 2021).

Third, despite positive expressions toward internationalization, students did not mention it as a competitive advantage in the global labor market. It could also be connected to social integration resulting in a more profound knowledge about intercultural communication and global career prospects. Hence, universities should consider external incentives for student involvement in social life. To that end, Marangell and others (2018) suggested that activities geared toward boosting social integration should be included in the internationalized curriculum "for credit and in a facilitated, purposeful manner, rather than on an elective, make-your-own-experience basis" (p. 1450). This can be done through, for instance, various joint programs with host students, such as volunteering work, team-based projects, experiential learning, or other formal courses in which students can develop their competencies of intercultural communication. However, a lack of experience of participating in joint activities should be a particular concern of faculty (Novgorodtseva & Belyaeva, 2020). Younger Russian students can be encouraged to participate in social activities for the purpose of, for example, enhancing their respective resumes or portfolios. All of the above means that educators should develop an introductory course for students in their early twenties, to stimulate participation in social life of the university, turning back to more student-oriented practices from inclusion in education.

Finally, the findings provide a more detailed portrayal of students' friendship networks. In Russian educational settings, several region-specific factors affect cross-cultural adaptation, one of them being the lack of English proficiency among staff members. As a result, multi-national networks, consisting of Russian-speaking students, mostly from post-Soviet countries, exist in the informal university culture. International participants indicated such social associations to be supportive and helpful for recreational and academic involvement in university life. When this is the case, administrators and student leaders should identify and support individuals who can link different social and linguistic groups, naturally making these persons university ambassadors. Hence, institutions can use such networks, through which to provide additional support to international students and to listen to student voices about university life (Hendrickson et al., 2011). Identifying similar networks in different settings can be a direction for future studies.

Overall, consistent with the recent study of international students in the United States (Bittencourt et al., 2021), these findings emphasized that social integration practices cannot fully satisfy domestic and international students' needs in terms of adaptation to an EMI university in a non-Anglophone emerging country. Both groups of learners described different challenges. Therefore, university leaders should reconsider the current adaptation practices, instead focusing on student diversity and mechanisms from the concept of inclusion in education (Ainscow, 2005), leading to an atmosphere of mutual engagement among all learners (Rose-Redwood & Rose-Redwood, 2013).

REFERENCES

Agnew, M. (2012). A false dichotomy of serving either the local or the global community and its impact on internationalisation of the university. *Journal of Higher Education Policy and Management, 34*(5), 473–489. https://doi.org/10.1080/1360080X.2012.715997

Ainscow, M. (2005). Developing inclusive education systems: What are the levers for change? *Journal of Educational Change, 6*(2), 109–124. https://doi.org/10.1007/s10833-005-1298-4

Akanwa, E. E. (2015). International students in western developed countries: History, challenges, and prospects. *Journal of International Students, 5*(3), 271–284. https://doi.org/10.32674/jis.v5i3.421

Arefyev, A. L., & Sheregi, F. E. (2014). *Иностранные студенты в российских вузах* [Foreign students in Russian universities]. Center for Sociological Research Publishing. https://www.5top100.ru/upload/iblock/be8/inostrannye_stydenty.pdf

Baruch, Y., & Holtom, B. C. (2008). Survey response rate levels and trends in organizational research. *Human Relations, 61*(8), 1139–1160. https://doi.org/10.1177%2F0018726708094863

Beregovaya, O. A., & Kudashov, V. I. (2019). The problems of linguistic and academic adaptation of international students in Russia. *Integration of Education, 23*(4), 628–640. https://doi.org/10.15507/1991-9468.097.023.201904.628-640

Berry, J. W. (1997). Immigration, acculturation, and adaptation. *Applied Psychology, 46*(1), 5–34. https://doi.org/10.1111/j.1464-0597.1997.tb01087.x

Berry, J. W. (2005). Acculturation: Living successfully in two cultures. *International Journal of Intercultural Relations, 29*(6), 697–712. https://doi.org/10.1016/j.ijintrel.2005.07.013

Bittencourt, T., Johnstone, C., Adjei, M., & Seithers, L. (2021). "We see the world different now": Remapping assumptions about international student adaptation. *Journal of Studies in International Education, 25*(1), 35–50. https://doi.org/10.1177/1028315319861366

Block, M., & Khvatova, T. (2017). University transformation: Explaining policy-making and trends in higher education in Russia. *Journal of Management Development, 36*(6), 761–779. https://doi.org/10.1108/JMD-01-2016-0020

Bochner, S., McLeod, B. M., & Lin, A. (1977). Friendship patterns of overseas students: A functional model. *International Journal of Psychology, 12*(4), 277–294. https://doi.org/10.1080/00207597708247396

Burnard, P. (1991). A method of analysing interview transcripts in qualitative research. *Nurse Education Today, 11*(6), 461–466. https://doi.org/10.1016/0260-6917(91)90009-Y

Deil-Amen, R. (2011). Socio-academic integrative moments: Rethinking academic and social integration among Two-Year College Students in career-related programs. *The Journal of Higher Education, 82*(1), 54–91. https://doi.org/10.1353/jhe.2011.0006

Dobbins, M., & Kwiek, M. (2017). Europeanisation and globalisation in higher education in Central and Eastern Europe: 25 years of changes revisited (1990–2015). *European Educational Research Journal, 16*(5), 519–528. https://doi.org/10.1177%2F1474904117728132

Fisher, G. G., Matthews, R. A., & Gibbons, A. M. (2016). Developing and investigating the use of single-item measures in organizational research. *Journal of Occupational Health Psychology, 21*(1), 3–23. https://doi.org/10.1037/a0039139

French, B. F., & Oakes, W. (2004). Reliability and validity evidence for the institutional integration scale. *Educational and Psychological Measurement, 64*(1), 88–98. https://doi.org/10.1177%2F0013164403258458

Froumin, I., Dobryakova, M., Barannikov, K., &Remorenko, I. (2018). *Универсальные компетентности и новая грамотность: чему учить се годня для успеха завтра* [Key competencies and new literacy: From slogan to school reality]. NRU HSE Publishing. https://ioe.hse.ru/data/2018/07/12/1151646087/2_19.pdf.

Frumina, E., & West, R. (2012). *Internationalisation of Russian higher education: The English language dimension.* British Council. https://www.britishcouncil.ru/sites/default/files/internationalisation_of_russian_higher_education.pdf

Furnham, A. (2004). Foreign students: Education and culture shock. *The Psychologist, 17*(1), 16–19. https://thepsychologist.bps.org.uk/volume-17/edition-1/foreign-students-education-and-culture-shock

Glass, C. R., Gómez, E., & Urzua, A. (2014). Recreation, intercultural friendship, and international students' adaptation to college by region of origin. *International Journal of Intercultural Relations, 42*, 104–117. https://doi.org/10.1016/j.ijintrel.2014.05.007

Golubkina, T. M., Efimova, S. A., Kipriyanova, N. V., Petrosyan, D. I., & Sokolova, M. V. (2018). Russian university through foreign students' eyes. *West – East, 11*, 223–239. https://doi.org/10.30914/2227-6874-2018-11-223-239

Guo, Y., & Guo, S. (2017). Internationalization of Canadian higher education: Discrepancies between policies and international student experiences. *Studies in Higher Education, 42*(5), 851–868. https://doi.org/10.1080/03075079.2017.1293874

Hendrickson, B., Rosen, D., & Aune, R. K. (2011). An analysis of friendship networks, social connectedness, homesickness, and satisfaction levels of international students. *International Journal of Intercultural Relations, 35*(3), 281–295. https://doi.org/10.1016/j.ijintrel.2010.08.001

Hill, C., Hell, S., & Van Cauter, K. (2019). Internationalising higher education in Cambodia, Lao PDR, Myanmar, and Viet Nam: Challenges and approaches. *Studies in Higher Education*, Advance online publication. https://doi.org/10.1080/03075079.2019.1680966

Ivanova, G. P., Logvinova, O. K., & Shirkova N. N. (2018). Pedagogical support of foreign students' sociocultural adjustment: The experience of implementation. *Higher Education in Russia, 27*(3), 60–69. https://vovr.elpub.ru/jour/article/view/1314

Jones, E., & Killick, D. (2013). Graduate attributes and the internationalized curriculum: Embedding a global outlook in disciplinary learning outcomes. *Journal of Studies in International Education, 17*(2), 165–182. https://doi.org/10.1177%2F1028315312473655

Knight, J. (2004). Internationalization remodeled: Definition, approaches, and rationales. *Journal of Studies in International Education, 8*(1), 5–31. https://doi.org/10.1177%2F1028315303260832

Kuzminov, Y. I., Froumin, I. D., & Zakharov, A. B. (2011). Russian school: An alternative to modernization from above. *Educational Studies Moscow, 3*, 5–54. https://doi.org/10.17323/1814-9545-2011-3-5-53

Li, J., Wang, Y., Liu, X., Xu, Y., & Cui, T. (2018). Academic adaptation among international students from East Asian countries: A consensual qualitative research. *Journal of International Students, 8*(1), 194–214. https://doi.org/10.32674/jis.v8i1.160

Marangell, S., Arkoudis, S., & Baik, C. (2018). Developing a host culture for international students: What does it take? *Journal of International Students, 8*(3), 1440–1458. https://doi.org/10.32674/jis.v8i3.65

Markina, D. M. (2018). Socio-economic factors exerting impact on motivation of training in Russia of foreign students on the example of the RANEPA. *Social-Economic Phenomena and Processes, 13*(2), 58–63. https://doi.org/10.20310/1819-8813-2018-13-2-58-63

Merola, R. H., Coelen, R. J., & Hofman, W. H. A. (2019). The role of integration in understanding differences in satisfaction among Chinese, Indian, and South Korean international students. *Journal of Studies in International Education, 23*(5), 535–553. https://doi.org/10.1177/1028315319861355

Nikolaeva, N. V. (2018). Investigation of the interdependence of adaptation characteristics and level of success in the training of students of senior classes. *Proceeding of Herzen's Readings: Psychological Studies in Education*, Russia, 1–1, 261–268.

Novgorodtseva, A. N., & Belyaeva, E. A. (2020). Internationalization of higher education in Russia: Sociocultural interaction of students from the BRICS countries (Russia, China). *Perspectives of Science and Education, 45*(3), 517–526. https://doi.org/10.32744/pse.2020.3.37

Organisation for Economic Co-operation and Development. (2013). *Education at a glance 2013: OECD indicators*. OECD Publishing.

Piller, I. (2016). *Linguistic diversity and social justice: An introduction to applied sociolinguistics*. Oxford University Press.

Plakhotnik, M. S., & Volkova, N. V. (2020). No longer a family: Employee perceptions of organizational culture of a Russian English-medium instruction university. *Journal of Management Development, 39*(1), 82–96. https://doi.org/10.1108/JMD-12-2018-0378

Presidium of the Presidential Council for Strategic Development and Priority Projects. (2017, May 30). *Project "Development of the export potential of the Russian education system."* http://static.government.ru/media/files/DkOXerfvAnLv0vFKJ59ZeqTC7ycla5HV.pdf

Pudelko, M., & Tenzer, H. (2019). Boundaryless careers or career boundaries? The impact of language barriers on academic careers in international business schools. *Academy of Management Learning & Education, 18*(2), 213–240. https://doi.org/10.5465/amle.2017.0236

Qu, S. Q., & Dumay, J. (2011). The qualitative research interview. *Qualitative Research in Accounting & Management, 8*(3), 238–264. https://doi.org/10.1108/11766091111162070

Rienties, B., Beausaert, S., Grohnert, T., Niemantsverdriet, S., & Kommers, P. (2012). Understanding academic performance of international students: The role of ethnicity, academic and social integration. *Higher Education, 63*(6), 685–700. https://doi.org/10.1007/s10734-011-9468-1

Rose-Redwood, C. R., & Rose-Redwood, R. S. (2013). Self-segregation or global mixing?: Social interactions and the international student experience. *Journal of College Student Development, 54*(4), 413–429. https://doi.org/10.1353/csd.2013.0062

Rosstat. (2020). *Russian statistical yearbook 2020*. https://gks.ru/bgd/regl/b20_13/Main.htm

Ryan, J. (2011). Teaching and learning for international students: Towards a transcultural approach. *Teachers and Teaching, 17*(6), 631–648. https://doi.org/10.1080/13540602.2011.625138

Smith, R. A., & Khawaja, N. G. (2011). A review of the acculturation experiences of international students. *International Journal of Intercultural Relations, 35*(6), 699–713. https://doi.org/10.1016/j.ijintrel.2011.08.004

Tinto, V. (1975). Dropout from higher education: A theoretical synthesis of recent research. *Review of Educational Research, 45*(1), 89–125. https://doi.org/10.3102%2F003465543045001089

Tinto, V. (1997). Classrooms as communities: Exploring the educational character of student persistence. *The Journal of Higher Education, 68*(6), 599–623. https://doi.org/10.1080/00221546.1997.11779003

Turner, S. F., Cardinal, L. B., & Burton, R. M. (2017). Research design for mixed methods: A triangulation-based framework and roadmap. *Organizational Research Methods, 20*(2), 243–267. https://doi.org/10.1177%2F1094428115610808

Uzhegova, D., & Baik, C. (2020). Internationalisation of higher education in an uneven world: An integrated approach to internationalisation of universities in the academic periphery. *Studies in Higher Education*, Advance online publication. https://doi.org/10.1080/03075079.2020.1811220

Ward, C., & Kennedy, A. (1993). Where's the "culture" in cross-cultural transition?: Comparative studies of sojourner adjustment. *Journal of Cross-Cultural Psychology, 24*(2), 221–249. https:///doi.org/10.1177/0022022193242006

Ward, C., & Kennedy, A. (1999). The measurement of sociocultural adaptation. *International Journal of Intercultural Relations, 23*(4), 659–677. https://doi.org/10.1016/S0147-1767(99)00014-0

Woolf, M. (2007). Impossible things before breakfast: Myths in education abroad. *Journal of Studies in International Education, 11*(3–4), 496–509. https://doi.org/10.1177%2F1028315307304186

World Bank. (2020). *Russia integrates: Deepening the country's integration in the global economy*. World Bank. http://hdl.handle.net/10986/34994

Yuan, R., Li, S., & Yu, B. (2019). Neither "local" nor "global": Chinese university students' identity paradoxes in the internationalization of higher education. *Higher Education, 77*(6), 963–978. https://doi.org/10.1007/s10734-018-0313-7

Yudkevich, M. (2014). The Russian University: Recovery and rehabilitation. *Studies in Higher Education, 39*(8), 1463–1474. https://doi.org/10.1080/03075079.2014.949537

Zachariadis, M., Scott, S., & Barrett, M. (2013). Methodological implications of critical realism for mixed-methods. *MIS Quarterly, 37*(3), 855–879. https://doi.org/10.25300/MISQ/2013/37.3.09

Zhou, Y., Jindal-Snape, D., Topping, K., & Todman, J. (2008). Theoretical models of culture shock and adaptation in international students in higher education. *Studies in Higher Education, 33*(1), 63–75. https://doi.org/10.1080/03075070701794833

NATALIA V. VOLKOVA (PhD in Psychology) is an associate professor in the Department of Management and the deputy of academic supervisor at English-medium instruction Master's program in Management and Analytics for Business at National Research University Higher School of Economics. Her research focuses on internationalization in higher education, student involvement in university life, and students' association with the university brand. Email: volkovanata1973@gmail.com

ANATOLII A. KOLESOV is a student of a Master's program in Applied Data Science at the School of Computing, Engineering and Digital Technologies, Teesside University in the UK. Among his research interests are the internationalization of higher education, cross-cultural communication, and student experience. Email: B1159927@tees.ac.uk

Research Article

© *Journal of International Students*
Volume 12, Issue 2 (2022), pp. 324-344
ISSN: 2162-3104 (Print), 2166-3750 (Online)
doi: 10.32674/jis.v12i2.3625
ojed.org/jis

The Impact of COVID-19 on International Student Support: A Global Perspective

Lisa Bardill Moscaritolo
American University of Sharjah, United Arab Emirates

Brett Perozzi
Weber State University, United States of America

Birgit Schreiber
University of Freiburg, Germany

Thierry M. Luescher
*Human Sciences Research Council and University of the
Free State, South Africa*

ABSTRACT

The COVID-19 pandemic caused unique challenges to international students. Student Affairs and Services (SAS) across the higher education sector played a key role in supporting students and institutions during the pandemic. This article reports the findings of an exploratory survey with SAS practitioners from around the globe on the ways in which SAS responded to the pandemic and sought to mitigate the impact of the pandemic on students, in general, and international students specifically. The results demonstrate that international students were among the primary groups of students impacted by the pandemic. Specific challenges identified include mental well-being, inability to return home, financial hardships, fear, and uncertainty. Discrimination of certain groups was also noted. SAS intervened to assist international students in navigating these challenges across world regions, including services declared essential for international student support. Finally, financial implications and the future of international student support are explored.

Keywords: COVID-19, international students, mobility, student affairs services, student support

COVID-19 wreaked havoc on higher education (HE) as it did on most areas of society, communities, and nations (Blankenberger & Williams, 2020; Ly, 2020; Marinoni et al., 2020; Organisation for Economic Co-operation and Development [OECD], 2020). In the course of 2020, an overwhelming number of national and international reports from various institutions, and governmental and not-for-profit organizations demonstrated how the pandemic was impacting international student experiences, travel, and overall mobility, describing it as a "Seismic Impact" (Fischer, 2020, p. i). Tesar (2020) argued that universities can no longer expect large numbers of international students on their campuses and need to adjust to different realities, as the implications from COVID-19 "shattered the overall structure of our degrees and programs and units, our plans, our academic rules and processes" (p. 556). The international student experience has changed along with the higher education context, and student affairs and services (SAS) practitioners who work in the international student domain have to adapt. International students are defined throughout this study as any student "who has crossed borders for the purpose of study" (Rebolledo-Gómez & Ranchin, 2013, p. 1).

The study's objectives are to capture how SAS colleagues around the world were responding to the impediments facing international students during this extraordinary time in history, establishing a base knowledge of contextual differences, and informing future practice.

LITERATURE REVIEW AND CONTEXT

SAS administrators are integral in managing emergencies and crises impacting students and higher education institutions (HEIs) (Treadwell & O'Grady, 2019; Zdziarski et al., 2007). It was evident in the early days of the onset of COVID-19 that this was no ordinary crisis and that there would be long-term global impacts on student mobility, internationalization, and international students.

As much as internationalization is not only conceptualized in quantitative terms (Brandenburg et al., 2019), it is impressive to note that in 2017, there were 5.2 million international students globally, which is more than a 60% increase from 2 million in 2000 (OECD, 2020). The top destinations for mobility are the United States, the United Kingdom, Australia, France, Germany, and the Russian Federation. There is also considerable consistency in the top countries of origin of international students over the past decade, whereby the number one source country of international students is China, followed by India, South Korea, and Saudi Arabia (Krsmanovic, 2021; OECD, 2020).

Researchers point out the importance of international students in academic communities through their invaluable impact on "diversity and internationalization of their classrooms" (Hsiao-ping et al., 2015, p. 1; Seeber et al., 2016). Other benefits include enhanced revenue for HEIs, prestige and rankings, increased talent and economic viability for the country and region, and personal development for students (Brown & Jones, 2007; Chao et al., 2017; Choudaha, 2016; OECD, 2020). Most recently, Brandenburg et al. (2019) discussed how the benefits should be expanded to include the socio-cultural impact through volunteerism and community engagement, and de Wit (2019) suggested that it should include "global learning for all" (p. 7).

HE and SAS practitioners are central in supporting international students in their personal, social, and academic goals. The support ranges from psycho-social development and support to assisting with pragmatic issues around permits and accommodation (Arthur, 2017; Ly, 2020; Perez-Encinas & Ammigan, 2016). Ludeman and Schreiber (2020) recently argued that "The impact SAS has on students, both academically and developmentally, proves to be essential and central to the HE mission and enterprise" (p. 10). Typically, SAS is the first staff who students studying abroad encounter when they arrive on their host campus (Wecker, 2017). The kind of support given to international students traditionally includes managing immigration and visa status (Choudaha, 2016; David, 2020). Much of this happens through orientation programs, or central offices dedicated to international student support, or is decentralized throughout the campus.

There are diverging views on the long-term impact of the COVID-19 pandemic. Marinoni et al. (2020) and others (e.g., Bilecen, 2020; Martel, 2020; "New EAIE Report", 2020) warned that the pandemic has stunted efforts to internationalize higher education via mobility and international students. Yet others are less pessimistic, arguing that other global influences including the pandemic pave the way for a new understanding of internationalization (Brandenburg et al., 2019; O'Malley, 2020). In the midst of this, Deardorff (2020) highlighted the risk of COVID-19 accentuating parochial populism and narrow-minded nationalism and calls for us "to reflect upon what matters most, what bonds us all together, and what it means to be a good neighbor" (p. xv), reminding us of the African concept of ubuntu: "I am because we are" (p. xvi). We are all part of a globalized world of HE (Altbach, 2010), and continuing the important work of HE internationalization, which includes supporting international students, is now more important than ever before.

This study is therefore designed to gain insight into the following areas related to international student support:

1. How and when was SAS involved in institutional decisions (and was support to international students considered)?

2. Which student population of students was most impacted?

3. What challenges were experienced by international students?

4. Were international students subjected to discrimination?

5. Which services were essential and how were international students supported?

6. What specific services or programs were offered to international students?

7. What changes do SAS professionals expect in the future?

METHODOLOGY

At the start of the COVID-19 pandemic, a research team of four higher education student affairs experts from Germany, South Africa, the United Arab Emirates (UAE), and the United States sought to understand the impact of COVID-19 and the related lockdowns, restrictions on practice, perceptions, and engagement of SAS in higher education across the globe.

Sampling and Sample

An online survey was distributed using the referral sampling method (also called snowball sampling) (Creswell, 2013). A non-probability sampling technique was used to generate a stratified but non-random convenience sample that reflects the broad spectrum of student affairs professionals globally but is not strictly speaking statistically representative. The referral sampling method is appropriate to reach 'hard to reach' groups during extraordinary times (Creswell, 2013). While the sample is not suitable for theory testing or making statistically reliable generalizations, it is appropriate to explore different kinds of practices as well as variations between contexts, and it enables theory and hypothesis development.

As a starting point, the survey was distributed by the International Association of Student Affairs and Services (IASAS) to its membership, as well as through email and social media (mainly Facebook, Twitter, and LinkedIn) and networks known to the researchers. In addition, more than 20 national and international SAS associations that are members of IASAS shared the survey with their respective membership and researchers distributed it further to their networks. This combination of methods facilitated rapid responses that reached a level deemed adequate (Goodman, 2011; Salganik & Heckathorn, 2004). It allowed the researchers to reach SAS professionals in countries and regions that could not have been reached in a timely manner by other means (compare for alternatives Baltar & Brunet, 2012; Salganik & Heckathorn, 2004).

After cleaning almost 1,000 responses for duplicates and incompleteness, there remained 781 responses (of which 46% fully completed the questionnaire and the rest completed it partially). Statistical Package for Social Sciences (SPSS) and NVivo tools were used for analysis. SPSS was used for descriptive statistics and cross-tabulation in quantitative analysis. NVivo was used for coding and thematic analysis of qualitative text responses.

The researchers used United Nations Educational, Scientific and Cultural Organization [UNESCO's] (2018) and IASAS' geographical regions as the primary guides to organize responses into seven world regions (i.e., Africa, Asia, Europe, Middle East, Oceania, North America, and Latin America & Caribbean/LAC), which allowed for interregional comparisons. Table 1 lists the respondents by regions based on respective IP addresses. The researchers acknowledge that the regions are diverse, however, a country comparison would not have been useful as some countries (especially those that do not use English in higher education) have low participation numbers.

Table 1: Number of Respondents by World Region, N = 781

Region	Number of participants
Africa	118
Asia	144
Europe	207
Middle East	35
Oceania	108
North America	149
Latin America and Caribbean	20
Total	**781**

Of these respondents, 35% reported that they had less than 5% international students on campus, 21% reported that 10% of their student body was international, and 20% reported that 25% or more were international students on their campus.

Instrument Design and Data Collection

Participants were asked to complete a questionnaire hosted on the Qualtrics platform, consisting of 53 questions, after voluntarily consenting. The questionnaire comprised many qualitative, open-ended questions as well as several questions with multiple choice, rank, and grading options. Specifically, there were nine questions on HEI and SAS involvement in decision-making, four questions on SAS responses to the pandemic, three questions on the possible financial implications of the pandemic, and three questions on thoughts on how the pandemic will impact practices and approaches in the future. In addition, there were eight questions on residence halls/student accommodations, and eight questions on SAS professionals working remotely, three questions on student outreach and engagement with student leaders, and seven questions on the impact on unique student populations. Included in this questionnaire were nine questions specifically related to international students and internationalization. The questionnaire ended with a set of demographic questions.

SAS practitioners were able to participate in the survey during the month of May 2020 and they did not have to answer all questions.

Analysis

NVivo qualitative data analysis software was used to analyze the qualitative responses. Specifically, it was used to extract themes via word frequency counts which were recorded and are reflected in the findings below (Woolf & Silver, 2018). SPSS offers statistical analysis of data and generates tables, visual graphs, and charts of the data which help us understand the SAS responses to COVID-19, i.e., describe observations rather than test hypothesis (Courtney & Gordon, 2013).

Limitations

Given the sampling methods used in order to access the hard-to-reach respondents under the uncertain conditions of the first COVID-19 wave, the data presented in this study are not fully randomized and should not be statistically generalized without further interrogation. As typical in exploratory empirical studies, statements of generality and comparison should be understood as propositions that require further testing (Bonevski et al., 2014).

Ethics

This research was approved by the institutional research review board of the American University of Sharjah in the UAE, the home institution of one research team member.

FINDINGS OF THE GLOBAL SAS COVID-19 RESEARCH

The coronavirus pandemic impacted international students in specific ways and higher education institutions and SAS rallied to devise innovative ways to support them. In this section, we discuss the experiences of SAS professionals around providing support to and engaging with the needs of international students. Provided that the data we discuss here are not statistically representative, we use the data to explore, describe, and try to understand the creative ways in which SAS engaged with the situation around international students across the globe and in specific regions.

SAS Involvement in Institutional Decision-Making

The majority of respondents (86%) indicated that SAS was key in the institutional decision-making during the pandemic on their campuses. When making decisions for their student communities, reasons around "community safety," "teaching and learning," and "ethics and care" were the top three considerations for institutional decision-making in all world regions, in this order. For Europe, Oceania, and North America, these three reasons were followed by how the decisions impacted international students, and then impact on students living in residence halls. The other regions considered residence halls first then international students. Overall, SAS across the seven regions was involved in the institutional decision-making by the second month (82%) of the institution being impacted by COVID-19. Our results suggest that SAS played a central role early-on in institutional decision-making around the pandemic and its impact on international students.

Impact on International Students and Other Student Groups

Research respondents identified international students as the student group that was impacted more significantly than others. Figure 1 shows that international students, in general, and Asian and Chinese students as a special group of international students, were identified as the student groups most impacted by the pandemic. The second group identified by respondents was students with lower socio-economic status (SES). This group was followed by students from difficult home situations that included violence, marginalized because of sexual identity, loss of a job, inadequate Wi-Fi, and students living and learning with disability. The categories are not mutually exclusive as there is some overlap; yet, there were clear regional variations, which are discussed below.

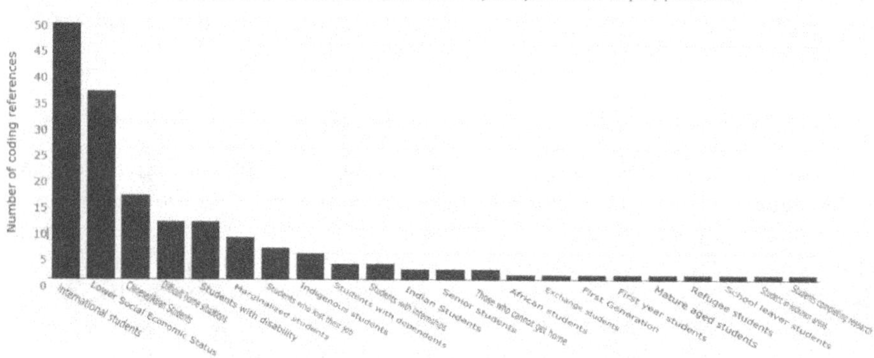

Figure 1: Populations of Students Impacted by COVID-19

Regional Variations

Respondents from Europe indicated that international students were the student group most impacted, followed by the student group who had lost their jobs, and then students who were living in difficult home situations. International students were considered the most impacted group of students in Oceania, Latin America and the Caribbean (LAC), and the Middle East. This is also the case for North America, followed by the group of lower-SES students.

Responses from the Africa and Asia regions diverged from this finding. African SAS respondents indicate that lower-SES students were most impacted, the second group most impacted were students living in difficult home situations including students living in overcrowded households, students who lacked access to Wi-Fi, and those exposed to gender-based and family violence. The third group in the African sample was students with disabilities. In the Africa region, the SAS respondents identified international students only as the fourth group most impacted by the COVID-19 pandemic.

Conversely in Asia, the data show that respondents from that region considered the student group most impacted as those living in difficult home situations, then lower-SES students, and third were international students.

The findings in this section illustrate several points. First, the fact that in all contexts SAS was involved from the earliest moments of the pandemic in institutional decision-making is an acknowledgment of the importance of SAS. Second, the finding that international students are considered the student group that was most impacted by the pandemic in five of the seven world regions is informative. The pattern of world regions also corresponds with patterns of international student mobility.

Specific Challenges Facing International Students

The survey asked SAS professionals what the most prevalent challenges were facing international students during the first wave of the COVID-19 pandemic. The respondents overwhelmingly noted emotional stress (96%), the challenges faced by international students to return home (88%), financial challenges (74%), and fear (67%) as impacts. This is explored further below and discussed in terms of emerging regional variations.

Mental Health and Emotional Well-being

Almost all of the responding SAS practitioners (96%) noted that international students faced enormous emotional stress during the pandemic. It is therefore not surprising that the most important essential SAS service noted by survey respondents across the globe was counseling services, which responded quickly to offer virtual mental health support. Along with the ongoing provision of mental health services, communication to international students was paramount according to the data. A North American colleague noted that among the specific support services established during the pandemic was the creation of "Specific Task Forces" for international students involving SAS and faculty partners who were assigned "to check in and support international students." Another respondent from North America referred to the increase of "First Alert Teams" in their SAS unit.

Other qualitative responses to the survey show the range of help developed for international students that included, for example, in Oceania, a "dedicated cross-functional team working with international students and communicating with them via phone, group chat, workshops and Moodle." A SAS staff member in the Middle East worked to pair up student leaders to answer questions and concerns in a peer support network, and offer support through "video content." In African universities and elsewhere, WhatsApp groups were created to communicate with students and answer specific queries, especially those from international students. Other help in North America included "storage for personal belongings for those who moved out" and "free food hampers for international students who needed it." In Asia specifically, SAS considered and supported the families of international students as well through outreach.

Inability to Return Home

A large majority of the survey respondents (88%) indicated that international students in their institution were impacted by the closing of borders and airlines not operating due to the pandemic. SAS navigated immigration issues for students during this time, assisted with continuing their studies, and ensured accommodations and food when needed. Indeed, there was a tremendous amount of support offered around immigration and the need to get students home. Respondents mentioned the following support services they offered to international students:

- "Facilitation of travel for aid from government and ability to study remotely from home country"; and "embassy connections" were comments from colleagues in LAC;

- "Regular communication about study permits" and "specific online sessions were offered to F-1 and J-1 students and advising was done remotely" were responses from North America staff. (Note: Under US law, F-1 and J-1 is a Visa status for international students studying in the US.);

- When returning home was not possible "due to war or other strife," a respondent from Middle East assisted by providing these students "with funds to reside with relatives in safer places."

This global survey further shows that SAS practitioners in all world regions assisted students in navigating ministry of health requirements and numerous visa challenges when they arose.

Financial Hardship

Seventy-five (75%) of respondents indicated that international students were suffering financially during the pandemic. SAS offered emergency grants to students for transportation, housing, and food. When asked how their institution supported international students a SAS practitioner in Oceania noted that "70+% of applicants" who applied for hardship monies were international students. Another Oceania colleague mentioned that other forms of help were offered by their institution, like grocery vouchers and food banks.

Even before COVID-19, financial resources were one of the challenges for international students (Hsiao-ping et al., 2015). In Europe, about 59% of students work to support themselves (Gil, 2014). European SAS professionals noted that due to the pandemic, many students lost their part-time jobs, which impacted their ability to meet expenses. SAS practitioners in Europe assisted students in obtaining government emergency grants and other forms of financial assistance.

Fear and Uncertainty

Along with the other three factors, respondents noted that fear was affecting international students in their institutional contexts. Even though there were no specifics in the multiple-choice questions on why this group of students faced fear, some of the qualitative responses suggest that the international students' fear was founded in the uncertainties they faced; how they would be able to study if they were away from campus, their inability to return home in some cases, and for some, food and housing insecurity. Adjusting to a new culture and acculturating (Berry, 2006) is a pressure that any new international student faces. The academic, day-to-day, and economic stresses facing the students were, of course, greatly intensified during the global health pandemic (Cao et al., 2020).

Survey results show that SAS worked to mitigate challenges facing international students while adapting to a different work mode. The uncertainty around if and how they were going to be able to finish the semester, fund housing and other necessities, along with the inability to be with family and networks familiar to them, clearly exasperated international students by May 2020 in the height of the pandemic. As noted above, it is not surprising that the number one concern for those from the sample was the mental health of international students.

COVID-19 Discrimination

A factor that may have aggravated the fears and impact on their mental well-being may have been discrimination experienced by international students in some contexts. International students make decisions on where to attend college based, among other reasons, on how welcoming the country is to international students (Choudaha, 2017; "International Student Survey-QS", 2020). International students typically chose to study across borders to improve socio-economic status for themselves and their families (Brown & Jones, 2017; Choudaha, 2016). According to an IEE study, one of the reasons a student chooses to study overseas is to improve their chances to find work back home (Arthur, 2017; Chao et al., 2017). International students are often facing financial struggles and need to find ways to fit in and adjust academically and socially (Hsiao-ping et al., 2015). With the recent wave of nationalism and populism around the world even though in some countries like the US new presidential changes may make the country more welcoming, many communities do not see the value of international students (Mittelmeier & Cockayne, 2020; Mok, 2018), which can lead to a hostile environment.

Three-fourths of the global sample of SAS practitioners (75%) did not feel that their international students were subject to discrimination. Yet, out of the 25% who responded affirmatively when asked which ones of their international student populations were targets of discrimination, the majority answered students from Asia.

Regional Variations

The 25% who noted that their international students faced discrimination were primarily from four regions: Oceania, North America, Asia, and Europe. No responses were received from Africa, LAC, and the Middle East.

A SAS professional from Oceania commented, "I have listed that Asian students experienced stigma, but this was not so much on campus, more in our country's social media and the reaction in community (e.g., people stopped frequenting Chinese restaurants and Chinatown areas)." Another respondent from Oceania noted, "International Chinese students were facing a lot of issues regarding entry into NZ during COVID19." The first comment could be more about the perceived discrimination felt by Chinese/Asian students that they heard about through media and in communities outside of the university; yet, these comments can send an unwelcoming message. Furthermore, a colleague in North America noted, "Yes, international students, and yes, Asian American/API students. Our campus didn't have any specific incidents of racism, but fear was increased, in general, for those populations and what has been happening."

The open-ended responses show that there may not have been many direct experiences of discrimination of international students as a result of the pandemic. However, some of the qualitative data indicate that the culture and political discourse around the coronavirus may have impacted international students, especially Asian/Chinese students. With a general increase in the level of xenophobia and prejudice toward international students (Beckstein, 2020; Deardorff, 2020), this can negatively impact well-being. A recent global study of social media posts confirmed that the overall public felt negative about overseas visitors to their country (Mittelmeier & Cockayne, 2020).

Specific SAS Support Offered to International Students

The survey asked SAS professionals what services SAS continued to offer during the lockdown and restrictions in the first wave of the COVID-19 pandemic and which services were specifically offered to international students.

Essential Services

When campuses moved to online teaching and learning, many SAS units were designated as "essential services." They typically included counseling and mental health services, health care, housing/student accommodation, and academic advising. The main essential SAS support offered to students across all seven regions was mental health and counseling services. Primarily, these services were offered virtually with some face to face (F2F) offering for emergency services, health care, and residential needs.

Categorizing SAS functions as essential services and offering these via virtual avenues occurred across all regions. As of May 1, 2020, 76% of respondents noted that the specific support for international students took place virtually, 20% offered support virtually and F2F, and a small percentage (4%) provided help in person only.

Regional Variations. Although nominal, respondents from Asia (10%) and the Middle East (7%) noted slightly more F2F provision of support to international students than respondents from other regions of the world, where, on average, their share of F2F services was low (3.5%). When asked how international student support would be delivered for the remainder of 2020, respondents were hopeful that they could implement more programs and services in a hybrid manner. Of the global SAS respondents, just over half (51%) indicated they would be able to offer virtual services, 45% indicated they would offer both F2F and virtual and 4% said they would only offer F2F. Respondents in Oceania more than any other region responded with a higher percentage (65%) than the 45% for all regions that they would operate support for international students in a hybrid fashion.

Because of the timing of new health and travel regulations for Oceania respondents, SAS was managing both students from China who just arrived for the semester and students who were still in their country of origin. Thus, it was a challenge for SAS to remotely support both F2F students and those who were remote. Further comments indicate again that the well-being of international students was a major concern, so it is not surprising that the main essential service for students globally was counseling.

How International Students Were Supported

Figure 2 illustrates the ways in which SAS supported international students to help their transition to online learning, provide accommodation and offer food security, and deal with various other challenges that students faced to continue their education. Travel restrictions prevented many international students from returning to their host campus after Christmas breaks, "spring breaks" or the Lunar New Year celebrations, or other reasons that had taken students home. Others needed housing/student accommodation, and counseling and health services were again among the most frequently offered. Other assistance mentioned most often included financial assistance, staff support, support around academic issues, and immigration-related challenges.

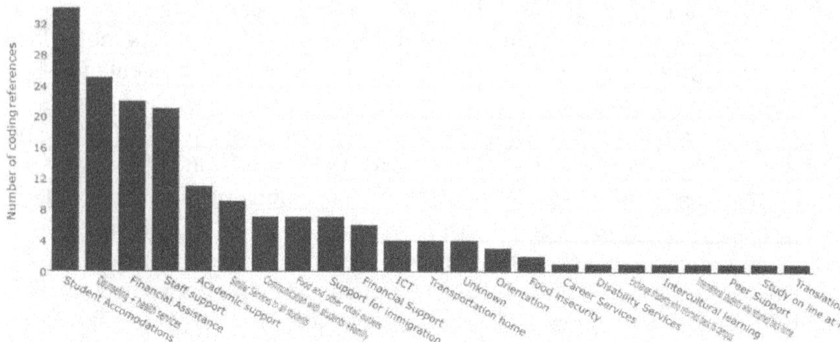

Figure 2: SAS Specific Support for International Students

Regional Variations. The diversity of higher education systems and institutional types across the globe provides for regional variances in the provision of services specific to international students during the pandemic. In Europe and Oceania, responses show that providing financial assistance was the most frequently provided service to international students. As mentioned above, this may be because in Europe, international students who support themselves lost part-time jobs. In Asia, student accommodation and financial help were not the primary service offered to international students. Instead, communication outreach to students, counseling services, and academic support ranked slightly higher. As one respondent from Asia indicated: "Students all have a 'case manager' from student affairs maintaining contact."

The top three services that North American SAS professionals continued to provide to international students, in particular, were student accommodations, communication outreach to students, and financial assistance. As indicated by a respondent in North America, "[Students were placed in] single rooms to ensure physical distancing and [provided meals at] staggered mealtimes for food pick up. We permitted international students to remain, without cost, because of border closures." Although counseling and mental health was the number one service offered to all students, SAS respondents indicated that housing and student accommodation was more of a concern for international students compared with local/domestic students due to travel restrictions.

The government and public restraints during the first wave of the pandemic were overwhelming and dictated much of what was going to happen for the international student population; whether they remained in their host country of study or returned home, or in the inverse case, whether they were confined to their home country or would be able to return to their chosen country of study eventually. As has been shown in this section, SAS professionals in different contexts and with different emphases were there to intervene and assist international students in meeting the guidelines, dealing with immigration policies and travel arrangements, or ensuring ongoing provision of accommodation, catering, as well as health and well-being services.

The Post-Covid-19 Future of SAS Support to International Students

When the survey was conducted in May 2020, every world region was still experiencing the first wave of the COVID-19 pandemic. Some countries were still under lockdown while in others lockdown restrictions had gradually begun to be lifted (Langer, 2020). Without a vaccine in the offing and a second wave looming, there was much uncertainty as to the lasting changes that the pandemic might have on higher education and international students.

In our study, SAS professionals commented that the way international students were supported would change as a result of the COVID-19 experience. In the process, they also made several critical comments. Thus, when asked about mistakes made by the institution or what they would do differently, a general comment was that HEIs and SAS needed to be smarter and more nuanced in their approach to serving international students to level the playing field for students from different backgrounds and abilities, and to ensure student success (also see, Bardill Moscaritolo & Roberts, 2016; Humphrey, 2020; Ludeman & Schreiber, 2020).

Our coding of open responses indicates a nuanced set of expectations. On the one hand, SAS practitioners hoped that the medium to long-term impact of the pandemic experience would be enhanced globalization efforts in the profession. On the other hand, respondents believed it was likely that there would be fewer international students that will negatively impact their institution's finances. In any case, they expected that there would be a restructuring of SAS organizations and that changes in services were likely. For example, a colleague from North America stated:

> Fewer international students will mean less demand for those services in the short term. However, if anything this pandemic has taught us the world is a small place that is highly connected. We need a continued focus on internationalizing our campuses to build awareness, cultural understanding, and nurture a global perspective.

With respect to what the future may hold, foremost on the minds of SAS professionals were the financial impact of the pandemic on HEIs and the provision of SAS support to international students.

Institutional Financial Impact of Less International Students

Three-fourths of the respondents (75%) believed that it would take more than two years for their institution to recover financially from the effects of the pandemic. Thus, SAS staff were concerned about layoffs and furloughs, especially in international student support and exchange offices/units, which they expected to be more affected. It is unclear if lack of international students was the main reason but based on the open-ended responses on internationalization and the future impact on SAS, a major fear for SAS professionals around the globe was that the impact of the pandemic would be restructuring and job losses.

In the European sample, international students were noted as the main population affected by COVID-19. With respect to the future, European respondents were therefore concerned about the impact of fewer international students on their internationalization efforts. Similarly, respondents from the Middle East noted that international students were the number one population affected by the pandemic. A respondent from the Middle East argued that less international mobility of students would increase the homogeneity of the campus and that this was concerning.

Possible Restructure of SAS Impact on International Student Support

As intimated above, the start of the pandemic required SAS practitioners to quickly adapt to delivering services and education in different ways. Remote working arrangements were hastily put in place as restrictions were implemented for staff and students on campus. With fewer international students, reduced budgets, a lack of F2F support (because of restricted activities on campus) has changed how students learn and develop outside of the classroom, which calls for SAS to support students differently. What has been learned from this experience and how will this translate into new models of support especially for international students? Will specific services for international students be combined into services for all students?

When asked to predict possible changes to SAS, themed coding of responses indicate that expected changes in how SAS might change involved more online provision of services and support for students. This can be seen, for example, in the following quote: "The philosophy or the basis of our work has been challenged and the how-to for our day-to-day work has drastically changed." This change in SAS philosophy and way of providing SAS will require creativity and re-invention. "It gives another way to think about [a] modern way to internationalize student affairs and services: that services can be given without social interaction."

DISCUSSION, IMPLICATIONS, AND FURTHER RESEARCH

This global COVID-19 study provides evidence from SAS practitioners around the world that international students were among the student groups most affected by the pandemic. In world regions that are typically destinations for international students, this group was noted without fail as the most impacted. In the world regions from where more globally mobile students originate, international students were among the top five groups but typically not the most frequently mentioned. Nonetheless, global SAS professionals made international students a priority in their efforts to mitigate the impacts of the COVID-19 pandemic.

Top exporting countries can leverage these results to leverage and engage SAS practitioners to help support international students. The pandemic has demonstrated the value and centrality of SAS programs and services for student success. Hosting international students at scale is a major undertaking for any institution, and knowing the essential and germane supports needed by international students and working together with those providing these supports can help policymakers and higher education professionals realize success for their institutions and students.

Focus on International Students and Support

A strong implication of this research is the attention that the pandemic has brought to international students, reopening questions around the purpose and value of international student mobility, and the nature and delivery of specific SAS services to appropriately support international students facing unique challenges in the context of the pandemic. These same questions present themselves in a post-COVID-19 future. As shown in this study, SAS professionals around the globe expect a restructuring and potential consolidation of SAS services, in general, along with an increased use of hybrid (virtual and F2F) models of providing SAS to international students.

Post-COVID-19 Continued Focus on International Student Support

The findings show the challenges experienced by international students during the pandemic, including their mental well-being, financial hardship, inability to return home (or to campus), related anxieties, and (a sense of) discrimination, and fear. With respect to lockdown travel restrictions and grants to alleviate students' financial hardships, there are lessons to be learned too. SAS professionals work with higher education institutional and system policymakers to decrease the impediments faced by international students whether it is in the way financial grants are determined and administered or interpreting immigration guidelines. The global birds' eye view of this study provides a rich source for developing and testing related propositions.

Partnerships for Improved Mental Health Services

The mental health of youth and adolescents must be a priority around the world. How can new partnerships among public and private sectors assist HEIs in meeting the mental health needs of students and give special attention to international students' well-being, not just during a pandemic? Research by Cao et al. (2020) on the impact of COVID-19 on Chinese students concluded that 26% of those studied presented with anxiety as a result of COVID-19. They call for institutions and government to work together to solve the problem "to provide high-quality, timely crisis-oriented psychological services to college students" (p. 4).

This study showed that mental well-being was the most persistent challenge, and student counseling and mental well-being services were therefore a key essential service mentioned in most regions as HE swiftly moved away from F2F modes of instruction Jand operation to other programs and service delivery modalities, throughout the pandemic. The rapid response teams, peer counseling models, and so forth, developed in the process, which were able to respond to international students' well-being challenges, need to be documented in-depth to diversify and enhance SAS provision to this group going into the future.

Managing Racism Impacting International Students Must Be a Priority

With the pandemic came more incidents of racism and xenophobia (Deardorff, 2020). We concur with Lee and Rice's (2007) call for institutions of higher education to evaluate how they manage racism impacting international students. Perhaps, with new relationships in place because of COVID-19 now is the time to have these conversations with internal and external stakeholders.

A common emergency across the globe presents tremendous challenge and hardship, yet provides an opportunity to review various perspectives and responses to the emergency. This study demonstrates that similar challenges for international students globally can be addressed and solved in different and culturally appropriate ways.

CONCLUSION

The primary objective of the study was to gain a comparative understanding of SAS response to the pandemic, particularly as it affected international students, to advise future practice. This survey describes and analyses the SAS responses to and engagements with international students at higher education institutions across the globe during the early days of the COVID-19 pandemic. International students were impacted in unique and distinct ways, primarily experiencing challenges around mental health, returning home, financial hardship, and dealing with acute issues around anxiety and uncertainty. Comparison across the world reveals that most regions listed international students as the most vulnerable group during the COVID-19 crisis at that time. The Africa and Asia region divert from this trend, with Africa listing students from lower-SES and students with disability, and Asia listing students living with difficult home situations as more vulnerable than international students at that time in that region. It emerges from these findings that SAS has played a vital role in mitigating the impact of COVID-19 on international students. Given that this research was done during crisis under time pressure, seeking responses from hard-to-reach participants, the results were not intended to test theory, but to illuminate the experiences of international students and the SAS responses to their needs along with regional variations. The understanding generated by this research guides higher education and SAS decision-makers to strengthen the support provided by SAS to international students.

REFERENCES

Altbach, P. (2010). The realities of mass higher education in a globalized world (p. 256). *In higher education in a global society* (Ser. [tiaa-cref institute series on higher education]). Edward Elgar Publishing.

Arthur, N. (2017). Supporting international students through strengthening their social resources. *Studies in Higher Education, 42*(5), 887–894. https://doi.org/10.1080/03075079.2017.1293876

Baltar, F., & Brunet, I. (2012). Social research 2.0: Virtual snowball sampling method using Facebook. *Internet Research, 22*(1), 55–74. https://doi.org/10.1108/10662241211199960

Bardill Moscaritolo, L., & Roberts, D. (2016). Global competencies for student affairs and services professionals. In K. Osfield, B. Perozzi, L. Bardill Moscaritolo, & R. Shea (Eds.), *Supporting students globally in higher education: Trends and perspectives for student affairs and services* (pp. 109–126). NASPA Publishers.

Beckstein, A. (2020, July 24). How are international students coping with the COVID-19 *pandemic?* https://www.timeshighereducation.com/student/blogs/how-are-international-students-coping-COVID-19-pandemic

Berry, J. W. (2006). Acculturative stress. In P. T. P. Wong and L. C. J. Wong (Eds.), *International and cultural psychology series. Handbook of multicultural perspectives on stress and coping* (pp. 287–298). Springer. https://doi.org/10.1007/0-387-26238-5_12

Bilecen, B. (2020, July 30). Commentary: COVID-19 pandemic and higher education: International mobility and students' social Protection. https://doi.org/10.1111/imig.12749

Blankenberger, B., & Williams, A. M. (2020). COVID and the impact on higher education: The essential role of integrity and accountability. *Administrative Theory & Praxis, 42*(3), 404–423. https://doi.org/10.1080/10841806.2020.1771907

Bonevski, B., Randell, M., Paul, C., Chapman, K., Twyman, L., Bryant, J., Brozek, I., & Hughes, C. (2014). Reaching the hard-to-reach: A systematic review of strategies for improving health and medical research with socially disadvantaged groups. *BMC Medical Research Methodology, 14*(42). https://doi.org/10.1186/1471-2288-14-42

Brandenburg, U., Leask, B., Jones, E., & de wit, H. (2019, April 20). Internationalisation in higher education for society. *University World News Global Window on Higher Education.* https://www.universityworldnews.com/post.php?story=20190414195843914

Brown, S., & Jones, E. (2007). Values, valuing and value in an internationalised higher education context. In E. Jones & S. Brown (Eds.), *Internationalising higher education* (pp. 1–6). Routledge.

Cao, W., Fang, Z., Hou, G., Han, M., Xu, X., Dong, J., & Zheng, J. (2020). The psychological impact of the COVID-19 epidemic on college students in china. *Psychiatry Research, 287.* https://doi.org/10.1016/j.psychres.2020.112934

Chao, C., Hegarty, N., Angelidis, J., & Lu, V. F. (2017). Chinese students' motivations for studying in the United States. *Journal of International Students, 7*(2), 257–269. https://doi.org/10.32674/jis.v7i2.380

Choudaha, R. (2016). Campus readiness for supporting international student success. *Journal of International Students, 6*(4). https://doi.org/10.32674/jis.v6i4.318

Choudaha, R. (2017). Three waves of international student mobility (1999–2020). *Studies in Higher Education, 42*(5), 825–832. https://doi.org/10.1080/03075079.2017.1293872

Courtney, M., & Gordon, R. (2013). Determining the number of factors to retain in EFA: Using the SPSS R-Menu v2 0 to make more judicious estimations practical assessment, research, and evaluation: Vol. 18, Article 8. https://doi.org/10.7275/9cf5-2m72

Creswell, J. (2013). Research design: Qualitative, quantitative, and mixed methods approaches. Sage.

David, D. M. (2020). A basic formula for effective international student services. *Journal of International Students, 10*(3). https://doi.org/10.32674/jis.v10i3.2000

Deardorff, D. K. (2020). (Re)learning to live together in 2020. *Journal of International Students*, 10(4), xv–xviii. https://doi.org/10.32674/jis.v10i4.3169

de Wit, H. (2019). Internationalization of higher education, a critical review. *Special Issue: Internationalization of Higher Education, 12*(3), 9–17. https://doi.org/10.21810/sfuer.v12i3.1036

Fischer, K. (2020). Confronting the seismic impact of COVID-19. *Journal of International Students, 10*(2). https://doi.org/10.32674/jis.v10i2.2134

Gil, N. (2014, August). One in seven students work full-time while they study. *The Guardian*, https://www.theguardian.com/education/2014/aug/11/students-work-part-time-employability

Goodman, L. A. (2011). Comment: On respondent-driven sampling and snowball sampling in hard-to-reach populations and snowball sampling not in hard-to-reach populations. *Sociological Methodology, 41*(1), 347–353. https://doi.org/10.1111/j.1467-9531.2011.01242.x

Hsiao-ping, W., Garza, E., & Guzman, N. (2015). International student's challenge and adjustment to college. *Education Research International*, 2015. https://doi.org/10.1155/2015/202753

Humphrey, D. (2020, August 17). Colleges must attend to three crucial areas. *Inside Higher Ed.* https://www.insidehighered.com/views/2020/08/17/higher-ed-responds-COVID-it-should-focus-three-areas-ensure-quality-and-equity

International Student Survey - QS. (2020). http://info.qs.com/rs/335-VIN-535/images/QS_EU_Universities_Edition-International_Student_Survey_2020.pdf

Krsmanovic, M. (2021). The synthesis and future directions of empirical research on international students in the United States: The insights from one decade. *Journal of International Students, 11*(1), 1–23. https://doi.org/10.32674/jis.v11i1

Langer, M. (2020). Coronavirus: Lifting lockdowns, European countries go their own way. *Deutsche Welle.* https://www.dw.com/en/coronavirus-lifting-lockdowns-european-countries-go-their-own-way/a-53264551-0

Lee, J. J., & Rice, C. (2007). Welcome to America? International student perceptions of discrimination. *Higher Education, 53*(3), 381–409. https://doi.org/10.1007/s10734-005-4508-3

Ludeman, R., & Schreiber, B. (2020). Student affairs and services in higher education: Global foundations, issues and best practices (3rd ed.). Deutsches Studentenwerk Publishers.

Ly, T. T. (2020). Teaching and engaging international students. *Journal of International Students, 10*(3), XII-XVII. https://doi.org/10.32674/jis.v10i3.2005

Marinoni, G., van't Land, H., & Jensen, T. (2020). The impact of COVID-19 on higher education around the world. International Association of Universities Global Survey. International Association of Universities Publishers. https://www.iau-aiu.net/IMG/pdf/iau_COVID19_and_he_survey_report_ final_may_2020.pdf

Martel, M. (2020) *COVID-19 effects on US higher education campuses,* (Report 3) IIE. https://www.iie.org/Research-and-Insights/Publications/COVID-19-Effects-on-US-Higher-Education-Campuses-Report-3

Mittelmeier, J., & Cockayne, H. (2020). Global depictions of international students in a time of crisis: A thematic analysis of Twitter data during COVID-19, SRRN. https://doi.org/10.2139/ssrn.3703604

Mok, K. H. (2018). Does internationalization of higher education still matter? Critical reflections on student learning, graduate employment and faculty development in Asia. *Higher Education Quarterly, 72*(3), 183–193. https://doi.org/10.1111/hequ.12170

New EAIE report on the impact of COVID-19. (2020, March 24). https://www.eaie.org/blog/coping-COVID-report.html

O'Malley, B. (2020, November 28). *Universities urge Biden to end curbs on foreign students.* https://www.universityworldnews.com/post.php? story= 20201128102119141

Organisation for Economic Co-operation and Development (2020), *Education at a glance 2020: OECD indicators*, OECD Publishing. https:// doi.org/10.1787/69096873-en

Perez-Encinas, A., & Ammigan, R. (2016). Support services at Spanish and US institutions: A driver for international student satisfaction. *Journal of International Students, 6*(4), 984–998. https://doi.org/10.32674/jis.v6i4.330

Rebolledo-Gómez, C., & Ranchin, J. (2013, July 5). *Education indicators in focus*, (14). http://www.oecd.org/education/skills-beyond-school/education-indicators-focus-other-languages.htm

Salganik, M., & Heckathorn, D. (2004). Sampling and estimation in hidden populations using respondent-driven sampling. *Sociological Methodology, 34*(1), 193–293. https://doi.org/10.1111/j.0081-1750.2004.00152.x

Seeber, M., Cattaneo, M., Huisman, J., & Paleari, S. (2016). Why do higher education institutions internationalize? An investigation of the multilevel determinants of internationalization rationales. *Higher Education, 72*(5), 685–702. https://doi.org/10.1007/s10734-015-9971-x

Tesar, M. (2020). Towards a post-COVID-19 'new normality?': Physical and social distancing, the move to online and higher education. *Policy Futures in Education, 18*(5), 556–559. https://doi.org/10.1177/1478210320935671

Treadwell, K. L., & O'Grady, M. R. (2019). Crisis, compassion, and resiliency in student affairs: using triage practices to foster well-being. NASPA Publishers.

United Nations Educational, Scientific and Cultural Organization. (2018). Definition of regions. https://unesdoc.unesco.org/ark:/48223/pf0000261751/PDF/261751eng.pdf.multi.page=142

Wecker, M. (2017). How to ensure your international student services program meets student needs. *International Educator, 26*(5), 38–41. https://www.proquest.com/docview/2124689873

Woolf, N., & Silver, C. (2018). *Qualitative analysis using NVivo*. Routledge.

Zdziarski, E. L., Dunkel, N. W., & Rollo, J. M. (2007). *Campus crisis management: A comprehensive guide to planning, prevention, response, and recovery* (1st ed., Ser. Jossey-bass higher and adult education series). Jossey-Bass.

LISA BARDILL MOSCARITOLO, PhD, is the Vice Provost for Student Life at the American University of Sharjah in the United Arab Emirates. Lisa teaches graduate classes in management and leadership for Purdue Global University. She is a founding member and secretary-general for the International Association of Student Affairs and Services (IASAS) and was instrumental in creating the *Global Summit for Student Affairs and Services* in its 6th reiteration. Lisa's research and writing interests are in international student affairs and services. Email: lmoscaritolo@aus.edu

BRETT PEROZZI, PhD, is Vice President for Student Affairs at Weber State University (WSU). He previously served in leadership roles at Arizona State, Indiana, Texas Tech, and Colorado State Universities, in the United States. Brett served as a faculty member in several higher education graduate programs and cofounded the Higher Education Leadership program at WSU. Brett has authored dozens of journal articles, and book chapters and monographs. He has published three books, two on international student affairs and services, and one on student employment during college. Email: brettperozzi@weber.edu

BIRGIT SCHREIBER, PhD, is a consultant for the higher education sector, has served in senior leadership positions for the past 25 years. She is a member of the Africa Centre for Transregional Research at the Freiburg University, Germany. Birgit has over 50 publications on social justice, student affairs, and higher education policy. She was the founding member and is the editorial executive of the *Journal for Student Affairs in Africa*. Email: birgitdewes@gmail.com

THIERRY M. LUESCHER, PhD, is a research director in the Human Sciences Research Council and an Associate Professor in Higher Education Studies affiliated to the University of the Free State in South Africa. Thierry is an NRF-rated researcher with expertise in the politics of higher education; higher education development in Africa; the student experience and student affairs. Thierry has extensive experience in the editing of journals and books and is a founding editor of the *Journal of Student Affairs in Africa*. Email: tluescher@hsrc.ac.za

Research Article

© *Journal of International Students*
Volume 12, Issue 2 (2022), pp. 345-365
ISSN: 2162-3104 (Print), 2166-3750 (Online)
doi: 10.32674/jis.v12i2.3158
ojed.org/jis

Social Media for Social Support: A Study of International Graduate Students in the United States

Annalise Baines
Muhammad Ittefaq
Mauryne Abwao
*William Allen White School of Journalism & Mass Communications,
University of Kansas, Lawrence, KS 66045, USA*

ABSTRACT

Based on 15 in-depth interviews, the present study aims to understand the common challenges international graduate students face and the coping strategies they employed, types of social networking sites (SNS) used, and social support sought from their relationship during graduate school. Common challenges faced are loneliness, stress, feeling overwhelmed with graduate school, and difficulties adjusting to a new culture. Coping strategies include sharing experiences with relations whom they trust and understand their situation, and joining online communities via SNS. The participants use both public and private SNS to seek social support depending on the various functionalities offered. SNS use depends on the affordances such as convenience, affordability, trust issues, and privacy. Most sought-after types of social support are emotional and informational via SNS.

Keywords: higher education, international graduate students, interview, SNS, social support

INTRODUCTION

Graduate students, including international graduate students, cope with feelings of social isolation and are prone to more stress than the general public and report that their stress is attributed to their graduate programs (Ali & Kohun, 2006; Cahir & Morris, 1991; Jairam & Kahl, 2012; McAlpine et al., 2020; Natriello, 2002; Stubb et al., 2011; van Rooij et al., 2019). Particularly international graduate students find it difficult to maintain and build new relationships, create a professional identity, and manage their socialization process into their new roles (Jairam & Kahl, 2012; Lee, 2009).

College students are digital natives on account of their usage of digital technologies to communicate and share information online (Kaplan & Haenlein, 2010; Xu & Jiang, 2018). They use social networking sites (SNS) to stay in contact with their friends and family members but also create and manage new connections. SNS are a subset of social media and are used to create public or private profiles, articulate a list of users with whom they share a connection with, and maintain existing relationships through online interactions using the platform (boyd & Ellison, 2007; Seo et al., 2016). In this paper, platforms to connect with people and share information online are referred to as social networking sites (SNS). These platforms offer communication affordances to maintain social relationships, engage in relational maintenance activities, and to access resources, like social support (Ellison et al., 2007, 2014). In this study, affordances are referred to as the potential for action that new technologies and SNS provide to users (e.g., connectivity, interactivity, and exchange of knowledge). SNS are popular among students because of their suitability and convenience, providing access to information, and social support (Elsaadani, 2012). Research indicates that SNS compensate for a lack of physical proximity and are a great source of emotional comfort (Correa et al., 2010). Facilitating relationships through SNS help people cope with challenging issues and provide a basis of communication to reach out for social support. In a new culture or environment, students' social media use increases to help them adjust (Lin et al., 2012; Seo et. al, 2016; Zhou et al., 2008).

Previous research in this scholarship has mainly focused on how first-year college students use SNS to seek social support (Kalpidou et al., 2011; McCarthy, 2010; Phua et al., 2017) and little research has been conducted on international graduate students (see Hyun, 2019, for a review). This study is important for several reasons. First, this population is understudied in media and communication research (Seo et al., 2016). Second, the number of international graduate students has increased over the last several years in the United States (McCarthy, 2019). Third, this population relies on SNS to stay in contact with their family, friends, and relations living abroad or at a geographical distance (Straumsheim, 2014). Fourth, it is worthwhile to explore how and why international graduate students in the United States use SNS to seek social support and if SNS help them cope with feelings of stress and enhance their well-being. Fifth, few studies have used qualitative methods to explore this population's experience with their graduate programs in the United States (Hyun, 2019).

Lastly, on average, international graduate students are prone to more stress-related environments, including academic responsibilities such as Graduate Teaching Assistants, Graduate Research Assistants, and Graduate Assistants (Khawaja et al., 2017; Zhou et al., 2018).

The present study aims to understand the common challenges international graduate students face and the coping strategies they use during their graduate degree programs. In addition, this paper examines how and why do international graduate students use SNS to seek social support from relationships. Furthermore, this paper explores the type of SNS used and social support (emotional, informational, and instrumental) sought from their relationships.

Conceptualizing Social Support

Most conceptualizations agree that social support is relational and defined as a function of aid that is obtained from an individual's social network such as family members, friends, and co-workers (Lin & Kishore, 2021; Thompson, 2008). Social support has various forms, including emotional, informational, and instrumental. Emotional support alleviates negative affect in another person, knowing that someone is understanding and can help accept and deal with an issue, having empathy for a person's situation or problem, and enabling a person to communicate their anxieties and fears, trust, respect, and even love them (House, 1981). Informational support happens when information is shared with others to help address a problem and mentor or guide a person. Instrumental support occurs when others provide specific help or assistance to a person and financial support. The perception for individuals to seek social support from their social network can lead to a reduction in the perceived threat of the stressful situation by helping a person's perceived ability to deal with the potential demand (Jairam & Kahl, 2012). Stress-related research implies that stress has damaging effects on a person's physical and psychological health (Jairam & Kahl, 2012). However, social support has shown to help reduce stress. Generally, those individuals who have strong social support have less stress, less physical and psychological problems, as well as lower mortality rates than those with less frequent and weaker social support (Jackson, 1992; Reblin & Uchino, 2008).

The mentioned studies highlight the importance of having social support networks during a person's life, but more research is needed to understand how and why SNS influence the composition of international graduate student's social networks. Particularly when international graduate students often rely on SNS for social support from their loved ones in their country of origin.

Social Support and International Graduate Students

Graduate students experience new and daunting life changes. Oftentimes, they find themselves transitioning from their parental households, experience an increase in their autonomy, and face new responsibilities. Their worldviews, values, and even identities are challenged by new academic and social circles (Kaufman & Feldman, 2004; Seo et al., 2016). Graduate students might have already gone through the process of leaving their parental households and experience an increase in their autonomy through their undergraduate years in college, but many still face the challenge of adapting to a new environment, coping with financial and academic stress, handling new academic responsibilities and workloads, and familiarizing themselves with a new culture (El-Ghoroury et al., 2012; Jairam & Kahl, 2012; Schwartz-Mette, 2009). These challenges can result in difficulty developing and exhibiting professional competence as well as having an impact on their psychological well-being (Colman et al., 2016). Therefore, it is important for students, particularly international graduate students, to alleviate the stress associated with graduate school.

Past literature suggested that social support from friends, families, and classmates is an important factor in dealing with these challenges (El-Ghoroury et. al., 2012). Goplerud (1980) studied psychology graduate students perceived levels of stress and social support during the first six months of the program and found that students who reported higher support were less stressed and had less health and emotional problems. Similarly, in another study, researchers examined college students' emotional, social, and academic adjustment to college and argued that local support networks are important for this to be a positive adjustment (Mallinckrodt & Leong, 1992). Social support helps reduce stress by offering emotional or other types of support to an individual as well as making them feel cared for and belong to a network of communication (Jairam & Kahl, 2012). Turning to friends, family members, peers, or supervisors for social support can be an effective strategy in coping with challenges of a graduate student's life such as combating feelings of social isolation and reducing stress (Byers et al., 2014; Jairam & Kahl, 2012).

Uses and Gratifications as Theoretical Framework

Since the 1940s, uses and gratifications theory (U&G) has been widely used to understand why people engage in and use certain types of media to satisfy their needs (Wimmer & Dominick, 1994). In the field of media and communication science, scholars have applied this theory to explore digital technologies like SNS to understand specific reasons that motivate users to engage with online content (Ruggiero, 2000). Each SNS yields unique affordances and functionalities, allowing users to use each site for a variety of motivations and reasons. Research has found that people use SNS for entertainment purposes, to obtain information about others, pass time, seek information, maintain interpersonal relationships, connect with like-minded people, receive companionship, and seek social support (Alhabash & Ma, 2017; Lampe et al., 2006; Seidman, 2013). Little attention has been given to the relationship between the use of SNS and social support in the context of U&G theory (Wang et al., 2019), particularly studying international graduate students and their use of SNS to seek social support. Methodologically, previous studies have applied quantitative methods with U&G such as surveys and experiments (Ahmad et al., 2016; Ellison et al., 2007; Wang et al., 2019), however, in the context of our study, the theoretical framework of U&G allows us to understand participants' reasons for SNS use and the type of social support sought (i.e., emotional, informational, and instrumental).

SNS and Social Support

Early studies of online social support investigated how supportive communication patterns emerged in online environments, particularly compared with face-to-face interactions (Baym, 1998). A study undertaken by Braithwaite et al. (1999) suggested that people develop unique features such as employing emoticons and signatures to deliver nonverbal cues and facilitate strong relationships for social support. Other studies of online support found relationships among mediated social support, online social networks, and health outcomes. People who spend more time communicating via online support groups are more likely to have a larger online support network and higher level of support network satisfaction (Rains & Young, 2009; Wright, 1999; Wright & Bell, 2003). These studies reveal that people who communicate online receive increased social support reception and satisfaction.

Extending these findings to SNS, scholars have found a similar effect on social support exchange over the last decade. SNS such as Facebook, Twitter, and WhatsApp have become an integral part of people's daily routines and are used for social support exchange (Li et al., 2015). One of the most popular SNS among millennials (18–34 years old) is Facebook with many users logging in more than once per day (Perrin & Anderson, 2019). These sites help foster, develop, and create interpersonal relationships and findings have shown that SNS emerged as a new avenue for two-way communication (Bicen, 2015; Kwon & Yixing, 2010).

Many scholars have found that the use of SNS provides new affordances for relational maintenance, reinforces existing ones, and can play a positive role in enhancing interpersonal relationships and well-being (boyd & Ellison, 2007; Ellison et al., 2007). A few scholars found that when people use SNS, it not only promotes social capital (connections among individuals) and subjective mental well-being but also generates greater benefits for people suffering from low levels of self-esteem and life satisfaction (Ellison et al., 2007; Valenzuela et al., 2009). Also, individuals who use Facebook are shown to have closer, more trustworthy, and supportive relationships than people who don't use SNS. These findings imply that SNS have a profound impact on people with close relationships (Hampton et al., 2011). The number of Facebook friends has also shown to be positively associated with perceived social support that leads to a reduction in stress and increase in life satisfaction, particularly within groups who are prone to high stress (Kim, 2014; Nabi et al., 2013). This current study extends on previous empirical and theoretical findings and aims to understand perceived online social support using SNS and subjective well-being of international graduate students. The following research questions are posed:

RQ1: What are the common challenges and coping strategies international graduate students face and use during their time in college in the U.S.?

RQ2: How and why do international graduate students use SNS to seek social support from their relationships?

RQ3: What type of social support (emotional, informational, and instrumental) do international graduate students seek from their relationships?

METHOD

An in-depth, semi-structured interviewing technique (Rubin & Rubin, 1995) was used to collect data from 15 participants on how and why they use SNS to seek social support from their relationships and which SNS they use to do this. This approach was used as it provides a rich narrative account from each individual's point of view (Lamont & Swidler, 2014; Rufas & Hine, 2018). The interview guide was approved by the university's Institutional Review Board in early spring 2020. In total, 15 participants took part in this study. Eight participants participated in face-to-face interviews, while the remaining seven were conducted online via Zoom. All interviews were audio recorded.

A snowball sampling approach was used to recruit participants on campus. Flyers were distributed around campus and those interested were asked to recommend acquaintances who might be willing to participate in the study. Emails were also sent to international graduate student groups on campus. The flyers and emails provided a brief description of the purpose of the study, eligibility, how they can participate, and contact information of the researchers. The participants were between the ages of (22–35) years and either in the master's or PhD program. The characteristics of participants are presented in Table 1.

Table 1: Demographic Characteristics of Participants

Pseudonym	Gender	Age	Race	Graduate degree	Preferred SNS
Adam	Male	24	Asian	Masters	Facebook Messenger
Barbara	Female	30	Black	PhD	Instagram, WhatsApp, Facebook, Twitter, YouTube
Clarissa	Female	32	Other	PhD	Twitter
Diane	Female	30	Asian	PhD	WeChat, Facebook, Skype
Elsa	Female	30s (didn't want to specify age)	Black	PhD	WhatsApp, Twitter

Pseudonym	Gender	Age	Race	Graduate degree	Preferred SNS
Felix	Male	22	Hispanic or Latin American	Master	WhatsApp, Facebook Messenger, Snapchat
Greg	Male	27	Asian	PhD	Facebook, WhatsApp, Twitter
Heather	Female	24	Hispanic or Latin American	PhD	Instagram
Ivan	Male	29	Central Asian	Master	Facebook, Messenger Twitter, WhatsApp
Jonas	Male	29	South East Asian	PhD	WhatsApp, Facebook Messenger
Khalup	Male	27	Asian	PhD	Facebook, WhatsApp
Lenny	Male	27	Did not wish to specify	PhD	WhatsApp, Facebook, Instagram
Monica	Female	29	Asian	Master	WhatsApp, WeChat
Noel	Male	29	Black	PhD	WhatsApp
Oman	Male	25	Asian	PhD	WhatsApp, Facebook Messenger

Before the interviews commenced, each participant was asked to fill out a close-ended questionnaire pertaining to their demographic information and their general SNS use. Demographic questions such as age, gender, race, graduate degree, academic field of study, SNS use, and preferred SNS were asked. Interview questions were developed from a range of open-ended questions.

In qualitative research, scholars often follow an interview protocol by starting with opening questions, transition questions, key questions, closing questions, and follow-up questions (Castillo-Montoya, 2016; Jacob & Furgerson, 2012). For this study, participants were asked how they define social support in order to capture their understanding of the concept. Then, they were asked to relay their experience in their graduate program, types of challenges they face or have faced, and how these challenges impacted their physical, mental, and emotional state. These questions are aimed to understand how international graduate students cope with stress during their college years. Next, questions were asked how participants relieved those challenges, transitioning to questions asking them to talk about their relationships and why they approach these people to seek social support from. Questions were also asked which SNS they used to seek social support from their relationships (i.e., family members, colleagues, friends) to help them cope with difficult situations during graduate studies and why they chose those SNS. Special attention was paid to how and why participants use SNS to seek social support from their relationships. Each interview lasted approximately 30–45 mins.

Once participants were being interviewed, we commenced with transcription of the data. During and after the transcription and coding process, pseudonyms were used to allow for anonymity (see Toff & Nielsen, 2018). All interviews were transcribed using the software InqScribe. In the initial stage, interviews were coded in chronological order during the data collection process, using a combination of "open coding" by identifying themes line by line. In the next stage, the researchers used "focused coding" by searching for specific themes to group them into categories (Charmaz, 2006; Erba, 2018).

The researchers revised the list of codes and agreed on which codes should appear in each theme. In the final stage of transcribing the interviews, data were continually analyzed to achieve theoretical saturation of data. After each interview and analysis of transcriptions, the researchers compared notes and reached a consensus.

FINDINGS

The most common challenges international graduate students face are loneliness, stress, and feeling overwhelmed with graduate school, difficulties adjusting to a new culture such as language barriers, culture shock, and lack of guidance. In terms of coping with these issues, the most commonly mentioned coping strategies are sharing their experiences with those who understand their situation, relationships whom they trust, and reaching out to them via SNS. The type of SNS used includes WhatsApp, Facebook, Facebook Messenger, Twitter, Instagram, and WeChat and depends on the functionalities of the SNS, such as convenience, affordances, cost, trust issues, and privacy. The findings of the present study suggest that emotional support and informational support were the most sought-after types of support via SNS. Meanwhile only two participants mentioned that they use SNS to seek instrumental support from their relationships.

Challenges: Loneliness, Stress, and Feeling Overwhelmed With Graduate School (RQ 1)

International graduate students face unique challenges during their time in college. Most participants indicated that they felt "overwhelmed" and "stressed" about the workload, have difficulties "adjusting to their new environment," "having demanding professors," "meeting deadlines," and their new role of being both "teaching assistants and students." Many students mentioned that they "get tired and lonely" (e.g., Barbara, Elsa, Jonas, Monica & Lenny), finding it difficult to connect with people with similar interests, and the pressure of "performing well and living up to the expectations of instructors and family members." These challenges impacted them physically, emotionally, and mentally. Some interviewees indicated that they struggle physically with their weight due to unhealthy eating habits as well as having back and shoulder problems from sitting in front of a computer screen and working long hours in the lab. Some interviewees mentioned that they often feel lonely during graduate school. Mentally, some participants said that they have been seeking help from therapists during the first few semesters of their graduate degree program. It was also found that mental pressure and stress depend on the semester and the workload, and most participants "feel overwhelmed, tired, and homesick." Noel (a 29-year-old PhD student) struggled with health issues, suffered from homesickness, and had a challenging time finding the right resources at school. He often felt mentally overwhelmed coping with these issues. Similarly, Barbara (a 30-year-old PhD student) echoed:

> Yeah, it was lonely and emotionally I would say I was sad uh and then this impacted me I didn't know but this impacted me health wise because just to keep up with this culture [...] Also I had the fear that maybe these students would be better than me coming in from a different culture so my first semesters were like, [...] so it was really a lot of pressure and then I didn't know this was impacting me. So in my second semester toward the end I felt sick. So it kind of impacted me emotionally, I was really sad at that point and I felt like maybe I made a wrong choice to come and study in the U.S.

Oman (29-year-old PhD student), Jonas (29-year-old PhD student), and Noel further stated that their graduate programs feel self-isolating because they are studying in the Science, Technology, Engineering, and Mathematics (STEM) field and spend many hours doing lab experiments. As Jonas said, "The supervisor expects me to continue working and wouldn't care about my mental or physical health."

However, Khalup (a 27-year-old PhD student), Monica (a 29-year-old master's student), and Elsa (didn't want to specify age, Ph.D. student) were the only participants who mentioned that they didn't feel as overwhelmed during graduate school.

Challenges: Difficulties Adjusting to a New Culture (RQ 1)

Various socio-cultural factors such as academics, family, food, and friendship were the most mentioned challenges in adjusting to the American culture. Several participants indicated the culture they grew up in is more collectivist (e.g., Pakistan, China, or Kenya) in the sense that they could reach out for social support in-person more easily with their family members. Since they are living in the United States without their close relations, they rely on SNS to seek social support. For instance, Greg (a 29-year-old PhD student) stated "it's a cultural difference because this is kind of an individualistic society and we live together and we help each other and here people don't do it that way." Monica found it challenging to make friends in her new environment, as she stated "I had a very strong accent when I got here. People used to judge me and I used to find it weird that people judged me. I stopped expressing myself or talking to anyone." Felix (a 22-year-old master's student) also mentioned that English is not his native language and he had difficulty understanding his professors during lectures, especially when they talked too fast. Felix came from a culture in which he could easily make friends and talk about challenges during graduate school. While he has found friends in his master's program, the mentality of being competitive for some students in the United States can be challenging. Similarly, Ivan (a 29-year-old master's student) and Jonas had a difficult time during their graduate studies because they often felt "marginalized as foreigners."

Most international graduate students highlighted that they came from different cultures and most of their close relations live outside the United States. Using SNS to reach out and stay in contact with their close relationships helped many of the interviewees adjust more easily to their new environment.

Coping Strategies: Sharing Experiences and Understanding Situations (RQ 1)

The most commonly mentioned coping strategies among international graduate students included sharing experiences with those whom they trust and understand their situation, joining online communities, and reaching out to close relationships via SNS. Interestingly, many participants highlighted that they don't only seek social support from their close relationships (e.g., friends and family members) but also their distant relationships such as colleagues or friends. The students did not include their academic relations (e.g., professor, supervisor, fellow students, and colleagues) in their close circle. Lenny (a 27-year-old PhD student) pointed out "I like to talk about graduate school issues with my cohorts and advisors here rather than with my closer relationships. My department is very helpful and I can talk to my supervisor." Adam (a 24-year-old master's student), Jonas, Khalup, Lenny, Noel, and Oman mentioned that they reach out to their closest relationships whom they trust such as their girlfriend/fiancé or close family members such as mother, father, cousins, or childhood friends to seek emotional support. However, they don't talk about their challenges during graduate school as their close relationships can't understand and "identify with their situations." As Monica echoed:

> I can't connect to family members anymore because they don't know my situation in graduate school [...] I kept my feelings to myself because I didn't want to upset anyone and there was also a time difference in not being able to connect with my close relationships.

All interviewees said the type of social support they seek depends on the person's experience and objective in life. For instance, Diane (a 30-year-old PhD student) has joined a work-related group of people and a study-related group of people that she goes to for advice. Depending on their life experience and the problem, people in either group will resonate with or have similar experiences on a certain issue to give advice about some of the challenges they face during graduate school.

SNS Use: Affordances (RQ 2)

The type of SNS use depends on the affordances, such as ease of use, cost, convenience, surveillance policies, two-way communication, and privacy issues. Some interviewees mentioned that they feel uncomfortable seeking social support using public SNS such as Twitter, Facebook, and Instagram. One of the main reasons international graduate students do not prefer using public SNS is because they feel "judged and uncomfortable." For instance, Adam stopped sharing intimate thoughts on public SNS, instead he uses private messaging applications like Facebook Messenger that enable one-on-one conversation. Similarly, Khalup doesn't seek social support on a public platform like Facebook because it's an "attention seeking platform and the most he can get from posting content online are likes." Monica raised the issue that public platforms give her a feeling of "disconnectivity" and "lack of empathy for her situation in graduate school" as opposed to private sites like WhatsApp. While expressing advantages of SNS, she pointed out the dark side of public SNS saying that "Facebook is not a good friend when you are in the dark side, everybody is fake and everyone is faking it." Most participants prefer private applications like WhatsApp or Facebook Messenger. As Jonas said "I use Facebook Messenger since most of my family is online and it is the most efficient way to stay connected."

On the contrary to Adam, Khalup, and Monica, some of the participants (i.e., Greg, Barbara, Heather, and Clarissa) reported that they use Twitter to connect with online communities because of their unique affordances. For instance, Greg uses the hashtag #PhDLife on Twitter to engage and participate in conversations with fellow graduate students. Barbara prefers a more visually connected medium like Instagram and uses the hashtag #BlackWomenPhD's to connect with people who have similar academic experiences and objectives in life. Heather (a 24-year-old PhD student) added that she doesn't necessarily use Instagram to seek social support from her relationships but "shares pictures and stories" to let her close relationships know she is "coping as a graduate student." Clarissa started using Twitter just to "share ideas" but found that some people on Twitter valued her ideas and thoughts:

> On Twitter I will talk about my concerns, how to graduate or about being a Ph.D. student and all concerns I have about my personal life so I write everything and all of these things there. And people send me direct messages and ask if you are doing well or not, if you are sick and today I feel like you were depressed, these kinds of things. I mean I feel like I found friends.

Clarissa also mentioned that many people on Twitter have the same ethnic background, immigration status, and are PhD students with similar majors. A few participants revealed that they seek social support either on private or public sites depending on the type of social support they need. Lenny uses a WhatsApp research support group to hold a private conversation with colleagues from school. The affordance of WhatsApp is end-to-end encryption and allows users to feel a sense of safety and security in their private conversations. Lenny argued that he "likes to use the call option on WhatsApp and the group chat function as it uses less data and is convenient."

Other participants (e.g., Barbara, Elsa, Ivan, Jonas, Khalup, Victor, Noel, and Monica) divulged that they use "WhatsApp due to its accessibility and ease of use for one-on-one conversations." The application allowed other affordances such as sharing of visual content (i.e., videos and pictures), memes, as well as functions like phone or video calls. Barbara stated:

> I tend to use WhatsApp because it's more of a phone call and with them (family members) it's more like, we do a lot of talking and for my siblings there's a lot of texting and we use like Instagram and go to Facebook and all these other platforms. My parents are not conversant with Facebook.

A majority of the participants asserted that they prefer seeking social support "via text instead of phone calls." This is likely due to generational differences between the person they are communicating with.

Overall, most of the international graduate students who participated in this study use SNS like WhatsApp because it allows private conversations and offers international communication affordability, convenience, and safety features (e.g., encrypted messages) and "real-time" conversations.

Type of Social Support: Emotional, Informational, and Instrumental (RQ 3)

International graduate students revealed that the most sought-after type of social support through SNS includes emotional and informational. These types of support were sought from family members and friends outside their academic life and academic circle. Participants sought emotional support from family members because of their limited exposure to graduate school challenges. Diane says:

> Usually we (mother) communicate on the phone. So I didn't mention that much academic pressure to her, just the trivial life details like how's the canteen food, how's the dorm, how's the roommate and how's your classmate. Or who's your supervisor, that kind of thing, so we just talk about that kind of stuff and she's very supportive and says don't stress yourself out and eat healthy. Sleep early and she says your hair is more important than your graduate career, so keep your hair, you can quit your graduate studies but keep your hair (laughs) [...] Though my mom can't give me much academic help, the emotional support is really important. And financial support (laughs).

On the contrary, Clarissa's husband is also in graduate school and offers her "emotional as well as instrumental support," but not much informational support "because we have different majors." Monica expressed that she seeks emotional and informational support from her graduate advisor and does not reach out to her close relationships to discuss challenges during graduate school because she doesn't want her close relationships to worry about her struggles and issues. Khalup did not seek any social support from relationships through SNS. However, he struggled with financial challenges (instrumental support) and did not reach anyone using SNS.

In summary, findings show that students face unique challenges during graduate school and use different coping strategies to mitigate their challenges. Participants use various SNS depending on their affordances to seek social support from relationships. For many interviewees, seeking social support depends on the issue and problems they face during their college life.

DISCUSSION

This study investigated how international graduate students use SNS to seek social support from their relationships. Through 15 semi-structured interviews, the type of social support (emotional, informational, and instrumental) as well as use and preference of SNS were examined. Results indicate that international graduate students face challenges during graduate school and difficulties adjusting to a new culture. The participants use SNS to seek social support from their relationships, however, the chosen SNS depend on the technical and communication affordances (Bucher & Helmond, 2018), such as cost, ease of use, accessibility, private or public setting, and whether the participants' relationships use the site.

The types of SNS the participants mentioned to seek social support afford different cues, interactions, relational contexts, and perceived values to its users. Each site offers different ways for users to present themselves and how they interact with the people or groups on that platform (Wohn et al., 2016). All of the interviewees indicated that they seek some type of social support using SNS from people or a community of people who share similar experiences or objectives in life as they do. Emotional support and informational support are largely sought-after from close relationships such as family members or friends and academic circles. Instrumental support was rarely sought from relationships using SNS. One explanation why most of the participants seek emotional support from their close relationships is because they have little or no experience with academia. Another reason why instrumental support was not sought-after is because most international students' families can't afford to cater for their personal and academic expenses.

The findings in this study regarding SNS use for various types of social support aligned with the U&G theory. This theory postulates how and why people use certain SNS to fulfill their needs. In the context of this study, our findings suggest that a majority of the participants use SNS to seek emotional and informational support from different relations and groups but also depend on the particular affordance of SNS. Previous studies regarding U&G theory suggest that affordances like "convenience" is one of the largest motivations to use SNS. Our study validates that seeking social support is one of the motivations and reasons for choosing a particular SNS, as studies using U&G theory suggested (Alhabash & Ma, 2017).

As previous research indicates (Kahn & Antonucci, 1980; Kim, 2014), seeking social support from a person or group of people often depends on the emotional intensity, intimacy, reciprocal services, trust, and beneficial aspects for a person's well-being. Interestingly, results in this study showed that the seeking of different social support (emotional, informational, and instrumental) didn't depend on the closeness, but rather on the similar situations in life between the participants and their relationships.

While previous research shows that international graduate students face challenges such as stress, culture shock, heavy workload, and homesickness, our study not only confirms these challenges but found that the students use different strategies to cope with these challenges by using various SNS platforms to reach out for social support from different relationships.

Practical Implications and Recommendations

The United States higher education institutions need to continually share resources and remind international students about support programs to help them deal with their challenges such as mental well-being. Offering workshops to help overcome language barriers and discussions about mental health issues could help students. Schools should consider alternate ways (i.e., using popular SNS platforms among international students like WhatsApp and WeChat) to reach out to international graduate students to understand their needs and provide support. Besides providing more resources, facilitating intercultural, and interracial dialogue can help create an open and respectful exchange of views between students from different cultures. The findings of this study can be used to advance institutions' policies to make sure they provide an equitable learning environment. The higher education institutions should invest more resources for inclusivity, diversity, equity, and accessibility to international graduate students.

Limitations and Future Research

Our study has several limitations. First of all, we recommend that future research also includes the international undergraduate population to compare the two groups and include students from various schools to understand the challenges and coping strategies. Second, this study is confined to international students enrolled in United States institutions, and analyzing experiences of international graduate students in other countries might be helpful and yield similar or different findings. Lastly, more specific questions on how people use SNS to seek social support could be further investigated by doing a social media walkthrough as a method (Light et al., 2018). The walkthrough method could provide a detailed analysis on how the user navigates the SNS, which person or group of people they contact, and the type of support they seek. Future studies should investigate if individual cultural values have an impact on how international graduate students seek social support through online networking sites. Methodologically, future research should incorporate a mixed-method approach to understand the relationship between their individual cultural values, use of SNS, and the type of social support they seek online. Also, an interdisciplinary approach to study this scholarship can enhance our understanding to introduce new policies in higher education.

DECLARATION OF CONFLICTING INTERESTS

No potential conflict of interest was reported by the authors.

FUNDING

This work has not been funded.

REFERENCES

Alhabash, S., & Ma, M. (2017). A tale of four platforms: Motivations and uses of facebook, twitter, instagram, and snapchat among college students? *Social Media + Society, 3*(1), 205630511769154. https://doi.org/10.1177/2056305117691544

Ahmad, S., Mustafa, M., & Ullah, A. (2016). Association of demographics, motives and intensity of using Social Networking Sites with the formation of bonding and bridging social capital in Pakistan. *Computers in Human Behavior, 57*, 107–114. https://doi.org/10.1016/j.chb.2015.12.027

Ali, A., & Kohun, F. (2006). Dealing with isolation feelings in IS doctoral programs. *International Journal of Doctoral Studies, 1*(1), 21–33. https://doi.org/10.28945/58

Baym, N. K. (1998). The emergence of an on-line community. In S. G. Jones (Ed.), *Cybersociety 2.0: Revisiting computer-mediated communication and community* (pp. 35–68). SAGE Publications.

Bicen, H. (2015). Determination of university students' reasons of using social networking sites in their daily life. *Procedia-Social and Behavioral Sciences, 190*, 519–522. https://doi.org/10.1016/j.sbspro.2015.05.036

boyd, D. M., & Ellison, N. B. (2007). Social network sites: Definition, history, and scholarship. *Journal of Computer-Mediated Communication, 13*(1), 210–230. https://doi.org/10.1111/j.1083-6101.2007.00393.x

Braithwaite, D. O., Waldron, V. R., & Finn, J. (1999). Communication of social support in computer-mediated groups for people with disabilities. *Health Communication, 11*(2), 123–151. https://doi.org/10.1207/s15327027hc1102_2

Bucher, T., & Helmond, A. (2018). The affordances of social media platforms. In J. Burgess, A. Marwick, & T. Poell (Eds.), *The SAGE handbook of social media* (pp. 233–253). Sage Publications.

Byers, V. T., Smith, R. N., Hwang, E., Angrove, K. E., Chandler, J. I., Christian, K. M., & Onwuegbuzie, A. J. (2014). Survival strategies: Doctoral students' perceptions of challenges and coping methods. *International Journal of Doctoral Studies, 9*, 109–136. https://doi.org/10.28945/2034

Cahir, N., & Morris, R. D. (1991). The psychology student stress questionnaire. *Journal of Clinical Psychology, 47*(3), 414–417. https://doi.org/10.1002/1097-4679(199105)47:3<414::aid-jclp2270470314>3.0.co;2-m

Castillo-Montoya, M. (2016). Preparing for interview research: The interview protocol refinement framework. *The Qualitative Report, 21*(5), 811–831. https://doi.org/10.46743/2160-3715/2016.2337

Charmaz, K. (2006). *Constructing grounded theory: A practical guide through qualitative analysis*. Sage Publications.

Colman, D. E., Echon, R., Lemay, M. S., McDonald, J., Smith, K. R., Spencer, J., & Swift, J. K. (2016) The efficacy of self-care for graduate students in professional psychology: A meta-analysis. *Training and Education in Professional Psychology, 10*(4), 188–197. https://doi.org/10.1037/tep0000130

Correa, T., Hinsley, A. W., & De Zuniga, H. G. (2010). Who interacts on the web? The intersection of users' personality and social media use. *Computers in Human Behavior, 26*(2), 247–253. https://doi.org/10.1016/j.chb.2009.09.003

Ellison, N. B., Steinfield, C., & Lampe, C. (2007). The benefits of Facebook "friends": Social capital and college students' use of online social network sites. *Journal of Computer-Mediated Communication, 12*(4), 1143–1168. https://doi.org/10.1111/j.1083-6101.2007.00367.x

Ellison, N. B., Vitak, J., Gray, R., & Lampe, C. (2014). Cultivating social resources on social network sites: Facebook relationship maintenance behaviors and their role in social capital processes. *Journal of Computer-Mediated Communication, 19*(4), 855–870. https://doi.org/10.1111/jcc4.12078

El-Ghoroury, N. H., Galper, D. I., Sawaqdeh, A., & Bufka, L. F. (2012). Stress, coping, and barriers to wellness among psychology graduate students. *Training and Education in Professional Psychology, 6*(2), 122–124. https://doi.org/10.1037/a0028768

Elsaadani, M. (2012). Exploration of teaching staff and students' preferences of information and communication technologies in private and academic lives. *International Journal of Computer Science Issues, 9*(2), 396–402.

Erba, J. (2018). Media representations of Latina/os and Latino students' stereotype threat behavior. *Howard Journal of Communications, 29*(1), 83–102. https://doi.org/10.1080/10646175.2017.1327377

Goplerud, E. N. (1980). Social support and stress during the first year of graduate school. *Professional Psychology, 11*(2), 283–290. https://doi.org/10.1037/0735-7028.11.2.283

Hampton, K., Sessions Goulet, L., & Purcell, K. (2011, June). Social networking sites and our lives. https://www.pewinternet.org/2011/06/16/social-networking-sites-and-our-lives/

House, J. S. (1981). *Work stress and social support*. Addison-Wesley.

Hyun, S. H. (2019). International graduate students in American higher education: Exploring academic and non-academic experiences of international graduate students in non-STEM fields. *International Journal of Educational Research, 96*, 56–62. https://doi.org/10.1016/j.ijer.2019.05.007

Jackson, P. B. (1992). Specifying the buffering hypothesis: Support, strain, and depression. *Social Psychology Quarterly, 55*(4), 363–378. https://doi.org/10.2307/2786953

Jacob, S. A., & Furgerson, S. P. (2012). Writing interview protocols and conducting interviews: Tips for students new to the field of qualitative research. *The Qualitative Report, 17*(42), 1–10. https://doi.org/10.46743/2160-3715/2012.1718

Jairam, D., & Kahl Jr, D. H. (2012). Navigating the doctoral experience: The role of social support in successful degree completion. *International Journal of Doctoral Studies, 7*(31), 1–329. https://doi.org/10.28945/1700

Kahn, R. L., & Antonucci, T. C. (1980). Convoys over the life course: Attachment, roles, and social support. In P. B. Baltes & O. Brim (Eds.), *Life-span development and behavior* (pp. 254–283). Academic Press.

Kalpidou, M., Costin, D., & Morris, J. (2011). The relationship between Facebook and the well-being of undergraduate college students. *Cyberpsychology, Behavior, and Social Networking, 14*(4), 183–189. https://doi.org/10.1089/cyber.2010.0061

Kaplan, A. M., & Haenlein, M. (2010). Users of the world, unite! The challenges and opportunities of social media. *Business Horizons, 53*(1), 59–68. https://doi.org/10.1016/j.bushor.2009.09.003

Kaufman, P., & Feldman, K. A. (2004). Forming identities in college: A sociological approach. *Research in Higher Education, 45*(5), 463–496. https://doi.org/10.1023/b:rihe.0000032325.56126.29

Khawaja, N. G., Chan, S., & Stein, G. (2017). The relationship between second language anxiety and international nursing students stress. *Journal of International Students, 7*(3), 601–620. https://doi.org/10.32674/jis.v7i3.290

Kim, H. (2014). Enacted social support on social media and subjective well-being. *International Journal of Communication, 8*(1), 2201–2221.

Kwon, O., & Yixing, W. (2010). An empirical study of the factors affecting social network service use. *Computers in Human Behavior, 26*(2), 254–263. https://doi.org/10.1016/j.chb.2009.04.011

Lamont, M., & Swidler, A. (2014). Methodological pluralism and the possibilities and limits of interviewing. *Qualitative Sociology, 37*(2), 153–171. https://doi.org/10.1007/s11133-014-9274-z

Lampe, C., Ellison, N. B., & Steinfield, C. (2006). A Face(book) in the crowd: Social searching vs. social browsing. In *Proceedings of the 2006 20th Anniversary Conference on Computer Supported Cooperative Work* (pp. 167–170).

Lee, C. J. (2009). The experience of nurse faculty members enrolled in doctoral study. *International Journal of Doctoral Studies, 4*(1), 59–75. https://doi.org/10.28945/45

Li, X., Chen, W., & Popiel, P. (2015). What happens on Facebook stays on Facebook? The implications of Facebook interaction for perceived, receiving, and giving social support. *Computers in Human Behavior, 51*, 106–113. https://doi.org/10.1016/j.chb.2015.04.066

Light, B., Burgess, J., & Duguay, S. (2018). The walkthrough method: An approach to the study of apps. *New Media & Society, 20*(3), 881–900. https://doi.org/10.1177/1461444816675438

Lin, J. H., Peng, W., Kim, M., Kim., S. Y., & LaRose, R. (2012). Social networking and adjustments among international students. *New Media & Society, 14*(3), 4210–4440. https://doi.org/10.1177/1461444811418627

Lin, X., & Kishore, R. (2021). Social media-enabled healthcare: A conceptual model of social media affordances, online social support, and health behaviors and outcomes. *Technological Forecasting & Social Change, 166*, 120574. https://doi.org/10.1016/j.techfore.2021.120574

Mallinckrodt, B., & Leong, F. T. (1992). International graduate students, stress, and social support. *Journal of College Student Development, 33*(1), 71–78.

McAlpine, L., Skakni, I., & Pyhältö, K. (2020). PhD experience (and progress) is more than work: Life-work relations and reducing exhaustion (and cynicism). *Studies in Higher Education.* https://doi.org/10.1080/03075079.2020.1744128

McCarthy, J. (2010). Blended learning environments: Using social networking sites to enhance the first-year experience. *Australasian Journal of Educational Technology, 26*(6). https://doi.org/10.14742/ajet.1039

McCarthy, N. (2019). *Where America's international students come from.* Statista. https://www.statista.com/chart/20010/international-enrollment-in-higher-education/

Nabi, R. L., Prestin, A., & So, J. (2013). Facebook friends with (health) benefits? Exploring social network site use and perceptions of social support, stress, and well-being. *Cyberpsychology, Behavior, and Social Networking, 16*(10), 721–727. https://doi.org/10.1089/cyber.2012.0521

Natriello, G. (2002). Leaving the ivory tower: The causes and consequences of departure from doctoral study by Barbara E. Lovitts. *American Journal of Sociology, 108*(3), 679–681. https://doi.org/10.1086/378426

Perrin, A., & Anderson, M. (2019, April). Share of U.S. adults using social media, including Facebook, is mostly unchanged since 2018. https://www.pewresearch.org/fact-tank/2019/04/10/share-of-u-s-adults-using-social-media-including-facebook-is-mostly-unchanged-since-2018/

Phua, J., Jin, S. V., & Kim, J. J. (2017). Uses and gratifications of social networking sites for bridging and bonding social capital: A comparison of Facebook, Twitter, Instagram, and Snapchat. *Computers in Human Behavior, 72*, 115–122. https://doi.org/10.1016/j.chb.2017.02.041

Rains, S. A., & Young, V. (2009). A meta-analysis of research on formal computer-mediated support groups: Examining group characteristics and health outcomes. *Human Communication Research, 35*(3), 309–336. https://doi.org/10.1111/j.1468-2958.2009.01353.x

Reblin, M., & Uchino, B.N. (2008). Social and emotional support and its implication for health. *Current Opinions in Psychiatry, 21*(2), 201–205. https://doi.org/10.1097/yco.0b013e3282f3ad89

Rubin. J. H., & Rubin, I. S. (1995). *Qualitative interviewing. The art of hearing data.* Sage.

Rufas, A., & Hine, C. (2018). Everyday connections between online and offline: Imagining others and constructing community through local online initiatives. *New Media & Society, 20*(10), 3879–3897. https://doi.org/10.1177/1461444818762364

Ruggiero, T. E. (2000). Uses and gratifications theory in the 21st century. *Mass Communication and Society, 3*(1), 3–37. https://doi.org/10.1207/S15327825MCS0301_02

Schwartz-Mette, R. A. (2009). Challenges in addressing graduate student's impairment in academic professional psychology programs. *Ethics & Behavior, 19*(2), 91–102. https://doi.org/10.1080/10508420902768973

Seidman, G. (2013). Self-presentation and belonging on Facebook: How personality influences social media use and motivations. *Personality and Individual Differences, 54*(3), 402–407. https://doi.org/10.1016/j.paid.2012.10.009

Seo, H., Harn, R. W., Ebrahim, H., & Aldana, J. (2016). International students' social media use and social adjustment. *First Monday, 21.* https://doi.org/10.5210/fm.v21i11.6880

Straumsheim, C. (2014, April 7). *Social media scholarship.* Inside Higher Ed. https://www.insidehighered.com/news/2014/04/07/social-media-may-benefit-international-students-and-group-projects-researchers-argue

Stubb, J., Pyhältö, K., & Lonka, K. (2011). Balancing between inspiration and exhaustion: PhD students' experienced socio-psychological well-being. *Studies in Continuing Education, 33*(1), 33–50. https://doi.org/10.1080/0158037x.2010.515572

Thompson, B. (2008). How college freshmen communicate student academic support: A grounded theory study. *Communication Education, 57*(1), 123–144. https://doi.org/10.1080/03634520701576147

Toff, B., & Nielsen, R. K. (2018). "I just Google it": Folk theories of distributed discovery. *Journal of Communication, 68*(3), 636–657. https://doi.org/10.1093/joc/jqy009

Valenzuela, S., Park, N., & Kee, K. F. (2009). Is there social capital in a social network site? Facebook use and college students' life satisfaction, trust, and participation. *Journal of Computer-Mediated Communication, 14*(4), 875–901. https://doi.org/10.1111/j.1083-6101.2009.01474.x

van Rooij, E., Fokkens-Bruinsma, M., & Jansen, E. (2019). Factors that influence PhD candidates' success: The importance of PhD project characteristics. *Studies in Continuing Education, 43*(1), 48–67. https://doi.org/10.1080/0158037X.2019.1652158.

Wang, G., Zhang, W., & Zeng, R. (2019). WeChat use intensity and social support: The moderating effect of motivators for WeChat use. *Computers in Human Behavior, 91*, 244–251. https://doi.org/10.1016/j.chb.2018.10.010

Wimmer, R. D., & Dominick, J. R. (1994). *Mass media research: An introduction.* Wadsworth.

Wohn, D. Y., Carr, C. T., & Hayes, R. A. (2016). How affective is a "Like"?: The effect of paralinguistic digital affordances on perceived social support. *Cyberpsychology, Behavior and Social Networking, 19*(9), 562–566. https://doi.org/10.1089/cyber.2016.0162

Wright, K. (1999). Computer-mediated support groups: An examination of relationships among social support, perceived stress, and coping strategies. *Communication Quarterly, 47*(4), 402–414. https://doi.org/10.1080/01463379909385570

Wright, K., & Bell, S. B. (2003). Health-related support groups on the Internet: Linking empirical findings to social support and computer-mediated communication theory. *Journal of Health Psychology, 8*(1), 39–54. https://doi.org/10.1177/1359105303008001429

Xu, S., & Jiang, S. (2018). Understanding the digital native behaviors of college students from computer experience. In *2018 Seventh International Conference of Educational Innovation through Technology (EITT)*, Auckland, New Zealand, 53–56.

Zhou, Y., Jindal-Snap, D., Topping, K., & Todman, J. (2008). Theoretical models of culture shock and adaptation in international students in higher education. *Studies in Higher Education, 33*(1), 63–75. https://doi.org/10.1080/03075070701794833

Zhou, Y., Zhang, H., & Stodolska, M. (2018). Acculturative stress and leisure among Chinese international graduate students. *Leisure Sciences, 40*(6), 557–577. https://doi.org/10.1080/01490400.2017.1306466

ANNALISE BAINES is a PhD student in the William Allen White School of Journalism and Mass Communications, University of Kansas, United States. Her research focuses on environmental, health and marketing communications, digital technologies, and marginalized groups. Her research has been published in several academic journals including *Vaccines*, *Newspaper Research Journal*, and *Frontiers in Communication*. Email: annalise.baines@ku.edu, Twitter: @AnnaliseFBaines

MUHAMMAD ITTEFAQ is a Ph.D. candidate in the William Allen White School of Journalism and Mass Communications at the University of Kansas, United States. He obtained his M.A. in Media and Communication Science from Technische Universität Ilmenau, Germany. His research focuses on health communication, social media, misinformation, health disparities, racial minorities, and the Global South. His research has been published in various academic journals including International Journal of Communication, Journalism: Theory, Practice & Criticism, Journalism Practice, Media International Australia, Third World quarterly, Vaccine, Psychology & Health, American Journal of Health Education, and Health, Risk & Society. His dissertation focuses on the use of social media by US local health departments during COVID-19 and how they correct health misinformation during the early phase of the pandemic. Email: muhammadittefaq@ku.edu, Twitter: @IttefaqM

MAURYNE ABWAO is a PhD candidate at the William Allen White School of Journalism and Mass Communications at the University of Kansas. Her research concentrates on the following areas: health communication, environmental racism, culture, and media representation of persons with disabilities, and the reproductive health rights of persons with disabilities. Her research has been published in several journals including *Vaccine, Vaccines, Frontiers in Communication, Psychology & Health, American Journal of Health Education,* and *Vaccines*. Additionally, she has published a book chapter with Routledge Taylor & Francis Group. Email: mauryneabwao@ku.edu

Research Article

© *Journal of International Students*
Volume 12, Issue 2 (2022), pp. 366-383
ISSN: 2162-3104 (Print), 2166-3750 (Online)
doi: 10.32674/jis.v12i2.2459
ojed.org/jis

One Family, Different Experiences of Identity Formation: International Graduate Students and Their Spouses

Ana X. de la Serna
*California State University
Dominguez Hills*

ABSTRACT

In this study, we use the communication theory of identity (CTI) to analyze the disparate experiences of International Graduate Students (IGS) and their accompanying partners. In CTI, four layers constitute the concept of identity: (a) The way individuals see themselves (*personal*), (b) their communicative interaction through social roles (*relational*), (c) their construction of messages (*enactment*), and (d) their role within a group or social network (*communal*). Thus, CTI views identity as a communicative and relational phenomenon. We analyze the layers of identity of IGS and their spouses living in the United States and find that although there are some coincidences, individuals within the student-dependent dyad mostly do not follow a common path of re-construction of their identity frames. Each narrative reflects individual and dyads' struggles as they work to define their new identities. For this phenomenological study, we conduct individual in-depth interviews with 16 couples from 12 different countries.

Keywords: different experiences of identity formation, one family

---

Universities in the United States receive international students from all over the world. For International Graduate Students (IGS) and their families, this is perceived often as a path to raise their economic and social status, or even to flee violence in their home countries. Relocating can represent an opportunity not only for themselves but also for their families as well. Families tend to be the student, their spouse, and children if they have any. Those individuals who travel with the student may also be referred to as dependents (Department of Homeland Security [DHS], 2020). Moving to another country with dependents constitutes a more challenging task than relocating by themselves (Brooks, 2018).

Graduate international students and their spouses experience different processes of identity formation as they navigate their new context. Even when they share a living space and numerous experiences (Thompson et al., 2020), students and their accompanying spouses find dissimilar obstacles to overcome. Therefore, both individuals navigate through particular situations when they try to figure out their identity in the new context (Ting-Toomey, 2005). The disparity comes from sources such as the immigration laws in the host country, different social norms, or access to university resources.

As they adapt to the new culture, both students and dependents encounter the challenge of affirming or reinventing their identities. Identity formation is important for individual's mental health and well-being (Evans et al., 2018). As individuals enter a new context, identity is transformed, built, and sustained through communication. Numerous identity and communication studies have considered the international student population (Liu et al., 2017; Tran, 2009; Wadsworth, 2008; Zimmermann, 1995); however, few studies include accompanying family members (De Verthelyi, 1995; Doyle et al., 2016; Elfeel & Bailey, 2018). Thus, the focus of this study is the inequality in the experiences of IGS and their spouses in their processes of identity transformation.

AN EXAMINATION OF INTERNATIONAL GRADUATE STUDENTS, THEIR SPOUSES, AND IDENTITY FORMATION

To analyze identity, we examined the conditions of IGS in the United States. Every year, individuals from countries all over the world choose to enroll in higher education in this country (Institute of International Education [IIE], 2019). In particular, international students enroll in postgraduate education programs. As Krsmanovic (2021) noted, graduate students tend to have different characteristics than undergraduate students; they tend to be older and are more likely to travel with their families. In the 2018/2019 academic year, there were over 350,000 new international students enrolled in a graduate program in the United States (IIE, 2019); and the most recent data accounted for over 135,000 dependents (Immigration and Customs Enforcement [ICE], 2014). *Dependent* is a term used by the Department of Homeland Security to refer to spouses and children of international students. It is a term that refers to the dependence of family members' immigration status on the students' immigration status.

More than language barriers and acculturation which have been widely studied by Krsmanovic (2021), becoming a student or a dependent has implications on individual's perception of themselves and their relationships, given that identity is a life-long developmental process and is constantly changing (Hopkins, & Blackwood, 2011; Marcia, 1980). When identity development takes place continuously in a particular context, few life-altering events could lead to an in-depth exploration of the self that requires a person to reinvent their core notions of identity (Tajfel, 2010). This means that when individuals follow the status quo, there are fewer possibilities of catalytic events that provoke deep identity transformation. Thus, few people could foresee that acculturation involves a process of redefinition of their identity (De Araujo, 2011). Students and dependents enter a culture different from their own. This is one event that inherently prompts the re-evaluation of a previously established identity (Wee, 2019). Often, dependents are less prepared than students for the changes that will lead to that identity transformation (Elfeel & Bailey, 2018). Imposed limitations, such as immigration laws for dependents of international students in the United States, present major disruption to their established sense of self and their place in society. Dependents are not allowed to work or study, they are not eligible for social security numbers, and their own legal immigration status depends completely on their partners (DHS, 2019).

There is existing literature about the identity formation of international students (Jung & Hecht, 2004; Wee, 2019). Although there tends to be a focus on language difficulties and cultural differences in international students' identity formation (Andrade, 2006; Wee, 2019). However, there are multiple factors that contribute to this process. Although there are variations of the meaning of identity (Jung & Hecht, 2004), researchers have found that identity formation of international students is inevitably related to their student activities (Kamara, 2017). International students' new identities are inevitably related to their process of navigating, living, and learning in host universities (Kamara, 2017), and interacting with peers, faculty, and staff, which leads the process of identity construction of international students to identity inconsistencies or identity gaps (Jung & Hecht, 2004) between their self-concept, and how Americans see them.

However, a student's function as part of a family unit has been scarcely studied. Existing research that considers the experience of identity formation of dependents is even rarer (De Verthelyi, 1995; Doyle et al., 2016; Elfeel & Bailey, 2018). In these studies, dependents are recognized as a vulnerable population due to their constraints in mobility and lack of social capital (Elfeel & Bailey, 2018). Doyle et al. (2016) opted to look at dependents and students as a family and make the family the unit of analysis. In this study, we compare the experiences of the students and their spouses, because both go through the process of identity formation in a new context.

IGS, THEIR SPOUSES, AND THE COMMUNICATION
THEORY OF IDENTITY

International student identity is complex. This is a result of students' belonging to different communities in their home and host countries (Wee, 2019). Identity is a concept that is widely used in diverse areas of research; however, it is often difficult to define. Even within the study of communication, there are diverse conceptualizations of identity (Bardhan & Orbe, 2012). Earlier views of identity emphasized the Western notion of "self" as a single, unified identity. Views that are more recent recognize that identity is a layered structure comprising values, drives, abilities, and life history (Marcia, 1980).

Communication scholars have found identity to be inevitably related to communication processes. All of these communication scholars have in common the idea that people are inherently social beings; their lives revolve around communication, relationships, and communities (Kim, 2005; Tajfel, 2010; Ting-Toomey et al., 1999). Therefore, people operate from multiple and shifting identities that adapt to the different contexts (Hecht et al., 2004). Communication plays a central role in the negotiation of relationships and group membership. It allows us to find connections with others, independently of our location (Metro-Roland, 2018). As Anderson (2000) said, "The self is possible only in the web of connected lives" (p. 2). Along these lines, Hecht (1993) proposed the communication theory of identity (CTI). He considered identity to be situated within the individual, but also in spheres between and among people (Jung & Hecht, 2004).

Hecht and his colleagues (2005) envisioned identity as a multilayered construct. In this study, this layering allowed us to analyze identity transformation in a more focused manner. This view of identity includes four layers: personal, enacted, relational, and communal. This breakdown of identity in layers allowed us to compare the experience of international students and their spouses in a precise manner. The *personal identity layer* refers to a person's self-concept, it reflects how individuals define themselves. The personal layer includes how individuals see themselves, in general, as well as how they see themselves in particular situations (Hecht & Choi, 2012). The *enacted identity layer* resides in a person's messages that express identity. The communicative process of message construction is the main focus of enacted identity. The way people enact their identity can have implications for international students and their spouses. For example, Bergquist et al. (2019) found that for refugees, discursive assimilation was important. As such, many emphasized enacting their identity as a member of the new host culture by speaking English.

The *relational identity layer* is jointly negotiated with others through social roles and interactions (Hecht & Choi, 2012). Here, identity is a product of how others perceive that individual. For instance, a student may form a relational identity as a good student when their professors or other students describe them as such. A marital relationship can be a unit of identity itself (Hecht & Choi, 2012). When a dependent describes themselves as a patient parent, they are referring to relational identity.

Lastly, the *communal identity layer* is performed at the collective level. Communal identity places identity in group membership. The individual shares characteristics with other group members, which provides a sense of inclusion. Place identity (Ching, 2001), when a person identifies as an international student, is one example. This signifies that the person, in this case the student, shares common characteristics with other foreign students. This can be the social norms, ways of learning, or culture.

When a person relocates to a new country that has a different culture, all of the layers defined by CTI are affected. Students and dependents are bound by new roles, new social norms, amongst other changes. A new context also requires adjustments to the couple's relationship. These adjustments are negotiated through communication including message construction. As individuals redefine their self-perception, they also redefine their group membership. The in-groups and out-groups reflect the individual and couple's new roles.

The four layers of identity are not always consistent with each other (Hecht, 1993). Layers can be contradictory and still form a part of identity as a whole. For example, a dependent may view him or herself as a supportive individual, and at the same time, they may demand more time and attention from their partner. This dynamic is defined as an identity gap. When people interact and communicate, gaps are unavoidable. The interaction between the layers is a communicative act and therefore a convenient framework in the study of identity.

Communication researchers have used CTI to guide studies in diverse areas. CTI, for example, has been used in the study of ethnic and racial differences, and in relation to face and politeness. In comparison, fewer studies based on CTI have focused on family relationships (Colaner et. al, 2014). Existing research on CTI includes grandparents and grandchildren (Kam & Hecht, 2009), adoptive and birthparent relationships with the adopted child (Colaner et al., 2014), and close relationships including friends and family (Guerrero et al., 2017). Our study adds to the existing research of the relationship between spouses, as we compare the layers of identity of students and dependents.

METHOD

Our main goal was to understand the inequality in the experiences of IGS and their spouses in their processes of identity transformation. Thus, we chose a hermeneutic phenomenological approach for this study. Phenomenology fits a project when the research problem requires an in-depth understanding of human experiences common to a group of people (Creswell, 1998). Specifically, hermeneutic phenomenology analyzes the world as experienced by the subject through their life world stories. This school of phenomenology follows the principle that interpretations are all we have, and description itself is an interpretive process (Caputo, 1984). This allowed us to study our participants' experiences and to interpret the meanings of the phenomena that they experienced (Padilla-Diaz, 2015).

Participants

We used purposive sampling for this study because we required participants to have specific characteristics. The sample for this study ($N = 32$) was composed of 16 student-dependent dyads. The dyads included married couples in which only one person is an international student currently enrolled in a university or college. All student participants were enrolled in the same large, mid-western university. The other person in the dyad was accompanying the student as a dependent. It is important that one person of the dyad was a dependent and not a student themselves, so that we could compare the different experiences. Participants were required to be able to speak English, Spanish, Chinese, or Arabic. We included these languages because the majority of the international students at the university where we collected the data are proficient in one of these languages (ISSS, ND) (Table 1).

Table 1: Participant Data

	Countries of origin	Gender
Students	Albania (1)	M = 12 (75%)
	Chile (1)	F = 4 (25%)
	China (3)	
	Colombia (2)	
	Czech Republic (1)	
	Honduras (1)	
	India (2)	
	Iraq (2)	
	Mexico (1)	
	Russia (1)	
	Turkey (1)	
Dependents	Albania (1)	M = 4 (25%)
	Chile (1)	F = 12 (75%)
	China (3)	
	Colombia (2)	
	Czech Republic (1)	
	Honduras (1)	
	India (2)	
	Iraq (2)	
	Japan (1)	
	Russia (1)	
	Turkey (1)	

Participants ranged in age from 27 to 50 years with an average of 33.6 years ($SD = 5.8$). All couples were married, the range of time married varied from 3 to 25 years with an average of 7.3 years ($SD = 5.5$). Couples had been living in the United States from one to eight years, with an average of 3.6 years ($SD = 1.8$). Only two couples did not have children. All student participants were enrolled in a postgraduate program. Dependents had different education levels ranging from high school to doctoral.

Procedure

After approval from the institutional review board, the P.I. and a research assistant recruited participants via messages sent through the graduate and family housing office listserv, as well as the International Center listserv. Both listservs allow us to send messages that reach the international students directly. The second set of interviews came from snowball sampling. After each interview, participants were given printed information about the study in the case they knew of other couples interested in participating.

The dyads consisting of one enrolled international student and their accompanying spouse were each interviewed as close in time as possible and independently. One participant was interviewed after the other one so that they would not have the opportunity to comment on their responses before their participation. Eisikovits and Koren (2010) pointed out that one of the benefits of dyadic analysis is that interviewing each participant in a couple relationship separately, the similarity or overlap in answers can be identified, as well as the difference and contrast.

Before the interview, one participant required translation to Mandarin Chinese, therefore an interpreter was provided. Ten individual interviews were conducted in Spanish. The role of the interpreter was to translate the questions and answers during the interview. Interviews took place in a convenient location that afforded enough privacy for the interviewees to express their experiences freely (e.g., a meeting room, office). Before the beginning of any interview, participants were provided with the IRB-approved informed consent form (in English, Spanish, Chinese, or Arabic). We asked respondents to share their accounts through narrative elicitation (Lindlof & Taylor, 2010) (e.g., Please tell me a story that describes who you were before you came to the United States); Please tell me about a time when you felt you had changed from the person you were before you came to the United States). Interviews lasted between 35 and 65 mins. All interviews were audio recorded.

Data Analysis

Data were transcribed by a professional service once it was collected and verified for accuracy by a research assistant. We then read the transcriptions to ensure accuracy. We divided the transcripts into dependent and student interviews. Next, we chose to analyze each group separately. We met after coding four interviews (two couples) to compare the coding results and resolve any differences. For the initial analysis, we used descriptive coding. We used descriptive codes (i.e., Personal identity layer, relational identity layer) not only to help categorize but also to index the data contents for further analytic work (Saldana, 2011). For the second round of analysis, we used versus coding. Versus coding uses binary terms to describe groups and processes, in this case students and dependents.

Table 2: Versus Coding Example

Quote	Versus codes
"So, the first year I was F-2 visa holder, means I do nothing. Just cleaning the house and doing other housewife stuff. That's not me, because I'm not a traditional woman type. I don't stick in the room and do all this kind of things. I did an awful job at being a wife. We fought a lot because I don't feel happy. I feel like I sacrificed too much."	Original vs. new occupational identity

The goal of versus coding is to see which processes are in conflict with each other throughout the document. We chose this analytic method because we wanted to compare how students and dependents experienced the layers of identity.

FINDINGS

The purpose of this study was to explore the inequality in the processes of identity formation of IGS and their spouses. In this section, we present our findings, which are organized by the four layers of identity described in the theory. We use quotes from participants to illustrate and use pseudonyms to protect their confidentiality.

The Personal Layer of Identity

There are numerous reasons for a family's decision to relocate to a new country. This decision was a catalyst that initiated a gradual process into who am I *now*? We identified this early action as the beginning of the personal layer transformation because it was at that point individuals had a new goal. One person would become the international student, and the other would provide support. This is reflected in most couple's narratives of that moment. For example, Ivan, a Family Studies PhD candidate from Russia envisioned his new role

> It is my story before coming here, that I left a socioeconomic level that was not even middle, it was a little bit up, and coming to the United States, my role is to be a student again, so it's two levels down. OK, I got it, I know how to be a student.

Ivan's message first described the sacrifice of status as a necessary loss that would materialize his new desired role. The 'student' label was adopted as a favorable identity characteristic. Before departure, 'student' symbolized growth and progress.

In comparison, spouses' narratives characterized the decision as initiated by their partners. They found their role to be of support. This was reflected in the way they described their preparation to come to a new country. As Xi, a 27-year-old dependent from China said:

Mostly because he wanted to do his Ph.D., I was working in Beijing at that time. I said, actually he can come here alone, and I will stay in China, but he doesn't agree. He wanted to me to come together with him. So, I said OK, because I'm pretty flexible, I adapt to the environment pretty good. So, he was a student and I was F-2 visa holder.

Xi's description reflected the way most dependents envisioned themselves in their new role. Spouse messages reflected less involvement in decision-making, including emigrating, which is a life-altering event. Reduced input in this decision can be a result of spouses' self-perception. It also reflects the view that they are willing to adapt their self-concept if needed.

Although self-perception transformation started with a decision, the arrival at the host country presented a radical disruption. Student's first contact with their new context was a significant life experience. This moment represented the introduction of the labels "international" and "foreign" to students' self-perception. For dependents, the new label was: *dependent*. This is a word used by The U.S. Department of Homeland Security to describe spouses or children of international students. However, the use of 'dependent' in a different way denotes that a person is defenseless, vulnerable, or reliant. Although the label of 'dependent' was introduced by an immigration institution, it illustrates a deeper sense of the role of spouses who accompany international students. It became a part of spouses' self-perception as they arrived in the United States. Spouses, in general, do not perceive themselves as dependents although their actions reflect a reliance on the student. Linda, a 35-year-old from Chile expressed her opposition:

> The term dependent does not correspond, because we are not dependent of the person who is studying, we accompany them, even if we are not studying we are contributing by watching the children, working, I don't know. We do the other part because otherwise you cannot get ahead. Dependent is not the correct term for me.

Once in the new country, IGS usually devote the majority of their time to the completion of their degree. A person's occupation is often the most common referent when defining self-perception. However, although occupation was central for students, they defined themselves through values first. Values included honesty, family orientation, and respect. For example, Ron, a 27-year-old student from China, explained that he thought of himself as a researcher but more importantly, a person who always put his family first.

When dependent participants had to describe their new personal identity, their responses were much more detailed and complex than their spouses.' Through their narratives, dependents described a void in their self-perception; they found it difficult to describe themselves. The ways that they had envisioned themselves were stripped away when they became a dependent. Aisha, a 30-year-old from Iraq described challenges similar to other dependents: "I lost myself, I think because I lost my job, I just stayed at home with my kids. My husband is not with me. I don't know who I am now."

The personal layer of identity was deeply affected for dependents. Even when they rejected the term "dependent," their self-perception was mostly influenced by their limitations. In an attempt to describe her new self-concept, Anka, a 45-year-old from Russia described herself as an inanimate random object

> I am getting older, and I am on visa status, and I am not allowed to work or study or…I am suitcase! I think I would like to do something else with my life, but I don't know how or when.

Gender also has an important role in the personal layer. Male dependents dealt with their sense of loss of purpose and added their dissatisfaction with the reversed gender roles. Adjit, a 30-year-old from India, had such a difficult time transforming his personal identity that after a short time he returned to his country, leaving his student-wife not only to her academic endeavors but also to care for their young child. He described this difficult decision as a result of Adjit's dissonance with the role of a dependent. He refused to adapt to this new and different personal identity layer.

Enacted Layer of Identity

The IGS that participated in our study felt they had to perform exceedingly well in their academic endeavors in order to fulfil the 'student' enacted layer of their identity. In general, this meant that they continuously devoted most of their time to their academic activities. These activities included teaching undergraduate classes, conducting research, working with peers and advisors, and covering all class requirements. Ivan referred to his enacted layer of identity as a student when he said that it was impossible for him to fail as a student after his whole family had sacrificed so much for him.

Gender was again an influence of how students built their identity. For Deepti, whose husband had gone back to India, it was especially difficult to enact her identity as a student.

> When we came to the U.S. I left my place thinking that I would be able to study. I never thought that my husband would have to go back to our place to work. How can I be a great student when I also have to care for R*[her child]? This is not what a good student is supposed to be. Now I am lucky to complete my work and sometimes it is not the best.

While Deepti's spouse moved back to India to continue working, the other dependents found a way to enact their identity as supportive spouses. Dependents provided emotional and enacted support to their partners. This is reflected in their narratives, Anka, for example, said:

> Right now, I am just around the house and I am driving him, and my daughter, so I am taxi driver. Sometimes I will be in negative mood, and I would try to [grrr] with him. I realize that it's not just about him, and he would like to change it also, but I guess the Lord is teaching me to be more patient.

In this particular example, Anka talks about providing enacted support by driving her husband and daughter to where they needed to go. Anka also talks about emotional support. This is expressed through her conflict avoidance. Conflict avoidance also became an enacted layer of identity when dependents chose not to communicate problems or challenges to their partners. This part of the enacted identity of dependents can be identified in the actions of Lenka, a 29-year-old from the Czech Republic:

> It is difficult to keep the troubles to myself, but *P has so many other things to think about in school. Like, one time I was desperate, I didn't know what to do with the baby that wouldn't stop crying. I'm telling you this was a crisis. But I didn't call *P, I called my mother even though it was a bad time for her back home. My mother talked me through everything I had to do and finally *B fell asleep. But why would I tell *P all of this things when he is coming home all tired. He works so hard. I am his biggest fan! No. I keep to myself.

(*Pseudonyms used to protect the identity of the participant's partner and child.)

Although they were very different, in this case the enacted identities of students and spouses complemented each other: Good students and supportive partners.

Relational Layer of Identity

Students and dependents constantly communicate to negotiate their roles. Dependents considered their most important role to provide their partners with the appropriate conditions so that they could succeed in their academic work. Although they already had a defined relationship in their country, their new context required that they adapt the way they saw themselves in the relationship. The relational layer was negotiated between the couple, and it is reflected in narratives like Aisha's:

> We speak all the time about hospitals, when we take D* we say: Oh! You see? It's like this. So sometimes he says no, you can't go. I say I can, now I'm strong. I'm different, I'm not like last times. If I'm in Iraq I can't go shopping alone, or I can't take D* alone, I should need him with me. But now, no. I am stronger. I am changing. Like, in my country if my husband stays in another city, I can't stay alone. But here I can. It's hard for me, but I can do it. I should do it.

Aisha and her husband Mahmoud found themselves often in unfamiliar situations. They described their lives in Iraq as more restricted than their lives in the United States and often of their conversations reflected those changes in their relational identity. Her new identity in the relationship was that of a more independent woman. This allowed Aisha to feel able to perform tasks that she would not have performed in her original country. In her new relational identity, she had different responsibilities.

Generally, the negotiation of the relational identity itself had to adapt to the new place. In this example, June, a 26-year-old from China was forced to find new ways to work out conflict:

> Sometimes I complain a lot and I run away from the house, I just don't want to stay in the house, I go outside…how to say it…If I was in China, I can go to some night places and just have a drink or sing songs in the karaoke or find a friend, go to their place, talk to them. But here if I run out, the only place I can go is Kroger. You don't want to just go to a friend's house because that might surprise them and it's not OK, not good. I don't really want to go to the bars because I'm not used to the atmosphere there, and I've been told don't go outside after 10 p.m. because it's not safe. So, all I can do is take a break and talk to him, even if he is stubborn.

Participants in this study found that with their new personal and enacted identity layers came a new way of understanding themselves as individuals in a relationship and understanding themselves as a couple.

Communal Layer of Identity

International students and their spouses incorporate into diverse communities in their new context. Their membership in these groups shapes their identity layers because a community delineates social norms, and with that, the shared visions of group identity. IGS belong to a larger group of students that serve as examples of how to perform in an academic setting. For example, for Jan, a 33-year-old from Czech Republic, it was important to follow the recommendations of other students who had more experience. Jan described a moment when he did not know how to address an issue with a professor, so he asked other students for advice. It was important for him to follow the social norms of the new place. Although students in the study gave priority to their academic endeavors, they were part of other groups or communities. These were groups of co-nationals or spiritual groups, for example. For Miguel, an engineering student from Honduras, it was very important to belong to a Catholic church:

> As soon as I arrived, I had to find my place of worship. My religion is very important for me and my family. When we first went to the church, the people were very welcoming and helped us with things for our apartment. Everyone was very nice, and we felt like we were back home for a little bit.

We found from our participants' narratives that there were significantly more opportunities for group membership for students than for dependents. In their original countries, dependents had family, friends, jobs, and other groups that they belonged to. They spoke the same language and understood the social norms. In the new country, they did not have the same opportunities. This often resulted in feelings of isolation and at times anxiety or depression.

> Here, it happens often, for example, that I have to go buy something to the supermarket, and if E* is not here, I have to go with all the kids and not

having anyone here, like when I am sick, there is no one who will say I will come over and help you cook, or watch the kids, or if you have a problem and need somebody to talk to, you can't just be like I will go to your house and talk about my problem because I think I don't want to impose.

Communal identity represents a sense of belonging for both students and dependents. It creates a sense of comfort and support. Dependents had significantly less opportunities to enrich this layer of identity than their spouses did.

DISCUSSION

As Bergquist and colleagues (2019) noted, CTI represents a useful framework for assessing self-concept during times of change. Through this framework, we found that participants' narratives of their experiences through identity formation as international students or dependents were divergent. CTI allowed us to identify obstacles in identity formation in a new context.

We found that students had more resources than their spouses did when they re-defined their identity. This was reflected in the way participants described their different layers of identity. Students had mostly made the decision to study in a foreign country, as suggested by Tran (2009). This provided them with more agency than their spouses. Spouses started to identify their personal identity layer as supportive. Often, support meant the decision to sacrifice jobs, family, friends, or economic status. Once they arrived to the United States, Students' personal identity layer became inevitably linked to their occupation. Studies of occupational identity highlight that it gives meaning and direction to one's career, but it also increases coping abilities in the face of stress and challenges; and allows an individual to find work that reflects their personal strengths, interests, preferences, and goals (Skorikov & Vondracek, 2011). However, for spouses that link was not there. They described this important shift in their occupation, as a void in their personal identity layer. They could not describe themselves using their occupation, and this was aggravated by the limitations they encountered in the new country. They sacrificed so much that in extreme cases, dependents went back to their home country.

In the enactment of identity, again, students found their occupation to be of outermost importance. They dedicated their time to their studies. Spouses again found that their enacted layer of identity was linked to support for their partners. This led to a re-negotiation of roles in their relational identity; in the literature (Bergquist et al., 2019; Faulkner & Hecht, 2011) we can see how people in romantic relationships who have deep discrepancies between partner's personal layers need to negotiate their roles. Students and their spouses used new communication strategies that better fit the relational identity. For example, keeping problems from their spouse so that they could focus on school. They also learned new ways to manage conflict in accordance with their new context. In this new context, spouses had limited opportunities to define their communal layer of identity. While students were part of an academic community, it was up to spouses to actively seek opportunities to join a community. Similar to the study of layers of identity of refugees (Bergquist et al., 2019), for most spouses there were barriers like language, location, and social norms that made them feel isolated and sometimes anxious or depressed.

We can see how the struggles of dependents have been widely ignored, even in the lack of literature about that population. While colleges and institutions provide a range of services and accommodations for incoming students, their families do not receive the same support, if any at all (Brooks, 2018). This study provides insight into the experiences of international students, but also of their dependents. Institutions of higher education would benefit from the well-being of both.

Limitations and Future Directions

International students bring diverse viewpoints that enrich not only their academic program but also their communities both in their host and home countries (Bender et al., 2019). When international students experience reduced stress levels, they have the conditions to produce better outcomes (Lee, 2010). Therefore, institutions that are hosts to IGS would benefit from recognizing the common difficulties that their students encounter. In addition, these same institutions should recognize the relevance of dependents. When dependent experiences are overlooked, there may be detrimental outcomes for the dependent themselves (Evans et al., 2018), and for their family unit and the community. The barriers to identity formation, in particular, can be addressed with programs that promote the inclusion and provide resources for the dependents through the institution.

This study was limited to graduate students, because they are more likely to bring their dependents to the United States than undergraduate students are. It is an example of barriers that are specific to this educational group. There is a need for future research to continue to account for international students as graduate and undergraduate instead of looking at them as a homogeneous group. As Krsmanovic (2021) reported, "the future direction of the research on international students' needs to (a) clearly account for students' academic level and (b) limit the investigation and generalizability of findings to either undergraduate or graduate students" (p. 15).

Additionally, this study included participants from only one institution. It would be important to replicate it in different locations and identify other barriers. The way institutions attract and support IGS and their families varies greatly. For example, it would be useful to replicate the study in institutions that do provide resources to dependents and evaluate the success of those resources. When more information becomes available to colleges and universities, they will be able to adopt or discontinue their practices based on actual evidence. The result will benefit all of the involved stakeholders.

CONCLUSION

In this study, we examined the lived experiences of international students and their spouses. We found through the different layers of identity that there are common experiences for a majority of students and some common experiences for the group of dependents, even when participants came from very diverse cultures. The comparison between student and dependent groups presented differences in most aspects of identity re-construction. As students gain new aspects for their personal identity, dependents lose the ones that made them who they were in their original cultures. In the enacted layer of identity, we found that although dependents have a difficult time defining themselves, their enacted identity is one of support for their partners. In the relational layer of identity, students and dependents negotiate their new roles and have conversations that allow their relationships to function. In the communal layer, we found that it is important for both groups to belong to a community, whether social, academic, or spiritual. However, it is a challenge for dependents to find the opportunities to enter such groups.

REFERENCES

Anderson, J. (2000). The organizational self and the practices of control and resistance. *Australian Journal of Communication, 27*, 1–32.

Andrade, M. S. (2006). International students in English-speaking universities: Adjustment factors. *Journal of Research in International Education, 5*(2), 131–154.

Bardhan, N., & Orbe, M. P. (Eds.). (2012). Identity research and communication: Intercultural reflections and future directions. Lexington Books.

Bender, M., van Osch, Y., Sleegers, W., & Ye, M. (2019). Social support benefits psychological adjustment of international students: Evidence from a meta-analysis. *Journal of Cross-Cultural Psychology, 50*(7), 827–847. https://doi.org/10.1177/0022022119861151

Bergquist, G., Soliz, J., Everhart, K., Braithwaite, D. O., & Kreimer, L. (2019). Investigating layers of identity and identity gaps in refugee resettlement experiences in the Midwestern United States. *Western Journal of Communication, 83*(3), 383–402. https://doi.org/10.1080/10570314. 2018. 1552009

Brooks, R. (2018). The construction of higher education students in English policy documents. *British Journal of Sociology of Education, 39*(6), 745–761. https://doi.org/10.1080/01425692.2017.1406339

Caputo, J. D. (1984). Husserl, Heidegger and the question of a "hermeneutic" phenomenology. *Husserl Studies, 1*(1), 157–178.

Ching, L. T. (2001). Becoming Japanese: Colonial Taiwan and the politics of identity formation. University of California Press.

Colaner, C. W., Halliwell, D., & Guignon, P. (2014). What do you say to your mother when your mother's standing beside you?" Birth and adoptive family contributions to adoptive identity via relational identity and relational–relational identity gap. *Communication Monographs, 81*(4), 469–494. https://doi.org/10.1080/03637751.2014.955808

Creswell, J. (1998). Qualitative inquiring and research design: Choosing many fine traditions. Sage.

De Araujo, A. (2011). Adjustment issues of international students enrolled in American colleges and universities: A review of the literature. *Higher Education Studies, 1*(1), 2–8. DOI:10.5539/hes.v1n1p2

De Verthelyi, R. F. (1995). International students' spouses: Invisible sojourners in the culture shock literature. *International Journal of Intercultural Relations, 19*(3), 387–411. https://doi.org/10.1016/0147-1767(95)00028-A

Department of Homeland Security. (September 21, 2019). *Bringing Dependents to the United States.* https://studyinthestates. dhs.gov/students/bringing-dependents-to-the-united-states

Department of Homeland Security. (January 10, 2020). *Immigration data and statistics.* Retrieved February 23, 2020 from https://www.dhs.gov/immigration-statistics

Doyle, S., Loveridge, J., & Faamanatu-Eteuati, N. (2016). Counting family: Making the family of international students visible in higher education policy and practice. *Higher Education Policy, 29*(2), 184–198. https://doi.org/10.1057/hep.2015.20

Eisikovits, Z., & Koren, C. (2010). Approaches to and outcomes of dyadic interview analysis. *Qualitative Health Research, 20*(12), 1642–1655. https://doi.org/10.1177/1049732310376520

Elfeel, S., & Bailey, L. E. (2018). Sojourners navigating structural constraints: International student spouses learning English in an informal centre. *Gender and Education, 2*(8), 1034–1052. https://doi.org/10.1080/09540253.2018.1547371

Evans, T. M., Bira, L., Gastelum, J. B., Weiss, L. T., & Vanderford, N. L. (2018). Evidence for a mental health crisis in graduate education. *Nature Biotechnology, 36*(3), 282. https://doi.org/10.1038/nbt.4089.

Faulkner, S. L., & Hecht, M. L. (2011). The negotiation of closetable identities: A narrative analysis of lesbian, gay, bisexual, transgendered queer Jewish identity. *Journal of Social and Personal Relationships, 28*(6), 829–847.

Guerrero, L. K., Andersen, P. A., & Afifi, W. A. (2017). *Close encounters: Communication in relationships.* Sage Publications.

Hecht, M. L. (1993). A research odyssey: Toward the development of a communication theory of identity. *Communications Monographs, 60*(1), 76–82. https://doi.org/10.1080/03637759309376297

Hecht, M. L., & Choi, H. (2012). The communication theory of identity as a framework for health message design. *Health communication message design: Theory and practice,* 137–152.

Hecht, M. L., Faulkner, S. L., Meyer, C. R., Niles, T. A., Golden, D., & Cutler, M. (2002). Looking through Northern Exposure at Jewish American identity and the communication theory of identity. *Journal of Communication, 52*(4), 852–869. https://doi.org/10.1111/j.1460-2466.2002.tb02577.x

Hecht, M. L., Warren, J., Jung, E., & Krieger, J. (2005). The communication theory of identity. In: W. B. Gudykunst (Ed.), *Theorizing about intercultural communication* (pp. 257–278). SAGE Publications.

Hopkins, N., & Blackwood, L. (2011). Every day citizenship: Identity and recognition. *Journal of Community and Applied Social Psychology, 21,* 215–227. https://doi.org/10.1002/casp.1088.

Immigration and Customs Enforcement. (2014). Student and exchange visitor program. https://www.ice.gov/sevis

Institute of International Education (2019, October 20). Research and Insights. https://www.iie.org/en/Research-and-Insights

Kam, J. A., & Hecht, M. L. (2009). Investigating the role of identity gaps among communicative and relational outcomes within the grandparent–grandchild relationship: The young-adult grandchildren's perspective. *Western Journal of Communication, 73*(4), 456–480. https://doi.org/10.1080/10570310903279067

Kamara, A. (2017). International students and "the presentation of self" across cultures. *Journal of International Students, 7*(2), 291. https://doi.org/10.32674/jis.v7i2.382

Kim, Y. Y. (2005). A contextual theory of intercultural communication. In W. B. Gudykunst (Ed.), *Theorizing about intercultural communication* (pp. 323–349). Sage.

Krsmanovic, M. (2021). The Synthesis and Future Directions of Empirical Research On International Students In the United States: The Insights From One Decade. *Journal of International Students, 11*(1), 1–23.

Jung, E., & Hecht, M. L. (2004). Elaborating the communication theory of identity: Identity gaps and communication outcomes. *Communication Quarterly, 52*(3), 265–283. https://doi.org/10.1080/01463370409370197

Lee, J. J. (2010). International students' experiences and attitudes at a US host institution: Self-reports and future recommendations. *Journal of Research in International Education, 9*(1), 66–84. https://doi.org/10.1177/147524090 9356382

Lindlof, T. R., & Taylor B. C. (2010). *Qualitative communication research methods.* Sage Publications.

Liu, N., Zhang, Y. B., & Wiebe, W. T. (2017). Initial communication with and attitudes toward international students: Testing the mediating effects of friendship formation variables. *Journal of Intercultural Communication Research, 46*(4), 330–345. https://doi.org/10.1080/17475759. 2017.1344999

Marcia, J. E. (1980). Identity in adolescence. *Handbook of Adolescent Psychology, 9*(11), 159–187.

Metro-Roland, M. (2018). Community, identity, and international student engagement. *Journal of International Students, 8*(3), 1408–1421. https://doi.org/10.32674/jis.v8i3.63

Padilla-Diaz, M. (2015). Phenomenology in educational qualitative research: Philosophy as science or philosophical science? *International Journal of Educational Excellence, 1*(2), 101–110. https://doi.org/10.18562/ijee.2015.0009

Saldaña, J. (2014). Coding and analysis strategies. In: Patricia Leavy (ed.), *The Oxford Handbook of Qualitative Research* (p. 318–339). Oxford University Press.

Skorikov, V.B., & Vondracek, F.W. (2011). Occupational Identity. In: Schwartz, S., Luyckx, K., Vignoles, V. (eds) *Handbook of Identity Theory and Research* (pp. 693–714). Springer, New York, NY. https://doi.org/10.1007/978-1-4419-7988-9_29

Tajfel, H. (Ed.). (2010). *Social identity and intergroup relations* (Vol. 7). Cambridge University Press.

Thompson, M. J., Carlson, D. S., Kacmar, K. M., & Vogel, R. M. (2020). The cost of being ignored: Emotional exhaustion in the work and family domains. *Journal of Applied Psychology, 105*(2), 186. https://doi.org/10.1037/apl0000433

Ting-Toomey, S., Yee-Jung, K. K., Shapiro, R. B., Garcia, W., Wright, T. J., & Oetzel, J. G. (1999). Ethnic/cultural identity salience and conflict styles in four US ethnic groups. *International Journal of Intercultural Relations, 24*(1), 47–81.

Ting-Toomey, S. (2005). Identity negotiation theory. In W. B. Gudykunst (Ed.), *Theorizing about intercultural communication* (pp. 173–191). Sage.

Tran, L. T. (2009). Making visible 'hidden' intentions and potential choices: International students in intercultural communication. *Language and Intercultural Communication, 9*(4), 271–284. https://doi.org/10.1080/14708470902807693

Vakkai, R. J. Y., Harris, K., Crabbe, J. J., Chaplin, K. S., & Reynolds, M. (2020). Sociocultural factors that impact the health status, quality of life, and academic achievement of international graduate students. *Journal of International Students, 10*(3), 758–775. https://doi.org/10.32674/jis.v10i2.1222

Wadsworth, B. C., Hecht, M. L., & Jung, E. (2008). The role of identity gaps, discrimination, and acculturation in international students' educational satisfaction in American classrooms. *Communication Education, 57*(1), 64–87. https://doi.org/10.1080/03634520701668407

Wee, A. (2019). Space and identity construction: A study of female Singaporean undergraduates in the UK. *Journal of International Students, 9*(2), 384–411. https://doi.org/10.32674/jis.v9i2.643

Zimmermann, S. (1995). Perceptions of intercultural communication competence and international student adaptation to an American campus. *Communication Education, 44*(4), 321–335. https://doi.org/10.1080/03634529509379022

ANA X. DE LA SERNA, PhD, is an Assistant Professor of Communications at California State University Dominguez Hills. Her research focuses on intercultural communication and health communication. Email: adelaserna@csudh.edu

Research Article

© *Journal of International Students*
Volume 12, Issue 2 (2022), pp. 384-402
ISSN: 2162-3104 (Print), 2166-3750 (Online)
doi: 10.32674/jis.v12i2.1651
ojed.org/jis

"Rules You Have to Know": International and Domestic Student Encounters With Institutional Habitus Through Group Work

Laura C. Seithers
Zhuldyz Amankulova
Christopher J. Johnstone
University of Minnesota

ABSTRACT

As more universities internationalize, interest in engagement between international and domestic students has increased. University initiatives to bring students together often adopt a deficit approach dependent on international students' adjustment to the host culture, overlooking the need for engagement to be a two-way exchange and the role of the institution in this process. Focusing on academic group work as a salient site of cross-national interaction, this study draws on analysis of focus group data to explore how institutional habitus or unwritten rules are enacted at a large U.S. university. Findings indicated that domestic students were better socialized to understand the habitus of the institution and tended to take charge in group work. In contrast, international students were seen as linguistically and academically deficient and were relegated to passive roles in a group. Important implications for practitioners and scholars of U.S. higher education are discussed.

Keywords: cross-national interactions, group work, institutional habitus, internationalization, U.S. higher education

The internationalization of higher education has become a dominant trend among universities in the United States and worldwide over the last few decades. A significant internationalization strategy of higher education institutions (HEIs) is the recruitment of international students (Verbik & Lasanowski, 2007), who are purported to bring an intercultural and international dimension to campus life. This supports the strategy of internationalization at home (IaH) (Knight, 2012), which is built on the presumption that international students can expose domestic students to the world through everyday contacts and special events (Crowther et al., 2001).

IaH is both a strategy and an outcome among a variety of institutional initiatives designed to improve intercultural contact among students from across the globe. The classroom provides one of the most salient contexts of cross-national interaction at U.S. HEIs, and interaction is often facilitated by group work. Though group work is a pervasive practice in U.S. university classrooms today, little research has examined international and domestic students' perceptions of the group work experience. The aim of this study was to understand how international and domestic students experience and perceive group work interactions.

This study draws upon the concept of habitus (Bourdieu, 1990) to examine the collective or institutional habitus (Cornbleth, 2010; Reay et al., 2001) of the university in relation to everyday classroom practices. According to Cornbleth (2010), institutional habitus refers to "an intermediary construct through which individuals encounter school structures" (p. 281), conveyed through messages communicated by members of the school community. Institutional habitus represents the unwritten and taken-for-granted expectations governing behavior at an institution as perceived by students, faculty, and staff.

The research questions guiding this study focused on perceptions of group work among international and domestic students in focus groups conducted at a large public research university in the Midwest: (1) How do international and domestic students perceive cross-national interactions in the context of group work? and (2) How do international and domestic students understand the expectations for group work in their U.S. university classrooms?

LITERATURE REVIEW

Group work as a sound educational strategy has been given considerable attention in the education literature in recent decades (Johnson & Johnson, 2009). Group work benefits students in a number of ways, including through the enhancement of the learning experience (Chang, 2006; Denson & Zhang, 2010), exposure to new ideas and values (Levin, 2005), development of key graduate employability skills (Denson & Zhang, 2010), facilitation of international students' academic and social adjustments (Wang, 2012), and diversification of social networks within large classrooms (Rienties, Heliot, et al., 2013; Rienties et al., 2014).

Educational research has also documented the challenges of group work interactions. Scholars have observed students' negative experiences and attitudes toward group work (Fozdar & Volet, 2012), in addition to the social tensions that arise among group members (Takahashi & Saito, 2013). Other possible difficulties of group work include student resistance (Isaac, 2012), groups' differential levels of collaboration and productivity (Summers & Volet, 2010), and freeloading group members who avoid active participation in the group (El Massah, 2018).

As increasing numbers of international students study in the United States (Verbik & Lasanowski, 2007), cross-national group experiences have become a common phenomenon. Many internationalization proponents see group work as an opportunity for global engagement among students (Crose, 2011; Kimmel & Volet, 2010). Montgomery (2009), for example, found that international and home students in the United Kingdom saw group work as an opportunity for learning and self-development. Kimmel and Volet (2010) concluded that students' subjective experiences of culturally diverse group work varied according to the organizational and instructional patterns of the learning context. Understanding student perceptions of group work provides a window into international and domestic student experiences of internationalization, as many of their day-to-day interactions occur in a group work context.

Intercultural Interaction in the University Classroom

Although research has shown that intercultural learning occurs when students engage with one another (Beelen & Jones, 2015; Crowther et al. 2001), some literature has recognized that simply bringing international and domestic students together on campus does not necessarily result in meaningful interaction between them (Leask, 2009). For example, domestic and international students may feel negatively toward working with one another (Moore & Hampton, 2015) and choose to self-segregate by cultural background or nationality (Rienties, Hernandez Nanclares, et al., 2013). International students may prefer interacting with co-nationals or other international students over their domestic peers (Bittencourt et al., 2021; Chen & Ross, 2015; Lee, 2010). Horne et al. (2018) found that international students struggled to feel a sense of belonging through academic engagement, suggesting the need for modeling of social integration and mutual respect in academic settings.

In an effort to pinpoint what prevents meaningful interaction, universities and international education scholars may rely on deficit thinking by emphasizing the individual characteristics of international students as the root of the problem (Freeman & Li, 2019). However, a programmatic emphasis on international students' inadequacies and deficits allows institutions to dodge critical reflection on systemic adaptability toward diversity and inclusion (Bittencourt et al., 2021). Few studies consider how institutions and individual students, faculty, or staff may marginalize international students (Beoku-Betts, 2004; Lee, 2005; Lee & Rice, 2007).

This study aimed to understand how the host culture of the institution, or institutional habitus, was perceived by university students in the context of cross-national group work. Through qualitative analysis of students' words on navigating cross-national group work, this study describes how institutional habitus was encountered in interactions between domestic and international students.

THEORETICAL FRAMEWORK

The theoretical framework of this study draws on Bourdieu's concepts of habitus, field, and capital (Bourdieu, 1986, 1990; Bourdieu & Wacquant, 1992). These concepts help to explain the dynamics of internationalized higher education (Marginson, 2008) due to their focus on "the social world and the dispositions that shape behavior, thoughts, and feelings in social contexts" (MacArthur et al., 2017, p. 32). In the context of a U.S. university in which domestic and international students meet, Bourdieu's (1986, 1990) concepts link structure and agency as they are negotiated in the space of higher education. The university setting represents a structure defined in part by an institutional habitus influencing possibilities for engagement, but students also exert agency by resisting and reinterpreting this set of norms and dispositions. This paper applies these concepts to explore how domestic and international students' experiences of cross-national group work both shape and are shaped by the institutional habitus of the university.

Habitus refers to "an orientation or network of predispositions toward the social world and one's place in it, including a sense of one's resources and how they might be used" (Cornbleth, 2010, p. 281). In other words, habitus is directly linked to an individual's social situatedness, beginning with their early socialization within family, community, and school; all of which impact their actions and decision-making. According to Bourdieu (1990):

> The habitus tends to generate all the 'reasonable', 'common sense', behaviors (and only these) which are possible within the limits of these regularities, and which are likely to be positively sanctioned because they are objectively adjusted to the logic of a particular field. (pp. 55–56)

For the purposes of this study, we define the term institutional habitus at universities as the unwritten expectations, rules, and behaviors that everyone seems to know. These unwritten expectations are often implicit, but they guide the ways in which individuals act toward and evaluate each other, and thus indirectly influence their "ability and performance in the formal curriculum" (Smith, 2013, p. 22). Individuals also possess various forms of capital, "the skills, knowledge, and qualifications of a person, group, or workforce considered as economic assets" (Merriam-Webster, n.d.) or "power resources" (Swartz, 2016) influencing their understanding of the institutional habitus.

Students who have been socialized in the habitus of the institution are likely to have an easier time navigating the social and educational requirements of group work (Lin, 2014), a dominant pedagogical strategy of Western HEIs. Bourdieu and Wacquant (1992) described what happens when an individual's habitus aligns with that of their social world:

> [S]ocial reality exists, so to speak, twice, in things and in minds, in fields and in habitus, outside and inside social agents. And when habitus encounters a social world of which it is the product, it is like a 'fish in

water': it does not feel the weight of the water and it takes the world about itself for granted. (p. 127)

Bourdieu's (1986) work has been used across a variety of settings, but many applications of his theory of cultural capital omit the voices of communities of color and overlook the forms of capital that marginalized groups possess (Yosso, 2005). In response to these inadequacies of traditional cultural capital theory, Yosso's (2005) model of community cultural wealth puts forth six forms of capital nurtured in marginalized communities. Under the umbrella of cultural capital or community cultural wealth, social, navigational, and linguistic capital have the most explanatory power for our exploration of cross-national group work.

Cultural capital in the context of group work represents both students' educational backgrounds and their socialization within the shared habitus of the U.S. education system. Social capital refers to the networks of people and links to community resources students draw on (Yosso, 2005). Navigational capital represents skills of maneuvering through institutions and fields, often those which are unfamiliar or represent sites of inequality (Yosso, 2005). Linguistic capital refers not only to international students' multilingual backgrounds but also their skills and experiences communicating in more than one style (Yosso, 2005).

To identify the forms of capital which have currency in cross-national classroom encounters, and the ways in which institutional habitus informs group norms, we take classroom group work as our unit of analysis. Thus, we can better understand the underlying logics of the field of group work by exploring how domestic and international students make meaning of the group work experience during focus group discussions.

The amount of power an individual has within a field depends on their position within it and the amount of capital they possess. Groups or agents occupying a position of power have the advantage of determining what counts as authentic capital (Webb et al., 2002). For example, in Lin's (2014) work examining the written assignment in higher education as a field, the instructor legitimized international students' capital through comments, suggestions, and grades.

In our study, students' mastery of the rules of group work are granted legitimacy in part by their instructor, but legitimation must also come from the other members of the project group. In groups, students display different forms of capital and influence. In the case of cross-national group work, domestic students often wield greater power in the field. Institutional habitus thus predicts that domestic students possess the unwritten procedural and behavioral knowledge to have the upper hand in group work settings. Without instructor or classmate legitimation of the "capital portfolio" (Lin, 2014), or the forms of capital each international student presents, international students may find themselves excluded or ignored within groups, their contributions overlooked. In this study, we analyzed students' observations about their experiences to identify the role of habitus and capital within the field of group work.

METHODS

This study employed focus group methods; a qualitative approach designed to elicit individual experiences in a conversational format among individuals with similar experiences. The focus group data used for this study were originally collected as part of a larger university project examining cross-national interaction and educational contributions of international students to the broader institution. Data were collected in multiple group sessions ranging from two to nine members. In total, nine focus groups were conducted with 131 students at one university. Focus group interviews were chosen for data collection to engage as many students as possible and to examine common themes among participants. Focus group participants included the following: 50 undergraduate domestic students, 30 undergraduate international students, 21 graduate domestic students, and 20 graduate international students. Students were defined as domestic if they did not need a visa to enroll in the university. All international students held student visas.

The use of focus groups assumed that students who identified as either international or domestic had shared experiences that could be identified through guided conversation. According to Krueger and Casey (2000), focus groups elicit consensus or shared meaning-making when participants with common experiences are consulted on phenomena that they encounter.

The original framing of the university project was meant to disrupt conceptualizations of international students on campus as merely economic resources, as they have increasingly been framed over the past two decades (Stein & de Andreotti, 2016). The initial review of focus group data identified the cultural and/or academic contributions students make at the university. Researchers originally employed inductive, interpretive coding to identify how cross-national interactions engaged all students academically and cross-culturally (for a full description see Johnstone et al., 2018).

In the present study, our analysis identified group work as a prevailing mode of instruction and site of cross-national interaction, bringing up questions about the functioning of power and capital in this field. We analyzed focus group data through qualitative content analysis and found that our inductive coding aligned with a Bourdieusian framework of habitus. Thus, Bourdieu's (1986, 1990) concepts were applied to understand the phenomena present through a critical lens and to identify structures of power and legitimacy. However, we found that the dynamics of group work could not be fully understood without also incorporating Yosso's (2005) concept of community cultural wealth, a complement to Bourdieu's work. Through this critical lens, we identified how relevant forms of capital functioned in the field of group work based on the perceptions of domestic and international students.

FINDINGS

Findings indicated that institutional habitus was present in group activities. While domestic students described having a shared understanding of how to proceed and the roles students should play in group work, international students who lacked experience with the learning strategy of group work faced unique difficulties. The following exchange between domestic and international student participants in a focus group encapsulates the themes of habitus and cultural capital that emerged from the data. Participants A and B, who were domestic students, and Participant C, an international student, spoke to the unwritten rules of group work, who has power, and which forms of capital are valued.

Referring to group work as an educational strategy in classrooms, Participant A explained, "Yeah, but it's more innate for us, compared to an international student." Participant B concurred, adding, "It's more in place."

Participant A continued:

This is what we've grown up with generally, even though at the university level it might be different, but we've been taught these same things, the same skill set from elementary on where that's just carried on. And international students maybe haven't been taught that same skill set that we have.

Participant C replied, pointing out that that group work is not universal:

Group work is not a norm in every culture or in every educational system across the world, as far as I know, for the four countries that I have lived in …. [I]t was so difficult for me to get used to the group work dynamic in United States. And there's an assumption that when you start working everyone has the same power and intellectuality, but then later, … you understand what kind of different skills people are bringing and you try to adjust that to the group work … So it was so interesting for me to learn how to navigate that division of labor, division of responsibility. Who's going to lead? Why they should lead but not the others?

In this discussion, we see that the domestic students felt that they were already equipped with the cultural capital to comfortably navigate group work assignments. They described their understandings of how group work functions as innate or ingrained through previous educational experiences in the United States. Participant C explains that as an international student they had not been socialized within the habitus of group work and had to "learn how to navigate" group work assignments.

Institutional Habitus and Capital in Group Work

Our analysis further suggests that the forms of capital students displayed influenced the roles and behaviors they assumed in group work. The field of group work had its own valued currency of capital. Cultural capital was essential to the roles and behaviors of domestic and international students engaged in group work. As Participant D, an international student, explained:

I think one thing is you're here to learn how to navigate the U.S. academic system, you want to get successful, right? And so there are rules you have to know, otherwise you obey it or you fight against it …

> And [working] with American peers, you get to know some things that you don't know but they do, and that will bring out something that is not explicit in the brochure, in the workshops for international students.

This student implied that international students needed to develop particular capital portfolios to be successful at the university. International students needed to learn the "rules" to have their capital recognized and legitimated by their peers within the group. These rules are "not explicit in the brochure" and have to be learned by students on the go.

Linguistic Capital

Our findings further suggest that linguistic capital, in this case the ability to perform with a high level of academic English, was critical to how student roles played out in group work. Language, whether written or spoken, was a key concern of domestic students when it came to completing projects with their international peers. Some focus group participants adopted a deficit approach toward international students' linguistic capital by emphasizing the challenges international students faced in effectively demonstrating the English language skills that domestic students perceived as valuable. A successful display of linguistic capital became a key gatekeeping measure monitored by domestic students in relation to international students' abilities to navigate group work, as demonstrated in Participant E's comments:

> I could tell they were international students [because] obviously their writing wasn't great so I figured that they aren't fluent in English. So that was pretty challenging. And then having to rewrite a lot of sentences and stuff to fix the basic grammatical errors. I feel like they do kind of put in more effort, because they have to prove themselves, that they can compete on our level, even if it's a second language to them.

This domestic student saw international student partners as a potential liability because of the extra work needed to edit their peers' writing. International students failed to demonstrate possession of a narrow, yet valued, form of linguistic capital. This student's reactions did not reflect the broader narratives outlined in IaH around the benefits of international learning, but instead suggested a narrow understanding of the goals of education and the skillsets that are most valued in classrooms.

In another reference to the currency of linguistic capital in group work, international student writing was mentioned repeatedly by domestic students in the focus group interviews. Domestic students felt that they needed to closely monitor international student writing in group projects when a grade was on the line. According to Participant B:

> I think one of the biggest problems we ran into was we would have to overcompensate on our parts, 'cause the writing level wasn't there. So that was a more frustrating experience, because I would be reading stuff

sometimes and I'm like … we can't submit this portion of the paper, 'cause it won't cut it.

International students expressed awareness that their language skills were a primary concern for domestic peers in cross-national interactions and used as a rationale for exclusionary behavior by domestic students. As Participant F, an international student, stated, "And also for Caucasian friends, they [are] not one hundred percent waiting to talk to international students, [be]cause they know there's a language barrier and a cultur[al] barrier between them."

Deficit Perspective Toward International Student Capital Portfolios

Although some domestic students highlighted the benefits of working with international students for learning about different cultures, many did not perceive international students as equal contributors to group work. Instead, they perceived international students as in need of domestic student guidance to navigate the system. As Participant E, a domestic student, explained:

> A lot of international students that I meet tend to be more quiet and reserved, and so they don't seem to really speak up … that's why the American students take over, because they're not speaking up so they just take charge of it, but I feel like if they would they could bring some really good different viewpoints to the table.

A view of international students as lacking skills and needing additional help seemed to be a default assumption among U.S. students. This reflected the positionality of domestic students with experiential knowledge of how things work in U.S. HEIs.

The focus group excerpts above demonstrate that both domestic and international students adopted a deficit view toward international students, emphasizing their weaknesses in group work. Moreover, both domestic and international students acknowledged an institutional habitus and the position of power domestic students occupied. Domestic students' individual habitus aligned with habitus of the institution and they possessed more valued forms of capital for group work. Students also acknowledged that domestic students could "fix" (Participant E) the contributions of international students by serving as cultural interpreters, but such help inevitably led to unequal power dynamics.

Domestic Students in Cross-National Group Work

As a result of previous educational experiences, many domestic students are pre-equipped with a set of skills and expectations around studying, seeking resources, and assignments at U.S. HEIs. This institutional habitus prioritizing the needs and prior experiences of domestic students goes largely unquestioned, despite an increase in internationalization activity on campuses (Beelen & Jones, 2015; Crose, 2011; Knight, 2012). Domestic students are thus more likely to embark upon projects with preconceived notions of how a student group best functions. Consequently, domestic students self-ascribe credibility and often appoint themselves as guides for international students in group work, as described by Participants A and B. Participant A stated,

> They [international students] might learn how to navigate the American education system better by working with people who know what's going on, even though a lot of times we don't even know what's going on. But we know a little bit better than international students, so they might learn … how to approach a professor, or the type of writing style that professors are generally looking for, or even things like how to navigate some of the school systems here at the university.

Participant B added, "So, basically, everything that we as domestic students have to learn at some point."

The above interaction between domestic students shows that their implicit understanding of institutional habitus lent them the authority to dictate how the group work encounter unfolded. International students found themselves on the margins because their capital portfolios had less perceived value in this field. Specifically, they lacked cultural capital in the form of knowledge of the implicit rules governing group work. Domestic student participants observed that American students tend to take the lead in group work encounters. Participant G shared,

> Well in my experience, if I was being stereotypical, usually it's the American students that take charge first and… I mean it's not like they don't want input from the other people, but I think a lot of times people assume that the international students would rather not take charge, or are shyer, or they have a language barrier…. [O]ne of my friends is from Korea. He speaks English very well, but sometimes he [uses] the tenses wrong or speak[s] really slowly, and so they would almost cut him off, and finish his sentence … because they wanted to do their presentation well.

Participant H added,

> With my experience, it was the complete opposite. He was the only international student in our group, and he completely took charge … I just found it refreshing to see, 'cause it rarely ever happens … I see that they do get cut off a lot, and it's almost like we don't trust them enough to get things done.

From Participant G's perspective, domestic students approach group work with the assumption that international students who fail to display the valued forms of linguistic capital need domestic students to take a leadership role in the group. When international students demonstrated linguistic capital by taking charge in group work, as in Participant H's example, this was understood as an exception to the rule.

International Students in Cross-National Group Work

In contrast with deficit perspective toward international students adopted by domestic peers, interviews with international students revealed several examples of international student agency in group work. Their agency was revealed by the navigational and social capital they employed to succeed in cross-national group interactions.

Navigational Capital

Some international students developed strategies to avoid the stigmatizing beliefs that domestic students held about their language capabilities. These students navigated around the requirements of group work, finding ways to remain under the radar by completing behind-the-scenes tasks rather than confronting stereotypes about their language skills. In the following exchange, international students described coping strategies for avoiding uncomfortable conversations with domestic groupmates. As Participant I explained:

> I heard a lot of students say that they know if they need to work on a project, a lot of international students will choose to do some work, maybe prepare for PowerPoint or something... [so] that they will not have to speak publicly.

Participant D agreed, adding:

> You know, I have seen group work, like a group presentation. American peers take the lead in the group presentation and their English is like perfect, so they do the talking. And some international students will just click the PowerPoint, or do some preparation work. But not really the talking.

Avoiding group work with domestic students altogether was an additional navigational strategy among international students. Some students felt more comfortable connecting with other international students rather than facing the judgment and assumptions of their domestic peers. International students described how they felt "closer to other international students" and "naturally work[ed] together" because they "share[d] similar struggles" (Participant D).

These examples demonstrate various ways international students navigate systems not built for them. Rather than challenge the system head-on, students instead relied on navigational capital to avoid discriminatory, racist, or xenophobic conversations with domestic students. Social capital built through solidarity networks with other international students aided in this navigation.

Social Capital

Networks of international students who supported one another in group work and classroom encounters represented a form of social capital. International students drew on their broader social networks to better navigate group work. In the following focus group excerpt, Participant J, an international student, emphasized their comfort working with other international students:

> ... I think international students might approach more international students than American students. Some of my concerns might be, I'll be thinking, oh, if this question is stupid, or I might be twisting this word, if domestic students whose English is good, maybe the professor already addressed this issue so many times, but I just can't get the language. And you have these sort of concerns that you share more with international students, they will understand if this question is stupid.

In addition to creating diverse networks of peer support to help them maneuver successfully in the classroom, international students also sought out peer mentors outside of the classroom. Some international students were better positioned to navigate the institutional habitus because of their years of experience studying in the United States. International students who had lived in the United States longer were able to help guide their newly arrived peers. As international student Participant C explained:

> When it comes to international students my interaction with them, as you said, depending on how much you know about the US, then there's some sort of a power differential between, you know, international students. Someone might have been there longer than the other person, or might speak the language better than the other person, so it's kind of like "Okay, you're kind of like my mentor right now, you need to help me to get acclimated to the culture and the rest of it," so I had so many other international, you know, friends of mine coming to me and asking me questions if they came later to the United States, and I did the same thing to the other international students who were here before.

International students who were in the US longer developed a better understanding of the institutional habitus and could serve as mentors to other international students in learning the unwritten rules. This social capital, or network of international peers supporting each other, provided a mechanism for navigating and succeeding in the institution.

DISCUSSION

This study used focus group interviews to understand international and domestic student perceptions of cross-national interactions in group work. Our analysis sought to describe the unwritten expectations of group work by applying the concepts of institutional habitus and community cultural wealth. The findings of this study support the use of institutional habitus (Cornbleth 2010; Reay et al., 2001) and community cultural wealth (Yosso, 2005) as productive frameworks which complement Bourdieu's original habitus framing (1986, 1990) to examine cross-national interactions in higher education.

A key contribution of our findings is that focus group participants made sense of cross-national group work interactions by centering the forms of capital with currency in the field. Group work involved a delineation of roles among domestic and international students, with domestic students holding great power over what forms of participation were valued. Thus, domestic students often took charge of proceedings while international students were relegated to more passive positions. These positions within groups were reinforced by domestic students' perceptions of how international students could contribute or lead. When international students exhibited successful displays of capital in the group, this was seen as an exception to the rule. However, in these cases, international students were in fact developing their own strategies and capital resources to contribute to group projects.

As in Lin's (2014) study on international students and writing assignments, a successful display of linguistic capital held great value in group work, especially to the domestic students who were the dominant gatekeepers. Domestic students frequently referenced concerns about speaking, writing, and performing academic English in the university classroom, and many expressed a lack of confidence in international students' academic English abilities when a grade was "on the line." In turn, international students worried about making errors, avoided speaking during presentations, and often complied with their assigned roles.

The participants in this study strictly observed the conventions of presenting group work, a pressure that they put on themselves and their classmates as part of the group work process. In an increasingly multicultural and multilingual university space, it is perplexing that linguistic abilities carry so much weight in comparison with the content or quality of student work and learning outcomes. The monolingual mindset of the university (Liddicoat & Crichton, 2008) is one of the most entrenched and prominent principles of institutional habitus in majority English-speaking contexts, one that appears to be present at this study's research site. Further, after decades of internationalization research and strategy, including IaH, there appears to be little cultural shift in how teaching and learning are done in the United States. Institutional habitus seems to advantage domestic students over international students and reinforce narratives of U.S. superiority.

Institutional habitus as a theoretical lens reflected university students' understandings of the unwritten rules and standards operating at HEIs. Students can absorb rigid understandings of how to behave in the university learning environment, perpetuating the idea that international students are not prepared to be equal contributors. The results of this study indicate that both domestic and international students are aware of domestic students' privilege but are not necessarily aware of the root institutional assumptions that promote and reinforce such privileges. Our data suggest that the culture of the institution (and U.S. higher education, in general) influences cross-national interactions on campus and reinforces narrowly nationalistic stereotypes of expertise.

Though domestic students appreciated the perspectives of their international student peers, the wealth of linguistic, navigational and social capital international students brought to groups often went unrecognized. However, analyzing focus group data through the lens of navigational capital (Yosso, 2005) revealed the ways that international students draw on their rich capital portfolios to successfully navigate group work despite their unfamiliarity with institutional habitus and its narrow and stereotypic assumptions about international student roles in groups.

LIMITATIONS

A key limitation of this study was the lack of demographic data available to the researchers as part of our qualitative data set of focus group interviews, which had been previously conducted by a separate research team. Information on demographic characteristics of focus group participants, including their race, gender, nationality, field of study, and level of study was not available to the researchers. This information is needed because neither domestic nor international student groups can be treated as homogenous, as both represent diverse student populations. Though this study shines a light on the dynamics of group work among international and domestic students at one university, it provides limited insight into the perceptions of international students toward the unwritten rules they encounter at their universities—perhaps because it takes time to recognize such unwritten rules exist. The concept of institutional habitus from the perspective of internationalization should be further explored beyond group work to examine broader university functions.

IMPLICATIONS FOR RESEARCH AND PRACTICE

The findings of this study suggest that universities are not impartial spaces designed primarily to serve the needs of a diverse student body, nor has internationalization created a comprehensive space for rethinking how education is done in U.S. institutions. Diversity and internationalization seem to have become buzzwords for institutions which readily employ the terms without fully considering the structural barriers in place for diverse students.

One way to address these shortcomings is to revise how institutions and practitioners understand student participation. To shift the mindset from a deficit perspective toward international students, universities should recognize international students as competent contributors to the academic community in their approach to internationalization. Faculty should prioritize an awareness of the diverse learning preferences and communication styles of students when designing group work assignments and question the ways unstructured group assignments may reproduce inequalities in the classroom. For example, Kim et al. (2016) provided a number of suggestions for designing group work to incorporate different types of engagement, including by setting up rotating discussion leaders, creating groups which remain the same throughout the course, and allowing students to nominate a spokesperson.

While radically shifting the ingrained institutional habitus of a university cannot happen overnight, it might productively begin with expanding norms to include most comprehensible expressions of academic language. There are moments when correcting every non-standard grammatical and stylistic error might be productive, but a deeper focus on the content and overall quality of the work may disentangle the process of cross-national work from the internal language policing that domestic students currently perform in groups. Additionally, curriculum should be flexible enough to welcome a range of modes of participation to fit the diverse strengths and needs of today's college students. Not every goal needs to be accomplished in groups—especially if these groups introduce stereotypes and power differentials into the learning process.

Moreover, given the barriers to meaningful interaction between international and domestic student peers, more work needs to be done to promote organic, low-stakes connection between them. It is critical to consider the institutional habitus and the messages university programming sends about international students in designing programs for bringing these two groups together. Programming might center on what Thomas et al. (2018) described as "common grounds" of experience, such as cultural celebrations, faith, and shared challenges, to promote meaningful interactions among all students. At the same time, such programming runs the risk of superficially celebrating diversity without addressing structural teaching and learning practices that advantage some students over others.

Future research should investigate which configurations of group work in the university classroom are most inclusive, and which programming is most effective for cultivating inclusive social and academic environments for university students. This study has begun to pull back the curtain on the hidden habitus of higher education institutions and its potential to marginalize international students, in particular, but more work needs to be done to inform which alternative strategies best support students. Faculty and staff who utilize group work activities should engage directly with students to form expectations for cooperation and leadership roles in group work within a classroom community. Group assignments should be carefully designed and considered rather than assumed as a gold standard of university teaching.

CONCLUSIONS

In all cases, internationalization is a process that benefits from careful critique. The intended or unintended assumptions, prejudices, and power imbalances that emerge from everyday practices in HEIs, including the teaching strategy of group work, are rife with opportunity for research and scrutiny. Institutional habitus and cultural capital as a framework can indicate why particular actors engage with each other in the way they do within particular institutions. This qualitative study indicated that classroom-based group work is a useful unit of analysis for understanding how habitus is reproduced in institutions as part of internationalization practice.

The notion that international students alone are responsible for adapting to the U.S. university setting, and learning its habitus is evident in the findings of this study on the dynamics of group work. This approach sets a tone for group work interaction that overlooks the strengths and capabilities international students bring with them to their studies and elides the important role that domestic students and the habitus of the institution play in the integration of international students. Moving away from deficit thinking, higher education institutions and the students, faculty, and staff who comprise them should approach group work activities with intentionality to build cooperation skills and inclusivity rather than reinforce social hierarchy and division.

REFERENCES

Beelen, J., & Jones, E. (2015). Redefining internationalization at home. In A. Curaj, L. Matei, R. Pricopie, J. Salmi, & P. Scott (Eds.), *The European higher education area: Between critical reflections and future policies* (pp. 59–72). Springer.

Beoku-Betts, J. (2004). African women pursuing graduate studies in the sciences: Racism, gender bias, and Third World marginality. *NWSA Journal, 16*(1), 116–135. https://www.jstor.org/stable/4317037

Bittencourt, T., Johnstone, C., Adjei, M., & Seithers, L. (2021). "We see the world different now": Remapping assumptions about international student adaptation. *Journal of Studies in International Education, 25*(1), 35–50. https://doi.org/10.1177/1028315319861366

Bourdieu, P. (1986). The forms of capital. In J. G. Richardson (Ed.), *Handbook of theory and research for the Sociology of Education* (pp. 241–258). Greenwood Press.

Bourdieu, P. (1990). *The logic of practice*. Stanford University Press.

Bourdieu, P., & Wacquant, L. J. (1992). *An invitation to reflexive sociology*. University of Chicago Press.

Chang, J. S. (2006). A transcultural wisdom bank in the classroom: Making cultural diversity a key resource in teaching and learning. *Journal of Studies in International Education, 10*(4), 369–377. https://doi.org/10.1177/1028315306287905

Chen, Y., & Ross, H. (2015). Creating a home away from home: Chinese undergraduate student enclaves in US higher education. *Journal of Current Chinese Affairs, 44*(3), 155–181. https://doi.org/10.1177/186810261504400307

Cornbleth, C. (2010). Institutional habitus as the de facto diversity curriculum of teacher education. *Anthropology & Education Quarterly, 41*(3), 280–297. https://doi.org/10.1111/j.1548-1492.2010.01088.x

Crose, B. (2011). Internationalization of the higher education classroom: Strategies to facilitate intercultural learning and academic success. *International Journal of Teaching and Learning in Higher Education, 23*(3), 388–395. https://files.eric.ed.gov/fulltext/EJ946165.pdf

Crowther, P., Joris, M., Otten, M., Nilsson, B., Teekens, H., & Wächter, B. (2001) *Internationalisation at home: A position paper*. EAIE.

Denson, N., & Zhang, S. (2010). The impact of student experiences with diversity on developing graduate attributes. *Studies in Higher Education, 35*(5), 529–543. https://doi.org/10.1080/03075070903222658

El Massah, S. S. (2018). Addressing free riders in collaborative group work: The use of mobile application in higher education. *International Journal of Educational Management, 32*(7), 1223–1244. https://doi.org/10.1108/ijem-01-2017-0012

Fozdar, F., & Volet, S. (2012). Intercultural learning among community development students: Positive attitudes, ambivalent experiences. *Community Development, 43*(3), 361–378. https://doi.org/10.1080/15575330.2011. 621085

Freeman, K., & Li, M. (2019). "We are a ghost in the class": First year international students' experiences in the global contact zone. *Journal of International Students, 9*(1), 19–38. https://doi.org/10.32674/jis.v9i1.270

Horne, S. V., Lin, S., Anson, M., & Jacobson, W. (2018). Engagement, satisfaction, and belonging of international undergraduates at U.S. research universities. *Journal of International Students, 8*(1), 351–374. https://doi.org/10.32674/jis.v8i1.169

Isaac, M. L. (2012). "I hate group work!" Social loafers, indignant peers, and the drama of the classroom. *The English Journal, 101*(4), 83–89. https://www.jstor.org/stable/41415478

Johnstone, C. J., Yefanova, D., Woodruff, G., Montgomery, M. L., & Kappler, B. J. (2018). "It would be better if you can hang out with different people": An examination of cross- national interaction in postsecondary classrooms. *The Journal of Teaching and Learning, 12*(2), 23–37. https://doi.org/10.22329/jtl.v12i2.4927

Kim, S., Ates, B., Grigsby, Y., Kraker, S., & Micek, T. A. (2016). Ways to promote the classroom participation of international students by understanding the silence of Japanese university students. *Journal of International Students, 6*(2), 431–450. https://doi.org/10.32674/jis.v6i2.365

Kimmel, K., & Volet, S. (2010). University students' perceptions of and attitudes toward culturally diverse group work: Does context matter? *Journal of Studies in International Education, 16*(2), 157–181. https://doi.org/10.1177/1028315310373833

Knight, J. (2012). Student mobility and internationalization: Trends and tribulations. *Research in Comparative and International Education, 7*(1), 20–33. https://doi.org/10.2304/rcie.2012.7.1.20

Krueger, R. A., & Casey, M. A. (2000) Focus *groups: A practical guide for applied research* (3rd ed.). Sage.

Johnson, D. W., & Johnson, R. T. (2009). An educational psychology success story: Social interdependence theory and cooperative learning. *Educational Researcher, 38*, 365–379. https://doi.org/10.3102/0013189x09339057

Lee, J. J. (2005). *Experiences and satisfaction among international students* [Conference session]. American Educational Research Association, Montreal.

Lee, J. J. (2010). International students' experiences and attitudes at a US host institution: Self- reports and future recommendations. *Journal of Research in International Education, 9*(1), 66–84. https://doi.org/10.1177/1475240909356382

Lee, J. J., & Rice, C. (2007). Welcome to America? International student perceptions of discrimination. *Higher Education, 53*(3), 381–409. https://doi.org/10.1007/s10734-005-4508-3

Leask, B. (2009). Using formal and informal curricula to improve interactions between home and international students. *Journal of Studies in International Education, 13*(2), 205–221. https://doi.org/10.1177/1028315308329786

Levin, P. (2005). *Successful teamwork*. McGraw-Hill Education.

Liddicoat, A. J., & Crichton, J. (2008). The monolingual framing of international education in Australia. *Sociolinguistic Studies, 2*(3), 367–384. https://doi.org/10.1558/sols.v2i3.367

Lin, I. (2014). Realigning capital portfolios: International students' educational experiences in higher education. *Asia Pacific Journal of Education, 34*(3), 366–380. https://doi.org/10.1080/02188791.2013.860009

MacArthur, G. J., Jacob, N., Pound, P., Hickman, M., & Campbell, R. (2017). Among friends: A qualitative exploration of the role of peers in young people's alcohol use using Bourdieu's concepts of habitus, field and capital. *Sociology of Health & Illness, 39*(1), 30–46. https://doi.org/10.1111/1467-9566.12467

Marginson, S. (2008). Global field and global imagining: Bordieu and worldwide higher education. *British Journal of Sociology of Education, 29*(3), 303–315. https://doi.org/10.1080/01425690801966386

Merriam-Webster. (n.d.). Human capital. In *Merriam-Webster.com dictionary*. https://www.merriam-webster.com/dictionary/human%20capital

Montgomery, C. (2009). A decade of internationalisation: Has it influenced students' views of cross-cultural group work at university? *Journal of Studies in International Education, 13*(2), 256–270. https://doi.org/10.1177/1028315308329790

Moore, P., & Hampton, G. (2015). 'It's a bit of a generalisation, but...': Participant perspectives on intercultural group assessment in higher education. *Assessment & Evaluation in Higher Education, 40*(3), 390–406. https://doi.org/10.1080/02602938.2014.919437

Reay, D., David, M., & Ball, S. (2001). Making a difference?: Institutional habituses and higher education choice. *Sociological Research Online, 5*(4), 1–12. https://doi.org/10.5153/sro.548

Rienties, B., Alcott, P., & Jindal-Snape, D. (2014). To let students self-select or not: That is the question for teachers of culturally diverse groups. *Journal of Studies in International Education, 18*(1), 64–83. https://doi.org/10.1177/1028315313513035

Rienties, B., Heliot, Y., & Jindal-Snape, D. (2013). Understanding social learning relations of international students in a large classroom using social network analysis. *Higher Education, 66*, 489–504. https://doi.org/10.1007/s10734-013-9617-9

Rienties, B., Hernandez Nanclares, N., Jindal-Snape, D., & Alcott, P. (2013). The role of cultural background and team divisions in developing social learning relations in the classroom. *Journal of Studies in International Education, 17*(3), 332–353. https://doi.org/10.1177/1028315312463826

Smith, B. (2013). Mentoring at-risk students through the hidden curriculum of higher education. Lexington Books.

Stein, S., & de Andereotti, V. O. (2016). V.O. Cash, competition, or charity: International students and the global imaginary. *Higher Educa*tion, *72*, 225–239. https://doi.org/10.1007/s10734-015-9949-8

Summers, M., & Volet, S. (2010). Group work does not necessarily equal collaborative learning: Evidence from observations and self-reports. *European*

Journal of Psychology of Education, 25(4), 473–492. https://doi.org/10.1007/s10212-010-0026-5

Swartz, D. L. (2016). Bourdieu's concept of field. *Oxford Bibliographies* in sociology. https://doi.org/10.1093/obo/9780199756384-0164

Takahashi, S., & Saito, E. (2013). Unraveling the process and meaning of problem-based learning experiences. *Higher Education,* 66(6), 693–706. https://doi.org/10.1007/s10734-013-9629-5

Thomas, V. F., Ssendikaddiwa, J. M., Mroz, M., Lockyer, K., Kosarzova, K., & Hanna, C. (2018). Leveraging common ground: Improving international and domestic students' interaction through mutual engagement. *Journal of International Students,* 8(3), 1386–1397. https://doi.org/10.32674/jis.v8i3.61

Verbik, L., & Lasanowski, V. (2007). International student mobility: Patterns and trends. *World Education News and Reviews,* 20(10), 1–16. https://nccastaff.bournemouth.ac.uk/hncharif/MathsCGs/Desktop/PGCertificat e/Assignment%20-%2002/International_student_mobility_abridged.pdf

Wang, Y. (2012). Mainland Chinese students' group work adaptation in a UK business school. *Teaching in Higher Education,* 17(5), 523–535. https://doi.org/10.1080/13562517.2012.658562

Webb, J., Danaher, G., & Schirato, T. (2002). *Understanding Bourdieu.* SAGE Publications Ltd.

Yosso, T. J. (2005). Whose culture has capital? A critical race theory discussion of community cultural wealth. *Race Ethnicity and Education,* 8(1), 69–91. https://doi.org/10.1080/1361332052000341006

LAURA C. SEITHERS recently earned her PhD in Comparative and International Development Education program at the University of Minnesota. Her research interests include the internationalization of higher education, women's transnational mobility, and narrative inquiry research methodologies. Email: seith004@umn.edu

ZHULDYZ AMANKULOVA is a PhD candidate in Comparative and International Development Education at the University of Minnesota. Her research concerns student development and success, higher education internationalization, and social reproduction theory. Email: amank005@umn.edu

CHRISTOPHER J. JOHNSTONE is an associate professor of Comparative and International Development Education at the University of Minnesota. His research focuses on inclusive outcomes in education, internationalization of higher education, and international development. He currently serves as the faculty coordinator for the university's Leadership in International and Intercultural Education low-residency PhD program for international educators. Email: john4810@umn.edu

Research Article

© *Journal of International Students*
Volume 12, Issue 2 (2022), pp. 403-421
ISSN: 2162-3104 (Print), 2166-3750 (Online)
doi: 10.32674/jis.v12i2.3337
ojed.org/jis

Adventures into the Unknown: Exploring the Lived Experience of East Asian International Students as Foreign-Accented Speakers in Australian Higher Education

Eunjae Park
Steven Hodge
Helen Klieve
Griffith University, Brisbane, Australia

ABSTRACT

Second language (L2) international students are frequently blamed for miscommunication and even stigmatized and marginalized due to the way they sound. However, little is known about how their accent contributes to the L2 lived experience at foreign universities. Taking a mixed methods phenomenological approach, survey ($N = 306$) and semi-structured interviews with participants from East Asian countries ($N = 5$), this study reveals that their personal journey as foreign-accented speakers can be traced through a four-stage process: (a) surprise, (b) anticlimax, (c) learning to survive, and (d) feeling empowered. The first two themes are a period wherein participants experience high levels of stress and anxiety because of having to fit into new learning environments. The last two themes refer to a stage where they developed the ability to survive with increasing self-confidence. Practical implications for improving the campus climate for all L2 students are discussed.

Keywords: accent discrimination, communication barriers, East Asian students, foreign accents, phenomenology

INTRODUCTION

Studying abroad is a common aspiration in this globalized era, whether the experience is a short or long period. According to Hunley (2010), numerous studies suggest that this experience provides a wide range of benefits for L2 international students, including improving their language proficiency, developing intercultural awareness, achieving a greater understanding of international affairs, enhancing adaptability, and contributing to personal growth. However, the shift from the controlled environment in which they prepared for their study abroad to unfamiliar settings where language and culture are drastically different is highly complex. Research into the process of settlement and social and academic integration into new university settings have revealed psychological issues (e.g., anxiety, depression, stress, feelings of worthlessness), homesickness, loneliness, cultural differences, social isolation, academic performance stress, racial discrimination, and language barriers (Hunley, 2010; Jean-Francois, 2019; Khawaja & Stallman, 2011; Park, 2016; Sawir et al., 2012). Beginning a new university life in a foreign country can be daunting and overwhelming.

A considerable amount of research has been dedicated to understanding the challenges faced by L2 students during their transitional period, often concluding that limited language proficiency has a direct and adverse influence on their social and academic life on campus (Dooey, 2010; Khawaja & Stallman, 2011; Moon et al., 2020; Sawir et al., 2012). This contention implies that limited language proficiency is at the heart of international students' adjustment difficulties. Although L2 students' language use is clearly an element in these difficulties, it should not be viewed in isolation from its social and cultural context (Miller, 2003). Spoken language, the focus of this study, is neither simply a means of communication nor a linguistic competence. Rather, spoken language, when perceived as leading to troubled communication emerge as lived issues that initially produce deeply felt concern in L2 students.

L2 students' accent and speech style serve as a signal in their evaluation as an interlocutor that can undermine successful communication (Kettle, 2013). Having an accent can deprive interactions of meaning (Miller, 2003). Accent has been blamed for miscommunication, and it may become the root of stereotyping, racism, and other types of discrimination (Derwing & Munro, 2009). Even so, little empirical research has been conducted on how accent plays out in L2 students' social and academic life at foreign universities (e.g., Kettle, 2013; Park, 2016). The present study explored L2 East Asian students' lived experience as foreign-accented speakers at one Australian university. The research sought a deeper understanding of /the students' journey from the immediate challenges of being a foreign-accented speaker to the overall impact on their life experience.

BACKGROUND

East Asian International Students

The number of international students in Australia has greatly increased over the past two decades, from 60,914 in 1999 to 442,210 in 2019 (Australian Government [AG], 2020). In 2016–2017, these students contributed around $28.6 billion dollars to the Australian economy, with 70% of that income from the higher education sector (AG, 2017). Due to the COVID-19 pandemic, the Australian Government policies restricting access to cross-border education will impact future enrolments and may decrease the number of students undertaking tertiary programs in Australia for some time. However, Northeast followed by Southeast Asian students (henceforth East Asian) have consistently represented the largest student population in Australian higher education (AG, 2017). A large number of East Asian students are from English as foreign language countries (EFL), where English does not play a significant role in daily communication.

Communication Barriers Faced by L2 East Asian Students

While moving to a new country and being immersed in new cultures may be exciting, the language differences can make L2 students feel powerless and even intimidated in their transitional period (Park, 2016). One of the most noticeable aspects of L2 students' spoken language is their accent. Having an accent is an integral part of L2 acquisition (Derwing & Munro, 2009), and once established, it is difficult to change (Bourdieu, 1977). At the same time, "accent has been blamed for all sorts of things" (Derwing & Munro, 2009, p. 476). It has been deemed the cause of miscommunication and used as a cover-up for prejudice, racism, and discrimination (Derwing & Munro, 2009). While L2 students' spoken language skills are frequently taken for granted, this important area has been under-reported in the literature.

An extensive body of literature on L2 students' transition has repeatedly problematized accent as one of the causes of broad language barriers and racial and ethnic discrimination (Dooey, 2010; Hellstén & Prescott, 2004; Houshmand et al., 2014; Jean-Francois, 2019; Sawir et al., 2012). These studies, although they are not accent-specific, suggest that communication with L1 faculty members and peers was often one-way and exclusive, placing the communicative burden on L2 students to carry all responsibilities within the communicative act (Lippi-Green, 2012). Upon arrival in a host country, L2 students need to operate through their L2 within unfamiliar settings, and thus anxiety, loneliness, and an initial loss of confidence are common experiences (Hunley, 2010; Ryan & Viete, 2009). Therefore, non-reciprocal communication—where students are not heard or received by faculty members and peers—can have deleterious effects on self-esteem and self-representation, resulting in significant delays in their social and academic adjustment (Kettle, 2013; Miller, 2003).

While L2 students need confidence to actively participate in classroom discourses and group work, interactions with L1 students may be disempowering and alienating. L2 students have reported that their opinions were not included in decision-making or taken seriously due to their speech and accent, evoking a feeling that they were "looked down upon" (Dooey, 2010; Hellstén & Prescott, 2004; Sawir et al., 2012). Some students sensed an assumption of low intelligence and competence because they were not given important tasks in group work and suffered from a fear of being blamed for miscommunication, which later became a motivation to keep silent in classrooms (Park, 2016). Due to apparent unwillingness on the part of L1 students to engage in interactions with them, many believed that L1 students do not appreciate or respect their efforts to communicate and made judgments concerning their proficiency and abilities (Park, 2016; Sawir et al., 2012). Consequently, feeling excluded, passively or deliberately, being blamed for miscommunication, and detecting unwillingness to communicate on the part of others reduced participation in classrooms and inhibited relationship-building with L1 students (Jean-Francois, 2019; Park, 2016; Sawir et al., 2012).

In a similar vein, interactions with faculty members were sometimes frustrating and hurtful (Hellstén & Prescott, 2004; Houshmand et al., 2014; Jean-Francois, 2019). A student in Jean-Francois's (2019) study reported: "If a white student makes a mistake, they assume it is a mistake... but if an international student makes a mistake, they assume that you are at-risk or you are dumb" (p. 1075), and she believed her accent was the main cause of underestimation. East Asian students can feel nervous and anxious about speaking up in classrooms (Kettle, 2013; Park, 2016), possibly because they have not been exposed to student-centered learning (Moon et al., 2020). Asian students in Hellstén and Prescott's (2004) study expressed that they were treated /like children and were not valued as people. Given these findings, Hellstén and Prescott (2004) concluded that such experiences can be a threat to the students' self-esteem and sense of security in classrooms.

Accent has significance beyond the struggles of L2 students for participating in educational contexts and maintaining self-esteem. English as the dominant and preferred medium of instruction in education reproduces standard English as the norm, which largely undermines the way L2 students sound because they do not abide by the standard (Kettle, 2013; Lippi-Green, 2012). According to Bourdieu (1977, p. 648), for L2 speakers, competence is not just "the right to speech, i.e., to the legitimate language which is also the language of authority (but also) the power to impose reception." Meaningful communication and learning can take place when L2 students are accepted as legitimate members of the community. However, those who are not deemed "legitimate speakers" can be silenced, excluded, or marginalized compared with the dominant group (Bourdieu, 1992), creating an unequal social hierarchy in classrooms; L1 students (the dominant group) versus L2 students (the minority group). The role of accent in social positioning and power relationships appears to play a role in shaping L2 students' lived experience.

Therefore, the main research question guiding this study is "what is the experience of East Asian international students as foreign-accented speakers in Australian higher education?," with a primary focus on the challenges and coping strategies.

METHODOLOGY

To gain rich understanding of L2 East Asian students' lived experience, a mixed method phenomenological research approach was adopted. The initial survey outcomes provided a broad overview of the experiences of a large group of participants ($N = 306$), establishing a basic account of where the accent-related challenges existed and how participants mitigated those challenges to navigate the unfamiliar academic settings. Analysis of these findings paved the way for an in-depth phenomenological investigation into five participants' experiences as foreign-accented speakers. Focusing on the nature of "being-in-the-world," hermeneutic phenomenology served as the primary lens for explicating the experiential meaning of the phenomenon; this is done by exploring the structure of individuals' lifeworld as they live it and by exploring the meaning they make of their existence and their social world in its wholeness (van Manen, 2016). The following sub-sections explain how the concepts of hermeneutic phenomenology were applied in the study.

Procedure and Participants

Prior to the commencement of the study, ethical clearance was gained from the Human Ethics Committee at the selected university (Reference number GU:2018/159). The selection criteria were: (a) students from EFL countries enrolled at the university and (b) those who started second language acquisition after childhood. Since age of learning (AOL) is a crucial predictor of the degree of accentedness, the critical period of L2 learning was considered for inclusion of this study (Patkowski, 1990), and demarcated at the age of 15.

A total of 306 valid survey responses were collected through purposeful and snowballing techniques (Cohen et al., 2018). From the 78 participants who indicated a willingness to take part in follow-up interviews in the survey, five participants who reported a wide range of experiences via the survey were selected. These participants came from diverse cultural backgrounds, aged 24 to 37 years and studying different academic disciplines, and had been in Australia for several years (Table 1).

Table 1: Participants' Profile

Pseudonym	Gender	Age	Time in Australia	Nationality	Level of education	Field of study
Ann	F	24	4 years	Vietnam	Undergraduate	Business
Tim	M	22	3 years	Thailand	Undergraduate	Linguistics
Melissa	F	37	10 years	Korea	Undergraduate	Nursing
Jennie	F	30	6 years	China	Postgraduate	Education
David	M	29	5 years	Japan	Doctorate	Criminology

The participants had varying levels of language proficiency and views on their communication skills as well as accent strength (Table 2). Among the participants, Tim was the only one who had a previous study experience in an L1 academic environment (in the United States).

Table 2: Background Knowledge in L2

Pseudonym	Self-reported communication skills	Accent strength	IELTS (Overall)	Experience in other L1 countries
Ann	Poor	Mild	6.0	X
Tim	Very good	Weak	7.5	O
Melissa	Good	Strong	7.0	X
Jennie	Very good	Weak	8.5	X
David	Average	Strong	6.5	X

Data Collection

Data were collected at one regional university campus between November 2018 and February 2019. Adhering to the principle of hermeneutic interviewing (e.g., collaboration with participants through conversations about the phenomenon; van Manen, 2016), three semi-structured interviews were conducted at three-week intervals over a period of up to four months. With interview questions guided by the initial survey findings, interviews focused on four key areas relating to (a) experiences before and after arrival in Australia, (b) recent or current challenges as an L2-accented speaker, (c) developed strategies for coping with the challenges, (d) views about and attitudes toward themselves as an L2-accented speaker. Interviews were conducted in English, with the exception of one participant who spoke the same L1 as the lead author (Korean). Each interview lasted from 90 mins to 3 hrs and was digitally recorded and transcribed verbatim by a professional transcription service in an attempt to construct texts that accounted for participants' experience in its wholeness. Consequently, the concrete experience of participants and the meaning their experience held for them were explored.

Data Analysis

All data were considered as part-to-whole when uncovering or isolating thematic aspects of the phenomenon by following van Manen's (2016) techniques of phenomenological reflection. For example, three particular steps were followed to analyze the transcript and identify themes. The first step was the "holistic/sententious" approach where the researcher tried to "capture the fundamental and main significance meaning of the text as a whole" (van Manen, 2016, p. 93). The "selective/highlighting" approach was the second step, characterized by re-reading the text several times and highlighting statements or phrases that could be considered "essential or revealing about the phenomenon or experience being described" (van Manen, 2016, p. 93). The last step was the "detailed/line-by-line" step, where each sentence and paragraph was examined.

The highlighted statements, phrases, and paragraphs were treated as thematic statements.

The researcher used a research journal during data collection and recorded notes, memos, and comments during data analysis in developing themes prior to composing linguistic transformation. The review of the journal material assisted in clarifying ideas and elaborating on possible connections between different data types. Subsequently, through the horizontalization process, each statement was given equal value, and repetitive and overlapping statements that were not relevant to the phenomenon studied were set aside (Hays & Singh, 2012). The researcher clustered the meaning units and thematic statements identified by the data readings, which captured various elements of participants' lived experiences and created themes in a more phenomenological manner. Through this process, an interpretive description of what it is like to be a foreign-accented speaker was developed. Throughout the process, NVivo (Version 12) was used to manage data and facilitate analysis.

Writing as a phenomenological method, the analysis continued when the researcher started writing (van Manen, 2016). To bring meanings to the surface, the researcher frequently wrote, reviewed, studied deeply, and rewrote the findings to uncover meanings in data and reveal hidden complexities.

Both member-checking and sharing transcripts with participants were conducted to enhance the integrity of the data (Cohen et al., 2018). To reduce obvious bias in the interpretation of the data, analysis of one of the transcripts was verified by another researcher involved in this study.

RESULTS

From 15 transcripts, 545 significant statements were extracted and clustered into four main themes: (a) surprise, (b) anticlimax, (c) learning to survive, and (d) feeling empowered. In the following, participants' responses were not corrected for grammar.

Surprise

In this cluster, participants focused on their experience before and soon after arrival in Australia. All participants were excited about residing and studying in Australia. At the same time, feeling out of place, feeling surprised at different English sounds, and struggling with accent and pronunciation were commonly experienced by participants.

For the majority, communicating and learning through L2 within unfamiliar settings was the biggest concern. Feeling out of place was a common experience for participants. David recalled his experience of feeling overwhelmed:

> I couldn't even imagine how much it would be different from my culture
> and my first language. So, I thought I studied English a lot, but I found
> my English was not enough. I couldn't understand 100% and convey

what I wanted to say. I felt completely out of place. Native students are way more fluent in writing, speaking, and communicating and so forth. I thought I would have to work hard, study hard to compete with them.

Since Australia was a completely new country for him, he was worried about something beyond his imagination, something yet to be discovered. He realized that his English was not sufficient for communicating with others, despite his belief that he was well-prepared. His inability to communicate in classrooms made him feel out of place, with an increasing sense of insecurity in classroom interactions. He became concerned that he was facing some sort of barrier to studying with L1 students because they generally have better literacy and oracy skills.

Tim, who had previous experience in the United States, was excited to start a new life in Australia and initially was not worried about his L2 ability. However, he started to notice that the way he spoke English was different from most L1 speakers and he began to feel out of place: "When I first arrived, I was not very comfortable. I think, maybe feeling out of place? I just felt that I speak so much differently than other people on campus."

For participants coming from the EFL context, where the experience of English is limited to the controlled environment of classrooms, feeling surprised at diverse kinds of English could continue over months or even years. Tim mentioned: "I would say very different [L1 accent]. I am not gonna lie. I was amazed when I first arrived in Australia; this is so hard to understand what my friends and professors are saying?" Jennie also stated: "It sounded very different and very unique speech habits like mumbling and slurring...I was so frustrated, and it was so difficult to follow."

Although participants detected differences in accent between other speakers and themselves, paying detailed attention to their own speech sounds was beyond their competence. Melissa recalled the early period of her stay in Australia:

I didn't care because I had to think about what to say in English all the time. So, as long as I could speak something with subject, object, and verb, I couldn't think about other things because thinking about grammar was difficult. But I realised accent is important later I could speak and think in English a lot faster than before.

Melissa's account hints that, with increased exposure to the local language, she slowly understood the significance of accent. She implied that she was subconsciously aware of the notion of accent and pronunciation in communication, although she prioritized constructing grammatically correct sentences over producing intelligible sounds, because paying extra attention to these other linguistic areas was too demanding. In Tim's and David's cases, they were unaware of the notion of accent and thus did not view themselves as even having an accent. David commented, "accent was completely out of the picture."

Anticlimax

For the participants, new challenges were mounting as their transition unfolded. Participants shared their experiences related to accented English that contributed to shaping their social and academic lives on campus. *Feeling heightened demands in communication, experiencing stereotyping and discrimination*, and *difficulties in forming friendships with L1 students* were all issues resonating in their accounts.

Feeling heightened demands in communication was a multilayered issue and appeared to be linked with other areas such as anxiety, low confidence, and limited vocabulary. Ann, who evaluated her own communication skills as poor, found many factors played a role in her interactions with tutors:

> When I tried to explain my opinion to my tutor, I had to repeat many times. I think I picked the wrong words, and my pronunciation wasn't clear. I lost confidence every time I had to repeat. I felt… "oh… again…" I couldn't even ask any questions. So, I felt I was studying alone. I tried to google things I didn't understand. But you know sometimes information we find from the internet is not really correct.

As Ann indicated, her L2 performance and academic performance were weakened by her limited vocabulary and her feelings of tension, anxiety, and low confidence. While she tried hard to make herself understood, being asked to repeat her statement many times seemed to increase her sense of malaise. With a range of issues playing out simultaneously, seeking information from the internet appeared to be the last option for her, and her academic isolation is indicated in her comments: "I felt I was studying alone." Jennie and Melissa also expressed similar experiences with L1 students. Jennie stated:

> I still feel a bit shy because they're going to pick some mistakes I make, and they know my grammar and pronunciation mistakes immediately. So, I feel I'd better not talk much. Sometimes, we have a group discussion… We still don't want to communicate too much with Aussies, especially the young girls because they speak so fast.

Working with L1 students was not straightforward for Jennie because of her shyness and fear of making mistakes. Intense concerns over making mistakes and a limited ability to comprehend were related to her reluctance to work with L1 students in class, especially with young female students.

In culturally and linguistically diverse classrooms, participants were required to work with a wide range of students. In the process, experiences of stereotyping and discrimination were another problem evident in participants' accounts. When communication breakdowns took place, one common reaction to the participants' struggles was blame for miscommunication. David recounted:

> They [L1] just move to another topic, pretend things not happening. Just because we speak English as a second language… doesn't mean we're always wrong and we're the ones who always make mistakes and when

we don't understand, they simply blame us. You know feelings like someone just looks down on you. But when they think it's my fault... it's kind of true... I mean sometimes, not all the times.

In David's interpretation, the strategies of moving on to another topic and overlooking miscommunication were a sign that L1 students did not want to engage with him. As he explicitly acknowledged, miscommunication could not always be attributed to him. Unfortunately, experiencing dismissive behaviors and withdrawal from the communication process evoked frustration and undermined self-esteem.

Some L1 students reacted to the participants in an offensive manner. Stereotypes associated with L2 speakers could emerge unexpectedly. Melissa stated:

She was talking about a singer and a concert that she would go to. I told her that I don't know the singer and all of sudden... she said, "if you don't speak English, why are you in Australia?" I was like... "What?? I didn't say I don't speak English. I just don't know the singer." I was so offended when she said that. She didn't even listen to me carefully. She didn't say sorry and I was shocked.

While the L1 student certainly misheard Melissa, the response to her was aggressive and humiliating, assigning all blame to her. The response seemed to be triggered by pre-existing stereotyping associated with L2 speakers. Blame for miscommunication, judgment on her English, and receiving such an insulting response came as a shock to Melissa.

All participants expressed dissatisfaction in their relationships with L1 students. The participants experienced unresponsive and unreceptive attitudes during communication with L1 students. Tim believed that his American accent was a good conversation starter, but it did no more than that:

I'll be treated slightly differently from the local people. I kind of feel that: different vibes. I'm trying so hard to be their friend until one point I become tired... I was like, "F... it. I'm just gonna be friends with international student because they're more understanding about myself, and did not really make me feel bad about being myself or being who I am." I find that it's difficult to get along with local student just because of this look.

Even from the researchers' perspectives, Tim had a native-like accent. However, his experience of forming friendships with L1 students was not different from other participants. Although he showed a genuine willingness to mingle with L1 students, putting significant efforts into talking to them, he felt the interest was not reciprocated. Attributing such difficulties to his race rather than to accent, these experiences eventually stopped Tim from trying to build relationships with L1 students. He became reluctant to go beyond his existing social circle. Seemingly, he wished to protect his identity by refusing connections with L1 students.

Learning to Survive

Participants indicated that their struggles to fit into new learning environments were gradually transformed into a deep motivation to overcome the challenges. In relation to this critical point, three sub-themes emerged: *Disguising*, *self-protection*, and *being strategic*.

"Disguising" was a strategic response made by some participants to their communication problems. Melissa, Jennie, and Ann were motivated to pretend they were a completely new arrival to elicit more tolerant treatment from L1 speakers. Melissa elaborated:

> I say, "I'm new here, I didn't know." I can tell they can be patient at least for those who are new. I sometimes say my English is not great. It's one way to break the ice to initiate conversations. I see people become supportive and try to listen to me. I feel they wouldn't judge me… and I don't worry too much about making mistakes.

Melissa noticed that some L1 speakers were indulgent toward new L2 students. This observation prompted her to pretend that she herself was a new student in order not to provoke any negative reactions and feelings. Additionally, pretending to be a poor L2 speaker was one way of "breaking the ice" and taking the initiative in conversations and, further, to prevent misjudgments. In this way, she was able to manage her worries about communication demands and unjust criticism.

Self-protection (avoiding and distancing strategies) was frequently delineated within participants' efforts to control communication. Being inspired by a "TED talk," Tim reported that he intentionally avoided topics related to his and the listener's ethnicity or nationality. As he explained:

> I was inspired by Ted talk and I started using that as my guideline. I start a conversation and I will never bring up about my ethnicity or my nationalities. Not because I'm ashamed of, but it's because I don't want them to put me in a box or in a category. Because once they know that, they start forming this sort of stereotype in their head and they'd be like, Oh, you must be this guy, you must be this particular person.

In Tim's words, stereotypes are mistaken ideas that people have about a certain group. He noticed that knowing a person's ethnicity and nationality can possibly lead to unhelpful assumptions about that person. To prevent this, he affirmed that speakers should not raise any questions that could be related to their identity. As Tim highlighted, the main benefit of avoiding topics associated with each other's backgrounds was "heading off" conversation that could connect with stereotyping tied to a particular group.

Jennie and Ann reported that they preferred working with co-national students, especially for group activities. They intentionally avoided being grouped with L1 students. Jennie recounted:

> We're concerned about some Australian students. They don't regard Chinese students as very good. Some of them, I don't mean all of them.

That's why we try to avoid them… Sometimes… to avoid myself being nervous or looked down upon.

Although Jennie tried not to overgeneralize her experience to the entire L1 community, she developed a defensive stance in relation to misjudgment and underestimation of herself and other Chinese students.

All participants believed that putting consistent efforts into improving their communication skills was important because placement in L2 environments by itself is not a magic key to enhance their language skills. "Real English" was what participants wished to acquire through movies, dramas, news, and YouTube videos. Since the English they had been trained in back home and the English in Australia contrasted, they sought familiarity with diverse English accents. David stated:

> What I found useful was to watching movies and dramas, DVDs in English because it's real English, not fake English… like in CD or… English test. I learned a lot of expressions and vocabularies. It's helpful for speaking and listening. To improve my English listening skills, I try to watch dramas in English with subtitles. So, when I encounter the word I don't know, I can just search and understand what that mean and how that used and what context that word is used.

David utilized various resources to develop his communication skills. He compared a set of media resources he used and other learning resources, such as English test materials. Using a distinction between "real English" and "fake English", he emphasized the authenticity of some media resources that assisted in his articulation. He believed that media resources were useful for learning expressions and vocabulary for oral communication in a context-sensitive way.

Feeling Empowered

The participants eventually became resilient and strategic in managing the challenges they faced. They realized learning through difficulties, and improving skills through painstaking efforts were ultimately valuable processes. At the same time, the participants gained a wider perspective on the challenges faced by L2 students. *Communication difficulties are natural* was a sub-theme discerned in the data. Tim recounted:

> I don't see it as barrier, but it's something that people make errors naturally when we talk. And if you're just like, "Oh, what did you say?" It's not always because of accent… it's because the speaker might just miss it because she was focusing on something else. It's not a big deal, I feel like. I know there are some people who abruptly respond to those students with accents though.

Acknowledging the social consequences for L2 students of having a different accent, difficulties were not perceived as a problem in principle, and were interpreted as a natural process in any communication to establish a mutual understanding. Participants appreciated that miscommunication could take place for a number of reasons—not solely because of the accent itself, but because the speaker's message may be misinterpreted by the listener. Additionally, all participants used expressions such as "it's part of my life," and "it happens all the time," clearly indicating that they believed miscommunication is a common phenomenon in their life experience rather than a deficit or failure.

Having L2 is valuable was another sub-theme identified in participants' accounts. Although they had to endure tough times in unfamiliar settings as an L2-accented speaker, they eventually valued their L2 ability, irrespective of their level of accentedness or language proficiency. Ann stated:

> I didn't have much confident to talk to people and people's accent made me so worried and even quieter student. Every time I didn't understand people and people didn't understand me, I was embarrassed and very sad. But being a second language speaker, I define this term positively, because when I go for travelling, I can meet more people and talk to people. After living in Australia, I can understand many accents and I like that. I think that's like extra ability. I can't have that ability if I just stayed in Vietnam.

While being an L2 speaker and not being able to accommodate different accents impeded her L2 performance, thereby creating stress for her, Ann held positive attitudes toward her experience and herself. Instead of concentrating on what she could not do, she placed much emphasis on what she had achieved and what she could do in the future because, without any challenges and aspirations to improve her circumstances in Australia, she would not have accomplished similar outcomes and developed such resilience.

Being proud to be L2 was also a common sentiment among participants. Although they felt their L2 skills were often taken for granted in Australia, they were proud of their ability to speak two languages. They felt neither ashamed of having a different accent nor wished to acquire a native-like accent because their accent indicates that they are bilinguals. Melissa mentioned:

> As long as I can communicate with people in English and mingle with them, there's no problem having a Korean accent. I see people with a Spanish accent, Italian accent... I think when they have these accents and speak English as a second language, that makes their linguistic ability valuable. I admire their effort to speak more than one language. And I feel proud of myself as well.

Melissa believed that having a different accent should not be an impediment to successful social interactions. She appeared to be successful in establishing and representing her identity as a Korean-accented speaker, although she was not necessarily recognized as a "legitimate" speaker in the dominant language context. Noting that the ability to speak more than one language requires significant investment and long-term commitment, she affirmed that having an accent reveals underlying efforts to be bilingual and thus she felt proud of herself.

DISCUSSION

This study drew on the voices of five participants to understand their lived experience as foreign-accented speakers in an Australian university. Using evidence of their lived experience, our study revealed that meeting the demands of studying at a foreign institution could be a meaningful source of motivation for the speakers to pursue their personal and academic growth. Strategies developed by participants were a means of overcoming stressful life events and of assisting them to strengthen their ability and stability. Notwithstanding that such phenomenological results are not generalizable to all international students, the authors hope that findings from this study will assist in identifying knowledge gaps and highlighting areas to improve in the promotion of equality in education, ideally creating a more positive and productive campus climate for all international students.

In contrast to much research cited above (Dooey, 2010; Khawaja & Stallman, 2011; Moon et al., 2020; Sawir et al., 2012), which identified language proficiency of L2 students as a major problem in their adjustment, this research explored the experience of being an L2 speaker, or being identified as an L2 speaker, as a threat to participants' adaptation to Australian higher education. While the demand for English itself was overwhelming for some, the anticlimax experienced was partially the product of societal pressure for linguistic conformity. In this context, the power relations between L1 and L2 students were visible within interactions. Projecting a voice, being heard, and anticipating a response are basic to all communication per se; however, effective communications were not an easy accomplishment for participants. Their audible differences signified their status as an L2 speaker, so incidents of disrupted communication were not tolerated by L1 students and were even attributed to the participants, which accords with other research (Lippi-Green, 2012; Park, 2016). Such communication challenges appear to be one of the fundamental issues between L1 and L2 students. While communication barriers are left with L2 students to manage and minimize through enhancing language skills, the authors believe that real changes can be brought about by more active leadership from universities, starting with pedagogical strategies at the level of teaching and managing class interactions.

Results from this study contribute to scholarship concerning coping strategies in response to accent stereotyping and discrimination. Viewing participants' lived experiences through a positive and strengths-based lens, developing resilience as a means of learning to survive was apparent in the data. In particular, interacting with L1 speakers in real-life situations led participants to seek out and develop coping strategies. Some coping strategies under the themes, such as disguising (e.g., pretending to be a new student) and self-protection (e.g., avoiding topics related to their background), were developed to actively control communication, maintain communication, and try to go beyond fostering simple tolerance on the part of their interlocutors. On the one hand, participants were clearly not vulnerable, but resilient and competent in terms of these coping mechanisms because they tried to succeed in "imposing reception" in L1–L2 communication, where they were constructed as non-legitimate speakers of English (Bourdieu, 1992). On the other hand, it can be suggested that a heavy communicative burden was felt by participants, possibly because the dominant group may feel "perfectly empowered" to neglect their role in the communicative act (Lippi-Green, 2012). L2 students generally have a more uncertain command of English compared with L1 speakers; however, the point to recognize is that L1 varieties of English are not necessarily the most intelligible varieties for all English users (Jenkins, 2000). Other factors should be considered, such as unfamiliarity with local accents and speech styles, as indicated in this study. Communication barriers, therefore, can be regarded to some extent as a problem of L1 speakers because some may not feel the need to accommodate or adapt to others.

Several findings were consistent with existing literature that documents passive coping behaviors developed by L2 students. For example, participants had to deal with their language anxieties and acquired the fortitude to actively contribute to their learning and that of their peers. Therefore, worrying about anticipated communication breakdowns, about not being heard, and living with a fear of being negatively evaluated and experiencing stigmatization were clearly a painful reality. Consequently, passive coping strategies such as self-protection (e.g., not working with L1 speakers) were developed to help them continue their studies without being hurt. Houshmand et al. (2014) similarly found that some L2 Asian students regarded withdrawing from the learning sphere as the last option. In practice, East Asian students are often seen as silent, reticent, and embedded in their own learning styles that do not easily align with Westernized pedagogies (Moon et al., 2020). However, the findings indicate that a campus communication climate that is unproductive involves common stereotyping and misconceptions about East Asian students to some degree. Those who perceive their campus climate as unsafe and less accepting have been reported to limit their social boundaries and not participate in non-mandatory learning activities in classrooms (Jean-Francois, 2019).

While it is interesting to know at what point the accent-related challenges encountered by participants became less distressing, this is not the focus of this study. Nevertheless, to our knowledge, our study is the first report on how L2 students make sense of themselves as foreign-accented speakers in higher education settings. In EFL countries, where L2 accent is a commonplace, they did not feel marginalized. Conversely, when living in a situation where their accent is exceptional, their identity and accent became related issues. Interestingly, contrary to popular opinion (Derwing & Munro, 2009), participants developed an interest in retaining their accent as a marker of their identity, emphasizing the value of being bilingual regardless of how they were seen or heard by the dominant group. By working through the challenges and having communication experiences in the dominant language context, they demonstrated a heightened understanding of intercultural communication along with knowledge in the management of social communicative consequences that may result from stereotypes about L2 speakers, in general. As participants believed, miscommunication is an inevitable phenomenon of any communication itself, whether their native language is English or other. Therefore, they eventually felt empowered to speak English with a foreign accent. Although the participants lived through these stages and emerged stronger, perhaps other students may be less resilient, less successful, and lost within the education system. These groups of students need more attention, support, and direction from the university community.

Implications for Practice

The findings suggest that simply encouraging L2 students to be more active in classrooms, assimilate the host culture, and ask faculty members to be friendly and tolerant does not seem to be sufficient. Hence, we emphasize three implications for practice.

First, the role of faculty members is significant in creating the conditions that require hearing of and reception for L2 students (Kettle, 2013). A lack of shared responsibility in communication may be the core problem underpinning the lack of meaningful interactions between L1 and L2 students. Hence, more specific guidance for working with diverse students can be given; for example, sharing background information, being more receptive and responsive when miscommunication takes place (e.g., using simpler words, clarification, speaking slowly, avoiding colloquialism), and allowing L2 students more time to formulate their responses. The use of these localized English varieties along with particular knowledge limited to Australia may challenge the comprehension of those EFL students who did not have "authentic" exposure to different Englishes as well as culture.

Second, a "positive campus climate" for L2 students may mean that they enjoy freedom of speech, freedom from rebuke, and no fear of psychological harm within their learning environment. In that regard, intercultural communication training designed to raise social awareness for all members of the university community could be considered. Drawing on Vaccarino and Li's (2018) intercultural communication training in higher education, the training program can incorporate three themes through verbal activities and discussions: "knowledge of self", where participants reflect on their own culture and how their values can influence the way they communicate; "acknowledgement of cultural differences," where participants acknowledge how cultural differences impact on the way they think, behave, and communicate; and "knowledge of other cultures", where participants appreciate and recognize individuals with values different to their own (p. 4). In addition, some empirical research findings around the difficulties that L2 students face can take place in the form of non-academic reports. These endeavors, in turn, should contribute to creating a more welcoming and accepting campus climate for all international students.

Third, university orientation programs can include a separate session for L2 students. Critical information is often shared during orientations but providing copious amounts of information may not be effective because L2 students may not remember it all. Introducing the challenges that L2 students experience and how they mitigate these challenges (e.g., introducing strategies found in this study, including how to improve language proficiency in real-life contexts) in foreign institutions can also be useful. Understanding the problems associated with intercultural communication, cultural differences, social inclusion, and stability can be half of the solution. If international students are not prepared—in a realistic manner—for what to anticipate and how to cope with new challenges, there may be a significant delay in their adjustment and integration to new learning environments. Employing current L2 international students or graduates as advisors or mentors could be an inspiring and empowering strategy.

REFERENCES

Australian Government. (2017). *Export income to Australia from international education activity in 2016–2017.* https://internationaleducation.gov.au/research/Research-Snapshots/Documents/Export%20Income%20FY 2016–17.pdf

Australian Government. (2020). *International student enrolments in Australia 1994–2019.* https://internationaleducation.gov.au/research/International-Student-Data/Documents/INTERNATIONAL%20STUDENT%20DATA/2019/2019 %20Time%20Series%20Graph.pdf

Bourdieu, P. (1977). The economics of linguistic exchanges. *Social Science Information, 16*(6), 645–668. https://doi.org/10.1177/053901847701600601

Bourdieu, P. (1992). *Language and symbolic power.* Polity Press.

Cohen, L., Manion, L., & Morrison, K. (2018). *Research methods in education* (8th ed.). Routledge.

Derwing, T., & Munro, M. (2009). Putting accent in its place: Rethinking obstacles to communication. *Language Teaching, 42*(4), 476–490. https://doi.org/10.1017/S026144480800551X

Dooey, P. (2010). Students' perspectives of an EAP pathway program. *Journal of English for academic purposes, 9*(3), 184–197. https://doi.org/10.1016/ j.jeap.2010.02.013

Hays, D. G., & Singh, A. A. (2012). *Qualitative inquiry in clinical and educational settings.* Guildford Press.

Hellstén, M., & Prescott, A. (2004). Learning at university: The international student experience. *International Education Journal, 5*(3), 344–351. https://files.eric.ed.gov/fulltext/EJ903859.pdf

Houshmand, S., Spanierman, L. B., & Tafarodi, R. W. (2014). Excluded and avoided: Racial microaggressions targeting Asian international students in Canada. *Cultural Diversity & Ethnic Minority Psycology, 20*(3), 377–388. https://doi.org/10.1037/a0035404

Hunley, H. A. (2010). Students' functioning while studying abroad: The impact of psychological distress and loneliness. *International Journal of Intercultural Relations, 34*(4), 386–392. https://doi.org/10.1016/j.ijintrel.2009.08.005

Jean-Francois, E. (2019). Exploring the perceptions of campus climate and integration strategies used by international students in a US university campus. *Studies in Higher Education, 44*(6), 1–17. https://doi.org/10.1080/03075079. 2017.1416461

Jenkins, J. (2000). *The phonology of English as an international language.* Oxford University Press.

Kettle, M. (2013). *The right to a voice and the fight to be heard: The experience of being an ESL user in Australia.* Paper presented at the 13th International Pragmatics Conference (IPrA): Implicit discrimination in public discourse symposium, New Delhi, India.

Khawaja, N. G., & Stallman, H. M. (2011). Understanding the coping strategies of international students: A qualitative approach. *Australian Journal of Guidance and Counselling, 21*(2), 203–224. https://doi.org/10.1375/ ajgc.21.2.203

Lippi-Green, R. (2012). *English with an accent: Language, ideology, and discrimination in the United States* (2nd ed.). Routledge.

Miller, J. (2003). *Audible difference: ESL and social identity in schools.* Multilingual Matters.

Moon, C. Y., Zhang, S., Larke, P. J., & James, M. C. (2020). We are not all the same: A qualitative analysis of the nuanced differences between Chinese and South Korean international graduate students' experiences in the United States. *Journal of International Students, 10*(1), 28–49. https:// doi.org/10.32674/jis.v10i1.770

Park. (2016). *Social and educational challenges of international students caused by accented English in the Australian context: A sociolinguistic analysis of linguistic experience* [Master's thesis, Griffith University]. https:// doi.org/10.25904/1912/177

Patkowski, M. S. (1990). Age and accent in a second language: A reply to James Emil Flege. *Applied Linguistics, 11*(1), 73–89. https://doi.org/10.1093/ applin/11.1.73

Ryan, J., & Viete, R. (2009). Respectful interactions: Learning with international students in the English-speaking academy. *Teaching in Higher Education, 14*(3), 303–314. https://doi.org/10.1080/13562510902898866

Sawir, E., Marginson, S., Forbes-Mewett, H., Nyland, C., & Ramia, G. (2012). International student security and English language proficiency. *Journal of Studies in International Education, 16*(5), 434–454. https://doi.org/ 10.1177/1028315311435418 van Manen, M. (2016). *Researching lived experience: Human science for an action sensitive pedagogy* (2nd ed.). Routledge.

Vaccarino, F., & Li, M. (2018). Intercultural communication training to support internationalisation in higher education. *Intercultural Communication, 2018*(46), 1–14. http://search.proquest.com.libraryproxy.griffith.edu.au/scholarly-journals/intercultural-communication-training-support/docview/2059074858/se-2?accountid=14543

Dr EUNJAE PARK is a research fellow at Griffith University. Eunjae's primary research interests include international higher education, sociolinguistics, and research methods. Email: eunjae.park@griffith.edu.au

Dr STEVEN HODGE is a senior lecturer and researcher at Griffith University. Steven's research work focuses on curriculum design and development and teacher use of curriculum documents. Email: s.hodge@griffith.edu.au

Dr HELEN KLIEVE is an adjunct lecturer and researcher at Griffith University. Her current research is focused on the contribution of education in the context of social disadvantage and social justice. Email: h.klieve@griffith.edu.au

Research Article

© *Journal of International Students*
Volume 12, Issue 2 (2022), pp. 422-443
ISSN: 2162-3104 (Print), 2166-3750 (Online)
doi: 10.32674/jis.v12i2.2512
ojed.org/jis

The Domains of Cross-cultural Adjustment: An Empirical Study With International Students

Joana Campos
Luisa Helena Pinto[1]
*School of Economics, University of Porto,
Porto, Portugal*

Thomas Hippler[2]
National University of Ireland, Ireland

ABSTRACT

This study examines the dimensionality of a new measure of international students' adjustment using a sample of 189 international students. Drawing on earlier conceptualizations of cross-cultural adjustment as a person-environment fit and a previous scale measuring adjustment from the expatriate literature, this study shows that this scale can be meaningfully adapted to the higher education context. Confirmatory factor analyses identified a stable 8-factor structure with adequate psychometric properties. Descriptive analysis confirms that international students are fairly adjusted in a number of distinct domains. The findings also provide criterion-related validity by showing positive associations between host social interaction and host connectedness and students' adjustment. This study contributes to the literature by offering a theoretically based scale that assesses international students' adjustment on a wide range of dimensions. It puts forward a useful tool for higher education counsellors and support services to monitor international students' adjustment and avoid adjustment difficulties.

---

[1] Corresponding author

[2] Passed away during the writing process of this paper. After having co-authored and co-presented an earlier version of this manuscript at the 15th Annual Conference of EURAM, 17–20 June 2015 in Warsaw, Thomas Hippler first revised and edited this manuscript.

Keywords: domains of cross-cultural adjustment, higher education students, international students' adjustment, person–environment fit

The number of mobile students worldwide has expanded massively over the last two decades and is expected to grow further in the next 15 years (Organisation for Economic Co-operation and Development [OECD], 2019). According to the Organization for Economic Co-operation and Development (OECD), in 2017 approximately 3.7 million foreign students were engaged in higher education programs across the OECD countries, a figure which reached 5.3 million for the world as a whole (OECD, 2019). Worldwide, most students choose the United States (US), the United Kingdom (UK), and Australia to study abroad (Abdullah et al., 2014), although other non-traditional destinations are emerging, like the United Arab Emirates (UAE) and Russia (Johnson, 2020). In Europe, the proportion of international students has increased markedly in the past decade, and in 2018, 1.3 million students from abroad were undertaking tertiary-level studies across the EU Member States (European Commission [EC], 2021). Compared with other parts of the world, European students go abroad for shorter periods mostly under the umbrella of the Erasmus$^+$ mobility program (Mikulas & Jitka, 2019). Multiple factors drive this worldwide increase in students mobility, such as European policies that foster mobility within the region (as is the case of Erasmus and Erasmus$^+$) and other countries' policies aiming to provide access to quality learning environments in science, technology, engineering, and maths (STEM), including computer science (OECD, 2019).

In this research, we follow the OECD (2019) definition of international student to include all tertiary students *"who received their prior education in another country and are not residents of their current country of study"* (p. 236), thus including foreign students (i.e., students who are not citizens of the country in which they study); credit mobility students (i.e., students who are temporarily studying abroad to gain academic credit within the framework of a tertiary education program at their home institutions, such as Erasmus+ exchange students); and other degree mobility students (i.e., external students enrolled as regular students with the aim of graduating in the country of destination).

It has long been recognized that studying in an unfamiliar cultural environment and through the medium of a foreign language poses a myriad of challenges for international students (Conroy & McCarthy, 2019; Spencer-Oatey & Dauber, 2019) and that failure to integrate the new cultural and academic environment can impact both their mental well-being as well as their academic achievement (Duru & Poyrazli, 2011; Gómez et al., 2014) and satisfaction (Merola et al., 2019). Consequently, the study of student adjustment has attracted attention from at least the 1950s (e.g., Abdullah et al., 2014; Smith, 1955; for an overview see Church, 1982) to the present day (e.g., Harzing, 2004; Jing et al., 2020; Li & Gasser, 2005; Mesidor & Sly, 2016). This growth in interest was accompanied by a proliferation of both conceptualizations and operationalization of student adjustment with no consensus emerging (Pedersen et al., 2011). This prevented a meaningful integration of research findings and impeded the growth of a cumulative body of knowledge (Heng, 2020; Spencer-Oatey & Dauber, 2019). Some commonly used instruments to assess students adjustment, such as the Student Adaptation to College Questionnaire (SACQ; Baker & Siryk, 1984), have been shown to be seriously deficient with regard to their psychometric properties (Taylor & Pastor, 2007). Moreover, the uncritical application of instruments developed to measure adjustment among domestic students has been criticized for missing issues uniquely relevant to international students and for being possibly culturally biased (Anderson et al., 2016). Lacking a valid and reliable instrument for assessing international students' adjustment is unfortunate because having a precise diagnosis of adjustment problems is of great interest to a number of stakeholders. Pinpointing international students' adjustment challenges would allow higher-education institutions (HEIs) to target their counseling and support where it is most likely to be effective, benefitting both the international students and university budgets.

So far, and up to our knowledge, there still remains a need for more information about students' experience outside the leading countries (i.e., United States/Canada, United Kingdom, and Australia/New Zealand) and for non-English-speaking destinations (Abdullah et al., 2014), including an analysis of the dimensions of the host environment that are important to international students' matching (Jing et al., 2020). Although international students' cross-cultural adjustment is a popular topic in global research, this research addresses earlier calls (e.g., Abdullah et al., 2014; Jing et al., 2020) to (i) understand students' experience and cross-cultural adjustment outside the countries that are the major hosts of international students globally; and (ii) complement the existing literature on examining the role of host social interactions and students' social integration.

In the remainder of this article, we will provide a brief overview of the instruments that have been used to assess international student adjustment and identify some of the weaknesses connected to their use. We will then draw on a parallel discussion in the business and management community, which has grappled with similar problems when measuring the adjustment of business expatriates. Borrowing from this literature, we will suggest an alternative approach to conceptualizing and measuring the adjustment of international students before presenting a preliminary test of this instrument with an international student sample from a public European university. We will then establish criterion-related validity by showing positive associations between host social interaction and host connectedness and students' adjustment. Finally, we will discuss how the findings contribute to a wider understanding of students' experience abroad including their cross-cultural adjustment, namely into non-English-speaking destinations.

APPROACHES TO MEASURING INTERNATIONAL STUDENTS' ADJUSTMENT

An early review by Church (1982) identified a plethora of indicators researchers chose to assess international students' adjustment, among them academic/professional performance, degree of social interaction with locals, students' satisfaction, and other outcomes, such as an international perspective, including a positive attitude toward the destination along with personal and professional growth. A later review by Searle and Ward (1990) added other factors, such as students' acceptance of other cultures, skills and coping, emotions, and behavioral changes. They also deplore the proliferation of terms adopted for the phenomenon of coming to terms with cultural contact, such as adaptation, acculturation, adjustment, and accommodation, which are often used interchangeably.

In terms of the theoretical frameworks used to guide the study of intercultural contact, Searle and Ward (1990) identified three distinct approaches: clinical perspectives, social learning models, and social cognition approaches. A review by Zhou et al. (2008) essentially comes to the same conclusion, distinguishing between stress and coping models, culture learning, and social identification, which they identify as affective, behavioral, and cognitive models. A look at recent studies of international student adjustment shows that this multitude of theoretical approaches, conceptualizations, and operationalizations persists (e.g., Shafaei & Razak, 2016), especially with regard to the stress and coping and behavioral perspectives (Smith & Khawaja, 2011). Brisset et al. (2010) studied psychological distress using Bradley's (1994) well-being questionnaire; Duru and Poyrazli (2011) employed Stroebe et al.'s (2002) Utrecht Homesickness Scale; Wang et al. (2012) relied on Derogatis' (2001) Brief Symptom Inventory; and Yang and Noels (2013) on Radloff's (1977) Center for Epidemiologic Studies Depression Scale.

A number of studies still employ the SACQ (e.g., Gómez et al., 2014; Gonzalez et al., 2012) despite Taylor and Pastor's (2007) scathing criticism of its psychometric properties. With regard to social learning approaches, a consensus emerged pertaining the use of Ward and Kennedy's (1999) Socio-cultural Adaptation Scale (SCAS) (or a variant thereof). This scale was used recently by Yu et al. (2019), and previously by Brisset et al. (2010), Kashima and Loh (2006), Lee and Ciftci (2014), Li and Gasser (2005), or Yang and Noels (2013).

With the possible exception of comparatively widespread adoption of the SCAS, we have to conclude that the study of international student adjustment is as fragmented as ever, both in terms of theoretical approach as well as instrumentation, preventing meaningful integration, and the growth of a cumulative body of knowledge. The closest we have come might be a meta-analysis by Wilson et al. (2013), exploring the correlates of cultural adjustment as assessed by the SCAS. This meta-analysis included samples of business expatriates, immigrants, and mixed samples, including international students (57.6%) that accounted for the largest proportion of participants.

WEAKNESSES IN PAST APPROACHES TO MEASURING INTERNATIONAL STUDENT ADJUSTMENT

While the SCAS may have "the most empirical foundation of any measure used in the study of intercultural relations" (Gudykunst, 1999, p. 553), it is not without problems. Wilson (2013) drew attention to valence, the assumption implicit in the SCAS that adjustment is inherently difficult, as expressed in the item wording and the response options ("Please indicate how much difficulty you experience in…", 1 = No difficulty; 5 = Extreme difficulty), and the fact that most researchers employing the SCAS conceive socio-cultural adjustment as taking place in a single domain (i.e., treating the SCAS as unifactorial), when it is known that students' adjustment abroad is inherently multidimensional (Gilbreath et al., 2011; Hua et al., 2020).

In the related international human resource management literature, it has long been acknowledged that the cross-cultural adjustment of international employees is a multi-faceted phenomenon (e.g., Black & Gregersen, 1991; Thomas, 1998). However, the single conceptualization and operationalization of adjustment from Black and colleagues (Black et al., 1991; Black & Stephens, 1989), had arguably been even more dominant in the expatriate literature than the SCAS is in the students' adjustment literature. This conceptualization conceives adjustment as "the perceived degree of psychological comfort with various aspects of the host country" (Black & Gregersen, 1991, p. 463) and distinguishes three separate environmental domains: adjustment to the workplace, to interacting with host nationals and to the general environment (Black et al., 1991), represented by a total of 14 items (Black & Stephens, 1989).

Similar to Wilson's (2013) critique of the SCAS, Hippler et al. (2014) have questioned whether the item wording ("How adjusted are you to…") adequately reflects the construct's intended conceptualization. Moreover, Hippler et al. (2014) raised concerns about how the environmental facets represented in the items were selected and the implicit assumption—that could equally be leveled against the SCAS—that all environmental aspects are of equal importance.

In response to these concerns, Hippler et al. (2014) developed an alternative scale to measure the cross-cultural adjustment of business expatriates. As we believe that this alternative scale addresses a number of parallel concerns pertaining to the measurement of the adjustment of international students, this study intends to establish whether this approach can be meaningfully used in the higher education context and the new scale adapted and applied with international student populations from multiple origins and located in different destinations.

In the following, we will anchor international student adjustment in the person–environment fit literature before then defining students' adjustment by introducing the new scale and outlining how it addresses the concerns identified.

INTERNATIONAL STUDENTS' ADJUSTMENT AS A PERSON–ENVIRONMENT (P–E) RELATIONSHIP

The wider psychological literature conceives of adjustment as person–environment (P–E) fit, as "the goodness of fit between the characteristics of the person and the properties of the environment" (French et al., 1974, p. 316). Students cannot simply 'adjust'; they can only 'adjust to' something or someone. It is thus immediately obvious that the environment is integral to the understanding of adjustment (Gilbreath et al., 2011). Yet every environmental facet will not be of equal importance to every individual (Conroy & McCarthy, 2019); for some students' new friendships at the host location or institution may emerge as more important than coming to terms with the local public transport; for other students maintaining contact with family back home might be more important. Hippler et al. (2014) maintained that it is the interaction between the degree of adjustment to a particular environmental facet and the importance ascribed to that facet rather than the degree of adjustment alone that determines overall student adjustment, well-being, and other more distal outcomes. Finally, adjustment is not determined by the individual or the environment alone, but by the interaction between them. Studying through the medium of a foreign language may be perceived as an unwelcome threat by some students, yet by others as a welcome challenge or an opportunity to finally put to good use the language skills they have acquired. Being in a culturally unfamiliar environment may be experienced as exciting (positive) or frightening (negative). With any relocation an individual's environment changes, and it is thus important that any measure of adjustment takes the perceived direction of change into account—is the change in a particular facet a change for the better or a change for the worse?

To accommodate the fact that (1) environmental facets are unlikely to be of equal importance and (2) the direction of change might differ from one individual to the next. Hippler et al. (2014) developed a 35-item alternative adjustment scale, established its dimensionality, and provided preliminary validity evidence. This scale, developed for international employees from multiple origins and locations in a business context, tapped into ten different life domains (language, work environment, job or task characteristics, work-life balance, leisure time, family life, local friendships, contact to those left behind, living quarters, and urbanity). Criterion-related validity was established by positive associations with self-rated performance, self-rated development, and general satisfaction.

It is our purpose in this study to draw on the person–environment fit approach and operationally define students' cross-cultural adjustment as the perceived harmony (or satisfaction, or comfort) within the P–E relationship in different life domains. We aim to establish whether the scale developed by Hippler et al. (2014) can be meaningfully adapted to the higher education context and applied with international student populations from multiple origins and locations. We believe that the concerns it was designed to address in the business expatriate literature are equally pertinent in international tertiary student populations (i.e., foreign students, credit mobility students, and other degree mobility students). Furthermore, this intent addresses Gilbreath et al.'s (2011) call to use more specific and precise measurement of fit factors relevant to international students.

To assess whether the adapted instrument can be used with international student populations, we (a) tested whether the dimensionality of the scale holds with a sample of international students from a public European university; and (b) started building the nomological network by relating student adjustment as measured with our scale to theoretically related constructs, such as social interaction with host nationals and social connectedness with host nationals (Zhang & Goodson, 2011a). We expect social interaction and social connectedness to be linked to the "social" facets of our adapted scale (e.g., language, local friendships, or leisure time), but not related to the inanimate facets such as urbanity or the living quarters.

METHOD

In 2018, there were 1.3 million students from abroad who were undertaking tertiary-level studies across the EU-27 (EC, 2021). For most EU Member States, the principal country of origin for students was another Member State, although in Southern Europe (e.g., France, Spain, Portugal, and Cyprus), a large proportion of students from abroad came from Asia, Africa, the Caribbean, and the Central and South America. This makes Southern Europe an ideal context to understand international students' experience in non-English-speaking locations, including the assessment of their cross-cultural adjustment. To this purpose, a survey was developed based on Hippler et al.'s (2014) scale to collect the data on students' cross-cultural adjustment while abroad.

International students enrolled in a Southern European public university were invited by email to participate in this study. An initial invitation was sent to the 2,173 international students who were enrolled for the first time in the fall semester of the school year of 2013/2014. To make the results as broadly applicable as possible, incoming and outgoing international students (i.e., foreign students, credit mobility students, and degree mobility students) were surveyed. The email informed them about the research purpose and contained a link to the survey. A reminder was sent two weeks after the initial invitation. All data were collected following students' arrival (late September) and during the first four weeks of the semester (i.e., October), to make comparable the length of time they were in the host country. Participation was voluntary and replies were anonymous, except for students aiming to qualify for a dinner voucher, who were asked to leave an email address at the end of the survey.

Sample

Overall, 189 international tertiary students replied. The sample consisted of international students originated from 33 countries and located in 22 countries, but all were under the umbrella of the Erasmus+ program, as 2014 was the first year of the program (EC, 2021). Of those reporting, 60.6% were female, 72.6% were undergraduates and had host language skills. Of those mentioning the field of study 30.2% were from business, administration, and law, followed by engineering (23.8%), and others (23.3.5%). Table 1 summarizes the demographic characteristics of the sample, which are comparable to other Erasmus samples (e.g., Mikulas & Jitka, 2019).

Table 1: Sample Characteristics

	n	*%*	*Mean*	*SD*
Age			23.21	3.83
Gender			0.39	0.49

		n	*%*	*Mean*	*SD*
	Male	69	39.4		
	Female	106	60.6		
Home region				0.77	0.42
	EU countries	131	74.9		
	Non-EU countries	44	25.14		
Host region				0.99	0.08
	EU countries	172	98.3		
	Non-EU countries	3	1.71		
Host Language skills	Yes	127	72.6	0.73	0.45
	No	48	27.4		

Note: *n* varies between 175 and 189, mean and standard deviation calculated for dummy code variable.

Measures

The survey instrument was designed in English and made available online. The questionnaire took approximately 15 mins to complete. A preliminary version was pilot tested with a similar (but smaller) international student sample, and the instrument was revised in accordance with their feedback.

Cross-cultural Adjustment

This was measured adapting Hippler et al.'s (2014) expatriate adjustment scale. The original 35 items were reworded to fit the student context. For each domain, participants were asked to indicate "How significant is the change you are experiencing" on a scale ranging from (1) *"this change is insignificant in my life"* to (4) *"this change is very significant in my life."* Sample items included: *"How significant is the change you are experiencing regarding the host students' method of studying, in general"* or *"How significant is the change you are experiencing regarding the autonomy in organizing and structuring the tasks at the host school."* For each item respondents also had to indicate if the change they experienced was positive (+1), neutral (0), or negative (−1). Therefore, the students' level of adjustment was computed by multiplying the direction of the change with the significance of the change, resulting in a range from (−4) to (+4), extending from *"a very significant negative change"* to *"a very significant positive change"*. Cronbach's alpha coefficient for the entire scale was 0.87.

Social Interaction with Host Nationals

Items were adapted from Zhang and Goodson's (2011a) nine-item scale, which measures two dimensions of social interaction with host nationals: quantity and quality. This scale was adapted to the exchange student context (e.g., *"During the last weeks, how often did you visit host nationals' homes?"*). For the items assessing the quantity of social interactions with locals, a five-point Likert scale was used, ranging from (1) *"rarely or never"* to (5) *"very often"*, while for the quality items a five-point Likert scale ranging from (1) *"not at all"* to (5) *"very"* was used. Cronbach's alpha coefficient for the nine-item scale was 0.86. The separate scales (quantity and quality) had reliability coefficients of 0.85 and 0.81, respectively.

Social Connectedness with Host Nationals

The eight items from Zhang and Goodson (2011a) were used and reworded to fit the study context. To answer, the respondents used a six-point Likert scale, ranging from (1) *"strongly disagree"* to (6) *"strongly agree"*. Cronbach's alpha coefficient for this scale was 0.91.

Control Variables

Demographics known to influence international students' adjustment (Zhang & Goodson, 2011b), such as age, gender, home, and destination regions, and host language skills were used as control variables. Age was computed in years. Gender was dummy-coded (1 = Male; 0 = Female) as well as host language skills (1 = Yes; 0 = No) and home and host regions (1 = EU region; 0 = non-EU region).

Data Analysis and Scale Validity

Given that the dimensionality of the expatriate adjustment scale is known (from Hippler et al., 2014), we considered conducting a confirmatory factor analysis (CFA) more appropriate than applying exploratory factor analysis to assess the factor structure. At the same time, we expected possible variations in the scale throughout the analysis, given that some items may function differently in a student population compared with business expatriates. For example, it is possible, if not likely, that students will think of their parents and siblings when asked about their family, whereas business expatriates are more likely to have their spouse or partner and children in mind.

To check for univariate normality, skewness and kurtosis were assessed for all 35 adjustment items. All skew indices were in the range -1.41 and 0.50, and all kurtosis indices were between -1.34 and 0.70. According to Kline (2005), only variables with skewness values greater than 3 and kurtosis values greater than 10 are of concern. We therefore proceeded to the CFA.

The CFA was conducted with AMOS 21 to confirm and refine the 10-factor structure established by Hippler et al. (2014). To evaluate model fit, we used several indices: Chi-square statistic, root-mean-square error of approximation (RMSEA), comparative fit index (CFI), and Tucker–Lewis index (TLI). In assessing model fit, we followed recommendations by Hu and Bentler (1999), who suggested that RMSEA of 0.08 or less and CFI and TLI above 0.90 indicate at least adequate fit, with RMSEA of 0.05 or less indicating close fit.

The results of the initial CFA did not indicate good model fit (Chi-square = 915.18; df = 515), whereas the RMSEA indicated adequate fit (0.064), the CFI and the TLI did not (0.813 and 0.785, respectively). A look at the factor loadings revealed that four items did not reach the minimum threshold of 0.45, which Comrey and Lee (1992) considered fair. We therefore removed these four items from further analysis. This resulted in 'work-life balance' and 'family life' becoming single item factors. These single items were therefore also removed, and we proceeded with the remaining 8-factor structure. We reran the analysis and repeated the process twice more until no further factor loadings below 0.45 remained. While model fit improved as a consequence, it still fell short of the desired threshold for the TLI (Chi-square = 423.88, DF = 271; RMSEA = 0.055; CFI = 0.905; TLI = 0.886). We therefore proceeded to examining the modification indices. This suggested allowing two of the error variances for items reflecting the language factor to covary. Adding this path resulted in a further improvement and overall adequate fit (Chi-square = 401.712, df = 270; RMSEA = 0.051; CFI = 0.918; TLI = 0.901).

This 26-item, 8-factor scale was therefore retained as the final model (see Table 2), so the key adjustment domains are work/academic environment, language, study or task characteristics, leisure time, urbanity, living quarters, local friends, and contact to those left behind. Most subscale internal consistency reliability coefficients were acceptable at 0.70 and above (Nunnally, 1978) except for the dimensions that had items deleted and are composed by two or three items, which usually have lower reliability scores (Peterson, 1994).

Table 2: International Students' Adjustment: 26 Items and 8-factor Scale Retained as the Final Model

Factor	Items	N Items	Cronbach alpha	*Mean*	*SD*
Work environment	1–7	7-item Factor	0.798	0.95	1.45
Language	8–12	5-item Factor	0.863	1.01	2.14
Study or task characteristics	14–15	2-item Factor	0.608	1.37	2.04
Leisure time	19–21	3-item Factor	0.732	1.84	1.82
Urbanity	22–24	3-item Factor	0.662	0.61	1.75

Factor	Items	N Items	Cronbach alpha	*Mean*	*SD*
Living quarters	28–29	2-item Factor	0.662	1.00	2.12
Local friendships	32–33	2-item Factor	0.757	1.38	2.24
Cantact to those left behind	34–35	2-item Factor	0.677	0.91	2.19
Overall Adjustment Scale		26-item scale	0.868	1.09	1.15

To determine the criterion-related validity of this new students' adjustment scale, the validity was assessed by examining the associations between students' social interaction in the destination and host connectedness (Zhang & Goodson, 2011a) as antecedents of students' adjustment, as measured by the new 26-item scale and its subscales.

RESULTS

Table 3 presents the descriptive statistics and zero-order correlations for all variables. There are significant and positive relationships between the composite adjustment measure and all subscales, as well as between self-rated host social interaction and connectedness and self-rated adjustment except for the facets of urbanity, living quarters and contact to those left behind. These results provide initial evidence of criterion-related validity.

Given that students' adjustment could vary from (−4) meaning a very negative change to (+4) for a positive change, one can observe that participants experienced a positive life change, especially pertaining to their leisure time ($M = 1.84$; $SD = 1.82$), local friendships ($M = 1.38$; $SD = 2.24$), and local study/task characteristics ($M = 1.37$; $SD = 2.04$). The quality of host social interactions and host connectedness were also fairly positive respectively ($M = 3.83$; $SD = 0.85$; and $M = 3.95$; $SD = 1.15$).

To determine whether host social interaction and host connectedness predict the 'social' facets of students' adjustment, several stepwise regression analyses were performed. In step one, the demographic variables that were correlated with the criterion (e.g., students age, home region, and host language skills) were entered, while in step two, social interaction (quantity and quality) and social connectedness were entered as predictors of each cross-cultural dimension. Potential multicollinearity was investigated, using tolerance and the variance inflation factor (VIF) (Cohen & Cohen, 1983). The values for the tolerance were all close to one, and the maximum VIF obtained in all regression models was far below the reference point of 10, which suggest that multicollinearity was not a problem (Cohen & Cohen, 1983). Table 4 presents the results of these multiple regressions.

Table 3: Means, Standard Deviations, and Correlations for All Variables

	Variable	M	SD	1	2	3	4	5	6	7	8	9	10	11	12
1	Adjustment 26	1.09	1.15												
2	Work environment	0.95	1.45	0.80**											
3	Language	1.01	2.14	0.64**	0.33**										
4	Study or task characteristics	1.37	2.04	0.61**	0.55**	0.20**									
5	Leisure time	1.84	1.82	0.67**	0.44**	0.33**	0.30**								
6	Urbanity	0.61	1.75	0.38**	0.27**	−0.09	0.24**	0.22							
7	Living quarters	1.00	2.12	0.55**	0.35**	0.21**	0.35**	0.36**	0.18**						
8	Local friendships	1.38	2.24	0.58**	0.35**	0.38**	0.18**	0.38**	0.10	0.23**					
9	Contact to those left behind	0.91	2.19	0.44**	0.24**	0.07	0.28**	0.23**	0.20**	0.27**	0.22**				
10	Host social interaction (quantity)	0.78	1.09	0.34**	0.36**	0.21**	0.13	0.23**	0.07	0.08	0.35**	0.04	(0.85)		
11	Host social interaction (quality)	3.83	0.85	0.34**	0.36**	0.21**	0.13	0.23**	0.07	0.08	0.35**	0.06	0.51**	(0.81)	
12	Host connectedness	3.95	1.15	0.46**	0.46**	0.26**	0.19**	0.36**	0.12	0.12	0.46**	0.08	0.68**	0.58**	(0.91)

Notes: n = 175–189; two-tailed Significant at *p < 0.05, **p < 0.01/ Cronbach's alpha estimates in parentheses, along main diagonal.

Table 4: Multiple Stepwise Regressions of the Hypothesized Relationships between Host Social Interaction (Quantity and Quality) and Host Connectedness and the Dimensions of Adjustment

Predictors	Adjustment-26 item		Work environment		Language		Study or task characteristics		Leisure time		Urbanity		Living quarters		Local friendships		Contac to those left behind	
	Step 1	2	Step 1	Step 2	Step 1	Step 2	Step 1	Step 2	Step 1	Step 2	Step 1	Step 2	Step 1	Step 2	Step 1	Step 2	Step 1	Step 2
Intercept	0.78**	−1.01***	−1.44***	−2.36***	−0.22	−1.97**	2.03**	0.62	1.34***	−0.81	1.51***	0.59	−2.26**	−2.79**	0.5	−2.84*	1.34	0.81
Step 1-Control variables																		
Age													0.25**	0.25***				
Home region (0 = Non-EU)							−0.82**	−0.94**			−0.30***	−0.32**			0.20**	0.15**		
Host language skills (0 = No)	0.16**	0.14**			0.36***	0.35***			0.17*	0.15**				015*			−0.16*	−0.17*
Step 2-Predictors																		
Host social interaction (quantity)																		
Host social interaction (quality)			0.239*															
Host connectedness		0.46***		0.33**		0.24**		0.38**		0.35**		0.17**				0.46**		
Overall F	4.63*	27.35***	50.30***	30.55**	26.18***	20.30***	5.08***	6.87**	5.10*	15.52***	17.19***	11.44***	11.37***	7.95***	7.49**	28.72***	2.76*	1.76
R^2	0.03	0.24	0.23	0.26	0.13	0.19	0.03	0.07	0.03	0.03	0.09	0.09	0.06	0.09	0.04	0.25	0.05	0.06
Adjusted R^2	0.02	0.23	0.22	0.25	0.13	0.18	0.02	0.06	0.02	0.14	0.09	0.11	0.09	0.07	0.04	0.24	0.03	0.03
Changein R^2	w	0.21	0.23	0.04	0.13	0.06	0.03	0.04	0.03	0.12	0.09	0.03	0.06	0.02	0.04	0.21	0.05	0.01

Notes: Significant at: *$p < .05$, **$p < .01$, ***$p < .001$; standardized β coefficients are reported after Z-score transformation, $n = 189$. Because gender and host region are not significantly correlated with the criterion, they have not entered into the regression analysis.

As shown, host social interaction (in quality) is a positive predictor of students' adjustment to the work environment (F = 30.55; p < 0.001). Self-reported host connectedness is a positive predictor of students' adjustment (F = 27.35; p < 0.001) as well as of the remaining social facets. As expected, social interaction and social connectedness are not predictors of the inanimate facets of students' adjustment, such as living quarters and contact to those left behind. Regarding urbanity, the results show that students' adjustment to this facet is easier among the EU-students (β = −0.32; p < 0.001), who reported higher host social connectedness than non-EU students (β = 0.35; F = 11.44; p < 0.001). Furthermore, no other demographic effects were observed, except for the dimension of living quarters, as its importance increases with students' age. However, the percentage of variance for this dimension that was accounted by age was small with a value of 4.7%. The pattern of these relationships suggests preliminary criterion-related validity evidence for the proposed 26-item student adjustment scale as well as some of the subscales (see Appendix 1 for the full list of items).

DISCUSSION

This study follows an alternative approach to conceptualizing and measuring the adjustment of international students and puts forward a preliminary test of a new scale drawn from Hippler et al.'s (2014) expatriate adjustment scale. First, the 35 items comprising the original scale for measuring expatriates' adjustment were rewritten and adapted to the HE context. Second, the answer scale accounted for the various facets of the students' environment by requiring an assessment of the importance and direction of the changes observed during the exchange period, as called by Gilbreath et al. (2011). This procedure conveys an alternative approach to the assessment of students' adjustment that stems from the assumptions that not all changes are equally important (Conroy & McCarthy, 2019). As shown, a final 26-item and 8-factor solution accounts for international students' adjustment and portrays the changes encountered in the new environment. As expected, host social interaction and connectedness are antecedents of the 'social' facets of the adapted scale (e.g., language, local friendships, or leisure time), but are not related to the facets of urbanity and the living quarters, which is consistent with earlier findings with international students (e.g., Duru & Poyrazli, 2011; Yeh & Inose, 2003; Zhang & Goodson, 2011a, 2011b) and supports the scale validity. Furthermore, the findings identify the dimensions of adjustment that were more challenging for international students, consisting of keeping contact with home family and friends and host urbanity (i.e., environmental pollution, street traffic, and people punctuality). Host language, which was not a specific pressure point for the surveyed students predicted their cross-cultural adjustment. This contradicts previous reports (Jing et al., 2020) but highlights the power European languages can have in attracting international students (Mikulas & Jitka, 2019).

The contributions of this study have to be interpreted bearing its limitations in mind. First, we relied on self-report data which incur the risk of same-source bias. Following Podsakoff et al. (2003), we followed several recommendations to reduce the sources of common-method variance, such as (a) assuring respondents anonymity and informing that there were no 'right' or 'wrong' answers; (b) randomizing the questions order; (c) using different response formats; (d) pilot testing the survey to avoid unclear and suggestive items and decrease social desirability. Finally, we used the single-common-method-factor approach to statistically control for method biases. As shown, the factor analyses confirmed the underlying constructs and the independence of the variables, which supports our theoretical approach.

Second, the sample includes international students from different origins and locations, but European countries are over-represented, accounting for 74.9% of all home countries and 98.3% of all destination countries. Given that the Erasmus mobility program in the context of the Bologna process has contributed to increase students' mobility as well as decrease academic differences (Papatsiba, 2006), the findings confirm that European students are now more aware of and receptive to lifestyle differences (Lesjak et al., 2015; OECD, 2019) compared with students from other world regions (Zhou & Todman, 2008) and are less likely to experience acculturative stress (Yeh & Inose, 2003). These features observed among European international students might account for the high levels of adjustment observed in this study. However, as no significant adjustment differences were observed according to students' demographics, including students' home and host location, we trust this adjustment scale may prove useful in other international settings.

Finally, another limitation of the study regards the reliability levels of some adjustment factors that were slightly below .70. As a result, the conclusions regarding these dimensions (e.g., study/task characteristics, urbanity, living quarters) must be analyzed with caution although our results would be more conservative since we found significant results with a low reliability. Future studies are needed to further examine the reliability of these measures with other international students' samples.

Implications for Future Research

This study puts forward a new instrument to assess the multidimensionality of international students' adjustment, bearing in mind that not all changes are unpleasant or equally important. The findings confirm most students experienced relevant and positive changes once they arrive at destination, which provides empirical evidence of the internal consistency of the subscales used, as well as preliminary criterion-related validity. Given its limitations, future research may extend its contributions by drawing on other samples of international students outside the EU and further examining the convergent and divergent validity of this scale by investigating the relationships with other theoretically related constructs such as cultural competence, stress, anxiety, psychological well-being, and satisfaction. The findings of this study also encourage more research on the main coping strategies and coping skills that international students use, notably those related to fostering host interaction and connectedness. While we have controlled for the time spent abroad by inquiring all respondents within the first weeks of mobility, future research may usefully employ an experimental design to measure adjustment variations throughout students' international stay.

Finally, this study highlights the importance of the host language for international students. As shown, knowing the host language is a positive antecedent of international students' adjustment within the EU, even when English is the instruction language. The importance of second-language acquisition has been reported before (Abdullah et al., 2014; Jing et al., 2020); however, less is known about the experiences of international students coming from and going to different countries, where English is not widely spoken. Such non-English-speaking contexts are ideal to advance our understanding of international students, including how language skills are relevant and can promote international students' intercultural competence.

Managerial Implications

This study offers a new approach for assessing the multidimensionality of international students' adjustment, that relies on P–E fit. Fit information can result in a better match between higher education institutions and students aiming to faster international mobility. As shown, not every host environmental facet is of equal importance to every individual nor inherently difficult. Therefore, the use of this adapted scale to assess international students' adjustment will enable HE institutions, notably counsellors and support services, to assess international students' level of preparedness (Brutt-Griffler et al., 2020) and cross-cultural adjustment that goes beyond study/task characteristics, thus identifying critical issues and taking remedial actions to avoid adjustment difficulties affecting academic performance and personal well-being. As shown, and even within Europe, where distances and stays are shorter (Mikulas & Jitka, 2019), international students can experience concerns about keeping contact with home family and friends, which emphasizes the need of continuing home support. Being able to pinpoint the key concerns of each student, early in the exchange program, may allow HE managers to proactively intervene as needed. Moreover, the refinement of this tool in the HE context will allow for the use of a common, yet tailored, metric for both the incoming and outgoing institutions that might help introduce timely and effective supporting practices.

The findings of this research also have practical implications to international students. First, this study provides a self-assessment tool that students can use to diagnose the dimensions they consider important to adjust abroad. Second, as students' cross-cultural adjustment is furthered by more and better interactions with host nationals and by host connectedness, HE institutions and international students may foster the engagement in host activities intended to promote the immersion in the local community and increase the sense of belongingness. Third, better fit also result from contact with those left behind, which includes students' family and friends. Thus, keeping contact with friends and relatives at home remains important to international students' adjustment in the destination. This is an issue that has been largely neglected in the literature, so further research down this line may consider how to design support systems geared toward students' engagement with home relatives and friends.

CONCLUSION

By addressing a number of concerns pertaining to the measurement of international student adjustment, this study aims to establish a new scale that can be meaningfully used in the higher education context and applied with international student populations. We anchored students' adjustment in the person–environment fit literature and offered a multidimensional instrument that takes account of the level of importance that international students place on various aspects of the host environment. The adapted scale includes eight different adjustment domains: work/academic environment, language, study or task characteristics, leisure time, urbanity, living quarters, local friends, and contact to those left behind. Criterion-related validity indicated positive associations between social interaction and social connectedness with host nationals and international students' adjustment, which highlights the importance of social interaction at destination. Although our new instrument provides a way forward to deal with the weaknesses in past approaches to measuring international students' adjustment, further research is required to replicate and validate its multidimensionality and prevent the outcomes of a poor adjustment.

ACKNOWLEDGMENTS

Thanks goes to Professor Daniela Noethen (ESADE) for her detailed comments on an earlier draft of this manuscript. We would also like to show our gratitude to Professor Anne-Will Harzing (Middlesex University London) for her encouragement throughout the process of completing this work.

HONOR NOTE

This paper honors Thomas Hippler's academic work on cross-cultural adjustment. Sadly, Thomas passed away in November 2018. True to his passion for research, we went on with this work until publication. The international students' adjustment scale is now available to the research community, including higher education institutions, advisory centers, academics, students, and families. Those less familiar with the contributions of Thomas Hippler may find inspiration here: A tribute to Thomas Hippler (1972–2018). https://harzing.com/blog/2019/02/a-tribute-to-thomas-hippler-1972-2018.

NOTE

Appendices for this article can be found on the JIS website at https://www.ojed.org/index.php/jis.

REFERENCES

Abdullah, D., Abd Aziz, M. I., & Mohd Ibrahim, A. L. (2014). A "research" into international student-related research: (Re)Visualising our stand? *Higher Education, 67*(3), 235–253. https://doi.org/10.1007/s10734-013-9647-3.

Anderson, J. R., Guan, Y., & Koc, Y. (2016). The academic adjustment scale: Measuring the adjustment of permanent resident or sojourner students. *International Journal of Intercultural Relations, 54*, 68–76. https://doi.org/10.1016/j.ijintrel.2016.07.006

Baker, R. W., & Siryk, B. (1984). Measuring adjustment to college. *Journal of Counseling Psychology, 31*(2), 179–189. https://doi.org/10.1037/0022-0167.31.2.179

Black, S., & Gregersen, H. B. (1991). The other half of the picture: Antecedents of spouse cross-cultural adjustment. *Journal of International Business Studies, 22*(3), 461–477. https://doi.org/10.1057/palgrave.jibs.8490311

Black, S., Mendenhall, M., & Oddou, G. (1991). Toward a comprehensive model of international adjustment: An integration of multiple theoretical perspectives. *Academy of Management Review, 16*(2), 291–317. https://doi.org/10.5465/amr.1991.4278938

Black, S., & Stephens, G. K. (1989). The influence of the spouse on American expatriate adjustment and intent to stay in Pacific Rim overseas assignments. *Journal of Management, 15*(4), 529–544. https://doi.org/10.1177/014920638901500403

Bradley, C. (1994). The well-being questionnaire. In C. Bradley (Ed.), *Handbook of psychology and diabetes: A guide to psychological measurement in diabetes research and practice* (pp. 89–109). Harwood Academic Press.

Brisset, C., Safdarb, S., Lewisb, J. R., & Sabatier, C. (2010). Psychological and sociocultural adaptation of university students in France: The case of Vietnamese international students. *International Journal of Intercultural Relations, 34*(4), 413–426. https://doi.org/10.1016/j.ijintrel.2010.02.009

Brutt-Griffler, J., Nurunnabi, M., & Kim, S. (2020). International students' level of preparedness. *Journal of International Students, 10*(4). https://doi.org/10.32674/jis.v10i4.839

Church, A. T. (1982). Sojourner adjustment. *Psychological Bulletin, 91*(3), 540–572. https://doi.org/10.1037/0033-2909.91.3.540

Cohen, J., & Cohen, P. (1983). Applied multiple regression/correlation analysis for the behavioural science. Lawrence Erlbaum.

Comrey, A. L., & Lee, H. B. (1992). *A first course in factor analysis* (2nd ed.). Lawrence Erlbaum.

Conroy, K. M., & McCarthy, L. (2019). Abroad but not abandoned: Supporting student adjustment in the international placement journey. *Studies in Higher Education*, 1–15. https://doi.org/10.1080/03075079.2019.1673718

Derogatis, L. R. (2001). Brief symptom inventory (BSI)-18: Administration, scoring and procedures manual. NCS Pearson Inc.

Duru, E., & Poyrazli, S. (2011). Perceived discrimination, social connectedness, and other predictors of adjustment difficulties among Turkish international students. *International Journal of Psychology, 46*(6), 446–454. https://doi.org/10.1080/00207594.2011.585158

European Commission (2021). Erasmus[+] worldwide factsheet, 2014–2020. European Union. https://ec.europa.eu/programmes/erasmus-plus/about/factsheets_en

French, J., Rodgers, W., & Cobb, S. (1974). Adjustment as person-environment fit. In G. V. Coelho, D. A. Hamburg, & J. E. Adams (Eds.), *Coping and adaptation* (pp. 316–333). Basic Books.

Gilbreath, B., Kim, T. Y., & Nichols, B. (2011). Person-environment fit and its effects on university students: A response surface methodology study. *Research in Higher Education, 52*(1), 47–62. https://doi.org/10.1007/s11162-010-9182-3

Gómez, E., Urzúa, A., & Glass, C. R. (2014). International student adjustment to college: Social networks, acculturation, and leisure. *Journal of Park & Recreation Administration, 32*(1), 7–25. https://search.ebscohost.com/login.aspx?direct=true&AuthType=ip,shib&db=asn&AN=95740581&lang=pt-pt&site=ehost-live&scope=site

González, M. S., Tinajero, V. C., Guisande, C. M. A., & Páramo, M. F. (2012). The student adaptation to college questionnaire (SACQ) for use with Spanish students. *Psychological Reports, 111*(2), 624–640. https://doi.org/10.2466/08.10.20.PR0.111.5.624-640

Gudykunst, W. B. (1999). Theory and research on intercultural relations: An introduction. *International Journal of Intercultural Relations, 23*(4), 529–534. https://doi.org/10.1016/S0147-1767(99)00008-5

Harzing, A. W. (2004). Ideal jobs and international student mobility in the enlarged European Union. *European Management Journal, 22*(6), 693–703. https://doi.org/10.1016/j.emj.2004.09.032

Heng, T. T. (2020). The role of theory in qualitative research: Insights from studies on Chinese international students in higher education. *Journal of International Students, 10*(4). https://doi.org/10.32674/jis.v10i4.1571

Hippler, T., Caligiuri P., Johnson, J., & Baytalskaya, N. (2014). The development and validation of a theory-based expatriate adjustment scale. *The International Journal of Human Resource Management, 25*(4), 1938–1959. https://doi.org/10.1080/09585192.2013.870286

Hu, L.-T., & Bentler, P. M. (1999). Cut-off criteria for fit indexes in covariance structure analysis: Conventional criteria versus new alternatives. *Structural Equation Modeling, 6*(1), 1–55. https://doi.org/10.1080/10705519909540118

Hua, J., Zhang, G., Coco, C., Zhao, T., & Hou, N. (2020). Proactive Personality and Cross-Cultural Adjustment: The Mediating Role of Adjustment Self-Efficacy. *Journal of International Students, 10*(4). https://doi.org/10.32674/jis.v10i4.1274

Jing, X., Ghosh, R., Sun, Z., & Liu, Q. (2020). Mapping global research related to international students: A scientometric review. *Higher Education, 80*(3), 415–433. https://doi.org/10.1007/s10734-019-00489-y

Johnson, K. (2020). 21st century international higher education hotspots. *Journal of International Students, 10*(1), v–viii. https://doi.org/10.32674/jis.v10i1.1851

Kashima, E. S., & Loh, E. (2006). International students' acculturation: Effects of international, conational, and local ties and need for closure. *International Journal of Intercultural Relations, 30*(4), 471–485. https://doi.org/10.1016/j.ijintrel.2005.12.003

Kline, R. B. (2005). Methodology in the social sciences. Principles and practice of structural equation modeling (2nd ed.). Guilford Press.

Lee, J., & Ciftci, A. (2014). Asian international students' socio-cultural adaptation: Influence of multicultural personality, assertiveness, academic self-efficacy, and social support. *International Journal of Intercultural Relations, 38*(1), 97–105. https://doi.org/10.1016/j.ijintrel.2013.08.009

Lesjak, M., Juvan, E., Ineson, E., Yap, M., & Axelsson, E. (2015). Erasmus student motivation: Why and where to go? *Higher Education, 70*(5), 845–865. https://doi.org/10.1007/s10734-015-9871-0

Li, A., & Gasser, M. B. (2005). Predicting Asian international students' sociocultural adjustment: A test of two mediation models. *International Journal of Intercultural Relations, 29*(5), 561–576. https://doi.org/10.1016/j.ijintrel.2005.06.003

Merola, R. H., Coelen, R. J., & Hofman, W. H. A. (2019). The role of integration in understanding differences in satisfaction among Chinese, Indian, and South Korean international students. *Journal of Studies in International Education, 23*(5), 535–553. https://doi.org/10.1177/1028315319861355

Mesidor, J. K., & Sly, K. F. (2016). Factors that contribute to the adjustment of international students. *Journal of International Students, 6*(1). https://www.ojed.org/index.php/jis/article/view/569

Mikulas, J., & Jitka, S. (2019). Statistical analysis of study abroad experiences of international students in five major host countries of Europe. *Journal of International Students, 9*(1), 1–18. https://doi.org/10.32674/jis.v9i1.262

Nunnally, J. C. (1978). *Psychometric theory* (2nd ed.). McGraw-Hill.

Organisation for Economic Co-operation and Development (2019). *Education at a Glance 2019*, OECD Publishing. Retrieved September 25, 2019, from: https://www.oecd-ilibrary.org/content/publication/f8d7880d-en

Papatsiba, V. (2006). Making higher education more European through student mobility? Revisiting EU initiatives in the context of the Bologna Process. *Comparative Education, 42*(1), 93–111. https://doi.org/10.1080/03050060500515785

Pedersen, E. R., Neighbors, C., Larimer, M. E., & Lee, C. M. (2011). Measuring sojourner adjustment among American students studying abroad. *International Journal of Intercultural Relations, 35*(6), 881–889. https:// doi.org/10.1016/j.ijintrel.2011.06.003

Peterson, R. A. (1994). A meta-analysis of Cronbach's coefficient alpha. *Journal of Consumer Research, 21*(2), 381–391. https://doi.org/10.1086/209405

Podsakoff, P. M., MacKenzie, S. B., Lee, J.-Y., & Podsakoff, N. P. (2003). Common method biases in behavioral research: A critical review of the literature and recommended remedies. *Journal of Applied Psychology, 88*(5), 879–903. http://doi.org/10.1037/0021-9010.88.5.879

Radloff, L. S. (1977). The CES-D scale: A self-report depression scale for research in the general population. *Applied Psychological Measurement, 1*(3), 385–401. https://doi.org/10.1177/014662167700100306

Searle, W., & Ward, C. (1990). The prediction of psychological and sociocultural adjustment during cross-cultural transitions. *International Journal of Intercultural Relations, 14*(4), 449–464. https://doi.org/10.1016/0147-1767(90)90030-Z

Shafaei, A., & Razak, N. A. (2016). International postgraduate students' cross-cultural adaptation in Malaysia: Antecedents and outcomes. *Research in Higher Education, 57*(6), 739–767. https://doi.org/10.1007/s11162-015-9404-9

Smith, M. B. (1955). Some features of foreign student adjustments. *Journal of Higher Education, 26*(5), 231–241. https://doi.org/10.1080/00221546. 1955.11779399

Smith, R., & Khawaja, N. (2011). A review of the acculturation experiences of international students. *International Journal of Intercultural Relations, 35*(6), 699–713. https://doi.org/10.1016/j.ijintrel.2011.08.004

Spencer-Oatey, H., & Dauber, D. (2019). What is integration and why is it important for internationalization? A multidisciplinary review. *Journal of Studies in International Education, 23*(5), 515–534. https://doi.org/10.1177/ 1028315319842346

Stroebe, M., Van Vliet, T., Hewstone, M., & Willis, H. (2002). Homesickness among students in two cultures: Antecedents and consequences. *British Journal of Psychology, 93*(2), 147–168. https://doi.org/10.1348/000712602162508

Taylor, M., & Pastor, D. A. (2007). A confirmatory factor analysis of the student adaptation to college questionnaire. *Educational and Psychological Measurement, 67*(6), 1002–1018. https://doi.org/10.1177/0013164406299125

Thomas, D. C. (1998). The expatriate experience: A critical review and synthesis. In J. L. C. Cheng & R. B. Peterson (Eds.), *Advances in international comparative management* (pp. 237–273). JAI.

Wang, K. T., Heppner, P. P., Fu, C.-C., Zhao, R., Li, F., & Chuang, C.-C. (2012). Profiles of acculturative adjustment patterns among Chinese international students. *Journal of Counseling Psychology, 59*(3), 424–436. https://doi.org/ 10.1037/a0028532

Ward, C., & Kennedy, A. (1999). The measurement of sociocultural adaptation. *International Journal of Intercultural Relations, 23*(4), 659–677. https:// doi.org/10.1016/S0147-1767(99)00014-0

Wilson, J. K. (2013). Exploring the past, present, and future of cultural competency research: The revision and expansion of the Sociocultural Adaptation Construct. Unpublished Doctoral Thesis from the University of Wellington. Retrieved September 25, 2019, from: http://hdl.handle.net/10063/2783

Wilson, J., Ward C., & Fischer, R. (2013). Beyond culture learning theory: What can personality tell us about cultural competence? *Journal of Cross-Cultural Psychology, 44*(6), 900–927. https://doi.org/10.1177/0022022113492889

Yang, R. P.-J., & Noels, K. A. (2013). The possible selves of international students and their cross-cultural adjustment in Canada. *International Journal of Psychology, 48*(3), 316–323. https://doi.org/10.1080/00207594. 2012. 660161

Yeh, C. J., & Inose, M. (2003). International students reported English fluency, social support satisfaction, and social connectedness as predictors of acculturative stress. *Counselling Psychology Quarterly, 16*(1), 15–28. https://doi.org/ 10.1080/0951507031000114058

Yu, B., Bodycott, P., & Mak, A. S. (2019). Language and interpersonal resource predictors of psychological and sociocultural adaptation: International students in Hong Kong. *Journal of Studies in International Education, 23*(5), 572–588. https://doi.org/10.1177/1028315318825336

Zhang, J., & Goodson, P. (2011a). Acculturation and psychosocial adjustment of Chinese international students: Examining mediation and moderation effects. *International Journal of Intercultural Relations, 35*(5), 614–627. https://doi.org/10.1016/j.ijintrel.2010.11.004

Zhang, J., & Goodson, P. (2011b). Predictors of international students' psychosocial adjustment to life in the United States: A systematic review. *International Journal of Intercultural Relations, 35*(2), 139–162. https://doi.org/ 10.1016/j.ijintrel.2010.11.011

Zhou, Y., Jindal-Snape, D., Topping, K., & Todman, J. (2008). Theoretical models of culture shock and adaptation in international students in higher education. *Studies in Higher Education, 33*(1), 63–67. https://doi.org/10.1080/ 03075070701794833

Zhou, Y., & Todman, J. (2008). Patterns of adaptation of Chinese postgraduate students in the United Kingdom. *Journal of Studies in International Education, 13*(4), 467–486. https://doi.org/10.1177/1028315308317937

JOANA CAMPOS, M.Sc., received her master's in management from the School of Economics in University of Porto. She is currently a Middle Office Analyst at a Portuguese energy company. Research interests include international students' adjustment, cultural orientation, and issues of multiculturalism and diversity. Email: jpinheirocampos@gmail.com

LUISA HELENA PINTO, PhD, is an Associate Professor at School of Economics in University of Porto. Her teaching interests include international human resource management, negotiation, and business methods research. Her research interests include global mobility, expatriation, tertiary education, recruiters' biases, and perceived employability. Email: lhpinto@fep.up.pt

THOMAS HIPPLER, PhD, was a Senior Lecturer in Management at National University of Ireland, Galway, when he passed away in November 2018. He held previous faculty positions at the University of Essex, at Swansea University, Queen's University Belfast, and Webster University, Missouri. His research interests included global mobility management, mainly in the topics of international assignments and expatriates cross-cultural adjustment.

Research Article

© *Journal of International Students*
Volume 12, Issue 2 (2022), pp. 444-466
ISSN: 2162-3104 (Print), 2166-3750 (Online)
doi: 10.32674/jis.v12i2.2351
ojed.org/jis

The Role of Language and Culture in Postgraduate International Students' Academic Adjustment and Academic Success: Qualitative Insights From Malaysia

Jasvir Kaur Nachatar Singh
*Department of Management and Marketing, La Trobe Business School,
La Trobe University, Australia*

Gavin Jack
*Department of Management, Monash Business School,
Monash University, Australia*

ABSTRACT

How do language and culture pose adjustment challenges that hinder the academic success of postgraduate international students? This article answers this question based on a thematic analysis of 55 semi-structured qualitative interviews conducted with postgraduate international students and academic and professional staff members at a Malaysian research-intensive public university. The results show that language and culture are influential in a range of academic (language, supervision, research training) and social (group work, friendship) adjustment challenges. The analysis highlights how these challenges hinder academic success as a result of limited or frustrated pathways for students' linguacultural development. We conclude that future academic research and university policy to support postgraduate international students may pay greater attention to cross-cultural, linguistic, and linguacultural issues.

Keywords: academic success, adjustment, culture, international students, language, linguaculture, Malaysia, postgraduate

INTRODUCTION

The purpose of this study is to investigate the role of language and culture in the adjustment issues that have an impact on the academic success of postgraduate international students. International students seek education abroad to gain better quality education, achieve academic success, develop career prospects, and enhance employability skills (Sam et al., 2013). Along their international education journey, international students face academic and social challenges that can impede realization of these goals, especially as they adjust to their new environments. International students' linguistic proficiency in a second/foreign language and cultural differences in an unfamiliar environment are prime amongst these challenges. To date, the majority of studies that highlight such difficulties are conducted in English-language education settings in the Global North and often on Asian students' adjustment to new academic and cultural environments (Andrade, 2006; Wolf & Phung, 2019; Xiong & Zhou, 2018). While a growing body of work about international students moving between locations in the Global South highlight similar dynamics (for example, international students in China and their adjustments: Nadeem et al., 2015; Tian and Lu, 2018), studies on the experiences of non-English-speaking postgraduate international students taught in English in Malaysia are limited (Shafaei & Abd Razak, 2016; Talebloo & Baki, 2013).

Malaysia presents a distinctive context in light of its colonial history, multiethnic and multilingual society, and growth as a regional hub for international education. English is the language of instruction in Malaysian universities that welcome international students, even though the national language is Bahasa Malaysia. Given the colonial histories of many nations in the Global South that are the source of many international students in Malaysia, qualitative study of the experiences of non-English-speaking postgraduate international students may help to shed new insights into issues of adjustment and academic success. Theoretically, the article draws upon the concept of linguaculture (Risager, 2020) to problematize the manner in which the literature separates language and culture into two discrete pillars of analysis, overlooking their interconnection. Using this concept to interpret the results of this qualitative interview study, we develop insights that can be generalized analytically beyond the specific Malaysian context.

The article begins with a selective literature review to guide the research question and the theoretical framework. Research design and methods follow. The discussion interprets the significance of the findings through the lens of the theoretical frame and notes the study's limitations and directions for future research. The theoretical contribution highlights how the academic and social challenges identified in the findings can hinder academic success as a result of limited or frustrated pathways for students' linguacultural development. The article provides implications for policy and practice.

LITERATURE REVIEW

International students experience a range of challenges in their chosen overseas educational institution (Alsahafi & Shin, 2017). In regard to academic success in Malaysian universities, Sam et al. (2013) and Singh as well as Jack (2018) revealed that postgraduate international students from countries in Asia, Africa, and the Middle East perceive academic success as a composite of attainment of overseas tertiary-level qualifications, timely study completion, employment upon graduation, developing research and transferable skills, experiencing international life, and contribution to their home country. Studies have shown that achievement of academic success is influenced by a range of factors related to students' adjustment to new academic and cultural environments (Ren & Hagedorn, 2012; Singh, 2018). Commonly reported types of adjustment-related challenge faced include academic (Trahar, 2014), social (Kim, 2019) and physiological/ psychological (Li et al., 2014) factors. Cross-cultural differences and linguistic issues are key factors (Xiong & Zhou, 2018; Yassin et al., 2020).

Most research to date about international students is predicated on Western settings (Nadeem et al., 2015; Singh & Jack, 2018), although studies from non-Western settings are growing, especially on international students' adjustment in China (Tian & Lu, 2018). A predominant focus has been placed on international students from diverse cultural backgrounds whose first language is not English undertaking study at academic institutions in the United States, Europe, Australia, and New Zealand. A common impediment to international students' adjustment in such contexts is lack of English proficiency (Sherry et al., 2010). Brown's (2008) ethnographic study of postgraduate international students from non-English-speaking countries, for example, found that they face problems when they communicate (in writing and orally) in English in both academic and social settings in the United Kingdom. A majority felt disadvantaged by having poor English skills, despite scoring well in their IELTS examination. Brown further discovered problems such as "insufficient comprehension of lectures, seminar discussion and day-to-day conversation; limited fluency, grasp of grammar and vocabulary" (p. 77) that affected academic adjustment and outcomes. Participants reported these problems restricted their participation in the classroom, resulting in poor reading and writing skills. In a study of Asian students in New Zealand, similar linguistic challenges were associated with non-timely completion of assignments, thesis chapters, exams, and tests (Campbell & Li, 2008); in another, they had a negative impact on the experience of postgraduate supervision (Li et al., 2010). As for social adjustment, international doctoral students from Korea in the United States in Kim's (2007) study highlighted how mistakes in wording their sentences and improper grammar usage frustrated them in expressing their ideas in English with friends. Language limitations also interfered with their daily conversations in their social space.

Providing a counter-balance to the Western dominance of the literature, a nascent body of Malaysian studies offers insights into international students' adjustment experiences that also encompass cultural and linguistic issues. Studies to date have explored, for example, international students' general challenges related to facilities, social environment, academic systems and international office programs (Talebloo & Baki, 2013), and psychological and socio-cultural adaptations in Malaysia (Shafaei & Abd Razak, 2016). One stream of work in Malaysia notes how international students experience friendship barriers with local students (Malaklolunthu & Selan, 2011), caused by communication gaps. Although Malay students were polite and friendly, they spoke the national language among themselves and international students felt ignored and isolated (Singh, 2018). Another stream of Malaysian studies focuses on supervision challenges. Here postgraduate international students from Arabic-speaking countries have reported negative experiences due to English language barriers (Al-Zubaidi & Rechards, 2010), which impacted their academic writing abilities and communication with supervisors. Differences in academic culture are also known to play a major role in supervisory relationships: students from some countries are taught to state their opinions and ideas directly and assertively rather than indirectly in discussions (Al-Zubaidi & Rechards, 2010). These differences in cultural communicative preferences can result in offensive or unpleasant relationship outcomes for both parties. In a Malaysian study, Sidhu et al. (2014) found that strained supervisory relationships were experienced by students due to supervisors' lack of research methodology knowledge and personality clashes between students and supervisors. These students reported feeling demoralized, fearful of their supervisors, and lacking confidence to complete research projects on time. A high attrition rate and non-timely completion of PhD studies is evident among PhD students in Malaysia (Ismail & Abiddin, 2009), attributable to such problematic supervisory relations.

In sum, language and culture have been shown to play a significant role in international students' adjustment and academic success across a range of Western and non-Western settings. While this article addresses the need for more study about international students (especially from the Global South), it also tackles a conceptual shortcoming in Western and non-Western literature. The current literature separates language and culture into two discrete pillars, highlighting how students encounter *either* cross-cultural differences (e.g., culturally distinct preferences in communication style) *or* linguistic issues (e.g., difficulties writing in English). Such a division overlooks how language and culture are interconnected human phenomena, as established by scholars in linguistic anthropology (Agar, 1994). We therefore turn to Risager's (2006, 2020) concept of 'linguaculture' and Astin's (1993) 'I-E-O' model as part of the theoretical framework to instead explore how the interface of language and culture influences postgraduate international students' experience of academic and social adjustments and thereby shapes their academic success.

THEORETICAL FRAMEWORK

Astin's (1993) Input-Environment-Output (I-E-O) model provided a starting point. It posits that academic success is a function of the interaction between a set of students and environment-specific factors. Input could include characteristics of the student at the time of initial entry to the institution such as race, high aspirations, and past educational experiences. Environment is described as "the various programs, policies, faculty, peers and educational experiences to which the student is exposed" (p. 7). Outcome or output refers to students' academic achievement in terms of grades, degree completion, critical thinking, attitudes, values, beliefs, and behaviors after exposure to the environment element. The model indicates that the individual student who takes part in the environment or educational experience tends to have an impact on their own development and outcomes (Astin, 1976).

Risager's (2006, 2020) writing on the concept of 'linguaculture'—"a domain of experience that fuses and intermingles the vocabulary, many semantic aspects of grammar, and verbal aspects of culture" (Friedrich, 1989, p. 306, quoted by Risager, 2020)—offered a framework for analyzing the mutually imbricated nature of language and culture. She identified three inter-related dimensions of linguaculture:

- constancy and variability in the semantics (relating to the meaning of words independent of context) and pragmatics (meaning in relation to context) of individual languages and language use, including how discourses circulate meanings beyond specific languages;
- the poetics of language (e.g., rhythms or puns as authors play with the form and content of language); and
- the identity dimension of language, related to social and personal variations in language use, which shows that language is never a neutral phenomenon. For example, English has considerable symbolic power as *lingua franca* in the hierarchy of global languages produced by imperial histories (Sharifian & Sadeghpour, 2020).

Linguaculture is part of the linguistic resources of an individual, and, according to Risager, will vary depending on whether the language a person (the student) is using is their first, second, or a foreign language (for purposes of written or oral communication). Individuals develop and have an intimate relationship with their linguaculture in their first/native language. They will draw upon that linguaculture when learning (or using) a foreign language and transfer associated cultural and social experiences from the mother tongue into this new linguistic and cultural realm.

According to Risager, the task for the language learner (or international student using a foreign language) was

> to establish an association between his/her *new* language and his/her life experiences and cultural knowledge, and this task has to be accomplished on the basis of a growing understanding of some of the life experiences and cultural knowledge common among first language speakers. (2020, p. 117)

When externalized through writing or speaking, an individual's linguaculture shows their communicative intentions and exhibits a high degree of semantic and pragmatic variabilities. Readers/listeners in turn interpret these intentions/texts through their own linguaculture. We use this framework to answer the research question: *How do language and culture pose adjustment challenges that hinder the academic success of postgraduate international students?*

METHOD

Research Design and Setting

This article is part of a wider study into international students' understanding of academic success. It adopts an interpretive methodology underpinned by hermeneutic phenomenology (van Manen, 1990), which "addresses experience from the perspectives of meanings, understandings and interpretations" (Pernecky & Jamal, 2010, p. 1056). It is appropriate for this study, given the interests in language and culture, and how postgraduate international students make sense, and thus meaning, of the lived experiences that arise from their adjustment to a new academic environment. It also aligns with qualitative emphasis on studying phenomena of interest from the viewpoint of research participants, and with due regard to context (Tracy, 2020).

Malaysia as a setting for this study is a key part of the research design and sampling. It is in the Global South, whose universities have growing numbers of international postgraduate students whose first language is not English but who are taught in English. Malaysia is a student hub (Knight, 2014) based on the exponential growth of international students in recent years (Ministry of Education [ME], 2019).

The Federation of Malaya gained political independence from Britain in 1957 (Lee, 2004) and became Malaysia in 1963. As of 2020, its population was 32.7 million; its multiethnic and multilingual society is 69.6% Bumiputra (Malay ethnicity), 22.6% Chinese, 6.8% Indians, and 1.0% other ethnicities (Department of Statistics Malaysia [DSM], 2020). Bahasa Melayu is the official language and widely used by Malaysians in verbal and written communication. English is the second language, but it is the medium of instruction at Malaysian higher learning institutions. This is the contemporary linguistic context of Malaysian universities in the neoliberal international education space where English is the lingua franca.

PARTICIPANTS

The study is based on qualitative interviews with 55 participants all based at a Malaysian research-intensive public university: 33 postgraduate international students (IS), 12 professional staff (PS), and 10 academic staff (AS). Purposive and snowball sampling methods were used to identify and recruit participants, including professional staff providing academic and non-academic support services to students (rarely covered in international student research). We deployed snowball sampling where research participants accepted for participation were then invited to suggest the names of other students who might be interested in participating (Minichiello et al., 2008). The study was conducted with institutional ethics approval (74/11PG) and confidentiality and anonymity of all participants and the university itself were assured. The majority of the student participants were from Iran, India, Iraq, Yemen, Indonesia, and China, and thus representative of the countries that dominate the postgraduate international student profile. Because the majority of such students are enrolled in popular courses in pharmacy, education, communication, architecture, and humanities, the majority of participants are drawn from these courses, as illustrated in Table 1. There were in total 33 postgraduate students interviewed in this study.

Table 1: Postgraduate International Students (IS)

Information		Number
Gender	Male	21
	Female	12
Total		**33**
Nationality	India	4
	Iraq	4
	Iran	4
	Yemen	3
	Nigeria	3
	China	3
	Indonesia	3
	Sri Lanka	2
	Pakistan	2
	Cambodia	1
	Bangladesh	1
	Somalia	1
Faculty	Pharmacy	5
	Education	5
	Communication	4
	Humanities	3
	Computer Science	3

Information		Number
	Architecture	3
	Biology	2
	Management	2
	Language	2
	Industrial Technology	1
	Physics	1
	Mathematics	1
	Business	1
	PhD	23
	Masters	10
	0–11 months	8
	1st year	10
	2nd year	4
Degree	3rd year	5
	4th year	3
Length of Candidature	5th year	1
	Graduated	2

Professional and academic staff came from a number of areas and Faculties. Table 2 shows academic staff members demographic details. There were in total 10 academic staff members interviewed for this study.

Table 2: Academic Staff (AS)

Information		Number
Gender	Male	7
	Female	3
Position	Dean	2
	Deputy Dean for Graduate Study	1
	Deputy Dean for Postgraduate and Research	2
	Senior Lecturer	2
	Language Instructor	1
	Language Coordinator	1
	Lecturer	1
Male	Professor	2
	Associate Professor	5
Female	Professor	1
	Language Teachers	2

A total of 12 professional staff participated from the Postgraduate Student Office, language support services, the library, and housing administration and faculties that offer academic assistance to postgraduate international students. Table 3 presents their demographic details.

Table 3: Professional Staff (PS)

Information		Number
Gender	Female	8
	Male	4
Position	Deputy Registrar	1
	Assistant Registrar	3
	Senior Assistant Registrar	1

Information		Number
	Residential Manager	2
	Librarian	3
	Statistical Administrator	1
	Editing Advisor	1
Department	Postgraduate Student Office	6
	Library	3
	Hostel	2
	Faculty	1

PROCEDURES

Semi-structured interviews were utilized. They are the most common method of data collection in qualitative and phenomenological research to obtain, understand, unfold, and explore in-depth the experiential views of participants (Kvale, 2007). The first author conducted face-to-face interviews over a three-month period. All interviews (except with one professional staff member who spoke in Malay) were conducted in English, audio-recorded (with participants' permission) and transcribed. Interviews lasted between 45 and 60 mins and the average length was 49 mins. The interview schedule for the wider study included questions about participant demographics, interviewees' understanding and experiences of academic success, factors and challenges that affect it, and how the university supports it. The first author was the interview facilitator to whom participants could reveal their perspectives and experiences of academic success. This required consistent effort on her behalf to avoid moving too fast in the interview and imposing preconceived thoughts on the phenomena under investigation (Green & Bowden, 2009).

ANALYSIS

Van Manen's (1990) method of thematic analysis was used to code the data. The first author adopted an inductive approach to first manually analyse, code, and generate a thematic map (Braun & Clarke, 2006). The coding process began with selecting the shortest transcript from each participant group and separately assigning key words or phrases that describe what the meaning the participants wished to convey about their experiences (Tesch, 1990). Van Manen's (1990) selective reading approach was adopted to see which phrases represent the phenomena under investigation. The first author asked "What statement(s) or phrases(s) seem particularly essential or revealing about the phenomenon or experience being described" to formulate meanings (van Manen, 1990, p. 93). The next step was to group similar sub-codes and redundant codes; this reduced the list to a smaller and more manageable number of codes (Braun & Clarke, 2006; Tesch, 1990). The first author highlighted quotes which supported the codes (Creswell, 2008; Tesch, 1990). As the coding process progressed and themes emerged, the analysis became more structured and organized (Ezzy, 2002). Reduction of codes then led to establishment of themes, and interpretation of data in relation to the research question.

RESULTS

The two main sets of adjustment-related challenges reported by participants as impacting their academic success were academic and social challenges. Figure 1 presents the thematic map of these and is used to structure the findings.

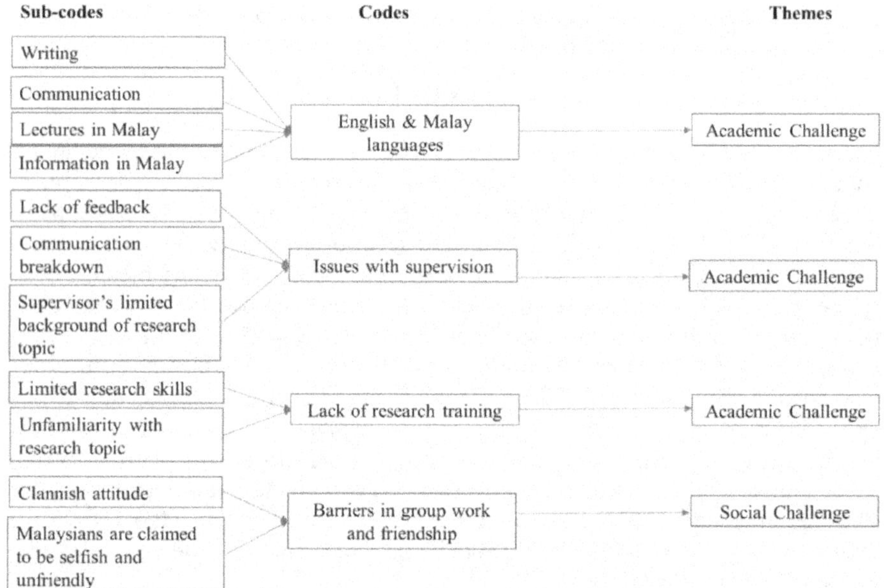

Figure 1: Thematic Structure

ACADEMIC CHALLENGES

English and Malay Language Challenges

English proficiency was perceived as a barrier to academic success. Students specifically reported issues with grammar and sentence structure in their communications in English, similar to Novera's (2004) finding. Academic staff also found that some students from Middle Eastern countries (first language Arabic) tend to have problems with the way they write Roman alphabets. Although these students have their IELTS/TOEFL scores as an admission requirement, there are issues when they translate Arabic words into English. Arabic has a 28-letter alphabet (all consonants), whereas English alphabet has 26 letters, including vowels. Arabic letters take on different shapes depending on whether they are the initial, medial, or final (Auty et al., 1993). As a result, students are confused when writing the Roman alphabet if they have limited writing experience in English:

> They come from a background where they have been trained to follow the wrong structure, and some of them have problems with their writing of the alphabet also *(AS 7, Female, Language Instructor).*

In regard to sentence structure, an editor explained that Middle Eastern students with Arabic as native tongue struggle with English grammar and using conversational language, as opposed to academic style language, which leads to mistakes:

> These students, especially from Arab countries, they have a tendency to write long sentences without full stops, and then, of course, the grammatical problems. They have the knowledge, but if you cannot express yourself properly, it is difficult to carry yourself at the international level *(PS 7, Male, Editor).*

International students also reported the tendency to think in their mother tongue first before translating their ideas into English and writing in English:

> I had a slight problem with changing the language. My problem was not really with my English but having a thought in my mind in Persian, but to write in English was not so easy. I couldn't find the best word to write. Sometimes I just translated them and it was not a good translation *(IS 10, Female, Iran).*

Such practical difficulties can certainly have an impact on the quality of students' written work and articulation of ideas. This may hinder students' academic success in terms of non-timely study completion because they can take a longer time to complete assignments or theses (Mori, 2000). A student pointed out that he faced challenges in writing his PhD thesis:

> I still have a lot to go because thesis writing is very tough. However, I am planning within six months I will finish it *(IS 18, Male, Bangladesh).*

A Master's student argued that thesis or assignment writing is a very difficult task as you need to perfect your writing in English, and this requires many drafts and redrafts, and a lot of time: "If we are unable to write to some academic standards, we are unable to receive good grades for our assignments" (IS 29, Male, Yemen), and

> English is our second language; so, when you write your assignment or thesis, this is a very difficult task. You need to write ten times over anything you write and rewrite, but you don't have the enough time to do it, especially in the course work, as you have limited time to do your

assignment and if you don't do your assignments neatly you don't have good marks at the end.

Academic staff associated communication challenges mainly with the *viva-voce* or oral examination. The *viva-voce* is a mandatory requirement for postgraduate students to defend their Master's or doctoral research project at Malaysian universities. According to staff, international students were sometimes unable to understand basic questions posed by panel members. In an extreme case, international students might experience academic failure due to their lack of English language competency. A Deputy Dean pointed out that international students tend to experience problems in their *viva-voce*:

> When it comes to the viva, who will talk on behalf of them, how would you defend yourself? So, there are students who couldn't do that. They fail maybe *(AS 6, Male, Deputy Dean)*.

He added: *'We have seen many students who couldn't cope or were demotivated because of the language barrier.'*

Students in this study had not only experienced difficulties in English. They also faced challenges in communicating in Bahasa Melayu, particularly if they themselves were Indonesians. They are, however, permitted to write their theses in Bahasa Melayu due to its linguistic similarities with Bahasa Indonesia. Thus, while the medium of instruction is English, some flexibility is applied in the case of Indonesian students to allow them to write either in English or in Bahasa Melayu, but, according to academics, even with this choice, Indonesian students tend to write their thesis in Bahasa Indonesia, which is not one of the two approved languages:

> The Indonesian students, they feel that it is easy here, because we have the common language, yet the language is still a problem for Indonesians, because you have to write in the Malay language, not the Indonesian language. Indonesian students write in the Indonesian language. It is better to ask them to write in English, because certain words are simply vulgar: the meaning is different *(AS 6, Male, Deputy Dean)*.

The structure of sentences and some specific words do not convey accurate definitions in both languages. As a result, academic staff members tend to edit and revise students' writing style. This may contribute to non-timely completion and poorly written quality of theses and publications. A PhD student commented: *'It is not just getting PhD within the time frame but completing with quality'* *(IS 30, Male, Nigeria)*.

Further, international students acknowledged that they faced problems in lectures and tutorials, because lecturers unconsciously or habitually used Malay to teach or to convey information, which impacted students' learning processes and led to feelings of exclusion:

> The lecturer will give a lecture in the Malay language. There is a tutorial for two hours in Bahasa. There are only a few sentences in English and

most, 90%, in Bahasa. Some slides were in English, so I can read them, but the lecture is mixed English and Bahasa in the teaching *(IS 7, Male, Somalia).*

Similar findings emerged in a Korean study (Kim, 2019), which reported that Korean was used in classrooms and had great influence on international students' academic socialization in class.

A Palestinian Master's student claimed that she faced difficulties in catching up on course materials due to the mixed languages used by lecturers:

Lecturers use Bahasa and English during the class, so I face some difficulties in this case, as it is difficult for international students to understand, to get the idea [behind it] *(IS 19, Female, Palestine).*

Newly arrived international students reported facing issues understanding information in Malay on campus noticeboards. Lack of understanding of Malay affected their academic success, because they were unable to comprehend vital information such as timetables or non-academic activities that could help them excel:

I read the notice board, I read banners, but all of them are in Malay. Every poster, every word is in Malay, and that sometimes irritates me. I find it very difficult, because I am yet to register in the Malay [language class] *(IS 25, Female, Pakistan).*

If it is written in English and Malay, we can learn. All is written in Bahasa. Even if we try to search it is difficult, and, in the timetable, it might be written in Bahasa *(IS 7, Male, Somalia).*

Malay language classes are offered to international students, and it is a requirement for all international students to pass in Malay before they graduate. It is recommended that international students take these classes in their first semester to assist them in their learning and social environment.

Issues With Supervision

Previous scholars have linked lack of supervision to differences or conflicts between supervisors and students in terms of cultural misunderstanding, lack of day-to-day contact, inadequate critical supervision that offers analysis and evaluation of work in progress, and time management (Abiddin & West, 2007; Krauss & Ismail, 2010). The findings here echo these themes, with students citing disorganized meeting appointments, feedback that lacks specificity or focus, and supervisor availability (because supervisors may have too many postgraduate students and they themselves may hold multiple leadership roles. Such issues were barriers to effective supervision:

My supervisor is very busy and when I pass my chapters to her, she needs a lot of time to read and give feedback to me. So that's the big challenge for me. She has a lot of students, so she is extremely busy with them too.

> She is also a Deputy Dean and also at the same time she needs to travel
> a lot. She doesn't have a lot of time to correct so many students' work
> and at the same time she is a lecturer *(IS 6, Female, Indonesia)*.

Due to the university's status, academic staff members have experienced increases
in their workload in recent years. The ratio of graduate students to supervisors has
increased, high-impact research needs to be conducted, and additional
administrative work is required, coupled with increased teaching workload.
Limited supervisor expertise in students' research topics was also an issue:

> Sometimes you feel your supervisor is disconnected from your field or
> on what you are going to do or what you are thinking. You feel you didn't
> make progress or fail in making progress. This is the main measure that
> makes me feel depressed *(IS 8, Male, Palestine)*.

Some students were prompted to take the extreme measure of changing their
supervisors:

> We notice now that the conflicts between the international students and
> the supervisor are increasing. For example, they always ask to change
> their supervisor, because they are having problems with their supervisor
> in terms of interaction, communication, human relations – I think
> because of the different backgrounds and different cultures *(PS 3,
> Female, Assistant Registrar)*.

While the government's Internationalisation Policy document (Ministry of Higher
Education [MHE], 2011) states that universities are responsible for providing
positive learning experiences to international students, these supervision
challenges undermine students' engagement and experience. Notably, no students
raised any concerns in regard to their supervisors' English proficiency during
supervision.

Lack of Research Training

International students from Arab and Asian countries acknowledge that they
have insufficient research knowledge due to their limited research experience in
their previous education systems. For example, a Yemeni student observed that
research was never a part of his undergraduate or Master's degrees in Yemen:

> I did my Bachelor and Master's degrees in my [home] country. So the
> academic challenge first [in the new country] was I didn't have the
> knowledge about doing research, the steps that should be done for
> preparing proposals, how to deal with databases, trying to analyse the
> articles you read, what are the things that you should read – is it articles
> only or books? *(IS 4, Male, Yemen)*.

Another student from Cambodia mentioned that only document analysis was
primarily used for research in his home country. He, therefore, faced difficulties

in understanding research methods in Malaysia, especially in initial years of candidature:

> Research method in my country is different. During the French time, there was only a focus on reading documents and then we can compile and analyse the documents. So here I need to conduct interviews. It is different. My background is law, so I changed to study education. This [new study field] was so different, and [hence] difficult for me *(IS 15, Male, Cambodia).*

Limited awareness of research culture was reported as impeding their research growth in terms of preparing a research proposal, reading and analyzing articles and books, conducting research, and writing thesis-related chapters. While Ismail and Abiddin (2009) claimed that issues of unfamiliarity with research topics and lack of research methodology knowledge are normal experiences faced by postgraduate international students, at this university this affected students' academic success in terms of timely completion: it took longer to start projects and completion tended to exceed the official timeframe:

> I should find the topic, the area and the gaps. It was very difficult to find the topic: I read for a year and a half, and I want to start to do it, but I don't find what to do, then I change the topic, I change the topic, [and] after a year and half I change the topic again. 'What is the objective you want to do, what is your contribution?' The topic is quite difficult for me *(IS 13, Male, Yemen).*

SOCIAL CHALLENGES

Barriers in Group Work and Friendship

International students faced barriers in group work with Malaysian students, which impacted their friendship. This study found negative perceptions on Malaysian students' personal characteristics. For example, local students were labelled selfish, for example, in not sharing research information, they were seen as unfriendly and limited discussion around stimulating ideas in group assignments. Group work issues impacted formation of friendships with domestic students, and in consequence international students were sometimes unable to complete their assignments:

> The way to study, to do group assignments, for us is really different with them. They start to do something, then they don't share with you. And then, whenever we ask them to explain to us what they are doing, they don't do anything. [That's the] end of the assignment, because we don't have any discussion. That's why we've got problems with the assignment, we cannot finish sometimes, also, the relationship between us and the Malaysian students. They don't explain. They just expect you do all the things *(IS 17, Female, Iraq).*

Malaysians are also considered to have a 'clannish' attitude. This is because they only make friends with the same race groups, according to student participants:

> In my country we don't have races. There was difficulty in trying to make friendship and communicate with Malaysians, with all races. We can say that Indians, they are friends with Indians, Malays are friends with Malays, and Chinese, they are friends with Chinese. I think there are barriers between friendship relationships between foreigners and Malaysian students *(IS 4, Male, Yemen)*.

This factor is also identified in Trahar (2014), where it is reported as apparent unwillingness of these three local ethnic groups to integrate; this reluctance may 'complicate' the international dimension if there is less integration between Malaysian and international students. Studies have suggested that such 'dis-integration' further impacts postgraduate international students' academic success because they are unable to experience international (Malaysian) life and communication barriers impede research ideas and study discussion (Singh & Jack, 2018). While studies (Nguyen, 2013; Zhu & Bresnahan, 2018) have claimed that international students are unreceptive to befriending local students, however, this study has found the opposite to be the case.

DISCUSSION

The purpose of this study was to investigate the role of language and culture in the adjustment issues that have an impact on the academic success of postgraduate international students in a particular university. In terms of Astin's model, the notion of linguaculture provides a novel variable of study that can advance understanding of international students' adjustment. Linguaculture may be viewed as both input (characteristics of the individual student) and linked to particular facets of the institutional environment (e.g., as manifest in the use of English as the official language of classroom instruction) within Astin's model.

The study addresses two limitations in the literature. The first is the need for more studies about international students whose first language is not English, and undertaking postgraduate degrees delivered primarily in English at non-Western institutions. Second, while studies have shown the role of cross-cultural differences and linguistic matters in international student adjustment, they are conceptually limited in not recognizing the interconnected nature of culture and language. Accordingly, we now discuss the results through the conceptual lens of 'linguaculture.'

The results section showed linguistic and cultural issues to be embedded in a series of academic and social adjustment challenges and reported by all participants to be detrimental to academic success. Risager's (2006) concept of linguaculture assisted in analysis as to how the *interface* of language and culture across different dimensions is at work. First, we view some challenges reported as related to the semantic and pragmatic dimensions of linguaculture. Prominent empirical instances include the academic and support staff reports on weaknesses in Arabic-first-language Middle Eastern students' use of English in written texts, and international students' difficulties expressing themselves verbally in English in oral examinations. Academic staff also criticize Indonesian students' unreflective and problematic use of Bahasa Melayu in thesis writing. It is also evident in students' accounts of their time-consuming cognitive approaches to translating literally from their first language to English before moving to speech or writing.

Second, the ambivalence and frustration of everyday experiences of international students are connected to the pragmatics of language and identity dimensions of linguaculture. Students noted that teachers made inconsistent use of English as the mandated language for classroom work, they posted important notice-board signs in Bahasa Melayu rather than English. There were difficulties, too, in undertaking group work with local Malaysian students and these thwarted opportunities for friendships among students from different backgrounds. Challenges reported by all participants about students' research and methodological knowledge—that is, the particular academic discourse and its domain-specific meanings and practices—transcended the boundaries of particular (national) linguistic and cultural groups. These difficulties played out in students' questioning of their budding academic identities and competencies.

We argue that these semantic, pragmatic, and identity dimensions of linguaculture in the data show that language and culture do matter in postgraduate international students' academic and social adjustment, but they also point to *how* they matter. They matter because they constitute barriers that undermine and frustrate opportunities for postgraduate international students to experience linguacultural development in academic and social settings during overseas study. Whether in classroom settings, feedback on grammar and writing or barriers to group integration, students are thwarted in their attempts to develop associations between their new language and existing life experience or cultural knowledge through "a growing understanding of some of the life experiences and cultural knowledge common among first language speakers" (Risager, 2020, p. 117). As a result, students are unable to access and accumulate the resources needed to fully operate interculturally and cross-linguistically in their new context, and to develop successful academic subjectivities. Such an interpretation does not seek to sideline the role of proficiencies in the English and Bahasa languages, or of cross-cultural differences as important issues in and of themselves. Instead, by considering the human experiential domain that "fuses and intermingles the vocabulary, many semantic aspects of grammar, and verbal aspects of culture" (Friedrich, 1989, p. 306, quoted by Risager, 2020), we offer a novel line of argument that explains how international student adjustment and the students' academic success is linked fundamentally to linguacultural development—to the inextricability of language and culture in the experience of international students.

LIMITATIONS AND FUTURE DIRECTIONS

The generalizability of this study is limited contextually, since its findings are based on information gathered from semi-structured interviews from a single public research university in Malaysia. It is also limited to a sample of postgraduate students. Further research could overcome these limits by using a mixed-methods research design from a wider range of public and private educational institutions in Malaysia. It could extend such research to other cultures and language backgrounds. Scholars could also investigate whether the insights presented here are echoed in the experiences of undergraduate international students at similar universities. Future studies could use ethnographic methods to document interactions and teaching and learning challenges faced by international students in lectures and tutorials in real time. We contend that the analytic generalizability of the findings lies in the use of the concept of linguaculture to interpret the results. Future work related to the role played by language and culture in research on the linkages between international student adjustment and academic success will benefit from further deployment of this notion.

CONCLUSION

This article has examined the role of language and culture in generating adjustment-related challenges that have an impact on international students' academic success. It is based on a qualitative interview study of postgraduate international students, academic and support staff at a Malaysian public university. The article pushes beyond linguistic deficit or cross-cultural arguments to suggest that postgraduate international students' academic success is a reflection of the extent to which they are given opportunities to engage in linguacultural development in their new educational setting.

The article may have implications for policy and practice in Malaysian universities, first of all, because Malaysia is the country under study and higher education the principal sector. Targeted and specific institutional programs oriented by language and cultural nuances may need to be offered to postgraduate international students. Universities may not only offer English but also Bahasa Melayu programs to support language proficiency and broader cultural understanding. On the student side, it is vital that students participate in any such programs, engage in institutional student orientation and workshops on supervision, and systematically address language and research training. A policy stating that all lecturers and tutors must use English as the medium of instruction in classrooms seems important to ensure inclusivity in the learning and teaching process. Malaysian research policy and supervision practices need to be clearly communicated to postgraduate international students via a Handbook and compulsory workshops. Finally, academic and support staff might be offered regular cross-cultural training, including introduction to the concept of linguaculture.

REFERENCES

Abiddin, N. Z., & West, M. (2007). Effective meeting in graduate research student supervision. *Journal of Social Sciences, 3*(1), 27–35. http://doi.org/10.2139/ssrn.962230

Agar, M. (1994). *Language shock: Understanding the culture of communication.* William Morrow.

Alsahafi, N., & Shin, S. C. (2017). Factors affecting the academic and cultural adjustment of Saudi international students in Australian universities. *Journal of International Students, 7*(1), 53–72. https://doi.org/10.32674/jis.v7i1

Al-Zubaidi, K. O., & Rechards, C. (2010). Arab postgraduate students in Malaysia: Identifying and overcoming the cultural and language barriers. *Arab World English Journal, 1*(1), 107–129. http://doi.org/10.2139/ssrn.2777058

Andrade, M. S. (2006). International students in English-speaking universities: Adjustment factors. *Journal of Research in International Education, 5*(2), 131–154. https://doi.org/10.1177/1475240906065589

Astin, A. W. (1976). *Academic gamesmanship: Student-oriented change in higher education.* Praeger.

Astin, A. W. (1993). *What matters in college?* Jossey Bass.

Auty, N., Holes, C., & Harris, R. (1993). *Just listen 'n learn Arabic.* McGraw-Hill.

Braun, V., & Clarke, V. (2006). Using thematic analysis in psychology. *Qualitative Research in Psychology, 3*(2), 77–101. https://doi.org/10.1191/1478088706QP063OA

Brown, L. (2008). Language and anxiety: An ethnographic study of international postgraduate students. *Evaluation & Research in Education, 21*(2), 75–95. https://doi.org/10.1080/09500790802152167

Campbell, J., & Li, M. (2008). Asian students' voices: An empirical study of Asian students' learning experiences at a New Zealand university. *Journal of Studies in International Education, 12*(4), 375–396. https://doi.org/10.1177/1028315307299422

Creswell, J. W. (2008). *Educational research: Planning, conducting and evaluating quantitative and qualitative research* (3rd ed.). Pearson Prentice Hall.

Department of Statistics Malaysia. (2020). *Current population estimates, Malaysia, 2020.* https://www.dosm.gov.my/v1/index.php?r=column/pdfPrev&id=OVByWjg5YkQ3MWFZRTN5bDJiaEVhZz09

Ezzy, D. (2002). *Qualitative analysis: Practice and innovation.* Routledge.

Green, P., & Bowden, J. A. (2009). Principles of developmental phenomenography. *Malaysian Journal of Qualitative Research, 2*(2), 55–74.

Ismail, A., & Abiddin, N. Z. (2009). The importance of graduate students' needs on supervisory contribution in a Malaysian public university. *The Social Sciences, 4*(4), 355–365. https://medwelljournals.com/abstract/?doi=sscience.2009.355.365

Kim, J. (2019). International students' intercultural sensitivity in their academic socialisation to a non-English-speaking higher education: A Korean case study. *Journal of Further and Higher Education*, 1–17. https://doi.org/10.1080/0309877X.2019.1627298

Kim, Y. (2007). Difficulties in quality doctoral academic advising: Experiences of Korean students. *Journal of Research in International Education, 6*(2), 171–193. https://doi.org/10.1177/1475240907078613

Knight, J. (2014). Introduction. In J. Knight (Ed.), *International education hubs: Student, talent, knowledge-innovation models* (pp. 1–12). Springer.

Krauss, S. E., & Ismail, I. A. (2010). PhD students' experiences of thesis supervision in Malaysia: Managing relationships in the midst of institutional change. *The Qualitative Report, 15*(4), 802–822.

Kvale, S. (2007). *Doing interviews*. Sage Publications.

Lee, M. N. N. (2004). *Restructuring higher education in Malaysia* (Vol. Monograph Series No: 4/2004). Universiti Sains Malaysia, School of Educational Studies.

Li, G., Chen, W., & Duanmu, J.-L. (2010). Determinants of international students' academic performance: A comparison between Chinese and other international students. *Journal of Studies in International Education, 14*(4), 389–405. https://doi.org/10.1177/1028315309331490

Li, J., Wang, Y., & Xiao, F. (2014). East Asian international students and psychological well-being: A systematic review. *Journal of International Students, 4*(4), 301–313. https://www.ojed.org/index.php/jis/article/view/450

Malaklolunthu, S., & Selan, P. S. (2011). Adjustment problems among international students in Malaysian private higher education institutions. *Procedia – Social and Behavioral Sciences, 15*, 833–837. https://doi.org/10.1016/j.sbspro.2011.03.194

Minichiello, V., Aroni, R., & Hays, T. (2008). *In-depth interviewing: Principles, techniques, analysis* (3rd ed.). Pearson Education Australia.

Ministry of Education (2019). *2018 Higher education statistics*. Kuala Lumpur.

Ministry of Higher Education. (2011). *Internationalisation policy for higher education Malaysia 2011*. Kuala Lumpur.

Mori, S. C. (2000). Addressing the mental health concerns of international students. *Journal of Counseling and Development, 78*(2), 137–144. https://doi.org/10.1002/j.1556-6676.2000.tb02571.x

Nadeem, A., Pratt, C. B., & Bo, S. (2015). Factors in the cross-cultural adaptation of African students in Chinese universities. *Journal of Research in International Education, 14*(2), 98–113. https://doi.org/10.1177/1475240915592107

Nguyen, H. M. (2013). Faculty advisors' experiences with international graduate students. *Journal of International Students, 3*(2), 102–116. https://doi.org/10.32674/jis.v3i2.504

Novera, I. A. (2004). Indonesian postgraduate students studying in Australia: An examination of their academic, social and cultural experiences. *International Education Journal, 5*(4), 475–487.

Pernecky, T., & Jamal, T. (2010). (Hermeneutic) phenomenology in tourism studies. *Annals of Tourism Research, 37*(4), 1055–1075. https://doi.org/10.1016/j.annals.2010.04.002

Risager, K. (2006). *Language and culture: Global flows and local complexity.* Multilingual Matters.

Risager, K. (2020). Linguaculture & transnationality. In J. Jackson (Ed.), *The Routledge handbook of language and intercultural communication* (2nd ed., pp. 109–123). Routledge.

Ren, J., & Hagedorn, L. S. (2012). International graduate students' academic performance: What are the influencing factors? *Journal of International Students, 2*(2), 135–143. http://lib.dr.iastate.edu/edu_pubs/4

Sam, R., Zain, A. N. M., Jamil, H. B., Souriyavongsa, T., & Quyen, L. T. D. (2013). Academic adjustment issues in Malaysian research university: The case of Cambodian, Laotian, Burmese and Vietnamese postgraduate students' experiences. *International Education Studies, 6*(9), 13–22. http://doi.org/10.5539/ies.v6n9p13

Shafaei, A., & Abd Razak, N. (2016). International postgraduate students' cross-cultural adaptation in Malaysia: Antecedents and outcomes. *Research in Higher Education, 57*(6), 739–767. https://doi.org/10.1007/s11162-015-9404-9

Sharifian, F., & Sadeghpour, M. (2020) World Englishes and intercultural communication. In J. Jackson (Ed.), *The Routledge handbook of language and intercultural communication* (2nd ed., pp. 299–311). Routledge.

Sherry, M., Thomas, P., & Wing, C. H. (2010). International students: A vulnerable student population. *Higher Education, 60*(1), 33–46. https://doi.org/10.1007/s10734-009-9284-z

Sidhu, G. K., Kaur, S., Fook, C. Y., & Yunus, F. W. (2014). Postgraduate supervision: Comparing student perspectives from Malaysia and the United Kingdom. *Procedia-Social and Behavioral Sciences, 123*, 151–159. https://doi.org/10.1016/j.sbspro.2014.01.1409

Singh, J. K. N. (2018). What are the factors that contribute to postgraduate international students' academic success? A Malaysian qualitative study. *Higher Education Research & Development, 37*(5), 1035–1049. https://doi.org/10.1080/07294360.2018.1467383

Singh, J. K. N., & Jack, G. (2018). The benefits of overseas study for international postgraduate students in Malaysia. *Higher Education, 75*(4), 607–624. https://doi.org/10.1007/s10734-017-0159-4

Talebloo, B., & Baki, R. B. (2013). Challenges faced by international postgraduate students during their first year of studies. *International Journal of Humanities and Social Science, 3*(13), 138–145.

Tesch, R. (1990). *Qualitative research: Analysis types and software tools.* The Falmer Press.

Tian, M., & Lu, G. (2018). Intercultural learning, adaptation, and personal growth: A longitudinal investigation of internantional student experiences in China. *Frontiers of Education in China, 13*(1), 56–92. https://doi.org/10.1007/s11516-018-0003-3

Tracy, S. (2020). *Qualitative research methods: Collecting evidence, creating analysis, communicating impact*. Wiley Blackwell.

Trahar, S. (2014). 'This is Malaysia. You have to follow the custom here': Narratives of the student and academic experience in international higher education in Malaysia. *Journal of Education for Teaching: International Research and Pedagogy, 40*(3), 217–231. https://doi.org/10.1080/02607476. 2014.903023

van Manen, M. (1990). *Researching lived experience: Human science for an action sensitive pedagogy*. Althouse Press/Routledge.

Wolf, D. M., & Phung, L. (2019). Studying in the United States: Language learning challenges, strategies and support services. *Journal of International Students, 9*(1), 211–224. https://doi.org/10.32674/jis.v9i1.273

Xiong, Y., & Zhou, Y. (2018). Understanding East Asian graduate students' socio-cultural and psychological adjustment in a U.S. midwestern university. *Journal of International Students, 8*(2), 769–794. https://doi.org/10.32674/jis.v8i2.103

Yassin, A. A., Abdul Razak, N., Qasem, Y. A., & Saeed Mohammed, M. A. (2020). Intercultural learning challenges affecting international students' sustainable learning in Malaysian higher education institutions. *Sustainability, 12*(18), 7490. https://doi.org/10.3390/su12187490

Zhu, Y., & Bresnahan, M. (2018). "They make nocontribution!" versus "We should make friends with them!"—American domestic students' perception of Chinese international students' reticence and face. *Journal of International Students, 8*(4), 1614–1635. https://doi.org/10.32674/jis.v8i4.221

Dr JASVIR KAUR NACHATAR SINGH, PhD, is an award-winning Lecturer at the Department of Management, Sport and Tourism, La Trobe Business School, La Trobe University, Australia. Dr Singh's research expertise is in higher education with a particular interest in exploring international students' lived experiences of academic success, employability, career aspirations, and learning experiences in a blended learning environment. Dr Singh also explores lived experiences of international academics with leadership positions. Email: j.nachatarsingh@latrobe.edu.au

Dr GAVIN JACK, PhD, is the inaugural Associate Dean Research Impact and Professor of Management. His multidisciplinary research interests and expertise include workplace diversity and inclusion, postcolonial organization studies, sustainable agricultural development, and qualitative and critical management research methods. He has been a co-chair of the Critical Management Studies Division of the Academy of Management. Email: Gavin.Jack@monash.edu

Research Article

© *Journal of International Students*
Volume 12, Issue 2 (2022), pp. 467-488
ISSN: 2162-3104 (Print), 2166-3750 (Online)
doi: 10.32674/jis.v12i2.3198
ojed.org/jis

The Duality of Persistence: Academic Enclaves and International Students' Aspirations to Stay in the United States

Vasundhara Kaul
Linda Renzulli
Purdue University

ABSTRACT

International students have been a growing presence in U.S. higher education institutions for over a decade. Feelings of belonging play a crucial role in the adjustment of these students to campus life in American universities, and their co-nationals play a significant role in facilitating this adjustment process. However, the role of belonging and co-national communities in facilitating the persistence of international students toward and beyond degree attainment remains understudied. In our examination of the aspirations of 642 international students across 9 U.S. universities, we establish that stronger feelings of academic and social belonging are associated with a higher likelihood of aspiring to stay in the United States after graduation. In particular, we demonstrate the presence of an academic enclave effect wherein larger communities of co-nationals have a stronger influence on the aspirations of international students with low social belonging but does not affect the aspirations of socially well-integrated international students.

Keywords: belonging, ethnic enclaves, higher education, international graduate students, international students, student persistence

INTRODUCTION

Every year, tens of thousands of international students arrive in the United States to pursue their career ambitions in higher education (Institute

International Education [IIE], 2020a). For many, the beginning of their higher education journey also marks the start of the gradual process of incorporation into American society. A critical moment in this incorporation process is whether these students choose to stay in the United States upon graduating from their institutions. In this paper, we examine the factors that determine the outcome of this critical juncture in an international students' life. In particular, we ask two key questions: how do feelings of belonging shape international students' aspirations to stay in the United States? And how do university-level factors—co-national diversity specifically—alter this association?

The role of feelings of belonging in facilitating international students' adjustment to campus life (Glass & Gesing, 2018; Kaya, 2020; Tang et al., 2018; Wang & Freed, 2021) and its positive impact on international students' psycho-social well-being is well-established (Cho & Yu, 2015; Khanal & Gaulee, 2019). There is also a growing body of scholarship on recruitment and retention of international students. However, these studies primarily focus on factors such as institutional funding and support services, and immigration policy (Bista & Foster, 2011; Glass et al., 2013; Srivastava et al., 2010). The role of feelings of belonging in shaping the persistence of international students in U.S. higher education institutions remains understudied (Garcia et al., 2019; Mamiseishvili, 2012). Further, while the importance of co-nationals in engendering feelings of belonging amongst international students is recognized (Rivas et al., 2019; Tang et al., 2018), whether these groups create different paths of persistence for different groups of international students has not been examined.

Our concept of academic enclaves, defined as the concentration/density of students from the same country of origin (co-nationals) in the same university, provides a more nuanced model of international student persistence. In particular, we demonstrate the duality of structure (Giddens, 1979) wherein communities of co-nationals encourage persistence by facilitating feelings of belonging for one group of international students and have no effect on another group. We contribute to the scholarship on belonging of international students by demonstrating how these feelings in tandem with institutional characteristics give rise to heterogeneity in the international student experience and persistence in the United States.

LITERATURE REVIEW

Belonging and Persistence

We emphasize the importance of understanding the lived experiences of international students in this study instead of focusing on individual students' ability to incorporate themselves into the dominant culture of their universities. Since the concept of belonging acknowledges the inherent subjectivity of the incorporation process, we employ it to understand international students' experiences in higher education institutions. Further, we anticipate these feelings will play a critical role in ensuring the retention of international students just as they do for American students, particularly students of color (Hausmann et al., 2007; Museus et al., 2017).

Feelings of belonging are contingent on individual student characteristics as well as the student's evaluation of their educational environment. Belongingness is understood as the feeling of connectedness and the idea that one matters to others (Rosenberg & McCullough, 1981) and students' psychological sense of connection to their campus community (Hurtado & Carter, 1997). Belonging is also operationalized as a function of perceived support from peers, teachers, and family members (Johnson et al., 2007; Strayhorn, 2008). Drawing on Strayhorn's definition of belongingness as "students' perceived social support on campus, a feeling or sensation of connectedness, the experience of mattering or feeling cared about, accepted, respected, valued by, and important to the group (e.g., campus community) or others on campus (e.g., faculty, peers)" (2012, p. 3), we use a conceptual definition of belonging that allows us to examine how supported and included international students feel not only in their interactions but also with respect to the resources and networks they need to succeed.

Using the concept of belonging allows us to acknowledge that students engage in subjective evaluations of their integration which vary based on the context (Strayhorn, 2012) rather than adhering to a set of universal and objective criteria for integration. Further, it allows for the recognition that students' feelings of belonging can be fostered in multiple ways across different contexts and does not necessitate their integration into the dominant culture of the university. After all, "some student communities are developed as forms of resistance to the larger institutional culture, but they will still represent unique areas where students' views of themselves and their aspirations converge" (Strayhorn, 2012, p. x).

International Students' Belonging

Feelings of belonging often take on heightened significance in certain contexts and certain times (Strayhorn, 2012). One such instance is when individuals are in unfamiliar and foreign contexts where they are more likely to perceive themselves as being marginal to the mainstream life of college (Anderman & Freeman, 2004; Strayhorn et al., 2013). Academic and social interactions that constitute campus life in American universities present such unfamiliar and foreign contexts to international students. In fact, the marginalization and isolation that international students experience in U.S. universities, particularly in social interactions with American colleagues and local community members, is well documented (Kaya, 2020; Khanal & Gaulee, 2019; Wang & Freed, 2021). In addition to facilitating academic achievement and psychological well-being, feelings of belonging play a central role in facilitating the persistence of American students toward the final goal of degree attainment in higher education institutions (Maestas et al., 2007; Museus et al., 2017). Preliminary examinations of international undergraduate students' experiences in U.S. colleges also suggest that an increase in their sense of belonging reduces their withdrawal from college (Garcia et al., 2019; Mamiseishvili, 2012).

We build on this evidence in two key ways. First, we make international students' aspirations to stay in the United States after graduation our focal point of inquiry. Thus, we are able to extend the understanding of international student persistence beyond the commonly examined outcome of degree attainment. Although an international student's presence in the United States after graduation is constrained by several legal factors, aspirations to persist are foundational to the movement toward this final goal. We propose that these aspirations are indicative of the probability of international students transitioning into the U.S. labor market, an area of the immigrant experience that remains underexamined. Second, we only focus on graduate student experiences because being a graduate student comes with its own set of challenges which are distinct from the challenges faced by undergraduate students (Brunsting et al., 2018; Le et al., 2016).

Experiences of domestic and international students indicate the presence of two key dimensions to feelings of belonging—one engendered by the students' academic interactions (i.e., academic belonging) and another by the students' social ties (i.e., social belonging). Increased academic interactions and engagement—discussions with peers about course content, tutoring other students, frequent discussions with faculty members—are strongly associated with feelings of belonging (Horne et al., 2018; Hurtado & Carter, 1997; Maestas et al., 2007). Social interactions that result in the establishment of meaningful relationships with other students and faculty on campus and participation in student organizations also play an important role in bolstering feelings of belonging (Glass & Gesing, 2018; Hurtado & Carter, 1997; Strayhorn, 2012; Yao, 2016). Further, preliminary evidence also suggests that academic and social integration influence international students' persistence in opposite directions (Mamiseishvili, 2012). Thus, we examine academic belonging and social belonging separately.

Given the centrality of feelings of belonging in reducing social isolation and improving academic achievement, we propose that international students' feelings of academic and social belonging are critical in determining their persistence within and beyond their universities in the United States. We hypothesize:

H1(a): International students with higher levels of academic belonging are more likely to aspire to stay in the United States than those with low levels of academic belonging.

H1(b): International students with high levels of social belonging are more likely to aspire to stay in the United States than those with low levels of social belonging.

The Academic Enclave Effect

Co-national students play a critical role in facilitating feelings of belonging for international students (Glass et al., 2013; Rivas et al., 2019; Tang et al., 2018). Students from the same country studying in U.S. universities help each other maintain connections with their home culture and language (Du & Wei, 2015; Rivas et al., 2019), provide alternatives to participating in mainstream campus culture (Rose-Redwood & Rose-Redwood, 2013), and are a source of valuable information on how to survive in a foreign country (Tang et al., 2018). Rather than assume that all international students respond similarly to the presence of co-nationals, we build on this evidence to examine whether the presence of co-nationals has a differential impact on the aspirations of persistence for different groups of graduate international students.

Drawing on the concept of ethnic enclaves, we propose that a concentration of international students from the same country in the same U.S. university creates "academic enclaves." Ethnic enclaves are best characterized as tight knit networks of co-ethnic migrants within a specific geographical location. Typically, these areas have a high concentration of residency and business operations of a particular migrant minority group that has a distinct cultural character (Hikido, 2018; Kosta, 2019; Toussaint-Comeau, 2008). Further, ethnic enclaves serve multiple economic and social functions including the provision of economic opportunities and encouraging feelings of belonging (Bouk et al., 2013; Portes & Manning, 2013).

The primary utility of ethnic enclaves lies in the close social networks that they help foster since these networks provide access to resources and help members navigate racial hostility and discrimination (Portes & Jensen, 1989; Portes & Manning, 2013). Close social networks serve similar functions for communities of co-national international students; they insulate their members from physical harm and social stigma, facilitate academic engagement, help in the maintenance of one's national identity, and facilitate social cohesion through cultural activities (Guo & Chase, 2011; Page, 2019). In our conceptualization, we emphasize the academic nature of enclaves because they are created by the transnational inflow of co-nationals into the very specific organizational setting of academic institutions.

While the importance of co-nationals in facilitating international students' feelings of belonging is well supported (Glass et al., 2013; Rivas et al., 2019; Tang et al., 2018), this evidence does not account for the heterogeneity in the distribution of international students across the United States. The overall population of international students is not equally distributed across all universities with some universities attracting larger proportions of international students than others (IIE, 2020c). Furthermore, not all nationalities are equally represented in the growing diversity of U.S. higher education institutions (IIE, 2020b). For instance, the international student population from China and India is usually larger than that from Somalia and Morocco. Thus, some nationalities in the international student community constitute an "ethnic majority" while others form an "ethnic minority" (Geven et al., 2016).

The ethnic density hypothesis posits that members of immigrant groups are more likely to experience better mental health outcomes when they are surrounded by higher proportions of people of the same ethnicity (Bécares & Nazroo, 2013; Das-Munshi et al., 2010). The presence of co-ethnics buffers the detrimental effects of interpersonal racism and discrimination on the health of ethnic minorities. Similar positive effects of co-ethnic ties in the form of social support and increased feelings of belonging have been noted for students studying in schools with a higher share of co-ethnics (Geven et al., 2016). Immigrants' income is also positively influenced as the proportion of co-ethnics living in their residential communities increases (Andersson et al., 2014).

Building on this density proposition, we anticipate that variations in the concentration of co-nationals of international students will shape the environment in which international students operate and the extent to which their feelings of belonging translate into aspirations to persist in the United States For instance, between two international students with the same level of academic or social belonging, we expect the student surrounded with more co-nationals to be more likely to aspire to persist in the United States after graduation. After all, preliminary evidence suggests that both international and domestic students find their campus climates to be more inclusive in the presence of more international students (Zhao et al., 2005), which is likely to impact their belongingness and persistence. Thus, we hypothesize that:

H2(a): The association between academic belonging and aspirations is moderated by the size of a student's co-national community. As the size of a student's co-national community increases, the association between academic belonging and aspirations is stronger.

H2(b): The association between social belonging and aspirations is moderated by the size of a student's co-national community. As the size of a student's co-national community increases, the association between social belonging and aspirations is stronger.

METHODS

We utilize several data sources to examine our research questions.

International STEM Graduate Student in the U.S. Survey

The "International STEM graduate student in the United States Survey 2015" (Han et al. 2015) is the most recent, publicly available dataset on the experiences of international students. The online survey was conducted with domestic and international graduate students who were enrolled in STEM disciplines at the 10 U.S. institutions with the largest total number of enrolled international students in 2013–2014—Arizona State University, Columbia University, Michigan State University, New York University, Northeastern University, Purdue University, University of California-Los Angeles, University of Illinois-Urbana Champaign, University of Southern California, and University of Washington at Seattle (Han & Appelbaum, 2016). In 2019–2020, nine of these ten institutions continue to be amongst the top 15 U.S. schools with the highest international student population (IIE, 2020c).

A total of 2,810 graduate students from 114 departments across the 10 institutions participated in the survey (see Han et al. (2015) for response rate details). Of the 2,493 students who completed the survey, 836 students were international students. The analysis presented in this paper draws on information collected from these 836 students. We were able to identify the university affiliation of 667 of these students across the 10 universities using their email addresses and the latitude-longitude coordinates collected by Qualtrics. More details about this process are available on request from the authors. After accounting for missing data, our final sample consists of 642 international students across nine universities. The sample characteristics are presented in Table 1.

Table 1: Sample Characteristics ($N = 642$)

Variable	Frequency	Percentage
Gender		
Men	394	61.00
Women	237	37.00
Do not want to respond	11	2.00
Country of Origin (Top 3)		
China	190	29.60
India	170	26.48
Taiwan	21	3.27
Discipline		
Life Sciences	103	16.04
Physical Sciences	89	13.86
Engineering	221	34.42
Mathematics	61	9.50
Computer Science	85	13.24
Other	83	12.93

International Student Enrollment

Nine of the ten universities in the sample make their international student enrollment data, including their distribution by country of origin, publicly available. The only exception is Northeastern University and therefore it was dropped from the sample. We utilize the Fall 2014 enrollment reports of the remaining nine universities to determine the proportionate representation of each country in the international student population of each university. Of these nine universities, two universities—Arizona State University and the University of Southern California (Los Angeles)—only provide data for the top 15 countries from where they receive the highest enrollment of international students. In our sample, only eight students' country of origin, across both universities, was not included in the top 15 countries. Hence, these students were removed from our analysis.

U.S. News & World Report 2018

U.S. News provides education rankings and is a popular resource to access institutional-level data. We rely on their latest department rankings since rankings from past years are not publicly available.

University Websites

Information pertaining to the type of institution (private or public) and the location of the university (rural or urban) is drawn from individual university websites

ETS Test Taker Data 2014

The ETS publishes annual reports on the population of individuals taking the GRE every year across various demographic characteristics such as age, gender, race, U.S. citizenship status, and country of citizenship. We utilize the average quantitative and verbal GRE scores in 2014 for test takers from each country in our analysis.

Variables

Dependent Variable (DV). The key concept of interest in this study is international students' aspirations to stay in the United States after graduation. Aspirations is measured by asking international students whether they hope to remain in the United States after graduation.

Focal Independent Variable (IV). We employ two variables to measure the dimensions of belonging, i.e. (a) academic belonging, and (b) social belonging. Academic belonging is conceptualized as the feelings of belonging engendered by a student's interaction and engagement with faculty and peers on academic issues (Hurtado & Carter, 1997). We extend the definition to include engagement in different parts of the research process such as access to books and journals, and freedom to pursue self-proposed research. We measure academic belonging using seven items where each international student is asked to rate seven different facets of their U.S. academic experience, compared with their home country.

Feelings of belonging in each area are recorded on a 5-point scale ranging from very much worse (1) to very much better (5). The areas of interest are as follows: (a) open classroom discussions; (b) professors' teaching styles; (c) subject teaching matter; (d) access to books, magazines, journals, and databases; (e) freedom to openly debate established theories; (f) freedom to pursue new, self-proposed research directions; (g) collaboration with other graduate students in your lab. An aggregate academic belonging score is computed for each student by taking an average of responses across the seven areas (Chronbach's $\alpha = 0.8294$).

Social belonging is conceptualized as the feelings of belongings kindled by a student's interactions with their peers and friends in non-work settings (Hurtado & Carter, 1997; Maestas et al., 2007; Walton & Cohen, 2007). We measure social belonging using the question "how do you feel you are treated by your colleagues and professors in the U.S. in comparison with those in your home country?" We recognize that this measure is limiting since (a) it does not refer to social interactions alone, and (b) it does not examine social interactions across multiple settings but condenses them into a single, aggregate measure. Nevertheless, in the absence of widely available secondary data on international students, we utilize it as a conservative measure to examine our theory.

International students' feelings of social belonging are recorded on a 5-point scale ranging from 'treated much worse (1)' to 'treated much better (5)'. Given the categorical nature of the dependent variable and limited sample size, social belonging was recoded into a binary variable with the categories of 'Better' (1) and 'Not Better' (0) to facilitate meaningful comparisons.

A key characteristic of all the items used to construct these two measures of belonging is their relational nature; the items capture a students' feelings of academic and social belonging in the United States compared with their home country. Such a conceptualization reaffirms a key premise of the belonging framework that feelings of belonging are subjective in nature and vary across contexts. Further, a framing of this nature ensures that the same subjective experience is being captured for all international students, i.e., their experience in the United States compared with their home country.

Moderating Variable (MV). To examine the effect of academic enclaves on students' integration and aspirations, we employ co-national concentration as the key moderating variable in our analysis. Thus, we measure the concept of academic enclaves as the concentration of each nationality in an individual university. The international students in the survey reported their nationality across 79 different countries. Since most of these countries have extremely low representation (less than 1% of the total international student population) in each university, the distribution of the percentage of country representation was skewed to the right. To address this skewness, we performed a log transformation of the percentage of the international student population represented by each country in a university to arrive at a more normally distributed curve.

Control Variables

We control for several factors that are associated with our dependent and independent variables: department prestige, gender, type of institution and location of institutions, and GRE scores. Details of these variables can be found in Table 2.

Table 2: Variables of Interest: Definitions and Descriptive Statistics ($N = 642$)

Variable	Description and coding	Frequency	%	Mean	S.D.
Dependent variable					
Aspirations to stay in the United States	International students' plan to stay in the United States after graduation. Binary variable.	642	100		
	No (0)	68	11		
	Possible (1)	574	89		
Independent variables					
Academic belonging	International students' feelings of belonging engendered by academic systems and communities in the United States compared with their home country. Continuous variable.	642		3.87	0.65
Social belonging	International students' feelings of belonging engendered by social interactions in the United States compared with their home country. Dichotomous variable.	642			
	Not Better (0)	340	53		
	Better (1)	302	47		
Moderating variable					
Academic enclave	Logged percentage of international students from each country in a university (Co-national Concentration). Continuous variable.	642		2.06	1.42
Control variables					
Discipline prestige	Prestige of a department within a university in relation to the same department across other U.S.	642		28.43	17.62

Variable	Description and coding	Frequency	%	Mean	S.D.
	universities. Continuous variable.				
Gender	Self-identified gender identity of international students. Dichotomous variable.	642	100		
	Men (0)	394	61		
	Women (1)	237	37		
	Do not want to respond (88)	11	2		
Type of institution	The funding status of a university Dichotomous variable.	642	100		
	Private (0)	192	30		
	Public (1)	450	70		
Location of institution	The location of a university Dichotomous variable.	642	100		
	Rural (0)	222	35		
	Urban (1)	420	65		
GRE Score—Quantitative	The average GRE quantitative score of all test takers from each country	642		157.19	5.30
GRE Score—Verbal	The average GRE verbal score of all test takers from each country	642		147.15	3.44

Data Analysis

The analysis of this study proceeds in two steps. First, we examine the relationship of academic and social belonging with students' aspirations to stay in the Unite States (H1a and H1b). We then analyze how co-national concentration moderates this relationship (H2a and H2b). Since aspirations to stay in the United States is a nominal variable, we employ multinomial logistic regression models to test all our hypotheses and calculate the predicted probabilities of aspiring to stay in the United States across different degrees of belonging. In addition to aforementioned theoretical reasons, we run separate models for academic and social belonging because there is a moderate amount of correlation (polyserial correlation of 0.5.) between the two variables. To account for clustering and heteroscedasticity, we use robust standard errors in our models.

All analyses rely on predicted probabilities and marginal effects. Marginal effects represent the difference between two predictions. While marginal effects are identical to regression coefficients in linear regression models, this is not the case when nonlinearities are introduced in the models. We examine the association between belonging and aspirations (H1a and H1b) by interpreting the coefficients of the belonging variables in the predicted probabilities metric and computing its marginal effect. For our second set of hypotheses (H2a and H2b), we test how the association between belonging and aspirations varies depending on the size of a student's co-national community, our measure of academic enclaves. Although we include the interaction term between co-national concentration and belonging in the logit models, we do not utilize its coefficient to draw conclusions about the significance of statistical interaction because it "does not provide a test for whether the effect differs in the predicted probability metric" (Mize, 2019, p. 98).

Instead, we test for equality of multiple marginal effects. The first effect that we examine, i.e., first level differences, is the marginal effect of the belonging on the aspirations (DV) at different levels of co-national concentration (MV). In the case of second level difference, we use Wald's test to examine whether these first-level differences are significantly different across levels of co-national concentration (Berry et al., 2010; Long & Freese, 2014; Mize, 2019). More specifically, we test whether the marginal effect of belonging when co-national concentration is 5 is significantly different from the marginal effect of belonging when co-national concentration is 0.

Predicted probabilities and marginal effects are computed using Stata's 16.1 margins command and Long and Freese's (2014) user-written command for Stata called mtable (program name is spost13). The Wald's tests underlying the computation of second differences are evaluated using the user-written command mlincom within the spost13 program (Long & Freese, 2014).

RESULTS

Importance of Belonging

We find support for the first set of hypotheses that greater feelings of belonging—academically and socially—are more likely to be associated with stronger aspirations to stay in the United States after graduation (H1a and H1b respectively). In Figure 1A, we see that international students who report one unit higher on academic belonging than their peers have a 0.115 higher probability of aspiring to stay in the United States ($p < 0.001$) (Figure 1). Further, students who are higher on the academic belonging scale are significantly less likely than their peers to feel undecided about their aspirations to persist in the country (ME = -0.101, $p < 0.001$). Overall, the more a student feels like they belong academically, the more likely they are to aspire to stay in the country and less likely to feel undecided about their future plans.

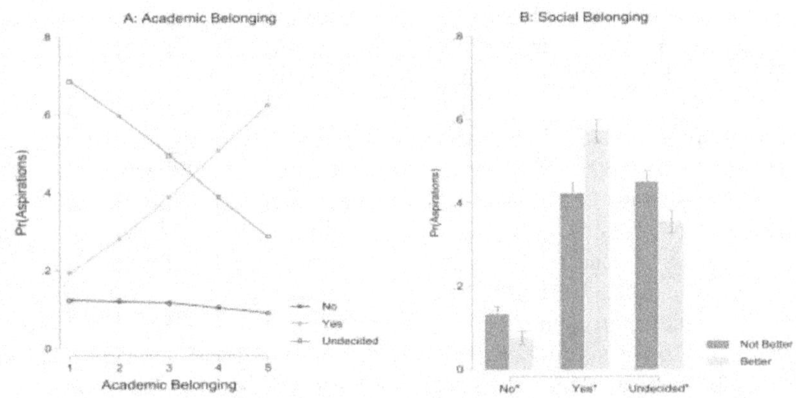

**Figure 1: Probability of Aspiring to Stay in the United States
Based on Feelings of Belonging**

Note: Outcomes for social belonging with
significant differences are starred

We find a similar positive relationship between social belonging and the aspirations to persist in the United States. In Figure 1B, we see that international students who report 'better' levels of social belonging in the United States compared with their home country have a 0.152 higher probability of aspiring to stay in the United States ($p < 0.001$) and 0.057 lower probability of aspiring to leave ($p < 0.05$) than international students with 'not better' levels of social belonging. Students with better levels of social belonging also have a 0.095 lower probability ($p < 0.05$) of feeling undecided about their future aspirations compared with their less socially integrated peers.

Thus, our findings corroborate the importance of feelings of belonging in ensuring the persistence of international students. Students who feel more like they belong in the United States—academically or socially—are more likely to aspire to stay in the country upon graduation.

Academic Enclave Effect

Our second set of hypotheses propose that academic enclaves, as measured by co-national concentration, will have a positive moderating effect on the association between feelings of belonging and aspirations. Thus, the marginal effect of belonging on aspirations should be larger as co-national concentration increases. We anticipate that international students who feel like they belong more are less likely to want to leave the United States after graduation and more likely to want to stay when they are enrolled in universities with a larger share of co-nationals than universities with a smaller share.

The results only provide support for our social belonging hypothesis (H2b). In our test for H2a, the marginal effect of academic belonging for all categories of aspirations does not change significantly between high and low levels of co-national concentration. Thus, there exists no moderating effect of co-national concentration on the association between academic belonging and aspirations.

However, we find support for the social belonging hypothesis albeit through a different pathway, i.e., co-national concentration shapes the effect of social belonging on aspirations to not stay in the United States/leave the United States after graduation instead of the aspiration to stay in the United States. At initial levels of co-national concentration, the marginal effect of social belonging (better—not better) on aspirations to not stay is negative and significant at $\alpha < 0.1$ (see Mize, 2016 for significant testing approaches).[1] Thus, students who report better levels of social belonging have a lower probability of aspiring to leave after graduation than those who report not better levels of social belonging. After the logged value of co-national concentration exceeds 2, this marginal effect is no longer significant (dotted section of Figure 2).

To ascertain whether these changes in the marginal effect of social belonging are meaningful, we compute the difference between the marginal effects of social belonging at the highest (5) and lowest level of co-national concentration (0) and find the difference to be significantly different (second difference = 0.132, p < 0.1). The second level difference is not significant for the remaining outcome categories of 'Yes' and 'Undecided' and thus not reported here. In keeping with H2b, we conclude that the effect of social belonging on a student's aspirations varies based on the size of their academic enclaves made up of co-nationals. However, the moderation does not take the pathway we had anticipated, i.e., the association between social belonging and aspirations does not become stronger as the density of academic enclave increases.

Nevertheless, a closer examination of the factors driving the changes in the marginal effect of social belonging still lends support to the positive role of dense academic enclaves in ensuring international student persistence. The probability of aspiring to leave/not stay for students with 'better' levels of social belonging (blue line in Figure 2) does not vary at different degrees of co-national concentration. However, as the size of the co-national concentration increases, students who report 'not better' levels of social belonging are less likely to aspire to want to leave.

---

[1] Marginal effects of social belonging outcome category 'No': (a) ME at concentration 0 $= -0.128$ ($p < 0.05$); (b) ME at concentration 1 $= -0.078$ ($p < 0.05$); (c) ME at concentration 2 $= -0.042$ ($p < 0.1$); (d) ME at concentration 3 $= -0.019$; (e) ME at concentration 4 $= -0.004$; and ME at concentration 5 $= 0.004$.

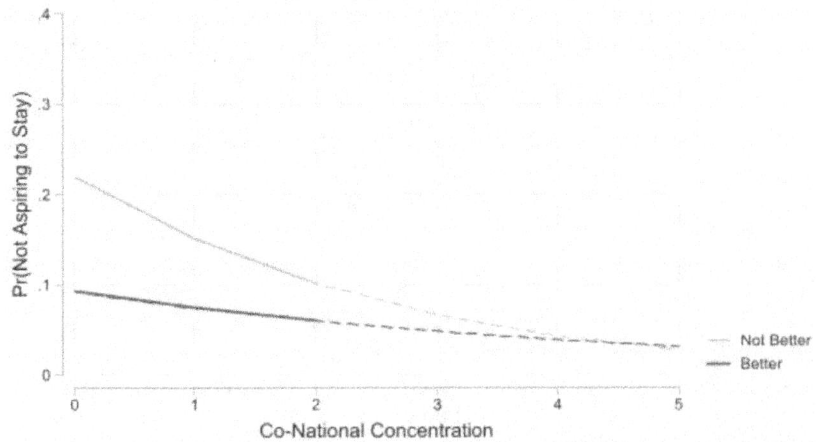

Figure 2: Probability of Aspiring to Stay in the United States Across Social Belonging and Co-National Concentration

Note: Group difference (better vs. less better) is
significant at the $p < 0.1$ level when lines are solid

Thus, changes in the marginal effect of social belonging are driven by two unanticipated factors. First, only the aspirations of students who experience lower social belongingness change in response to an increasing presence of co-nationals. Students who report stronger feelings of belonging are less likely to be influenced by the presence or absence of co-nationals. Second, co-nationals do not bolster the aspirations of students with low levels of social belongingness to "stay" in the United States. Instead, academic enclaves temper international students' "desire to leave" but that is also only up to the point when they become as well-adjusted as their peers. We refer to these dual paths of persistence that emerge when we account for heterogeneity in the presence and experiences of international students as the "academic enclave effect."

DISCUSSION AND CONCLUSION

Our findings demonstrate the importance of "academic enclaves" in ensuring the persistence of international graduate students in the United States. Building on scholarship that emphasizes the importance of co-nationals in improving academic outcomes, reducing loneliness, and bolstering the psycho-social well-being of international students (Glass & Gesing, 2018; Kaya, 2020; Khanal & Gaulee, 2019; Wang & Freed, 2021), we draw attention to the positive association between feelings of belonging (academic and social) and the persistence of graduate international students. Our examination of international student persistence extends into aspirations to stay in the United States upon graduation. We emphasize the importance of this extension because factors contributing to the transition of international students into the American labor market, beyond legal factors, remain underexamined (Wadhwa et al., 2009).

By accounting for the heterogeneity in the distribution of the international student community across universities, we are also able to establish a more nuanced model of international student persistence. We find that students with lower levels of social belonging are more likely to persist in the United States, when they are enrolled in universities with a higher density of co-nationals. In contrast, co-national density does not have a significant bearing on the aspirations of students with higher levels of social belonging. We refer to these dual paths of persistence as the "academic enclave effect" because we conceptualize co-national communities as "academic enclaves" that support international students in the same way ethnic enclaves support immigrant communities (Hikido, 2018; Kosta, 2019). However, academic enclaves differ from ethnic enclaves on account of the "enclave ceiling effect" present in the former—co-national communities only shape the likelihood of persistence for those students who are experiencing a certain level of paucity in their social belonging and have no bearing on socially well-integrated international students.

Limitations

The analysis presented in this paper is based on cross-sectional data and therefore associational and not causal. Further, given the sampling frame, our results are generalizable only to the experiences of international graduate students enrolled in universities with relatively large international student populations. Another limitation lies in the measure of aspirations. Aspirations to not leave do not imply that students are more likely to stay—they could simply feel undecided. Nevertheless, the reduced probability of leaving is still a movement in the direction to retain valuable, yet overlooked, members of the American society (Hagedorn & Lee, 2005). Finally, we also recognize that individuals of the same nationality can be of different racial identities and that these identities shape their feelings of belonging and persistence within U.S. higher education institutions (Mwangi, 2016). Although we focus on the national identity of international students, we hope that future research will take a closer look at how racial dynamics influence the academic enclave effect.

Implications and Future Research

Our findings demonstrate the important relationship between feelings of belonging and the persistence of international students, not only toward the completion of their degrees but also in terms of aspiring toward transitioning into the American labor market. Second, our explicit focus on the graduate international student population addresses an important gap in the international student scholarship that is predominantly focused on undergraduate students' experiences.

Finally, recognition of the academic enclave effect extends our understanding of how co-nationals influence international students' experiences in the United States. The pivotal role of co-nationals in creating inclusive spaces for international students where they feel like they belong is well established (Glass et al., 2013; Kaya, 2020; Rivas et al., 2019; Tang et al., 2018). Evidence also indicates that international students' reliance on their co-nationals as a primary source of social support changes as their duration of stay in the United State increases (Bhochhibhoya et al., 2017; Le et al., 2016). We contribute to this knowledge about co-national communities' influence on international students' experiences by demonstrating how variations in their density have implications on international students' persistence.

At a broader policy level, the discourse on the persistence of international students is often focused on visa and immigration policies. Our results demonstrate the importance of meso-level, institutional factors—the presence co-national communities—in shaping international students' aspirations to stay in the United States. International graduate students, especially those pursuing doctoral programs, spend long durations of time in the United States and are an integral component of American society. Future research should inquire into additional university-level factors that would similarly encourage international students to aspire for a life in the United States beyond degree attainment.

By highlighting the heterogeneity in international students' experiences and their differing responses to increasing co-national presence, we facilitate future research into other factors that engender variations in this community's experiences. In particular, future research should examine the factors that shape the persistence of students with higher levels of social belonging. It is critical to identify the factors engendering variations in international students' experiences so that universities can develop more inclusive policies and structures to best support all groups of international students instead of treating them a homogenous community.

REFERENCES

Anderman, L. H., & Freeman, T. M. (2004). Students' sense of belonging in school. In P. R. Pintrich & M. L. Maehr (Eds.), *Advances in motivation and achievement. Motivating students, improving schools: The legacy of Carol Midgley* (Vol. 13, pp. 27–63). Elsevier.

Andersson, R., Musterd, S., & Galster, G. (2014). Neighbourhood ethnic composition and employment effects on immigrant incomes. *Journal of Ethnic and Migration Studies, 40*(5), 710–736. https://doi.org/10.1080/1369183X.2013.830503

Bécares, L., & Nazroo, J. (2013). Social capital, ethnic density and mental health among ethnic minority people in England: A mixed-methods study. *Ethnicity & Health, 18*(6), 544–562. https://doi.org/10.1080/13557858.2013.828831

Berry, W. D., DeMerrit, J. H. R., & Esarey, J. (2010). Testing for interaction in binary logit and probit models: Is a product term essential? *American Journal of Political Science, 54*, 248–266. https://doi.org/10.1111/j.1540-5907.2009.00429.x

Bhochhibhoya, A., Dong, Y., & Branscum, P. (2017). Sources of social support among international college students in the United States. *Journal of International Students, 7*(3), 671–686. https://doi.org/10.5281/zenodo.570032

Bista, K., & Foster, C. (2011). Issues of international student retention in American higher education. *The International Journal of Research and Review, 7*(2), 1–10. Available at SSRN: https://ssrn.com/abstract=1958362

Bouk, F. E., Vedder, P., & Poel, Y. T. (2013). The networking behavior of Moroccan and Turkish immigrant entrepreneurs in two Dutch neighborhoods: The role of ethnic density. *Ethnicities, 13*(6), 771–794. https://doi.org/10.1177/1468796812471131

Brunsting, N. C., Smith, A. C., & Zachry, C. (2018). An academic and cultural transition course for international students: Efficacy and socio-emotional outcomes. *Journal of International Students, 8*(4), 1497–1521. https://doi.org/10.5281/zenodo.1467805

Cho, J., & Yu, H. (2015). Roles of university support for international students in the United States: Analysis of a systematic model of university identification, university support, and psychological well-being. *Journal of Studies in International Education, 19*(1), 11–27. https://doi.org/10.1177/1028315314533606

Das-Munshi, J., Becares, L., Dewey, M. E., Stansfeld, S. A., & Prince, M. J. (2010). Understanding the effect of ethnic density on mental health: Multi-level investigation of survey data from England. *British Medical Journal, 341*, c5367. https://doi.org/10.1136/bmj.c5367

Du, Y., & Wei, M. (2015). Acculturation, enculturation, social connectedness, and subjective well-being among Chinese international students. *The Counseling Psychologist, 43*(2), 299–325. https://doi.org/10.1177/0011000014565712

Garcia, H. A., Garza, T., & Yeaton-Hromada, K. (2019). Do we belong? A conceptual model for international students' sense of belonging in community colleges. *Journal of International Students, 9*(2), 460–487. https://doi.org/10.32674/jis.v9i2.669

Geven, S., Kalmijn, M., & Tubergen, T. (2016). The ethnic composition of schools and students' problem behaviour in four European countries: The role of friends. *Journal of Ethnic and Migration Studies, 42*(9), 1473–1495. https://doi.org/10.1080/1369183X.2015.1121806

Giddens, A. (1979). *Central Problems in Social Theory: Action, structure and contradiction in social analysis.* Berkeley: University of California Press.

Glass, C. R., Buus, S., & Braskamp, L. A. (2013). Uneven experiences: What's missing and what matters for today's international students. Global Perspective Institute.

Glass, C. R., & Gesing, P. (2018). The development of social capital through international students' involvement in campus organizations. *Journal of International Students, 8*(3), 1274–1292. https://doi.org/10.5281/zenodo.1254580

Guo, S., & Chase, M. (2011). Internationalisation of higher education: Integrating international students into Canadian academic environment. *Teaching in Higher Education, 16*(3), 305–318. https://doi.org/10.1080/13562517.2010.546524

Hagedorn, L. S., & Lee, M.-C. (2005). International community college students: The neglected minority? In *Online Submission*. ERIC: Institution of Education Sciences. https://eric.ed.gov/?id=ED490516

Han, X., & Appelbaum, R. P. (2016). *Will they stay or will they go? : International STEM students are up for grabs* (p. 50). Ewing Marion Kauffman Foundation.

Han, X., Appelbaum, R. P., Stocking, G., & Gebbie, M. (2015). *International STEM graduate student in the United States Survey 2015*. Inter-university Consortium for Political and Social Science Research. http://doi.org/10.3886/E43668V1

Hausmann, L. R. M., Schofield, J. W., & Woods, R. L. (2007). Sense of belonging as a predictor of intentions to persist among African American and White First-Year college students. *Research in Higher Education, 48*(7), 803–839. https://doi.org/10.1007/s11162-007-9052-9

Hikido, A. (2018). Entrepreneurship in South African township tourism: The impact of interracial social capital. *Ethnic and Racial Studies, 41*(14), 2580–2598. https://doi.org/10.1080/01419870.2017.1392026

Horne, S. V., Shuhui Lin, Anson, M., & Jacobson, W. (2018). Engagement, satisfaction, and belonging of international undergraduates at U.S. research universities. *Journal of International Students, 8*(1), 351–374. https://doi.org/10.5281/zenodo.1134313

Hurtado, S., & Carter, D. F. (1997). Effects of college transition and perceptions of the campus racial climate on Latino college students' sense of belonging. *Sociology of Education, 70*(4), 324–345. https://doi.org/10.2307/2673270

Institute of International Education. (2020a). *International scholars trends, 1999/00–2019/20* (Open Doors Report on International Educational Exchange). https://opendoorsdata.org/data/international-scholars/international-scholars-trends/

Institute of International Education. (2020b). *Leading places of origin of international scholars, 2000/01–2019/20* (Open Doors Report on International Educational Exchange). https://opendoorsdata.org/data/international-scholars/leading-places-of-origin/

Institute of International Education. (2020c). *Top 25 institutions hosting international students, 2000/01—2019/20* (Open Doors Report on International Educational Exchange). https://opendoorsdata.org/data/international-students/leading-institutions/

Johnson, D. R., Soldner, M., Leonard, J. B., Alvarez, P., Inkelas, K. K., Rowan-Kenyon, H. T., & Longerbeam, S. D. (2007). Examining sense of belonging among first-year undergraduates from different racial/ethnic groups. *Journal of College Student Development, 48*(5), 525–542. https://doi.org/10.1353/csd.2007.0054

Kaya, J. (2020). Inside the international student world: Challenges, opportunities, and imagined communities. *Journal of International Students, 10*(1), 124–144. https://doi.org/10.32674/jis.v10i1.1031

Khanal, J., & Gaulee, U. (2019). Challenges of international students from pre-departure to post-study: A literature review. *Journal of International Students, 9*(2), 560–581. https://doi.org/10.32674/jis.v9i2.673

Kosta, E. B. (2019). Becoming Italian, becoming American: Ethnic affinity as a strategy of boundary making. *Ethnic and Racial Studies, 42*(5), 801–819. https://doi.org/10.1080/01419870.2018.1432871

Le, A. T., LaCost, B. Y., & Wismer, M. (2016). International female graduate students' experience at a Midwestern University: Sense of belonging and identity development. *Journal of International Students, 6*(1), 128–152. https://doi.org/10.32674/jis.v6i1.485

Long, J. S., & Freese, J. (2014). Regression models for categorical dependent variables using Stata (Third). Stata Press.

Maestas, R., Vaquera, G. S., & Zehr, L. M. (2007). Factors impacting sense of belonging at a hispanic-serving institution. *Journal of Hispanic Higher Education, 6*(3), 237–256. https://doi.org/10.1177/1538192707302801

Mamiseishvili, K. (2012). International student persistence in U.S. Postsecondary Institutions. *Higher Education, 64*, 1–17. https://doi.org/10.1007/s10734-011-9477-0

Mize, T. D. (2016). Sexual orientation in the labor market. *American Sociological Review, 81*(6), 1132–1160. https://doi.org/10.1177/0003122416674025

Mize, T. D. (2019). Best practices for estimating, interpreting, and presenting nonlinear interaction effects. *Sociological Science, 6*, 81–117. https://doi.org/10.15195/v6.a4

Museus, S. D., Yi, V., & Saelua, N. (2017). The impact of culturally engaging campus environments on sense of belonging. *The Review of Higher Education, 40*(2), 187–215. https://doi.org/10.1353/rhe.2017.0001

Mwangi, C. A. G. (2016). Exploring sense of belonging among Black International Students at an HBCU. *Journal of International Students, 6*(4), 1015–1037. https://doi.org/10.32674/jis.v6i4.332

Page, A. G. (2019). Ethnic enclaves transcending space Chinese international students' social networks in a European University town. *Asian Ethnicity, 20*(4), 418–435. https://doi.org/10.1080/14631369.2019.1570816

Portes, A., & Jensen, L. (1989). The enclave and the entrants: Patterns of ethnic enterprise in Miami before and after Mariel. *American Sociological Review, 54*(6), 929–949. https://doi.org/10.2307/2095716

Portes, A., & Manning, R. D. (2013). The Immigrant Enclave: Theory and Empirical Examples. In J. Lin & C. Mele (Eds.), *The Urban Sociology Reader* (Second, pp. 202–213). New York: Routledge.

Rivas, J., Hale, K., & Burke, M. G. (2019). Seeking a sense of belonging: Social and cultural integration of international students with American College Students. *Journal of International Students, 9*(2), 682–704. https://doi.org/10.32674/jis.v9i2.943

Rosenberg, M., & McCullough, B. C. (1981). Mattering: Inferred significance and mental health among adolescents. *Research in Community & Mental Health, 2*, 163–182.

Rose-Redwood, C. R., & Rose-Redwood, R. S. (2013). Self-segregation or global mixing?: Social interactions and the international student experience. *Journal of College Student Development, 54*(4), 413–429. https://doi.org/10.1353/csd.2013.0062

Srivastava, S. K., Srivastava, A. K., Minerick, A., & Schulz, N. (2010). Recruitment and retention of international graduate students in US universities. *International Journal of Engineering Education, 26*(6), 1561–1574. https://krex.k-state.edu/dspace/bitstream/handle/2097/7514/SchulzIJEE2010.pdf?sequence=1

Strayhorn, T. L. (2008). Fittin' in: Do diverse interactions with peers affect sense of belonging for Black men at predominantly White Institutions? *NASPA Journal, 45*(4), 501–527. https://doi.org/10.2202/1949-6605.2009

Strayhorn, T. L. (2012). College students' sense of belonging: A key to educational success for all students. Routledge. https://doi.org/10.4324/9780203118924

Strayhorn, T. L., Long III, L. L., Kitchen, J. A., Williams, M. S., & Stenz, M. E. (2013). *Academic and social barriers to Black and Latino Male Collegians' success in engineering and related STEM fields*. 120th ASEE Annual Conference and Exposition, Atlanta, GA. https://commons.erau.edu/publication/295

Tang, X., Collier, D. A., & Witt, A. (2018). Qualitative study on Chinese students' perception of U.S. university life. *Journal of International Students, 8*(1), 151–174. https://doi.org/10.5281/zenodo.1134279

Toussaint-Comeau, M. (2008). Do ethnic enclaves and networks promote immigrant self-employment? *Economic Perspectives, 32*(4), 30. Available at SSRN: https://ssrn.com/abstract=1297315

Wadhwa, V., Saxenian, A., Freeman, R., & Salkever, A. (2009). *Losing the world's best and brightest: America's new immigrant entrepreneurs, Part V*. Ewing Marie Kauffman Foundation. https://www.immigrationresearch.org/report/other/losing-worlds-best-and-brightest-americas-new-immigrant-entrepreneurs-part-v

Walton, G. M., & Cohen, G. L. (2007). A question of belonging: Race, social fit, and achievement. *Journal of Personality and Social Psychology, 92*(1), 82–96. https://doi.org/10.1037/0022-3514.92.1.82

Wang, X., & Freed, R. (2021). A Bourdieusian analysis of the sociocultural capital of Chinese international graduate students in the United States. *Journal of International Students, 11*(1), 41–59. https://doi.org/10.32674/jis.v11i1.952

Yao, C. W. (2016). Unfulfilled expectations: Influence of Chinese international students' roommate relationships on sense of belonging. *Journal of International Students, 6*(3), 762–778. https://doi.org/10.32674/jis.v6i3.355

Zhao, C., Kuh, G. D., & Carini, R. M. (2005). A comparison of international student and American student engagement in effective educational practices. *The Journal of Higher Education, 76*(2), 209–231. https://doi.org/10.1353/jhe.2005.0018

VASUNDHARA KAUL is a PhD candidate in the Department of Sociology at Purdue University, West Lafayette. Her research integrates how culture and emotions shape inequality and social policy across different institutional contexts. Her current research focuses on the effect of culture and emotions on how lay citizens make sense of and protect their personal data privacy. Email: kaul9@purdue.edu

LINDA RENZULLI, PhD, is a professor of sociology and Department Head in the College of Liberal Arts Department of Sociology at Purdue University, West Lafayette. Her scholarly interests include sociology of education, organizational change, and stratification. She is also interested in the family school nexus to understand better educational opportunities and constraints. Email: lrenzull@purdue.edu

Research Article

© *Journal of International Students*
Volume 12, Issue 2 (2022), pp. 489-509
ISSN: 2162-3104 (Print), 2166-3750 (Online)
doi: 10.32674/jis.v12i2.3561
ojed.org/jis

The Role of Studying Abroad in Attitudes toward Immigration: A European Context

Yakup Öz
Enes Gök
Karamanoglu Mehmetbey University, Karaman, Turkey

ABSTRACT

International student mobility has been rising as a global phenomenon in the last few decades, while its impact could be various in different contexts. For the European Union (EU), studying in another EU member country could be regarded as an important factor for the solidarity and integrity of the Union. The current study elaborates on the role of studying abroad regarding the attitudes of people toward immigration in the EU. It shows that people who are studying in an EU member country, belonging to higher social classes and from EU15 countries, are more likely to have positive attitudes toward immigration. But after controlling several socio-demographic variables studying abroad still contributes positively to the attitudes of EU citizens toward immigration. Accordingly, current study provides promising pieces of evidence on the social contribution of studying abroad for both future research and policymakers.

Keywords: Eurobarometer, European Union, immigrants, migration, student mobility, study abroad

INTRODUCTION

One significant outcome of globalization is the increasing mobility of individuals across countries in recent decades. In addition to developments in technology and transportation, social, economic, cultural, and political issues, the situation has resulted in the migration of individuals from one country to another. As a result, discussions on refugees as forced migrants and the immigration issue continue to be an important topic in political agendas today.

In the case of Europe, the issue is more severe, since some developed countries in Europe become, what Triandafyllidou (2004) called, a "magnet" for people from both third world and eastern European countries. According to Eurostat (2019), there are 22.3 million non-EU citizens (5% of the EU-28) and 17.6 million other EU citizens residing in European countries as of January 2018. To this end, the number of people flowing into Europe as immigrants and refugees from unstable parts of the world has changed not only traditional national states in terms of social composition and ethnicity (Davidov & Semyonov, 2017) but also the attitudes of societies toward these newcomers. Specifically, negative attitudes toward immigrants and refugees derive mostly from problematic immigration policies, nationalism, and stereotypes toward other cultures and identities.

In addition to this severity of negative attitudes and increasing tension among cultures, as a result of the internationalization of higher education, a new type of short and medium-term immigration (student mobility/study abroad) began to emerge along with its consequences in social, political, cultural, and economic arenas. However, these migrants differ from non-student immigrants due to their desirability in the host country. In this type of experience, students are reportedly absorbing increasing cosmopolitan ideals and positive attitudes toward other cultures (Carlson & Widaman, 1988) and, as King and Raghuram (2013) put it, "students are solicited as desirable migrants because of the skills they bring and then subsequently develop in the countries into which they move" (p. 127). In short, such short-term immigration experience seems to have the potential to increase positive attitudes of both immigrants and the citizens who host them.

In terms of attitudes toward immigrants, the literature provides a rich coverage of the problem in a European context (Akrami et al., 2000; Davidov & Semyonov, 2017; Kleinschmidt, 2003; Leong & Ward, 2006; Rustenbach, 2010), global contexts (Fussell, 2014; Mayda, 2006; Ward & Masgoret, 2006). Although international students are arguably the least studied group in migration research (Bozheva, 2020; Findlay, 2011), a later study suggests that migration studies related to international student mobility and study abroad have a significant share in the literature (Gümüş et al., 2020). Considering the body of research partly addressed above, existing studies examining attitudes toward immigration lack the focus on the contribution of studying abroad to people's attitudes toward migration and immigrants, in general. However, people who have experience of immigration once in their lives might have attitudes toward immigration differing from people who have had no such experience. Therefore, this research aims to explore the role of studying abroad in people's attitudes toward immigrants and immigration. Accordingly, it attempts to answer two broad questions:

1.   What is the contribution of studying abroad to individuals' attitudes toward immigration?

2.   How does this contribution change over time and geography?

CONCEPTUAL BACKGROUND

Historically, immigration is not a new phenomenon in Europe, but its direction is impacted by the socio-economic and political circumstances of the time. As De la Rica et al. (2013) explained, Europe was characterized by emigration to the rest of the world before World War Two, and the second half of the 20th century witnessed a dramatic shift in direction, with European countries becoming a host region for immigrants. Today's picture is different. According to 2017 statistics, Europe and Asia in total hosted the largest immigrant population in the world, at a rate of 60%. And, from 1990 to 2017, the number of immigrants in Europe increased by 29 million; "Of the 29 million international migrants gained by Europe during this period, 46% were born in Europe, 24% in Asia, nearly 17% in Africa and 12% in Latin America and the Caribbean" (United Nations [UN], 2018).

In parallel with the increasing numbers and Europe becoming a continent of migration, issues related to immigration have become a major policy issue in countries affected by the demographic changes due to the inflow of immigrants (Bade, 2004). While major political discussions focus on the social, cultural, political, and economic integration of the immigrants, one part of the issue resides in the response of society to this changing landscape. The literature provides a wide range of concepts and discussions related to public reaction to immigration and the acceptance of newcomers. In addition, one of the most striking debates in the literature is related to how citizens of a host country see immigration and what attitudes they have toward the immigrants from within and outside of Europe. Considering the theoretical explanations, studies examining factors concerning public attitudes toward immigration could be grouped into two categories; studies focusing on the impact of individual-level factors and contextual-level factors.

The individual-level factors range from socio-economic status, welfare, and income (Bridges & Mateut, 2009; Genge & Bartolucci, 2019; Hoxhaj & Zuccotti, 2019; Huber & Oberdabernig, 2016), the position of individuals in the labor market (Gang et al., 2013), social capital (Economidou et al., 2020), education (Bilodeau & Fadol, 2011; Gang et al., 2013; Hatton, 2016), age (Barber et al., 2013; Calahorrano, 2013), race (Bridges & Mateut, 2009), and a number of other demographic and individual characteristics (Gang et al., 2013; Stöhr & Wichardt, 2016). For instance, Becchetti et al. (2010) found a negative relationship between both a job loss or reduction in household income and concerns about immigrants. As Pardos-Prado (2011) summarized this by arguing that the relationship between socio-economic status of individuals and their attitudes toward immigrants were mostly analyzed within the "xenophobic attitudes" from the perspectives of ethnic competition theory. Additionally, Paas and Halapuu (2012) suggested that "ethnic minorities, urban people, people with higher education and income, as well as people who have work experience abroad are, as a rule, more tolerant toward immigrants in Europe" (p. 161). Besides the link between individuals' socio-economic status and attitudes toward immigrants, some studies investigate if the people see immigrants as a socio-economic threat (Marozzi, 2016). From this perspective, Paas and Halapuu (2012) found that the lower the attitudes toward socio-economic risk the lower the concern toward immigrants.

The contextual factors examined vary from economic crisis (Hatton, 2016), changes over time (Hatton, 2016; Murard, 2017), skills of the immigrants (Facchini & Mayda, 2012; O'Connell, 2011), religion of the immigrants (Strabac et al., 2014), terrorism (Leclerc, 2018), and the concentration of immigrants (Hoxhaj & Zuccotti, 2019; Scipioni et al., 2019). In short, the findings suggest that the economic conditions of the country, competition for jobs, race, and the education level of the immigrants and the host country citizens are all significant determinants of attitudes toward immigration.

The above discussions in a European context allow for current research, focusing on the outcomes of student mobility from an immigration perspective. As summarized by Coleman and Chafer (2011), the impact of study abroad on individuals and the resulting learned outcomes are discussed in the following six dimensions in the literature: academic, personal, professional, linguistic, cultural, and intercultural gains. Among them, the social turn of study abroad and personality changes seem to be more related to the attitudinal changes of individuals toward immigrants. Students who have encountered different cultures and identities during their study abroad might develop a global identity, more positive attitudes toward other cultures and individuals, cosmopolitan ideals, and global citizenship (Carlson & Widaman, 1988; Hendershot & Sperandio, 2009; Tarrant et al., 2014).

METHOD

Data Source and Sample

Current study uses two different data sources: the Eurobarometer 77.3 (European Commission [EC], 2015) and the Eurobarometer 89.1 (EC, 2018). Eurobarometers are specifically designed surveys to understand the political, economic, or social conditions of EU citizens and to evaluate their perceptions regarding different EU policies or reforms. Both surveys were carried out by TNS Opinion & Social on request of the European Commission, Directorate-General for Communication in 2012 and 2018. Since the surveys are conducted by TNS Opinion & Social, and the data are publicly shared by the GESIS-Leibniz Institute for the Social Sciences, the researchers did not need IRB approval.

Surveys cover the population of the respective nationalities who are aged 15 years and over in each of the EU member countries. A multi-stage, random sample design was applied, and several sampling points were drawn with probability proportional to population size and population density in each member state. In this regard, the samples were composed of 26,637 and 27,988 respondents in 2012 and 2018, respectively.

Within this context, in 2012, of the respondents, 58.1% are from EU15 countries, 47.3% agree that immigrants contribute a lot to their country, 12.5% studied abroad, 54.0% are female, 47.9% are working, 27.5% live in large towns, and 51.8% are composed of the middle class, and the respondents who are 55 years old and over constitute the biggest share of the sample (39.5%).

In 2018, of the respondents, 56.0% are from EU15 countries, 44.4% agree that immigrants contribute a lot to their country, 69.5% feel positive about immigration from EU member states, 38.5% feel positive about immigration from outside the EU, 20.4% studied abroad, 54.2% are female, 50.1% are working, 27.8% live in large towns, and 68.5% are composed of the middle class (lower-middle, middle, and upper-middle classes in total), and the respondents who are 55 years old and over constitute the biggest share of the sample (46.8%).

Variables

Dependent Variables

In the surveys, three items were available for the attitudes toward immigration. However, only the first one below was included in both surveys. The other two were included in the 2018 survey only.

Immigrants' Contributions

This variable was derived from a set of items related to the question, "To what extent do you agree or disagree with each of the following statements?" One of the items is, "Immigrants contribute a lot to (our country)." Responses are Likert Type in four as 1: totally agree, 2: tend to agree, 3: tend to disagree, and 4: totally disagree. Accordingly, this item was transformed into a dichotomous variable representing whether participants agree (=1) or disagree (=0).

Feelings Regarding Immigration of People From EU Member States

This variable is one of the two items related to the question, "Please tell me whether each of the following statements evokes a positive or negative feeling for you?" One of the items is, "Immigration of people from EU Member States." This item is Likert Type in four as 1: very positive, 2: fairly positive, 3: fairly negative, 4: very negative. It was transformed into a dichotomous variable representing whether the participant has a positive feeling (=1) or not (=0).

Feelings Regarding Immigration of People From Outside the EU

This variable was derived from the other item, "Immigration of people outside the EU," for the same question represented in the second dependent variable. It has the same Likert Type rating, and the same transformation was applied to create a similar variable.

Independent Variables

Studying Abroad

This variable was derived from a set of items related to the question, "For each of the following achievements of the EU, could you tell me whether you have benefitted from it or not?" One of the items is, "Studying in another EU country." And answers are dichotomous: "has benefitted" (1) and "has not benefitted" (2). Has not benefited was taken as the reference category.

National Group

National group represents the two-broad groups of EU member countries, namely EU15 (Austria, Belgium, Denmark, Finland, France, Germany, Greece, Ireland, Italy, Luxembourg, Netherlands, Portugal, Spain, Sweden, and the United Kingdom) and New Member States (NMS [Bulgaria, Croatia, Cyprus, Czech Republic, Estonia, Hungary, Latvia, Lithuania, Malta, Poland, Romania, Slovakia, and Slovenia]). EU15 countries are those members of the EU up to 1995, and the NMS became members of the EU after 2004. The United Kingdom was included in this list since it was still an official member of the EU during the administration of the surveys. NMS was taken as the reference category.

Gender

Gender is simply male and female in both surveys. Male was taken as a reference category.

Age

Age was treated as a continuous variable.

Employment

Employment is represented as to whether the participant is 1: self-employed, 2: employed, or 3: not working. Self-employed and employed answers were transformed into another category as employed (=1) and not working (=0). Not working was taken as the reference category.

Type of Community

This variable represents the residential area. It is categorized into three items in both surveys; 1: Rural Area, 2: Small/Medium Size Town, 3: Large Town. The rural area was treated as the reference category.

Social Class

This variable is derived from the question preserved in both surveys, "Do you see yourself and your household belonging to…?" The social class is categorized as 1: the working class, 2: the middle class, and 3: the upper class in the 2012 survey. However, in 2018, the middle class was enlarged as "the lower middle class," "the upper middle class," and another item "the higher class" was added. Working class was taken as the reference category.

Analysis

Considering the dichotomous dependent variables, binary logistic regression analyses were performed, and weighting was applied in all of them. For the immigrants' contributions, analyses were made for both years, but for the feelings about immigration, analyses were only made for 2018, because of the absence of the last two dependent variables in the 2012 survey.

Before passing each analysis, several assumptions were also checked. For the linearity between the Logit of the outcome and each predictor variable (the only continuous variable is age), there is a linear relationship between the age and dependent variables in all models. We checked this assumption by controlling the pair-wise scatter plot between age and Logit values in each model, and there was not any violation of the linearity assumption.

Considering the independence of errors, in our data, the observations do not come from repeated measurements or matched data, since they are gathered by different respondents each year. To check the influential values, we used Cook's distance. According to Field (2009) values for Cook's distance should be lower than 1.0. And none of the values for Cook's distance in our analyses for all models were above 1.0. To control the multicollinearity, we used VIF and tolerance values. According to Hair et al. (2013), the VIF value lies between 1.00 and 10.00 and it should be closer to 1.00, with the Tolerance value lying between 0.10 and 1.00 and it should be closer to 1.00. In the analyses, none of the VIF values were no higher than 1.208, and Tolerance values were lower than 0.828. Lastly, the sample size is quite enough. According to Hair et al. (2013), there should be at least 10 observations per number of independent variables for sufficient sample size in logistic regression analysis.

Hence, a basic binary Logit model, Logit (P_i) = Log $[P_i/(1-P_i)]$ = p_i, was used, and a stepwise approach was followed in the analyses. Accordingly, national group is included in Model 1 only; Logit (P_i) = β_{0i} + β_{1i}EU15 + r_i. National group and studying abroad are included in Model 2; Logit (P_i) = β_{0i} + β_{1i}EU15 + β_{2i}STUDIEDABROAD + r_i. Model 3 represents the full model; Logit (P_i) = β_{0i} + β_{1i}EU15 + β_{2i}STUDIEDABROAD + β_{3i}FEMALE + β_{4i}AGE + β_{5i}WORKING + β_{6i}RURAL + β_{7i}WORKINGCLASS + r_i.

But these models are appropriate to work with the full data, including all members of the EU. Within national group analyses, there are only two models (Models 4 and 5), resulted by the exclusion of the national group. Accordingly, studying abroad is included in Model 4 only; Logit (P_i) = β_{0i} +

β_{1i}STUDIEDABROAD + r_i. Model 5 represents the whole model within EU15 and NMS; Logit (P_i) = β_{0i} + β_{1i}STUDIEDABROAD + β_{2i}FEMALE + β_{3i}AGE + β_{4i}WORKING + β_{5i}RURAL + β_{6i}WORKINGCLASS + r_i.

FINDINGS

Immigrants' Contributions

Immigrants' contributions were represented as to whether people agree or disagree that immigrants contribute a lot to their country. According to Table 1, along with being in the upper/higher class category and living in an EU15 country, studying abroad increased the odds of agreeing with immigrants' contributions in both years.

In 2012, studying abroad made a bigger contribution than living in an EU15 country when they are only two variables in the model. However, after controlling the other variables, being in the upper/higher social class makes the greatest contribution. On the other hand, the contribution of living in an EU15 country to the odds of agreeing increases in 2018. Still, studying abroad is the third biggest contributing variable in the model. Considering other variables, age doesn't make an important contribution, even if it is statistically significant, because β is equal to 1.00 in 2012 and is extremely close to 1.00 in 2018. Similarly, gender doesn't make an essential contribution for almost the same reasons. However, the contribution of being employed increases between 2012 and 2018, even if it is only small. Living in a large town always increases the odds of agreeing as opposed to living in a rural area in both years.

Apart from this, when the association of studying abroad and perceptions on immigrants' contributions are compared by national groups in different years, the role of studying abroad in an understanding of immigrants' contributions could become clearer. According to Table 2, studying abroad is an important contributor to the odds of agreeing, especially in the NMS. In 2012, studying abroad is responsible for 38.5% of the explained variance in EU15 countries, but it goes up to 59.3% in the NMS. In 2018 however, it decreases to 31.6% in EU15 countries, whereas it increases to 58.7% in the NMS. Moreover, in 2012, after controlling the other variables, studying abroad is the second biggest contributor to the odds of agreeing in EU15 countries, but in the NMS, it is first. In 2018, being in higher social classes re-establishes itself as the biggest contributor in both national groups. In the EU15, studying abroad increases the odds of agreeing 2.11 times more than not studying abroad in 2012, but it increases only 1.54 times in 2018. However, in the NMS, the contribution of studying abroad goes up between 2012 and 2018.

Age and gender do not make an important contribution. However, being employed positively contributes to the odds of agreeing in both national groups and years. In 2012 and 2018, living in large towns makes both positive and significant contribution than living in a rural area in the EU15. In the NMS, however, the contribution of living in small/middle size and large towns becomes negative between 2012 and 2018. Apart from this, being in higher social classes makes a relatively more positive and significant contribution than being working class to the odds of agreeing, especially in the NMS.

Table 1: Association of Studying Abroad and Perceptions Related to Immigrants' Contribution in 2012 and 2018

	2012 ($n = 22,396$[a])						2018 ($n = 24,306$[a])					
	Model 1 ($n = 22,087$[b])		Model 2 ($n = 22,086$[b])		Model 3 ($n = 22,087$[b])		Model 1 ($n = 23,892$[b])		Model 2 ($n = 23,892$[b])		Model 3 ($n = 23,892$[b])	
	SE	β	SE	β	SE	β	SE	β	SE	β	SE	β
Constant	0.031	0.75***	0.034	0.62***	0.060	0.52***	0.031	0.45***	0.034	0.37***	0.065	0.48***
National group												
EU15	0.035	1.67***	0.036	1.92***	0.037	1.91***	0.034	2.89***	0.035	3.22***	0.036	3.29***
Studied abroad												
Yes			0.046	1.99***	0.046	1.83***			0.034	1.73***	0.035	1.57***
Gender												
Female					0.028	0.98					0.027	0.95*
Age					0.001	1.00***					0.001	0.99***
Employment												
Working					0.029	1.10***					0.029	1.16***
Type of community												
Small/medium town					0.032	1.24***					0.032	0.89***
Large town					0.037	1.41***					0.036	1.05
Social class-2012												
Middle class					0.028	1.33***						
Upper class					0.088	1.99***						
Social class-2018												
Lower middle											0.042	0.91*
Middle											0.032	1.17***
Upper middle											0.057	1.77***
Higher											0.178	2.20***
Negalkarke R^2	0.013		0.027		0.047		0.056		0.070		0.092	
Model χ^2 (df)	222.239 (1)***		457.968 (2)***		793.951 (9)***		1024.196 (1)***		1281.794 (2)***		1702.097 (11)***	

*p ≤ 0.05; **p ≤ 0.01; ***p ≤ 0.001.

[a]Unweighted observations
[b]Weighted observations

Table 2: Comparison of the Association of Studying Abroad and Perceptions Related to Immigrants' Contribution by National Groups

	2012								2018							
	EU15 (n = 13,542[a])		Model 5 (n = 13,197[b])		NMS (n = 8,854[a])		Model 5 (n = 8,291[b])		EU15 (n = 13,818[a])		Model 5 (n = 13,533[b])		NMS (n = 10,488[a])		Model 5 (n = 10,081[b])	
	Model 4 (n = 13,197[b])		Model 5		Model 4 (n = 8,290[b])		Model 5		Model 4 (n = 13,532[b])		Model 5		Model 4 (n = 10,081[b])		Model 5	
	SE	β	SE	β	SE	β	SE	β	SE	β	SE	β	SE	β	SE	β
Constant	0.018	1.18***	0.070	0.90***	0.026	0.66***	0.083	0.69***	0.019	1.19***	0.075	1.65***	0.028	0.36***	0.099	0.37***
Studied abroad																
Yes	0.072	2.30***	0.073	2.11***	0.050	1.64***	0.051	1.54***	0.048	1.67***	0.049	1.49***	0.045	1.87***	0.045	1.74***
Gender																
Female			0.036	0.99			0.045	0.93			0.035	0.94			0.044	1.00
Age			0.001	1.00***			0.001	1.00***			0.001	0.99***			0.001	1.00***
Occupation																
Employed			0.038	1.12***			0.047	1.04			0.037	1.16***			0.048	1.19***
Type of community																
Small/medium town			0.041	1.32***			0.054	0.97			0.041	0.89*			0.052	0.86*
Large town			0.048	1.54***			0.056	1.05			0.048	1.12*			0.057	0.81***
Social class-2012																
Middle class			0.036	1.35***			0.048	1.33***								
Upper class			0.120	2.24***			0.128	1.47***								
Social class-2018																
Lower middle											0.054	0.88*			0.073	1.07
Middle											0.042	1.14*			0.055	1.35***
Upper middle											0.075	1.80***			0.103	1.74***
Higher											0.237	1.84*			0.256	4.38***
Negalkarke R^2	0.015		0.039		0.016		0.027		0.012		0.038		0.027		0.046	
Model χ^2 (df)	146.400 (1)***		392.094 (8)***		99.219 (1)***		166.923 (8)***		177.798 (1)***		390.783 (10)***		195.173 (1)***		334.992 (10)***	

*$p \leq 0.05$; **$p \leq 0.01$; ***$p \leq 0.001$

[a]Unweighted observations
[b]Weighted observations

Feelings About Immigration

Feelings about immigration are represented as being positive with regard to immigration from both inside and outside the EU. The first analyses were made using all the data in the 2018 survey, without comparing the national groups.

Accordingly, Table 3 shows that studying abroad increases the odds of having positive feelings by 1.57 times after controlling the other variables for immigration from inside and outside the EU. It is the third biggest contributor to having positive feelings regarding immigration from EU member countries, after being in the upper-middle and higher social classes. It preserves its place for having positive feelings regarding immigration from outside the EU, but this time, after being in higher class and living in the EU15.

Considering gender, employment, type of community, and age, some of them make significant contributions to having positive feelings about immigration from the EU and outside of the EU. However, these are also only small contributions. But social class differs from all of them. For having positive feelings about immigration from EU member countries, social class makes more contribution than it makes in having positive feelings about immigration outside the EU, which means geographical factors related to the direction of immigration prevail against the social factors.

When the national groups are investigated separately, studying abroad has a more essential role in having positive feelings regarding immigration, whether it is from both inside and outside the EU. According to Table 4, studying abroad is the second major contributor to having positive feelings about immigration from both directions, and in both national groups, after being in the higher social classes. For having positive feelings about immigration from EU member countries, studying abroad is responsible for 27.27% of the explained variance in the EU15, whereas in NMS, it is 40.74%. However, for having positive feelings about immigration from outside the EU, studying abroad is responsible for 31.25% and 56.25% of the explained variance in EU15 and the NMS, respectively.

Moreover, age and gender make certain significant contributions, but these are often minor, since either $\beta = 1.00$ or is very close to 1.00. Being employed makes only one significant contribution and increases the odds of having positive feelings regarding immigration from EU member countries in the NMS by 1.24 times. Living in large towns significantly increases the odds of having positive feelings about immigration from EU member countries in the NMS more than living in rural areas, whereas it significantly increases the odds of having positive feelings about immigration from outside the EU in the EU15. Lastly, social class, especially being in a higher social class compared with being working class, increases the odds of having positive feelings about immigration from both directions in both national groups. However, it could be said that the contribution of social class also diminishes when it comes to immigration from outside the EU.

Table 3: Association of Studying Abroad and Feelings toward Immigration From Inside/Outside the EU-2018

	Positive feelings about immigration from EU member states ($n = 24{,}554$[a])						Positive feelings about immigration outside the EU ($n = 24{,}347$[a])					
	Model 1 ($n = 24{,}173$[b])		Model 2 ($n = 24{,}173$[b])		Model 3 ($n = 24{,}173$[b])		Model 1 ($n = 23{,}915$[b])		Model 2 ($n = 23{,}915$[b])		Model 3 ($n = 23{,}917$[b])	
	SE	β	SE	β	SE	β	SE	β	SE	β	SE	β
Constant	0.031	2.24***	0.033	1.88***	0.069	2.88***	0.031	0.43***	0.034	0.36***	0.064	0.60***
National group												
EU15	0.035	1.03	0.035	1.13***	0.036	1.12**	0.034	2.11***	0.035	2.35***	0.036	2.40***
Studied abroad												
Yes			0.038	1.76***	0.039	1.57***			0.033	1.74***	0.034	1.57***
Gender												
Female					0.029	0.90***					0.027	0.99
Age					0.001	0.99***					0.001	0.99***
Occupation												
Employed					0.031	1.01					0.029	1.04
Type of community												
Small/medium Town					0.033	0.93*					0.032	0.90***
Large town					0.039	1.08*					0.036	1.07
Social class												
Lower middle					0.043	1.01					0.042	1.00
Middle					0.034	1.38***					0.033	1.19***
Upper middle					0.066	2.26***					0.055	1.45***
Higher					0.225	2.97***					0.167	1.69**
Negalkarke R^2	0.000		0.014		0.045		0.028		0.043		0.068	
Model χ^2 (df)	0.703 (1)		235.941 (2)***		773.335 (11)***		500.973 (1)***		778.428 (2)***		1244.786 (11)***	

*$p \leq 0.05$; **$p \leq 0.01$; ***$p \leq 0.001$

[a]Unweighted observations
[b]Weighted observations

Table 4: Comparison of the Association of Studying Abroad and Feelings Toward Immigration From Inside/Outside the EU by National Groups-2018

	Positive feelings toward immigration from the EU member states								Positive feelings toward immigration outside the EU							
	EU15 (n = 13,959[a])		NMS (n = 10,595[a])						EU15 (n = 13,790[a])				NMS (n = 10,557[a])			
	Model 4 (n = 13,693[b])		Model 5 (n = 13,693[b])		Model 4 (n = 10,194[b])		Model 5 (n = 10,194[b])		Model 4 (n = 13,518[b])		Model 5 (n = 13,519[b])		Model 4 (n = 10,173[b])		Model 5 (n = 10,173[b])	
	SE	β	SE	β	SE	β	SE	β	SE	β	SE	β	SE	β	SE	β
Constant	0.020	2.10***	0.083	3.65***	0.026	1.96***	0.096	1.91***	0.019	0.83***	0.075	1.63***	0.028	0.36***	0.099	0.33***
Studied abroad																
Yes	0.055	1.89***	0.057	1.65***	0.047	1.52***	0.048	1.46***	0.046	1.77***	0.048	1.57***	0.045	1.66***	0.046	1.56***
Gender																
Female			0.038	0.89***			0.044	0.96			0.035	1.00			0.044	0.95
Age			0.001	0.99***			0.001	1.00**			0.001	0.99***			0.001	1.00**
Occupation																
Employed			0.041	0.96			0.048	1.24***			0.037	1.03			0.048	1.09
Type of community																
Small/medium town			0.044	0.90*			0.051	0.99			0.041	0.87***			0.052	1.03
Large town			0.052	1.03			0.057	1.26***			0.048	1.11*			0.057	0.88*
Social class																
Lower middle			0.056	0.97			0.069	1.22**			0.055	0.93			0.071	1.39***
Middle			0.045	1.51***			0.052	1.03			0.043	1.15***			0.056	1.50***
Upper middle			0.086	2.48***			0.113	1.46***			0.071	1.44***			0.104	1.61***
Higher			0.296	3.06***			0.364	2.81**			0.221	1.59*			0.256	2.75***
Negalkarke R^2	0.015		0.055		0.11		0.027		0.015		0.048		0.018		0.32	
Model χ^2 (df)	144.551 (1)***		542.116 (10)***		81.020 (1)*		194.091 (10)***		154.381 (1)***		497.553 (10)***		126.710 (1)***		230.932 (10)***	

*$p \leq 0.05$; **$p \leq 0.01$; ***$p \leq 0.001$

[a]Unweighted observations
[b]Weighted observations

DISCUSSION AND CONCLUSION

In examining the contribution of the study abroad experience on people's attitudes toward immigrants and immigration, one major finding is that contribution of studying abroad is significant for having positive attitudes toward immigrants and immigration, regardless of time or geography. Earlier research that focuses on the learning outcomes of students' educational experience outside of their country links the study abroad experience with personal gains, such as language acquisition (Coleman & Chafer, 2011; Kinginger, 2009), cultural competence (Perez-Encinas & Rodriguez-Pomeda, 2019; Watson et al., 2013), identity creation (King & Ruiz-Gelices, 2003), and intercultural competence (Alred & Byram 2002; Avcılar & Gök, 2021). The findings of such research contribute to the literature on social gains of studying abroad by linking it with personal attitudes toward others, namely immigrants. And our findings also partly explain attitudes toward immigrants by arguing that an educational immigration experience influences people's perception of immigrants.

Moreover, people from EU15 countries are more likely to have positive attitudes toward immigrants and immigration. Similarly, findings emerge from a study by Meuleman et al. (2009) that there is a regional difference among European countries toward immigration. They found that, "populations of Northern European countries, especially Scandinavian countries, tend to hold more open attitudes toward immigration, while Southern and Eastern European countries, those that started to experience sizeable immigration only recently, are among the least immigrant friendly" (p. 359). Furthermore, national group differences also affect the contribution of studying abroad. In the NMS, studying abroad explains more variance in the odds of having positive attitudes toward immigrants and immigration than in the EU15.

Another implication of this research is that there is a close relationship between peoples' socio-economic status and their attitudes toward immigrants. In other words, being in higher social classes and employment (having a job) have a positive contribution on having positive attitudes toward immigrants and immigration regardless of national group. Theoretical explanations of people's attitudes toward immigrants argue from economic perspectives that people might have negative attitudes toward immigrants when they see the immigrants as threats to their jobs and wages (O'Rourke & Sinnott, 2006; Wilkes et al., 2008). These findings can partly be explained by the findings of earlier research that job insecurity is greater in lower classes. Näswall and De Witte (2003) suggested that "employees in jobs characterized by manual labor, contingent workers, and to some extent older workers, and those with lower levels of education, experience higher levels of job insecurity" (p. 189). The findings of this research are consistent with the individual level socio-economic factors (household income, job loss) impacting on people's attitudes toward immigrants as found by Becchetti et al. (2010). However, there is need for a more detailed up-to-date examination is needed in explaining the association between socio-economic status and attitudes toward immigrants by future research for a better policy recommendation. Because there is a contradiction between the findings in the literature. Gang et al. (2002) using the Eurobarometer survey of 1988–1997 found that Europeans, who are in economic competition with foreigners have a negative view of immigrants. In their later study (Gang et al., 2013), using 1988, 2003, and 2008 Eurobarometer surveys, they argue that during economic strains, negative attitudes toward immigrants increase. By contrast, Valentino et al. (2019), whose study sample from four continents, argued that "there is little support for the Labor Market Competition hypothesis, since respondents are not more opposed to immigrants in their own SES stratum" (p. 1201) leaving a space for future research. Besides the individual level socio-economic factors, state level (welfare distribution among the residents) concerns that impact individuals' attitudes toward immigrants are also noteworthy to consider in future research from the perspective of what is called "welfare chauvinism."

Additional findings from the research suggest that people living in larger towns in the EU15 are more likely to have/develop positive attitudes toward immigrants and immigration than people living in rural areas, confirming the findings of Garcia and Davidson (2013) that people in rural areas have negative attitudes toward immigrants in the United States. However, in the NMS, people living in large towns are less likely to feel positive about immigration from outside EU member countries than people living in a rural area, which requires further investigation as to whether this difference is related to people's cultural and economic differences or is related to continuing adaptation of NMS to the European Union.

Gender and age do not make an essential contribution to the development of positive attitudes toward immigrants and immigration regardless of year and national group. Calahorrano (2013) found a hump-shaped association between population age, peaking at around the 70s, and people's concerns toward immigration. However, the data of this research do not confirm this association; one possible reason is due to the cross-sectional secondary data use in the current research. According to one perspective, women are more "others-oriented" than men, who tend to be self-oriented, and women have a more favorable outlook toward other racial groups than men (Hughes & Tuch, 2003). But the findings of this research do not find supportive evidence for such a school of thought.

Overall, this study shows that studying abroad may play an important role in having positive attitudes toward immigrants and immigration, even after controlling certain socio-demographic factors. National group characteristics and time factors may lessen or strengthen the contribution of studying abroad, but its positive and significant contribution remains salient. A possible explanation for this could be the relatively similar experience that students studying abroad and people migrating have, because of the similar motives they may share. So, increasing the opportunities to study abroad among EU member countries could be an essential solution, especially for people living in the NMS, and from working or lower-middle-class sections of society in both national groups. Therefore, the findings of this research seem to provide promising pieces of evidence for those researchers who investigate the social outcomes of study abroad, and for those policymakers of EU countries struggling with an increasing number of immigrants and, as a result, an increase in the number of citizens who oppose them. As this study is limited to the European citizens' study abroad experience in other European countries, it leaves space for future research on the role of the European citizens' study abroad experience outside the EU, and the role of non-European citizens' study abroad experience in their attitudes toward immigration.

Limitations

There are several limitations of the study. First, the exact meaning of the term "studying abroad" is not clearly articulated in the surveys so it may include different types of degree and credit mobility or abroad voluntary activities covering short- or long-term study abroad periods. Second, unlike the experimental design surveys, the cross-sectional data utilized in this study hinder to make sharp decisions on the effect of studying abroad on the attitudes toward immigration and immigrants. Accordingly, we suggest further investigation to confirm whether this positive role of studying abroad in the attitudes toward immigrants and immigration is a result of the abroad study experience or just an overrepresentation of respondents who already have positive attitudes, considering the possible selection effects originating from the absence of pre-measure of those attitudes.

A similar limitation is related to the role of socio-economic status in both studying abroad and attitudes toward immigration. The current study shows that people from higher social classes have positive attitudes toward immigration. Besides, mobile students are often from the higher strata (Van Mol & Timmerman, 2014), and lack of financial means and study costs could be a hindering factor the mobility (Dabasi-Halász et al., 2019; Souto-Otero et al., 2013). So, socio-economic status might also be a preexisting factor for the mobility of the people, and the actual contribution of studying abroad could be limited because of such interaction effect.

REFERENCES

Akrami, N., Ekehammar, B., & Araya, T. (2000). Classical and modern racial prejudice: A study of attitudes toward immigrants in Sweden. *European Journal of Social Psychology, 30*(4), 521–532. https://doi.org/10.1002/1099-0992(200007/08)30:4%3C521::AID-EJSP5%3E3.0.CO;2-N

Alred, G., & Byram, M. (2002). Becoming an intercultural mediator: A longitudinal study of residence abroad. *Journal of Multilingual and Multicultural Development, 23*(5), 339–352. https://doi.org/10.1080/01434630208666473

Avcılar, A., & Gök, E. (2021). Intercultural effectiveness of international and domestic students: The case of a Turkish Public University. *Journal of International Students, 12*(1). https://doi.org/10.32674/jis.v12i1.2972

Bade, K. J. (2004). Legal and illegal immigration into Europe: Experiences and challenges. *European Review (Chichester, England), 12*(3), 339–375. https://doi.org/10.1017/S1062798704000316

Barber, C., Fennelly, K., & Torney-Purta, J. (2013). Nationalism and support for immigrants' rights among adolescents in 25 countries. *Applied Developmental Science, 17*(2), 60–75. https://doi.org/10.1080/10888691.2013.774870

Becchetti, L., Rossetti, F., & Castriota, S. (2010). Real household income and attitude toward immigrants: An empirical analysis. *The Journal of Socio-Economics, 39*(1), 81–88. https://doi.org/10.1016/j.socec.2009.07.012

Bilodeau, A., & Fadol, N. (2011). The roots of contemporary attitudes toward immigration in Australia: Contextual and individual-level influences. *Ethnic and racial studies, 34*(6), 1088–1109. https://doi.org/10.1080/01419870.2010.550630

Bozheva, A. (2020). Geographic embeddedness of higher education institutions in the migration policy domain. *Journal of International Students, 10*(2), 443–465. https://doi.org/10.32674/jis.v10i2.961

Bridges, S., & Mateut, S. (2009). *Should they stay or should they go? Attitudes towards immigration in Europe*. Sheffield Economic Research Paper Series. SERP Number: 2009008. ISSN 1749–8368. Department of Economics, University of Sheffield.

Calahorrano, L. (2013). Population aging and individual attitudes toward immigration: Disentangling age, cohort and time effects: Population aging and immigration attitudes. *Review of International Economics, 21*(2), 342–353. https://doi.org/10.1111/roie.12040

Carlson, J. S., & Widaman, K. F. (1988). The effects of study abroad during college on attitudes toward other cultures. *International Journal of Intercultural Relations: IJIR, 12*(1), 1–17. https://doi.org/10.1016/0147-1767(88)90003-X

Coleman, J. A., & Chafer, T. (2011). The experience and long-term impact of study abroad by Europeans in an African context. In F. Dervin (Ed.), *Analysing the consequences of academic mobility and migration* (pp. 67–96). Cambridge Scholars Publishing.

Dabasi-Halász, Z., Kiss, J., Manafi, I., Marinescu, D. E., Lipták, K., Roman, M., & Lorenzo-Rodriguez, J. (2019). International youth mobility in Eastern and Western Europe –the case of the Erasmus[+] programme. *Migration Letters: An International Journal of Migration Studies, 16*(1), 61–72. https://doi.org/10.33182/ml.v16i1.626

Davidov, E., & Semyonov, M. (2017). Attitudes toward immigrants in European societies. *International Journal of Comparative Sociology, 58*(5), 359–366. https://doi.org/10.1177%2F0020715217732183

De la Rica, S., Glitz, A., & Ortega, F. (2013). *Immigration in Europe: Trends, policies and empirical evidence*. IZA Discussion Papers, No. 7778. Institute for the Study of Labor (IZA), Bonn.

Economidou, C., Karamanis, D., Kechrinioti, A., & Xesfingi, S. (2020). The role of social capital in shaping Europeans' immigration sentiments. *IZA Journal of Development and Migration, 11*(1). https://doi.org/10.2478/izajodm-2020-0003

European Commission, Brussels. (2015). *Eurobarometer 77.3 (2012)* [Data set]. GESIS Data Archive. https://doi.org/10.4232/1.12050

European Commission, Brussels. (2018). *Eurobarometer 89.1 (2018)* [Data set]. GESIS Data Archive. https://doi.org/10.4232/1.13154

Eurostat (2019). Migration and migrant population statistics. https://ec.europa.eu/eurostat/statisticsexplained/index.php/Migration_and_migrant_population_statistics#Migrant_population:_22.3_million_non-EU_citizens_living_in_the_EU_on_1_January_2018. Accessed on 21/02/2020.

Facchini, G., & Mayda, A. M. (2012). Individual attitudes towards skilled migration: An empirical analysis across countries. *World Economy, 35*(2), 183–196. https://doi.org/10.1111/j.1467-9701.2011.01427.x

Field, A. (2009). *Discovering statistics using SPSS* (3rd ed.). SAGE Publications.

Findlay, A. M. (2011). An assessment of supply and demand-side theorizations of international student mobility: Theorizing international student mobility. *International Migration (Geneva, Switzerland), 49*(2), 162–190. https://doi.org/10.1111/j.1468-2435.2010.00643.x

Fussell, E. (2014). Warmth of the welcome: Attitudes toward immigrants and immigration policy. *Annual Review of Sociology, 40*(1), 479–498. https://doi.org/10.1146/annurev-soc-071913-043325

Gang, I. N., Rivera-Batiz, F. L., Yun, M. S. (2002), Economic strain, ethnic concentration and attitudes towards foreigners in the European Union. IZA Discussion Paper No. 578.

Gang, I. N., Rivera-Batiz, F. L., & Yun, M. S. (2013). Economic strain, education and attitudes towards foreigners in the European union: Attitudes towards foreigners. *Review of International Economics, 21*(2), 177–190. https://doi.org/10.1142/9789813208711_0017

Garcia, C., & Davidson, T. (2013). Are rural people more anti-immigrant than urban people? A comparison of attitudes toward immigration in the United States. *Journal of Rural Social Sciences, 28*(1), 80–105.

Genge, E., & Bartolucci, F. (2019). Are attitudes towards immigration changing in Europe? An analysis based on bidimensional latent class IRT models. https://mpra.ub.uni-muenchen.de/94672/1/MPRA_paper_94672.pdf

Gümüş, S., Gök, E., & Esen, M. (2020). A review of research on international student mobility: Science mapping the existing knowledge base. *Journal of Studies in International Education, 24*(5), 495–517. https://doi.org/10.1177%2F1028315319893651

Hair, J. F., Black, W. C., Babin, B. J., & Anderson, R. E. (2013). *Multivariate data analysis: Pearson new international edition* (7th ed.). Pearson Education.

Hatton, T. J. (2016). Immigration, public opinion and the recession in Europe. *Economic Policy, 31*(86), 205–246. https://doi.org/10.1093/epolic/eiw004

Hendershot, K., & Sperandio, J. (2009). Study abroad and development of global citizen identity and cosmopolitan ideals in undergraduates. *Current Issues in Comparative Education, 12*(1), 45–55.

Hoxhaj, R., & Zuccotti, C. V. (2019). How are attitudes towards immigrants in Europe shaped by regional contexts? A study of the conditioning relationship between immigrants' concentration and socioeconomic environment. *SSRN Electronic Journal.* https://doi.org/10.2139/ssrn.3393555

Huber, P., & Oberdabernig, D. A. (2016). The impact of welfare benefits on natives' and immigrants' attitudes toward immigration. *European Journal of Political Economy, 44*, 53–78. https://doi.org/10.1016/j.ejpoleco.2016.05.003

Hughes, M., & Tuch, S. A. (2003). Gender differences in whites' racial attitudes: Are women's attitudes really more favorable? *Social Psychology Quarterly, 66*(4), 384–401. https://psycnet.apa.org/doi/10.2307/1519836

King, R., & Raghuram, P. (2013). International student migration: Mapping the field and new research agendas: Mapping the field and new research agenda in ISM. *Population, Space and Place, 19*(2), 127–137. https://doi.org/10.1002/psp.1746

King, R., & Ruiz-Gelices, E. (2003). International student migration and the European Year Abroad?: Effects on European identity and subsequent migration behaviour. *International Journal of Population Geography, 9*(3), 229–252. https://doi.org/10.1002/ijpg.280

Kinginger, C. (2009). *Language learning and study abroad: A critical reading of research* (2009th ed.). Palgrave Macmillan UK.

Kleinschmidt, H. (2003). *People on the move: Attitudes toward and perceptions of migration in medieval and modern Europe*. Praeger.

Leclerc, J. (2018). *Terrorism and opinions towards migration* [Université Catholique de Louvain]. http:// hdl.handle.net/2078.1/thesis:14578

Leong, C.-H., & Ward, C. (2006). Cultural values and attitudes toward immigrants and multiculturalism: The case of the Eurobarometer survey on racism and xenophobia. *International Journal of Intercultural Relations: IJIR, 30*(6), 799–810. https://doi.org/10.1016/j.ijintrel.2006.07.001

Marozzi, M. (2016). Construction, robustness assessment and application of an index of perceived level of socio-economic threat from immigrants: A study of 47 European countries and regions. *Social Indicators Research, 128*(1), 413–437. https://doi.org/10.1007/s11205-015-1037-z

Mayda, A. M. (2006). Who is against immigration? A cross-country investigation of individual attitudes toward immigrants. *The Review of Economics and Statistics, 88*(3), 510–530. https://doi.org/10.1162/rest.88.3.510

Meuleman, B., Davidov, E., & Billiet, J. (2009). Changing attitudes toward immigration in Europe, 2002–2007: A dynamic group conflict theory approach. *Social Science Research, 38*(2), 352–365. https://doi.org/10.1016/j.ssresearch.2008.09.006

Murard, E. (2017). Less welfare or fewer foreigners? Immigrant inflows and public opinion towards redistribution and migration policy. IZA Discussion Papers, No. 10805. Institute of Labor Economics (IZA), Bonn.

Näswall, K., & De Witte, H. (2003). Who feels insecure in Europe? Predicting job insecurity from background variables. *Economic and Industrial Democracy, 24*(2), 189–215. https://doi.org/10.1177%2F0143831X03024002003

O'Connell, M. (2011). How do high-skilled natives view high-skilled immigrants? A test of trade theory predictions. *European Journal of Political Economy, 27*(2), 230–240. https://doi.org/10.1016/j.ejpoleco.2010.11.002

O'Rourke, K. H., & Sinnott, R. (2006). The determinants of individual attitudes towards immigration. *European Journal of Political Economy, 22*(4), 838–861. https://doi.org/10.1016/j.ejpoleco.2005.10.005

Paas, T., & Halapuu, V. (2012). Attitudes towards immigrants and the integration of ethnically diverse societies. *Eastern Journal of European Studies, 3*(2), 161–176.

Pardos-Prado, S. (2011). Framing attitudes towards immigrants in Europe: When competition does not matter. *Journal of Ethnic and Migration Studies, 37*(7), 999–1015. https://doi.org/10.1080/1369183X.2011.572421

Perez-Encinas, A., & Rodriguez-Pomeda, J. (2019). Geographies and cultures of international student experiences in higher education: Shared perspectives between students from different countries. *Journal of International Students, 9*(2), 412–431. https://doi.org/10.32674/jis.v9i2.271

Rustenbach, E. (2010). Sources of negative attitudes toward immigrants in Europe: A multi-level analysis. *The International Migration Review, 44*(1), 53–77. https://doi.org/10.1111/j.1747-7379.2009.00798.x

Scipioni, M., Tintori, G., Alessandrini, A., Migali, S. and Natale, F. (2019). *Immigration and trust in the EU: A territorial analysis of voting behaviour and attitudes.* Publications Office of the European Union. https://data.europa.eu/doi/10.2760/76114

Souto-Otero, M., Huisman, J., Beerkens, M., De Wit, H., & Vujić, S. (2013). Barriers to international student mobility. *Educational Researcher, 42*(2), 70–77. https://doi.org/10.3102/0013189X12466696

Stöhr, T., & Wichardt, P. C. (2016). Conflicting identities: Cosmopolitan or anxious? Appreciating concerns of host country population improves attitudes towards immigrants. Kiel Working Paper, No. 2045. Kiel Institute for the World Economy (IfW), Kiel.

Strabac, Z., Aalberg, T., & Valenta, M. (2014). Attitudes towards Muslim immigrants: Evidence from survey experiments across four countries. *Journal of Ethnic and Migration Studies, 40*(1), 100–118. https://doi.org/10.1080/1369183X.2013.831542

Tarrant, M. A., Rubin, D. L., & Stoner, L. (2014). The added value of study abroad: Fostering a global citizenry. *Journal of Studies in International Education, 18*(2), 141–161. https://doi.org/10.1177%2F1028315313497589

Triandafyllidou, A. (2004). Immigrants and national identity in Europe. Routledge.

United Nations. (2018). *International migration report 2017: Highlights.* Department of Economic and Social Affairs, United Nations.

Valentino, N. A., Soroka, S. N., Iyengar, S., Aalberg, T., Duch, R., Fraile, M. Hahn, K. S., Hansen, M. K., Harell, A., Helbling, M., Jackman, S. D., & Kobayashi, T. (2019). Economic and cultural drivers of immigrant support worldwide. *British Journal of Political Science, 49*(4), 1201–1226. https://doi.org/10.1017/S000712341700031X

Van Mol, C., & Timmerman, C. (2014). Should I stay or should I go? An analysis of the determinants of intra-European student mobility. *Population, Space and Place, 20*(5), 465–479. https://doi.org/10.1002/psp.1833

Ward, C., & Masgoret, A.-M. (2006). An integrative model of attitudes toward immigrants. *International Journal of Intercultural Relations: IJIR, 30*(6), 671–682. https://doi.org/10.1016/j.ijintrel.2006.06.002

Watson, J. R., Siska, P., & Wolfel, R. L. (2013). Assessing gains in language proficiency, cross-cultural competence, and regional awareness during study abroad: A preliminary study. *Foreign Language Annals, 46*(1), 62–79. https://doi.org/10.1111/flan.12016

Wilkes, R., Guppy, N., & Farris, L. (2008). "No thanks, we're full": Individual characteristics, national context, and changing attitudes toward immigration. *The International Migration Review, 42*(2), 302–329. https://doi.org/10.1111/j.1747-7379.2008.00126.x

YAKUP ÖZ, PhD, is a research assistant in the Department of Educational Sciences at Karamanoglu Mehmetbey University. His research interests lie in the area of internationalization of higher education, public diplomacy, European studies, and comparative and international education. Email: yakupoz@kmu.edu.tr

ENES GÖK is an associate professor of the Department of Educational Sciences at Karamanoglu Mehmetbey University. In the last four years, he has worked as the head of Educational Evaluation Center and Distance Education Center. He also served as the consultant at the Higher Education Quality Council of Turkey from 2018 to 2020. He currently is a visiting scholar at Indiana University-Bloomington. He holds an MEd (2010) and EdD (2013) in higher education management from the University of Pittsburgh. During his education, he also served as the project associate and program coordinator at the University of Pittsburgh's Institute for International Studies in Education, participating in national and international projects and events. His research interests include higher education administration, internationalization of higher education, and comparative education. Email: enesgok@kmu.edu.tr

Research Article

© *Journal of International Students*
Volume 12, Issue 2 (2022), pp. 510-530
ISSN: 2162-3104 (Print), 2166-3750 (Online)
doi: 10.32674/jis.v12i2.3642
ojed.org/jis

How International Students' Acculturation Motivation Develops over Time in an International Learning Environment: A Longitudinal Study

Adedapo T. Aladegbaiye
Menno D.T. De Jong
Ardion Beldad
University of Twente, The Netherlands

ABSTRACT

This research investigates how the acculturation motivation (AM) of new international students develops over time, and which factors play a role in this development. In the context of a Dutch university, we interviewed 25 students from 17 countries three times over eight months. The findings show that initial AM levels can be categorized as high or low. These AM levels evolved into four patterns in the three interview rounds: high-low-low, high-low-high, low-high-low, and low-high-high. After four months, twelve factors emerged as affecting the development of students' AM levels. Prominent factors were prior international experience, language issues, and perceived student identities. After eight months, seven additional factors contributed to subsequent changes in students' AM levels, including the perceived international learning environment, friendship networks, and teachers' role in intercultural contacts. Findings suggest that universities can introduce interventions which could improve international students' acculturation experiences at specific times.

Keywords: acculturation experience, acculturation motivation, international learning environment, international students, university

Student-migrants experience no linear process toward adaptation to new socio-cultural and academic environments (Zhou et al., 2008). The acculturation process unfolds over time and may differ among individuals (Rienties & Tempelaar, 2013). This means that some international students can adjust faster than others in their acculturation journey. Still, many international students continue to struggle to adjust to their new international learning environment (ILE). Part of the challenges they face is the mismatch between their expectations and their lived experiences (Smith & Khawaja, 2011). Such a mismatch may have psychological, academic, and socio-cultural consequences such as depression, homesickness, loneliness, and poor academic performances (Dentakos et al., 2017).

Unlike economic migrants who move for work, or refugees and asylum seekers who move for safety, international students are a special group of migrants called sojourners because of their temporary stay for educational purposes in a new society (Dentakos et al., 2017). The uniqueness of student-migrants makes current acculturation models insufficient to wholly explore their acculturation experiences (Smith & Khawaja, 2011). This means that their acculturation motivation (AM) may also significantly differ from other migrant groups over time (Berry et al., 1987). A congruence between migrants' expectation of the new society and their real experience can enhance their motivation to acculturate (Dentakos et al., 2017; Recker et al., 2017).

So far, little is known about how international students' AM develops over time and the factors that are responsible for these changes. This study tries to fill this gap by addressing two research questions: (1) how does international students' AM develop over time in an ILE, and (2) what factors play a role in this development in their AM? Past studies (e.g., Dentakos et al., 2017) have tried to understand AM via quantitative surveys, even though the use of longitudinal studies have often been recommended to gain more detailed insights into the acculturation experiences of international students (e.g., Smith & Khawaja, 2011). Therefore, this research longitudinally explores new international students' AM development via periodic, semi-structured interviews.

LITERATURE REVIEW

Acculturation

Acculturation is the change process that occurs when two cultures come into firsthand, unmediated, and continuous contact over time (Berry, 2005). International students who opt for studying abroad directly experience this change, albeit in differing degrees (Rienties & Tempelaar, 2013). Acculturation encompasses three dimensions of international students' experiences in a new ILE (Berry, 2006): a socio-cultural dimension, a psychological dimension, and an academic dimension. The socio-cultural dimension includes friendship networks and contacts (Ward & Kennedy, 1999). The psychological dimension includes mental health and well-being and identity (Berry & Hou, 2016). The academic dimension includes academic systems, academic performance, and academic satisfaction (Yu & Wright, 2016). Student-migrants need to successfully adapt in these dimensions for a wholesome acculturation experience while achieving personal and academic goals (Yakobov et al., 2019).

Expectations and Acculturation Experiences

Students transitioning to a new society have expectations of the associated benefits and difficulties in adapting to the three dimensions identified above (Berry, 2005). For example, Wintre et al. (2015) identified eight underlying themes of motivations for foreign study: new experiences, education, future career and immigration prospects, qualities of the host country, qualities of the institution, financial reasons, location, and friends and relatives in the host country.

Ward et al. (1998) noted that the U-curve hypothesis highlights the stages student-migrants go through before adaptation. This begins with the honeymoon stage, when everything is new and exciting. However, the euphoria of this stage may set unrealistic expectations of the new environment. Subsequently, the identified differences between the new system and what students were used to could result in degrees of culture shock while expectations become realistic (Berry, 2005). This is followed by the adjustment phase in which student-migrants learn to accept the new conditions. Finally, during the adaptation stage, students are getting used to the new conditions.

Fulfilled expectations have been found to have a positive impact on adjustment (Yakobov et al., 2019). When expectations are unfulfilled, students may experience depression, loneliness, and anxiety. International students, for example, experience higher levels of acculturative stress than other migrant groups with permanent residence intentions (Berry et al., 1987). Empirical studies established that factors such as personality, age, gender, acculturative stress, openness of the host society, attitudes, and cultural dimensions have consequences for the lived experiences of foreign students in their adaptation to the new ILE. However, such effects were examined regardless of how AM changes over time. This research, however, explores students' AM, which has been found to have stronger effects on adaptation than other socio-demographic and psychosocial variables (Dentakos et al., 2017).

Acculturation Motivation

Berry (2005) identified four acculturation orientations: assimilation, integration, separation, and marginalization. However, this approach has been criticized for being too reductionistic (Smith & Khawaja, 2011). Besides, it neglects the international and academic nature of the ILE because it was not specifically designed for student-migrants. Therefore, academic scholars have proposed other concepts for exploring international students' acculturation. Chirkov et al. (2007) advocated the use of AM instead of acculturation orientation in student studies. Dentakos et al. (2017) defined AM as the willingness of international students "to learn about the host culture, to develop friendships with host members, and to explore the host country's social and cultural environments"

(p. 29). This definition, though more applicable, also excludes the other international students in the acculturation process and the influence of the ILE on acculturation (Chirkov et al., 2007).

While an ILE operates within the context of the host society, it may be distinct from it because of its international nature. For example, the official language at the university may differ from the native language of the society (Carmit & Philip, 2006). Acculturation within the host university, therefore, differs significantly from acculturation in the host society. For the purpose of this work, AM in an ILE refers to the willingness of an international student to participate in academic activities, develop friendships with domestic and other international students, and engage in the university's socio-cultural environment.

Acculturation Motivation and Adaptation Outcomes

The effects of AM have been investigated in various studies. Recker et al. (2017) investigated AM from the lenses of motivation for cultural maintenance, which indicates interest to retain the home culture, and motivation for cultural expansion, which refers to the willingness to accommodate new cultural traits. They argued that motivations can change because migrants' adaptation is nonlinear. Chirkov et al. (2007) examined how self-determined motivation and goal contents for foreign study (e.g., good education) affect students' adaptation to the new society. They discovered that self-motivated students had better adaptation outcomes than non-self-motivated students. They also identified two key factors in international students' goals for foreign study: (1) preservation factors such as avoiding disadvantageous conditions back home were found to negatively affect adaptation, whereas (2) self-development factors were found to positively affect adaptation. Dentakos et al. (2017) found that AM predicts students' adjustment and intentions for permanent residence in the new society. International students with low AM levels had negative perceptions about socio-cultural adjustment, the university, and peer relationships compared with students with high AM levels. AM also affects academic adaptation, especially because students prioritize academic achievement above socio-cultural and psychological adjustment (Eshel & Rosenthal-Sokolov, 2000).

METHOD

This study employed a longitudinal approach based on in-depth, semi-structured interviews. This method was appropriate to allow participants to freely share their acculturation expectations and experiences (Owen, 2014). The study focused on the first eight months (end of August 2019—mid-April 2020) of the participants' experiences at the university. This was done in three interview rounds: at the start of the academic year, after four months, and after eight months. The research was approved by the Ethics Committee of the University of Twente, the Netherlands.

Participants

Twenty-five new international students of the University of Twente participated in this study. They held no dual Dutch nationality and had not previously lived or studied in the Netherlands. They were recruited during the August 2019 introduction program. Table 1 gives an overview of the demographic characteristics of the participants. As can be seen, the participants had diverse national backgrounds. There were 14 males. Most of the participants enrolled for a master's program. They had varying degrees of prior international experience. Their ages ranged from 19 to 31 years.

All 25 participants completed the first interview round. Only 23 participants participated in the second interview (after four months), while 22 participants also completed the third interview (after eight months).

Interview Guides and Procedure

The interviews aimed at gaining an understanding of participants' acculturation experiences, adjustment status, and expectations for the following months. The first interview round focused on participants' goals, pre- and post-arrival preparedness, expectations and anticipated challenges, and initial experiences. The second and third rounds predominantly looked back at participants' experiences but also addressed their expectations for the upcoming months.

Questions addressed their academic and social activities, their impressions of the university and their social environment, and their positive and challenging experiences.

Table 1: Participants' Demographics

Participant	Country	Gender	Age	Study level	Intl. experience
1	Estonia	M	22	Master	>12 months
2	India	M	22	Master	0–3 months
3	Mexico	F	23	Master	0–3 months
4	Colombia	F	31	Pre-master	>12 months
5	India	F	22	Master	0–3 months
6	Germany	F	23	Master	>12 months
7	Japan	F	21	Master	0–3 months
8	Mexico	M	25	Master	6–9 months
9	Belarus	M	21	Pre-master	>12 months
10	Spain	M	23	Master	>12 months
11	Germany	M	25	Pre-master	3–6 months
12	Mexico	F	22	Bachelor	>12 months
13	USA	F	25	Master	>12 months
14	France	M	23	Master	0–3 months
15	India	M	22	Master	0–3 months
16	India	M	22	Master	0–3 months
17	China	F	23	Pre-master	>12 months

Participant	Country	Gender	Age	Study level	Intl. experience
18	USA	M	24	Master	0–3 months
19	India	M	25	Master	0–3 months
20	New Zealand	M	20	Bachelor	>12 months
21	Poland	M	19	Bachelor	0–3 months
22	Taiwan	F	24	Master	0–3 months
23	Ireland	M	23	Master	>12 months
24	India	F	23	Master	>12 months
25	Zimbabwe	F	23	Master	>12 months

The interviews lasted between 25 and 70 mins. All interviews were audio-recorded and transcribed.

Data Analysis

We holistically assessed each participant's AM level using four metrics, each awarded one point. Therefore, AM level represented participants' willingness to: (1) participate in the university's academic activities (e.g., class attendance, personal and group study, assignments, projects, and examinations) (1 point), (2) develop friendships with domestic students (1 point), (3) develop friendships with other international students outside of their own countries (1 point), and (4) take part in the university's socio-cultural environment by participating in social activities, cultural events, and sports (1 point). An overall score of 0 means no motivation, a score of 1–2 stands for a low AM, and a score of 3–4 represents a high AM. For example, a participant who participated in academic activities, who developed friendships with domestic students and other international students, and who explored the university's socio-cultural landscape gets a total of four points and was considered to have a high AM.

Data were then analyzed following Wintre et al.'s (2015) approach for thematic analysis, including phases of data transcription, data reduction by excluding irrelevant information, highlighting key information, spotting and collating emerging themes, and, finally, coding the constructs. Specifically, all three transcripts of each participant were chronologically analyzed to have a feel of their AM at the different stages and scored appropriately. Emerging factors were then coded and compared among the participants and thematically categorized.

A second coder analyzed the transcripts of three randomly selected participants (nine transcripts in total). The Cohen's kappas for intercoder agreement appeared to be sufficient: .85 for AM measurement and .84 for the acculturation factors extracted.

FINDINGS

Overview of Students' AM Development

Table 2 gives an overview of participants' AM development. The findings suggest that students' AM fluctuates over time and that periods of lower AM levels are quite common among international students. Furthermore, they underline the individual and non-linear nature of students' acculturation processes. Some participants with high AM levels in the beginning saw a decline in their AM after four months. While some of them were able to attain a high AM level after eight months, others did not, and vice versa. We thus distinguished four patterns of AM development among the 22 participants who completed all interview rounds: high-low-low ($n = 6$), high-low-high ($n = 9$), low-high-low ($n = 3$), and low-high-high ($n = 4$).

Table 2: Development of Participants' AM Levels

Participant	Initial AM	After 4 months	After 8 months
1, 10, 13, 14, 15, 20	High	Low	Low
3, 4, 6, 8, 11, 19, 21, 23, 24	High	Low	High
9, 16, 22	Low	High	Low
5, 12, 18, 25	Low	High	High
17	Low	High	–
2, 7	Low	–	–

Factors Affecting Students' AM Levels

Table 3 presents factors that, according to their self-reports, affected participants' AM levels after four and eight months. Several observations can be made. Participants' AM levels were affected by different factors, which played their role simultaneously or subsequently (on average, about 11 factors per participant were mentioned). With only one exception (Participant 1), all participants experienced a mix of positive and negative factors. The ratio between factors playing a positive and a negative role differed per participant, but, on average, the positive and negative factors were relatively balanced (47% versus 53%, respectively). With only a few exceptions, factors were mentioned as playing both positive and negative roles. The exceptions were living costs, academic workload, discrimination and stereotypes (only negative), and university resources (only positive). Finally, seven new factors emerged from the third interview round, suggesting that there may be factors that only become salient after a longer stay. Below, we will elaborately discuss the findings.

Initial AM Levels

The analysis of the first interview round revealed two general AM levels—high ($n = 15$) and low ($n = 10$)—among the participants. The characteristics of both groups will be summarized below.

Participants with High Initial AM Levels

Most participants reported a high AM level at the beginning of their student experience. They consciously chose to study at the university. Some already had prior experience studying abroad. They displayed willingness to explore the ILE. They were open to interacting, working, making friends, and living with domestic and other international students and were motivated to put effort into these. They were eager to explore the socio-cultural and academic environment of the university. They had plans to learn Dutch and improve their English. One participant, for instance, said:

I grew up meeting people from different cultures and this made me curious about other cultures, especially how people think. So, I am excited about my new experience here in the university. [P24]

Participants with Low Initial AM Levels

Participants with low initial AM levels had no specific positive or negative expectations regarding their new situation. The university was not necessarily their first choice. Some had little or no prior experience abroad. They were more oriented toward staying within their own cultural group or within the international students' group than interacting with domestic students. They were open to interacting, working, making friends, and living with domestic or international students, but showed no intentions to put effort into this. They showed little interest in exploring the socio-cultural environment of the university. They were undecided on learning Dutch, but would improve their English skills. One participant said:

I'm worried I may have some problems, especially with making friends…. I don't want to suddenly feel lonely. Right now, I don't see any interests from other students. [P5]

Developments in Participants' AM Levels after Four Months

The analyses of the participants' experiences after four months showed an interesting shift in their AM levels. Most participants noted that they were not yet adjusted to the socio-cultural landscape of the ILE. They had varying interests to build friendships and explore the socio-cultural environment of the university. However, they were all motivated to participate in academic activities. Interestingly, participants who had initially displayed high AM levels reported low AM levels ($n = 15$), while those who had low initial AM levels showed high AM levels ($n = 8$) at this stage. The confrontation in the first months between expectations and experiences resulted in a dialectical process, in which positive initial positions were relativized by difficulties and disappointments and negative positions were counterbalanced by unforeseen positive events.

Some factors that were mentioned as having positive effects on the AM levels of some participants had negative effects on others. We distinguished 12 factors which contributed to these differences in experiences among participants and grouped them into three categories. First, there are *personal factors*, which reflect participants' past or current experiences and individual perceptions. Second, there are *social factors*, which emerged as a result of social contacts with others at the university. Third, there are *academic factors*, which are linked with academic activities, academic personnel, or academic processes at the university. These are discussed below.

Table 3: Participants' Responses Coded by Thematic Factors Identified

Participant	1	2	3	4	5	6	7	8	9	10	11	12	13	14	15	16	17	18	19	20	21	22	23	24	25
Initial AM level	H	L	H	H	L	H	L	H	L	H	H	L	H	H	H	L	L	L	H	H	H	L	H	H	L
AM Factors within 4 months																									
1. Prior intl. experience	−		−	−	+	−		−	+	−		+	−		+		+			+	+		−	−	−
2. Language issues	−		−	−	−	−		−	−		−	−	−	−	−			+	−	−	−			−	−
3. Perceived student identities	−		−	−	+			−		−	−	+	−			−	+			−	−	−	−	−	−
4. Extracurricular participation	−		−	+	+	−																			
5. Housing search experience										−	−					+		+			−			−	+
6. Living costs			−		−			−			−		−		−		−	−						−	−
7. Intl. in-group pressure	−		−	−	−		−	+		+	+			+											+
8. Other students' opinions		+			+		+	+		+	+														
9. University resources		+			+					+															+
10. Study program characteristic	−				+							+			+										+
11. Academic workload	−		−	−	−		−	−		−	−	−	−	−	−	−	−		−	−		−	−		
12. Information on procedures			−				−														+		+		
AM level after 4 months	L		L	L	H	L		L	H	L	L	H	L	L	L	H	H	H	L	L	L	H	L	L	H
Additional AM Factors within 8 months																									
1. Perceived discrimination & stereotype					−																	−		−	
2. Perceived ILE identity	−		+		+	+	+		−	−	+	+	−	−	−	−	−			+	+	−	+	+	+
3. Friendship networks		+	+	+	+	+	+		−	+	−			−	−					+	+	−	+	+	+
4. Interaction with other students				+			+				+				−	−				+	+	−	+	+	+

Participant	1	2	3	4	5	6	7	8	9	10	11	12	13	14	15	16	17	18	19	20	21	22	23	24	25
5. Intercultural exchange events			+	+	+		+				+		+		−	−				+	+			+	+
6. Interaction with teachers & uni. Staff	−		+	+	+	+	+	−	−	+	+	−	+		+					+	+		+	+	+
7. Teachers' role in intercultural contact	−		+		+			+	+							−			+		+			+	+
AM level after 8 months	L		H	H	H	H		H	L	L	H	H	L	L	L	L		H	H	L	H	L	H	H	H

Note: +/− indicates that factor was mentioned by participants as having a positive/ negative impact on their acculturation. L/H indicates participant has high or low AM at this stage.

Personal factors

Prior International Experience

The dynamics of participants' prior international experience had an impact on their AM level. Most participants who had had positive prior experiences had high initial AM levels, because they expected to replicate their positive prior experience. If this was not the case, their AM levels diminished. Participants with negative prior experiences had low initial AM levels, which improved if their Dutch experience was better than expected. One participant said:

> When I moved to Switzerland I thought it was a xenophobic place, but the Netherlands is a very open place. I meet different people when I get to work with others in my program and I find that nice. [P20]

Some participants without prior experience abroad made more plans to work, live, and make friends with Dutch and other international students. They did some background research regarding life at the university and showed a higher level of preparedness than participants with prior experience.

Language Issues

Language issues played a critical role in participants' AM development. A good mastery of English made interactions easier for some participants, while those with English language issues experienced fewer interactions with domestic and other international students who did not speak their own native language. One participant said:

> The Dutch speak pretty good English and I get along with them as well as other new international. People from China, for example, are usually isolated. They do their thing within their group, probably because they want to speak their own language. [P18]

Additionally, some Dutch language skills facilitated interactions with domestic students. Some participants felt excluded by the Dutch students, who often had the habit of using Dutch when conversing with one another. One participant said:

> I'm the only non-Dutch in my team for this module. They sometimes just switch to speaking Dutch. I told them it's fair we make a rule that when I'm here we speak English because I also want to know what's going on. [P12]

Perceived Student Identities

Participants' perceptions of their own student identities also had an impact at this stage. Participants who saw themselves only as 'international students' preferred interactions with other international students rather than with domestic students and reported lower AM levels at this stage. They mostly participated in social events within the international group. Those who perceived themselves only as 'members of an international community' were more motivated to learn about other cultures within the ILE and interacted with both domestic and other international students. One participant said:

> I see myself as a part of an international community. I consider even the Dutch as just one of the different countries present at the university. I engage well with other students regardless of where they are from. [P6]

Extracurricular Participation

Participants who participated in extracurricular activities showed higher AM levels than those who excluded themselves. For example, the introduction activities for new students were regarded by some participants as a positive experience because they formed friendships with other Dutch and international group members, who already had established networks at the university. These participants could therefore easily get information about the university or seek assistance when needed. This improved their AM. One participant said:

> I do some sports at the university, and I have joined some associations with very nice people who I now consider as friends. These help to have some social contacts. [P9]

However, participants who had limited extracurricular activities had significantly less contact with other students and reported subsequent difficulties in building intercultural friendships.

Housing Search Experience

The search for housing was a major challenge for some participants' AM. Participants who reported difficulty in finding housing, particularly because Dutch students rejected them as housemates, had a negative perception of domestic students, resulting in less interest to interact with them. One participant said:

It is difficult for me to find a place because the Dutch don't want internationals. The university also cannot help me because I am from Europe. [P10]

In contrast, some participants who secured housing with Dutch students had access to the friendship networks of their housemates. This gave them a positive impression of the Dutch with higher interest to engage with them. Moreover, these Dutch contacts helped them understand the Dutch socio-cultural and academic systems.

Living Costs

Living costs were a factor that had negative effects on some participants' experience. For instance, some participants worked part-time to support their living costs. Therefore, they had less time for academic work and social activities. This affected their AM level at this stage. One participant said:

> The Netherlands is really expensive to live in, especially if you want to do a lot of social things with your friends like travelling to other cities or maybe eating out together. I teach math online as a side-job to support myself here. [P4]

Social Factors

International In-group Pressure

Some participants, who had developed early friendships with other internationals, especially students from their own native countries, experienced an internal in-group mechanism that sought to retain them within the group, despite their own efforts to engage with other domestic and international students. One participant said:

> Sometimes when I make new friends, some of the guys complain that I was trying to leave the group. It's very subtle but I can feel the pressure they bring. [P19]

In contrast, some participants who developed friendship with internationals (who had been at the university longer) were able to gain access to their friendship networks consisting of many domestic and international students.

Other Students' Opinions

Opinions of both Dutch and international students, especially those who had been at the university longer, had an impact on participants' AM levels. When these opinions were negative, participants reported low AM levels, especially in terms of participating in the university's socio-cultural events and in engaging with Dutch students. One participant said:

I've heard a lot about the university from other people and it's not necessarily positive, especially when it comes to meeting the Dutch. So, I resolved not to stress myself with making Dutch friends. I won't worry about it. [P15]

Academic Factors

University Resources

Participants' perceptions of the university resources positively affected their AM. Resources include personnel (e.g., university psychologists, library assistants, and study advisors), technological resources (e.g., databases, software, labs, and tools), and physical facilities (workspace, library, and social spaces such as canteens, sports facilities, and shops) available to the students. Their expectations of good facilities were met; thus, improving their AM. One participant said:

I am very impressed with the university facilities…. I appreciate the cultural space in the Bastille for us to meet other people during lunch. [P16]

Study Program Characteristics

Some participants commended the programs' potential to design personalized studies and internship/exchange opportunities. This reflected positively in their AM level at this stage because it met their expectations of high-quality education. One participant said:

My program has more flexibility because it is a self-design…you get your pick of courses with a fixed structure. I'm adjusting easily at this stage. [P20]

However, participants with less flexibility in how their programs were organized were dissatisfied with the academic system, most of whom resorted to just completing their programs with aloof interest. Others noted disappointment with the contents of some courses when the course descriptions raised a different expectation than the actual course experience.

Academic Workload

This factor was only mentioned as having a negative impact on participants' acculturation experiences. All participants had issues with the workload of their studies. This was because they prioritized their schoolwork and wanted to perform well academically. However, the demands, especially for those taking multiple courses, were heavy. This affected the time they had for social activities. One participant said:

There's quite a lot of work to do compared to my country. I can't make time for other things. [P11]

Information on Academic Procedures

Some participants indicated that the university was effective in providing information on academic procedures such as the use of certain platforms, joining external projects, collaborations, and pathways to internship opportunities and exchange programs. This gave them a positive perception of the university's role in their adjustment. However, other participants who had difficulty obtaining the information they needed felt neglected by the university. This resulted in distrust in the academic system and, thus, diminished their AM. One participant said:

> I had a problem with understanding how to do a procedure and I asked some people about it. At the end of the day no one knew what to do or where to find the information. I felt really let down. [P13]

Developments in Participants' AM Levels after Eight Months

There was a general increase in AM levels of participants in the third round. The AM process, however, remained dialectical with some interesting outcomes. Some participants with a high AM after four months either sustained their motivation because their expectations were met after eight months or relapsed due to disappointing experiences, and vice versa.

Participants who reported high AM levels ($n = 13$) at this stage perceived themselves as adjusted to the ILE than those with low AM levels ($n = 9$). There were still varying interests to build friendships and explore the socio-cultural environment of the ILE. However, all participants were still motivated to participate in academic activities. Furthermore, all the factors identified above, especially language, international in-group pressure, academic workload, living costs, and extracurricular participation were still reported but as having less impact on their AM. This is because many participants have managed the challenges associated with those factors. Nevertheless, seven additional factors emerged which had more impact on the participants' AM development at this stage. We also categorized these as personal, social, or academic factors.

Personal Factors

Perceived Discrimination and Prejudice

Participants who encountered some degree of discrimination and prejudice from both domestic or other international students showed a reduction in their AM level at this stage. One participant said:

> There is still casual racism here at the university from the Dutch and even other internationals. This gives me a bad impression of the culture around here. [P20]

Some were particularly surprised that discrimination and prejudice occurred even within the international group. One participant said:

I expected internationals to be accepting because we are all in the same boat here. But some people still do or say things to me which are upfront discriminatory or condescending. [P12]

Perceived ILE Identity

In line with the role of their self-identities as international students, participants' perceptions of the university's identity appeared to affect their AM at this stage. Participants who perceived the university as internationalized showed a higher AM than those who perceived the university as a *Dutch* institution. They noted that an internationalized university contributes to their self-image as members of a community which facilitates their integration. Participants who perceived the university as not internationalized argued that the university played an inadequate role in their integration. One participant said:

I expected the university to be more international. You still have things done the Dutch way here. Otherwise, we internationals are what makes it seem like an international university. They can do more, especially in getting the Dutch students involved. [P10]

Social Factors

Friendship Networks

There were three kinds of friendship networks identified at this stage: those with international and domestic friends, those with only international friends, and those with only friends from their own countries. Participants who had diverse friends among the domestic and/or international groups showed higher AM levels than those without. Their diversified friend-groups exposed them to intercultural contacts with prospects to build new friendships. They were, therefore, willing to participate more in intercultural academic and social activities. Those who had only international friends showed little interest to proactively engage with Dutch students at this stage. Likewise, those with only friends from their native countries reported having only academic and social ties within their own cultural groups and showed little interest to engage outside of them. One participant said:

Most of my friends now are Asians like me. It is easier for us to understand each other because our cultures are similar. [P22]

Interactions with Other Students

Beyond friendship networks, participants who had mostly positive encounters with domestic and international students showed higher AM levels at this stage than those with negative encounters. However, participants' positive experiences with only other international students had a consequential reduction in their willingness to interact with domestic students. One participant said:

> I find the Dutch like a peach. They are soft and sweet on the outside but the more you eat the harder it gets. I work better with internationals at this stage of my study. [P1]

Intercultural Exchange Events

Some participants considered intercultural exchange events as a crucial factor in their AM at this stage. For example, intercultural dinners broadened their knowledge about other cultures and provided them with new contact opportunities to develop friendships. Therefore, they reported higher AM levels at this stage. However, participants who engaged mostly with people from their own culture experienced lower AM levels at this stage. One participant said:

> I had a putlock dinner last Friday where we all cooked nice foods from our countries and shared them. It was very nice to meet more people and learn about their cultures in this way. [P19]

Academic Factors

Interaction with Teachers and University Staff

Many participants commended the teachers and university staff for being friendly and accessible. These experiences improved their AM. Participants who were dissatisfied with their interactions with teachers and university staff judged their experiences negatively. These differences are illustrated in the following quotes:

> Professors here are very accessible and helpful. I have good interactions with them. I feel they make things easy for us internationals. [P19]

> I had a minor issue with a professor. I felt bad with how she handled the situation. But I did speak about this to the study advisor. She checked up on me earlier this month if things were okay. These are two people from the same university handling an issue differently. [P5]

Teachers' Role in Intercultural Contacts

A particularly acknowledged factor at this stage was the teachers' role in fostering intercultural contacts by diversifying student teams for class assignments. This gave some participants the impression that the university, represented by the teachers, facilitated their intercultural contacts, especially with the domestic students who generally prefer to work with other Dutch students. One participant said:

> I really like it when the professor encourages us to try to mix-up our group. It makes me feel like someone is helping with my integration. [P9]

However, participants who had opposite experiences perceived the academic system as ineffective in promoting intercultural relations among the student groups. This affected their willingness to work with domestic students and increased their preference to work and build friendships within their own cultural groups or only with other international students.

DISCUSSION

Earlier research acknowledges that acculturation experiences differ per student (Rienties & Tempelaar, 2013). Our results illustrate these differences, as highlighted by students' AM development. Dentakos et al. (2017) in their cross-sectional study also identified high and low AM levels among their student sample irrespective of how long these students had been at the institution. With our longitudinal approach, we established that students' AM levels are not static but evolve over time, not always in linear and predictable ways. Furthermore, Dentakos et al.'s (2017) categorization of peer relationship did not distinguish domestic from international students. Our findings fill this space, showing that the dynamics of interactions with domestic and other international students may be different and have different effects. Finally, Dentakos et al. (2017) limited university perceptions to students' experiences with university's internal structures and services. Our findings expanded this, showing that international students' perceptions of their own identities and the university's international identity affect their AM over time.

AM development may explain the U-curve acculturation process, as well as individual differences between students. AM development appears to be an important factor explaining why some international students adjust better than others. Our research showed that AM development is simultaneously affected by many different factors and that the nature and influence of these factors might change over time. As a result, the curve may not be *U-shaped* for every student.

Furthermore, our findings nuance and annotate various findings from earlier research. Prior international experience has often been found to have adaptational outcomes for migrants: People with earlier experiences abroad are better prepared for intercultural challenges (Bartlett et al., 2017; Smith & Khawaja, 2011). However, we found that the nature of the prior experience is equally crucial in shaping students' initial expectations and subsequent experiences. As a result, prior international experience may also have negative effects on AM.

Boring (2000) posited that second language acquisition can help migrants to easily adjust. Our study showed that some international students may even face a third language acquisition challenge. Most of our participants were non-native English speakers and had little or no Dutch language skills when they arrived. Many, therefore, had to sustain or improve their English language skills for academic and social purposes within the ILE, but also felt the need to learn some Dutch for social interactions with domestic students.

Regarding perceived discrimination and stereotyping, earlier research focused mainly on the migrants' perspectives about the host society (Abdullah,

2020). We discovered that there may also be perceived discrimination within the international student in-group.

Other factors such as living costs, academic workload, and housing challenges have been identified as stressors in previous studies (Smith & Khawaja, 2011). We found that these factors may also affect students' AM levels over time.

Academic goals are central to the experiences of international students and often take precedence over other adaptational goals (Kim, 2001; Wintre et al., 2015). Our findings support this, since there was sustained overall academic interest among the participants. Moreover, interaction with teachers, program designs, university facilities, and information of key academic procedures may indicate potential areas for intervention from universities to improve their international students' AM.

Limitations and Suggestions for Future Research

Several limitations must be considered when interpreting our findings. The first limitation is that we only focused on international students. However, if we take the concept of an ILE seriously, we would also need to consider the AM of domestic students. Future research should include the AM of domestic and international students in ILEs.

A second limitation involves the qualitative nature of our research. Our in-depth interviews with international students helped us to identify factors that might play a role in students' AM, but we cannot be sure to what extent all factors actually influence AM. Quantitative follow-up research could focus on the extent to which the identified factors indeed explain and predict international students' AM.

Due to the sample size, this study looked at international students as a homogenous group, not distinguishing between participants' cultural backgrounds. It is imaginable that the development of international students' AM is related to their cultural background, for instance, based on the width and depth of the cultural differences between their home country and their host country. Future research could differentiate between different cultural backgrounds and compare the development of students' AM.

It is also important to keep in mind that the majority of the participants were master (or pre-master) students. This means that they were older than students at the bachelor level and had other academic experiences before. Future research could also focus on bachelor students, who combine the international and intercultural experience with the transition from high school to university.

Finally, the research focused on students of a single university in the Netherlands. Although our participants enrolled in a wide variety of programs within the university, it would be interesting to include other universities and host countries in future research.

CONCLUSIONS

It is crucial for universities to provide their international students with the best possible experience and ensure that their AM helps them thrive in ILE. Our research showed that the development of international students' AM is not a linear process, which deserves attention over time. We identified a range of personal, social, and academic factors that potentially affect students' AM. These factors can already be used to sustain or improve international students' AM throughout their acculturation or to monitor their experiences. Undoubtedly, the challenges associated with adapting to a new society will continue to linger for many international students. Nevertheless, there is hope that the continued joint efforts between the students and their universities can help smoothen students-migrants' acculturation journeys.

ACKNOWLEDGMENTS

The authors would like to thank the international students who participated in this longitudinal study.

REFERENCES

Abdullah, S. (2020). Exploring the lived social and academic experiences of foreign-born students: A phenomenological perspective. *Journal of International Students, 10*(3), 590–612. https://doi.org/10.32674/jis.v10i3.1171

Bartlett, L., Mendenhall, M. & Ghaffar-Kucher, A. (2017). Culture in acculturation: Refugee youth's schooling experiences in international schools in New York City. *International Journal of Intercultural Relations, 60*, 109–119. https://doi.org/10.1016/j.ijintrel.2017.04.005

Berry, J. W. (2005). Acculturation: Living successfully in two cultures. *International Journal of Intercultural Relations, 29*(6), 697–712. https://doi.org/10.1016/j.ijintrel.2005.07.

Berry, J. W. (2006). Contexts of acculturation. In D. L. Sam & J. W. Berry (Eds.), *Cambridge handbook of acculturation psychology* (pp. 2735–2742). Cambridge University Press.

Berry, J. W., & Hou, F. (2016). Immigrant acculturation and wellbeing in Canada. *Canadian Psychology, 57*(4), 254–264. https://doi.org/10.1037/cap0000064

Berry, J. W., Kim, U., Minde, T., & Mok, D. (1987). Comparative studies of acculturative stress. *International Migration Review, 21*, 491–511. https://doi.org/10.1177/019791838702100303

Boring, R. (2000). Schumann's acculturation model: Cross-sectional and longitudinal evidence in second-language acquisition. *Canadian Linguistics Association Annual Conference Proceedings*, 51–62. https://doi.org/10.13140/RG.2.1.4639.7927

Carmit, T. T., V& Philip, E. T. (2006). Biculturalism: A model of the effects of second-culture exposure on acculturation and integrative complexity. *Journal of cross-cultural psychology, 37*(2), 173–190. https://doi.org/10.1177/0022022105284495

Chirkov, V. I., Vansteenkiste, M., Tao, R., & Lynch, M. (2007). The role of self-determined motivation and goals for study abroad in the adaptation of international students. *International Journal of Intercultural Relations, 31*, 199–222. https://doi.org/10.1016/j.ijintrel.2006.03.002

Dentakos, S., Wintre, M., Chavoshi, S., & Wright, L. (2017). Acculturation motivation in international student adjustment and permanent residency intentions: A mixed-methods approach. *Emerging Adulthood, 5*(1), 27–41. https://doi.org/10.1177/2167696816643628

Eshel, Y., & Rosenthal-Sokolov, M. (2000). Acculturation attitudes and sociocultural adjustment of sojourner youth in Israel. *The Journal of Social Psychology, 140*, 677–691. https://doi.org/10.1080/00224540009600509

Kim, Y. Y. (2001). Becoming intercultural: An integrated theory of communication and cross-cultural adaptation. Sage.

Owen, G. T. (2014). Qualitative methods in higher education policy analysis: Using interviews and document analysis. *Researchgate.* https://www.researchgate.net/publication/289764396

Recker, C., Milfont T., & Ward, C. (2017). A dual-process motivational model of acculturation behaviors and adaptation outcomes. *Universitas Psychologica, 16*(5), 1–15. https://doi.org/10.11144/Javeriana.upsy16-5.dmma

Rienties, B., & Tempelaar, D. (2013). The role of cultural dimensions of international and Dutch students on academic and social integration and academic performance in the Netherlands. *International Journal of Intercultural Relations, 37*(2), 188–201. https://doi.org/10.1016/j.ijintrel.2012.11.004

Smith, R. A., & Khawaja, N. G. (2011). A review of the acculturation experiences of international students. *International Journal of Intercultural Relations, 35*(6), 699–713. https://doi.org/10.1016/j.ijintrel.2011.08.04

Ward, C., Okura, Y., Kennedy, A., & Kojima, T. (1998). The U-curve on trial: A longitudinal study of psychological and sociocultural adjustment during cross-cultural transition. *International Journal of Intercultural Relations*, 22(3), 277–291. https://doi.org/10.1016/S0147-1767(98)00008-X

Ward, C., & Kennedy, A. (1999). The measurement of sociocultural adaptation. *International Journal of Intercultural Relations, 23*(4), 659–677. https://doi.org/10.1016/S0147-1767(99)00014-0

Wintre, M. G., Kandasamy, A. R., Chavoshi, S., & Wright, L. (2015). Are international undergraduate students emerging adults? Motivations for studying abroad. *Emerging Adulthood, 3*, 255–264. https://doi.org/10.1177/2167696815571665

Yakobov, E., Jurcik, T., Solopieieva-Jurcikova, L., & Ryder, A. G. (2019). Acculturation and expectations: Unpacking adjustment mechanisms within the Russian-speaking community in Montreal. *International Journal of Intercultural Relations, 68,* 67–76. https://doi.org/10.1016/j.ijintrel. 2018.11.001

Yu, B., & Wright, E. (2016). Socio-cultural adaptation, academic adaptation and satisfaction of international higher degree research students in Australia. *Tertiary Education and Management, 22*(1). https://doi.org/10.1080/ 13583883.2015.1127405

Zhou, Y., Jindal-Snape, D., Topping, K., & Todman, J. (2008). Theoretical models of culture shock and adaptation in international students in higher education. *Studies in Higher Education, 33*(1), 63–75. https:// doi.org/10.1080/03075070701794833

ADEDAPO T. ALADEGBAIYE, MSc, is a PhD candidate in the Department of Communication Science at the University of Twente. His research explores the acculturation experiences of international students with particular focus on the international learning environment as a distinct part of the new society. He investigates this phenomenon from the lenses of international students' expectation-experience, social and academic inclusion, and integration and internationalization policies of universities. Email: a.t.aladegbaiye@utwente.nl

MENNO D.T. DE JONG, PhD, is a full professor of technical and organizational communication in the department of Communication Science at the University of Twente. His research focuses on the role communication plays in societal and organizational challenges. His research involves a wide variety of practically relevant topics, for which communication is studied in close relation to organizational characteristics, technological developments, and the affordances of design. Email: m.d.t.dejong@utwente.nl

ARDION BELDAD, PhD, is an assistant professor in the Department of Communication Science at the University of Twente. He also lectures at the University College Twente. His primary research interests include trust creation and maintenance, online privacy, crisis communication, adoption and use of new communication technologies, prosocial behavior, and ethical and sustainable consumption. Email: a.d.beldad@utwente.nl

Research Article

© *Journal of International Students*
Volume 12, Issue 2 (2022), pp. 531-549
ISSN: 2162-3104 (Print), 2166-3750 (Online)
doi: 10.32674/jis.v12i2.2972
ojed.org/jis

Intercultural Effectiveness of International and Domestic University Students: A Case of Turkey

Ahsen Avcılar
Recep Tayyip Erdogan University, Rize, Turkey

Enes Gök
Karamanoglu Mehmetbey University, Karaman, Turkey

ABSTRACT

Among the vast and diverse discussions and research on international students, the intercultural status of university students holds a special place in terms of integration and academic success. One of the discussions is the intercultural competencies of the students in higher education. In this respect, this study aims to compare the intercultural effectiveness of international and domestic students, as well as examine their intercultural effectiveness status in terms of different background characteristics. The data were collected from a public university in Turkey using the Intercultural Effectiveness Scale developed by Portalla and Chen. The findings revealed that international students compared with domestic counterparts show a higher level of intercultural effectiveness. Additionally, some background characteristics are significant predictors of the intercultural effectiveness of university students: grade level, parent's nationality, being and living in a foreign country, and having a close friend(s) from a different culture. Some research and policy recommendations are provided.

Keywords: Intercultural effectiveness, international students, domestic students, Turkey, higher education

INTRODUCTION

Many people need to learn to communicate effectively with other individuals from different cultural backgrounds due to reasons such as global economy, global market and international partnerships, rapid development of communication technologies, wide-ranging international mobility, the developing multicultural profile of many societies around the world, and the internationalization of educational programs (Stone, 2006). In line with this need, individuals desire to benefit from a different intellectual experience outside their own country, mostly through international higher education.

International students' education in a foreign country provides benefit for both themselves and the host country. While these students meet their educational needs, they also bring their country's intellectual experiences to the country where they are receiving university education (Berry, 2005). Thus, they help increase awareness of and respect for different cultures in the host country (Bevis, 2002). In this context, international student mobility is an important foreign policy tool and a bridge that connects cultures in terms of increasing mutual cooperation, solidarity, and understanding between countries (Harrison, 2002). Internationalization in higher education institutions (HEIs) requires university students to acquire intercultural skills to successfully interact with students and academic members from other countries and to maximize their university experience (Griffith et al., 2016). Likewise, guest students need to have intercultural communication skills and intercultural effectiveness to interact with individuals in the host country and to socio-culturally adapt to the new environment (Hammer et al., 1978; Lee & Çiftçi, 2014). When the related literature is examined, it is seen that the relationship between intercultural effectiveness and factors such as personality traits, academic success, job performance, and socio-cultural adaptation or the relationship between intercultural effectiveness and various demographic variables has been investigated. However, it is noteworthy that the study groups of these studies investigating the intercultural effectiveness of higher education students only consist of either international students or local students. In the era where the global issues such as economic crisis and current Covid-19 pandemic seem to interrupt international movements of students and scholars and the increasing demand for internationalization at home requiring global citizenship of every participant (de Wit & Altbach, 2020), the examination of intercultural effectiveness of both incoming and domestic students of higher education is vital.

In the case of Turkey, internationalization is almost a new phenomenon as Turkish universities have begun to experience it massively in recent years with the help of both national policies/stimulates and the demand for internationalization by the HEIs. According to the statistics, with rapid growth, the number of international students has increased tenfold in the last 20 years, and the number reached up to around 154 thousand as of 2019 (YOK, 2020). However, as stated by Gök and Gümüş (2018), the majority of the students are from the neighboring countries who have either cultural or religious ties with Turkey. While there exist the examinations of the varying aspects of internationalization of Turkish higher education, the studies on intercultural effectiveness of international students are limited. Additionally, the lack of investigation on the comparison of the intercultural effectiveness of domestic and international students suggests the need for such an examination. In the light of discussions above, the purpose of this study is to compare the intercultural effectiveness status of international and domestic students in Turkey as well as investigating the correlation of various factors with students' intercultural effectiveness.

Intercultural Competence

As a broader term, intercultural competence or intercultural communication competence enables an individual to communicate effectively and acceptably with others in a group of members from different cultural backgrounds (Fantini et al., 2001). According to Chen and Starosta (1996), intercultural competence consists of three dimensions: intercultural awareness, intercultural sensitivity, and intercultural effectiveness. While intercultural awareness explains the cognitive process in which the individual gets to know his/her own culture and other cultures, intercultural sensitivity is the affective aspect of intercultural communication competence. However, intercultural effectiveness refers to the behavioral dimension of intercultural communication competence and the ability to achieve communication goals in the intercultural interaction (Chen & Starosta, 1996). It is important to have knowledge about cultures and to develop a positive attitude toward cultural differences for a successful intercultural interaction; however, for knowledge and attitudes to turn into a suitable action, the individual must also have intercultural skills (Bubas, 2006). In higher education systems, where internationalization is becoming a key component, acquiring intercultural competencies is crucial. As indicated by Almeida et al. (2016), the institutional interventions have a positive impact on increasing sojourners' intercultural competencies which in turn contribute to the efforts of HEIs in internationalization. Among the discussions on the nuance between the terms of intercultural competence ("demonstrating and acquiring culturally appropriate skills") and effectiveness ("getting a desired response/outcome") (Mamman, 1995, p. 43), intercultural effectiveness has been described differently (Simkhovych, 2009). While some definitions emphasize people from different countries living in a foreign country, there are more general definitions that do not emphasize sojourners. In the present study, intercultural effectiveness is conceptualized based on the definition of Stone in accordance with the purpose of the study. Intercultural effectiveness is "the ability to interact with people from different cultures so as to optimize the probability of mutually successful outcomes" (Stone, 2006, p. 338). There are different approaches that explain the factors affecting intercultural effectiveness and its dimensions.

The first approach explains intercultural effectiveness with the personality traits of individuals. According to this approach, intercultural effectiveness results from the personality of individuals (McGinty, 2011). Patience, tolerance, kindness, self-confidence, and entrepreneurship are considered as personality traits that play a role in ensuring intercultural effectiveness. Intercultural effectiveness is also influenced by individuals' self-awareness of their own values and beliefs (Paige, 1993). However, perfectionism, dogmatism, ethnocentrism, and egocentrism are traits that have a negative relationship with intercultural effectiveness (Hannigan, 1990). This approach, which focuses on personality, ignores the behavioral dimension of intercultural effectiveness. Therefore, this situation raises the question "How does someone who values other cultures show this in an intercultural interaction?" (Abe & Wiseman, 1983).

The second approach suggested to eliminate this problem, focuses on the behaviors and social skills required for intercultural effectiveness (Furnham & Bochner, 1982). According to this approach, intercultural effectiveness includes communication skills that involve both verbal and nonverbal behaviors and these skills help individuals to be in an effective and appropriate intercultural interaction with others (Portalla & Chen, 2010). Ruben (1976) identified seven behavioral dimensions associated with intercultural effectiveness: (1) display of respect, (2) interaction posture, (3) orientation to knowledge, (4) empathy, (5) role behavior, (6) interaction management, and (7) tolerance for ambiguity. In another study, Hawes and Kealey (1979, 1981) found that similar communication skills were predictive of intercultural effectiveness. These communication skills were determined to be flexibility toward the ideas of others; respect toward others; listening and accurate perceptions of the needs of others; trust, friendliness, and cooperation with others; calm and self-control when confronted by obstacles; and sensitivity to cultural differences (Hawes & Kealey, 1979). Furnham and Bochner (1982) suggested that seven skills could be important for intercultural effectiveness. These are perceptive skills, expressive skills, conversational skills, assertive skills, emotional expression skills, anxiety management skills, and affiliative skills.

Besides the approaches described above, Gudykunst et al. (1977) developed a model that focuses on both personality traits and behaviors. This model involves the characteristics such as open-mindedness toward new ideas and experiences; the ability to empathize with people from other cultures; accuracy in perceiving differences and similarities between the sojourner's own culture and the host culture; being nonjudgmental, astute noncritical observers of their own and other people's behavior; the ability to establish meaningful relationships with people in the host culture; and being less ethnocentric (Gudykunst et al., 1977). According to this model, the behavioral dimension of intercultural effectiveness and the skills that constitute it are explained as follows: ability to deal with psychological stress (frustration, social alienation, interpersonal conflict, etc.), ability to effectively communicate (ability to enter into meaningful dialogue with other people, ability to deal with communication misunderstandings, ability to effectively deal with different communication styles, etc.), and ability to establish interpersonal relationships (ability to develop and maintain satisfying interpersonal relationships with other people, ability to accurately understand the feelings of another person, ability to effectively work with other people, etc.) (Hammer et al., 1978). In this study, the model that puts emphasis on behaviors and social skills is employed to explain the intercultural effectiveness.

Objectives

In this study, it was aimed to examine the intercultural effectiveness levels of university students in terms of various variables. Specifically, it was hypothesized as follows:

1. Intercultural effectiveness levels of students show a significant difference in terms of:

    1.1. Gender

    1.2. Year of school

    1.3. Faculty

    1.4. Nationality of parents

    1.5. Education level of parents

    1.6. Accommodation (on-campus/off-campus)

    1.7. Previous international travel experience

    1.8. Having close friend(s) from a different culture

2. There is a significant difference between domestic and international students in terms of intercultural effectiveness.

3. Variables such as gender, year of school, nationality, parents' nationality, accommodation (on-campus/off-campus), previous international travel experience, parents' education level, and having close friend(s) from a different culture are significant predictors of intercultural effectiveness.

METHOD

Participants

The population of the study consists of 12,732 undergraduate students studying in the Middle East Technical University (METU) in the spring semester of the 2017–2018 academic year. The findings are expected to be of interest to both international and Turkish audience since the chosen university is one of the few Turkish universities where the teaching is in English with a diverse international student population compared with other higher education institutions. The sample of the study consists of a total of 300 students (63% female, 27% male) selected from the population using the snowball sampling method. Participants' age ranges from 18 to 29 years ($M = 21.51$ $SD = 2.031$). Of the participants, 80.7% are domestic students and 19.3% are international students. Students from 31 different countries participated in the study. Most of the students are from Pakistan, Azerbaijan, Iran, Kenya, Morocco, Palestine, and Albania; 33.3% of the participants are first-year students and 29.3 of them receive education in the Faculty of Arts and Sciences. While 81% of the participants' mothers are Turkish and 19% are foreign; 80.7% of their fathers are Turkish and 19% are foreign. As for parents' level of education, 32.2% of mothers and 37.7% of fathers are university graduates. In addition to these data, it was determined that 50.7% of the students participating in the study live on the campus and 74.7% have close friends from different cultural backgrounds. Besides, while 58.7% of the students have never been to a foreign country, 83.3% have not lived in a foreign country. In other words, the majority of the students participating in the study do not have any previous international travel experience.

Measures

Intercultural Effectiveness

In this study, a 20-item Intercultural Effectiveness Scale developed by Portalla and Chen (2010) was used to measure the intercultural effectiveness level of university students. The scale has six sub-dimensions: behavioral flexibility, interaction relaxation, interactant respect, message skills, interaction management, and identity maintenance. Answers were given on a 7-point scale ranging from 1 (strongly disagree) to five (strongly agree). Scale reliability was good in this study ($\alpha = .88$).

Demographic Variables

Participants were asked to state their gender, age, faculty, year of school, nationality, previous international travel experience, the place where they live (on-campus/ off-campus), whether they have close friends from different cultural backgrounds, their parents' nationality, and their parents' education level. The independent variables can be grouped under two broad categories to be tested. Personal or background factors (gender, age, and nationality) and previous experience with other cultures (previous international experience, the place where they live, close friends from other cultures, parents' nationality, and parents' education level) are included in the study. While personal factors mostly tested in social sciences are included, the previous experience with other cultures seems also promising to explain the status of an individual's intercultural effectiveness. For instance, Carlson and Widaman (1988) found that students with previous experience, for instance, living abroad, have more cross-cultural interest than the students who do not have any previous experience with other cultures. Additionally, parents' education level, and previous experience with other cultures (parents' nationality and close friend from other cultures) were included in the study to be tested for Turkish context, although the variables (growing up in bi- or multi-national family or having a close friend from another culture) were not evidenced as the core predictor of increasing intercultural competence in the study of Lantz-Deaton (2017).

Data Analysis

Based on the research questions, both descriptive and inferential statistics were used to analyze the data obtained. While descriptive statistics were conducted to show the trends within the data, inferential statistics including *t*-test and one-way analysis of variance (ANOVA) were conducted to test Hypotheses 1 and 2. Also, multiple linear regression analysis was employed to find the predictive power of the variables used in the study on intercultural effectiveness (Hypothesis 3). The significance level of the statistical analysis was selected as .05.

RESULTS

Descriptive Statistics

To determine the intercultural effectiveness level of the students, descriptive statistics on this variable and its sub-dimensions are presented in Table 1.

Table 1: Descriptive Statistics on Intercultural Effectiveness and Sub-dimensions

	N	Mean	*Ss*	Min.	Max.
Intercultural effectiveness	300	3.70	.54	2	5
Behavioral flexibility	300	3.73	.74	1.5	5
Interaction relaxation	300	3.62	.70	1.80	5
Interactant respect	300	4.33	.60	1.67	5
Message skills	300	3.44	.81	1.33	5
Interaction management	300	3.74	.81	1	5
Identity maintenance	300	3.39	.70	1.67	5

According to Table 1, students' intercultural effectiveness was found to be at a satisfactory level ($\overline{X}$ = 3.70; *Ss* = .54). In addition, it is seen that the highest average score among six sub-dimensions belongs to interactant respect ($\overline{X}$ = 4, 33; *Ss* = .60), and the minimum average score belongs to identity maintenance ($\overline{X}$ = 3, 39; *Ss* = .70).

Analysis of Intercultural Effectiveness According to the Demographic Variables

To test Hypothesis 1, the level of students' intercultural effectiveness was examined according to demographic characteristics (Tables 2 and 3). Demographic variables were categorized under three main categories: (a) personal variables (gender, year of school, faculty, accommodation), family variables (mother's nationality, father's nationality, mother's education level, father's education level), and internationalization related variables (being in a foreign country, living in a foreign country, having close friend(s) from a different culture, nationality).

Table 2: *t*-Test Results Regarding Intercultural Effectiveness of University Students in Terms of Different Demographic Variables

Variables		N	$\overline{X}$	Ss	sd	t	p
Gender	Male	111	3.70	.53			
	Female	189	3.70	.54	298	.10	.91
Grade level	1st grade	100	3.59	.55			
	Other grades	200	3.75	.52	298	−2.46	.01***
Mother's nationality	Turkish	243	3.64	.52			
	International	57	3.97	.52	298	−4.35	.00***
Father's nationality	Turkish	242	3.63	.52			
	International	58	3.98	.52	298	−4.51	.00***
Being in a foreign country (visit)	Yes	124	3.84	.52			
	No	176	3.60	.52	298	−3.87	.00***
Living in a foreign country (residency)	Yes	50	4.04	.54			
	No	250	3.63	.51	298	5.12	.00***
Mother's education level (HE)	Yes	138	3.76	.54			
	No	162	3.65	.53	298	−1.87	.06
Father's education level (HE)	Yes	187	3.73	.51			
	No	113	3.65	.57	298	−1.29	.19
Accommodation	On-campus	152	3.70	.55			

Variables		N	$\overline{X}$	Ss	sd	t	p
	Off-campus	148	3.69	.52	298	.16	.87
Having close friend(s) from a different culture	Yes	224	3.79	.52			
	No	76	3.43	.50	298	5.23	.00***

***$p < .05$.

In terms of personal characteristics, Table 2 shows that the average intercultural effectiveness scores of male and female students ($\overline{X} = 3.70$) are the same, but these scores are not statistically significant [t (298) = 0.107, $p > 0.05$]. In terms of the year of school, students were examined in two categories as those who are in the first year and those who are in the second, third, and fourth years. Accordingly, the t-test analysis results indicate that there is a significant difference in the intercultural effectiveness level between the first year students and the second, third, and fourth year students [t (298) = −2.467, $p < 0.05$]. According to the students' mean scores, the average intercultural effectiveness score of the first year students ($\overline{X} = 3, 59$) is lower than the average score of those studying in other grades ($\overline{X} = 3.75$). When the t-test results regarding intercultural effectiveness of the students are examined, it is seen that there is not any significant difference in the intercultural effectiveness level between the students living on the campus ($\overline{X} = 3.70$) and those living outside the campus ($\overline{X} = 3.69$) [t (298) = 0.163, $p > 0.05$].

Students' family backgrounds were also analyzed. It was found that there is a significant difference in the intercultural effectiveness level between the students whose mother has a foreign nationality and those whose mother is Turkish [t (298) = −4.355, $p < 0.05$]. When the mean scores of the students are examined, it is seen that the average intercultural effectiveness score of the students whose mother is not Turkish ($\overline{X} = 3, 97$) is higher than the average score of those whose mother is Turkish ($\overline{X} = 3.64$). Similarly, a significant difference was found between the intercultural effectiveness level of the students whose father has a foreign nationality and the level of those whose father is Turkish [t (298) = −4.516, $p < 0.05$]. When the average scores of the students are examined, it is seen that the average intercultural effectiveness score of the students whose father is not Turkish ($\overline{X} = 3, 98$) is higher than the average score of those whose father is Turkish ($\overline{X} = 3.63$). Education level is another component in the analysis as part of the family background. Education level of the participants was included in the study as the college effect. Parents' education levels are dichotomized as having a higher education and above degree or not. The findings show that there is not any significant difference between the intercultural effectiveness score of the students whose mother has a higher education or above degree ($\overline{X}$ = 3.76) and the score of those whose mother does not have a higher education degree ($\overline{X}$ = 3.65) [*t* (298) = −1.874, *p* > 0.05]. Similarly, any significant difference was not found between the average intercultural effectiveness score of the students whose father has a higher education or above degree ($\overline{X}$ = 3.73) and the average score of those whose father does not have a higher education degree ($\overline{X}$ = 3.65) [*t* (298) = −1.293, *p* > 0.05].

In the examination of internationalization variables in terms of students' intercultural effectiveness, being and living in another country, having a close friend from a different culture, and students' nationality (domestic and international students) are included. As findings indicate, there is a significant difference in the intercultural effectiveness level between the students who have previously been to a foreign country and those who have never been to a foreign country before [*t* (298) = −3.873, *p* < 0.05]. When the average scores of the students are examined, it is seen that the average intercultural effectiveness score of the students who have previously been abroad ($\overline{X}$ = 3, 84) is higher than the average score of those who have never been abroad before ($\overline{X}$ = 3.60). Similarly, there is a significant difference in the intercultural effectiveness level between the students who have previously lived in a foreign country and those who have never lived in a foreign country before [*t* (298) = 5.122, *p* < 0.05]. When the average scores of the students are examined, it is seen that the average intercultural effectiveness score of the students who have previously lived abroad ($\overline{X}$ = 4, 04) is higher than the average score of those who have never lived abroad before ($\overline{X}$ = 3, 63). Lastly, a significant difference was found between the intercultural effectiveness level of the students who have close friends from a different culture and the level of those who do not have any close friends from a different culture [*t* (298) = 5.234, *p* < 0.05]. When the average scores of the students are examined, it is seen that the average intercultural effectiveness score of the students having close friends from a different culture ($\overline{X}$ = 3, 79) is higher than the average score of those having no close friends from a different culture ($\overline{X}$ = 3, 43).

Table 3: Variance Analysis Results Regarding Intercultural Effectiveness of University Students in Terms of Faculty

Faculty	N	$\overline{X}$	Ss	sd	F	P	Significant difference
Education	47	3.60	.43	3			
Arts and Sciences	88	3.67	.57	296			

Faculty	N	$\bar{X}$	Ss	sd	F	P	Significant difference
Economics and Administrative Sciences	82	3.73	.59	299	.96	.40	–
Engineering and Architecture	83	3.76	.50				

Table 3 shows that there is not any significant difference among the students' average intercultural effectiveness scores in terms of faculty.

A series of *t*-tests and variance analysis conducted to determine the intercultural effectiveness level of students in terms of demographic characteristics showed that Hypothesis 1 was partially supported. To test Hypothesis 2, an independent samples *t*-test was conducted to compare the intercultural effectiveness levels of domestic and international students. *t*-Test results regarding intercultural effectiveness of the university students in terms of nationality are given in Table 4.

Table 4: *t*-Test Results Regarding Intercultural Effectiveness of University Students in Terms of Nationality

Variable		N	$\bar{X}$	Ss	sd	t	p
Nationality	Turkish	242	3.63	.52			
	International	58	3.99	.51	298	−4.65	.00***

***$p < .05$.

According to Table 4, there is a significant difference in the intercultural effectiveness level between domestic students and international students [t (298) = −4.650, $p < 0.05$]. When the students' average scores are examined, it is seen that the average intercultural effectiveness score of international students ($\bar{X}$ = 3.99) is higher than the average score of domestic students ($\bar{X}$ = 3.63). Thus, Hypothesis 2 was supported. To test Hypothesis 3, a stepwise regression analysis was conducted to determine the demographic variables predicting intercultural effectiveness best. Stepwise regression analysis results regarding intercultural effectiveness of the university students in terms of demographic variables are given in Table 5.

Table 5: Stepwise Regression Analysis Results Regarding Intercultural Effectiveness of University Students in Terms of Demographic Variables

	Predictor variables	B	β	t	TV	VIF	R	$R2$	$R2$ Change	F
Model 1	Constant	3.43		57.68						
	Having close friends from a different culture	.36	.29	5.23	1.00	1.00	.29	.08	.08	27.39
Model 2	Constant	3.42		59.03						
	Having close friends from a different culture	.30	.24	4.42	.96	1.04	.37	.13	.13	23.72
	Having lived in a foreign country	.34	.23	4.29	.96	1.04				
Model 3	Constant	3.40		59.89						
	Having close friends from a different culture	.25	.20	3.74	.92	1.07				
	Having lived in a foreign country	.33	.23	4.33	.96	1.04	.42	.18	.17	21.65
	Nationality	.28	.20	3.90	.96	1.03				

When Table 5 is analyzed, it is seen that the demographic variable that best predicts intercultural effectiveness alone is "Having close friends from a different culture" ($R = .290$, $p < .05$). The variable of having close friends from a different culture explains 8% of the change in the level of intercultural effectiveness. In the second stage of the regression analysis, "Having lived in a foreign country" was included in the model ($R = .371$, $p < .05$). It was determined that the variables of having close friends from a different culture and having lived in a foreign country explain 13% of the intercultural effectiveness level together. In the third stage of the analysis, "Nationality" was added to the model ($R = .424$, $p < .05$). The model formed by having close friends from different cultures, having lived in a foreign country, and nationality (being an international student) explains 18% of the change in the level of intercultural effectiveness. However, factors such as gender, year of school, parents' nationality, accommodation (on-campus/off-campus), being in a foreign country for less than three months, and parents' education level are not significant predictors of intercultural effectiveness. Thus, it can be said that Hypothesis 3 was partially supported.

DISCUSSION AND CONCLUSION

According to the study results, the intercultural effectiveness level of the students does not show any significant difference in terms of gender. Studies with similar results (Akın, 2016; Bekiroğlu & Balcı, 2014; Pedersen, 2010; Simkhovych, 2009; Yılmaz & Göçen, 2013) stated that the variable of gender does not have any significant effect on intercultural effectiveness and intercultural sensitivity levels. However, in his study on university students, Gonzales (2017) concluded that male participants are more emotionally resilient in intercultural communication compared with female participants, and females are able to better empathize culturally than males. Also, there are studies in which the intercultural sensitivity level of female students was found to be higher than that of male students (Margarethe et al., 2012; McMurray, 2007). In this context, it is seen that different results have been reached in the literature on intercultural effectiveness and gender.

It is seen that the variable of the year of school has a significant effect on the level of intercultural effectiveness. Accordingly, the intercultural effectiveness level of the second, third, and fourth year students is higher than that of the first year students. Based on this finding, it can be interpreted that the experiences of students at the university improve their intercultural effectiveness level. As Deardorff (2006) emphasized, higher education shapes students' intercultural effectiveness. Studies with similar results (Akın, 2016; Penbek et al., 2009) showed that students' intercultural sensitivity levels and respect for different cultures increase as they progress to higher school years.

The findings obtained from this study show that the variable of faculty does not have any significant effect on the level of intercultural effectiveness. When the relevant literature is analyzed, it is seen that "faculty" is replaced by "department" in most studies. Similar to the findings of the current study, Onur Sezer, and Bağçeli Kahraman (2016) found that there is not any significant difference between the intercultural sensitivity levels of students studying in different departments. However, Demir and Üstün (2017) concluded that the intercultural sensitivity level of the students of the Department of English Language Teaching is significantly higher than those who receive education in the Departments of Primary School Teaching and Turkish Language and Literature Teaching.

It is seen that whether parents are foreign or not has a significant effect on intercultural effectiveness. The transfer of experience, knowledge, and skills from adults to children is mainly carried out in the family (Biktarigova, 2016). Accordingly, it can be interpreted that parents convey their knowledge, attitudes, and skills regarding different cultures to their children. According to the findings of the current study, it was determined that the intercultural effectiveness level of students whose mother or father is not Turkish is higher than the level of those whose mother or father is Turkish. It can be said that it is an expected result considering the previous studies indicating that the intercultural sensitivity level of international individuals is higher than that of domestic ones (Morales, 2017; Ruiz-Bernardo et al., 2012). However, when the literature is examined, it is seen that there is no related research in which parents' nationality is regarded as a variable.

Any significant difference was not found in the intercultural effectiveness levels of university students in terms of the education level of their parents. Findings obtained from the research conducted by Akın (2016) support this result. According to the findings of the aforementioned study, parents' education level does not have a positive or negative effect on the intercultural sensitivity level of Turkish language teacher candidates.

Any significant difference was not found in the intercultural effectiveness levels of university students in terms of whether they live on the campus or outside the campus. Similarly, in the study conducted by Pedersen (2010), it was concluded that living with a local family instead of living on the campus does not have any significant effect on the intercultural effectiveness outcomes of international students. However, according to Pascarella and Terenzini (1991), the living space within the campus offers students an environment more open to diversity.

In the study, the variable of international travel experience was addressed in two ways: Experience of being abroad (less than three months) and experience of living abroad (three months and more). According to the study of Bekiroğlu and Balcı (2014), there is not any significant difference between the intercultural sensitivity level of students who have never been abroad and that of those who have been abroad at least once. Similarly, some studies (Pedersen, 2010; Vande Berg, 2007) also suggest that just sending students abroad is not enough for generating intercultural effectiveness outcomes for the intended students. However, some studies indicate that the intercultural effectiveness scores of students show a significant difference in favor of students who have been abroad or lived abroad in the previous period of their lives (Demir & Üstün, 2017; Penbek et al., 2009). In his study, Del Villar (2010) concluded that as the number of countries visited and the time spent abroad increases, students' intercultural sensitivity scores also increase. According to the qualitative findings of the same study, the participants who have lived in a foreign country for more than six months stated that this experience gave them the ability to be open-minded and to accept other cultures.

Intercultural effectiveness scores of students show a significant difference in favor of those who have close friends from a different culture. In the literature, it is possible to find other studies supporting this finding (Demir & Üstün, 2017; Onur Sezer & Bağçeli Kahraman, 2016). Also, Del Villar (2010) concluded that as the number of friends from different cultures increases, the intercultural sensitivity scores of students also increase. According to the qualitative findings of the same study, the participants with the highest number of international friends stated that their relations with foreigners made them more social, open-minded, tolerant, and self-confident. When the literature is analyzed, it is seen that there are also studies with different results. In the studies of Pedersen (2010) and Akın (2016), it was stated that making close friends from different countries does not have any significant effect on the intercultural sensitivity levels of university students.

In the study, the intercultural effectiveness level of international students was found to be significantly higher than that of local students. When the literature is examined, it is seen that there are other studies having similar results. Wang and Ching (2015), in their study conducted on students from different countries, revealed that the nationality of the participants has a significant effect on the level of intercultural effectiveness. In their study, Del Villar (2010) and Wu (2009) emphasized that international students have a higher level of motivation toward learning a foreign language and are more willing to accept different cultures. The possible explanation for this is that international students might get more exposure to different cultures compared with local students. When they get more experience and acculturation to the culture of the host country, they become more multicultural or at least bicultural. As Thomas et al. (2010) found, "bicultural individuals have more pronounced skills related to intercultural effectiveness than monocultural ones, including a higher level of cognitive skill called cultural metacognition that directly influences intercultural effectiveness" (*p*. 315).

The intercultural effectiveness level of university students participating in the study is significantly predicted by having close friends from different cultures, having lived in a foreign country for more than three months, and nationality (being an international student). Studies in the literature support this finding. The study conducted by Chocce et al. (2015) showed that the country where students come from and having friends from different cultures significantly predict the level of intercultural sensitivity. Similarly, Wu (2009) stated that being an international student is a significant predictor of the intercultural sensitivity level. It was stated by Pritchard and Skinner (2002) and Tanaka et al. (1997) that making international friends is a significant predictor of the intercultural sensitivity level. Tanaka et al. (1997) emphasized that international students' making friendship with individuals from the host culture will facilitate their getting used to this new culture. The study of Williams (2005) indicated that friendship or romantic relationship with one from a different culture and interacting with individuals from a different culture are significant predictors of intercultural communication skills. In addition, Del Villar (2010) revealed that the duration of international travel experience (being abroad for more than six months) and the number of international friends (having 11 or more international friends) significantly predict the intercultural sensitivity level.

In conclusion, this study highlights the important effect of the year of school, nationality, parents' nationality, previous international travel experience, and having friends from different cultural backgrounds on the intercultural effectiveness level of undergraduate students. The findings are significant to demonstrate that international students with their varying background characteristics show a higher level of intercultural effectiveness compared with domestic students. These findings are expected to provide significant insights for future research, for university administrators who deal with intercultural conflicts in their campuses, and policymakers who are in charge of articulating a quality higher education environment for the future of students and the citizens. Specifically, future research should examine the reasons and motivations behind the intercultural effectiveness gap between domestic and international students. University administrators and authorities, who deal with cultural conflicts or who want to increase their quality through diversity, should create a more culturally diverse teaching and learning environment for the students with intercultural competencies. Government authorities, higher education councils, and policymakers should aware of the gap between domestic and international students and consider these insights in designing the future of higher education for students as global citizens.

REFERENCES

Abe, H., & Wiseman, R. L. (1983). A cross-cultural confirmation of the dimensions of intercultural effectiveness. *International Journal of Intercultural Relations, 7*, 53–67. https://doi.org/10.1016/0147-1767(83)90005-6

Akın, E. (2016). Türkçe öğretmen adaylarının kültürlerarası duyarlılıklarının çeşitli değişkenler açısından incelenmesi: Siirt üniversitesi örneği. *International Periodical for the Languages, Literature and History of Turkish or Turkic, 11*(3), 29–42. https://doi.org/10.7827/turkishstudies.9276

Almeida, J., Fantini, A. E., Simões, A. R., & Costa, N. (2016). Enhancing the intercultural effectiveness of exchange programmes: Formal and non-formal educational interventions. *Intercultural Education, 27*(6), 517–533. https://doi.org/10.1080/14675986.2016.1262190

Bekiroğlu, O., & Balcı, Ş. (2014). Kültürlerarası iletişim duyarlılığının izlerini aramak: İletişim fakültesi öğrencileri örneğinde bir araştırma. *Türkiyat Araştırma Dergisi, 35*, 429–459. https://doi.org/10.21563/sutad.187110

Berry, J. W. (2005). Acculturation: Living successfully in two cultures. *International Journal of Intercultural Relations, 29*, 697–712. https://doi.org/10.1016/j.ijintrel.2005.07.013

Bevis, T. B. (2002). At a glance: International students in the United States. *International Educator, 11*(3), 12–17. https://doi.org/10.1177/1475240909356382

Biktarigova, G. F. (2016). The potential of 'family pedagogy' discipline in the formation of students' family values. *International Electronic Journal of Mathematics Education, 11*(4), 810–817.

Bubas, G. (2006). Competence in computer-mediated communication: An evaluation and potential uses on a self-assessment measure. Manuscript submitted for presentation consideration, University of Zagreb, Croatia.

Carlson, J. S., & Widaman, K. F. (1988). The effects of study abroad during college on attitudes toward other cultures. *International Journal of Intercultural Relations, 12*(1), 1–17. https://doi.org/10.1016/0147-1767(88) 90003-X

Chen, G. M., & Starosta, W. J. (1996). Intercultural communication competence: A synthesis. *Communication Yearbook, 19*, 353–384. https://doi.org/10.1080/23808985.1996.11678935

Chocce, J., Johnson, D. A., & Yossatorn, Y. (2015). Predictive factors of freshmen's intercultural sensitivity. *International Journal of Information and Education Technology, 5*(10), 778–782. https://doi.org/10.7763/ijiet.2015.v5.610

Deardorff, D. K. (2006). Identification and assessment of intercultural competence as a student outcome of internationalization. *Journal of Studies in Intercultural Education, 10*(3), 241–266. https://doi.org/10.1177/1028315306287002

de Wit, H., & Altbach, P. G. (2020). Internationalization in higher education: Global trends and recommendations for its future. *Policy Reviews in Higher Education, 5*, 1–19. https://doi.org/10.1080/23322969.2020.1820898

Del Villar, C. P. (2010). How savvy are we?: Towards predicting intercultural sensitivity. *Human Communication, 13*(3), 197–215.

Demir, S., & Üstün, E. (2017). Öğretmen adaylarının kültürlerarası duyarlılık ve etnik merkezcilik düzeylerinin çeşitli değişkenler açısından incelenmesi. *YYÜ Eğitim Fakültesi Dergisi, 14*(1), 182–204. https://doi.org/10.23891/yyuni.2017.7

Fantini, A. E., Arias-Galicia, F., & Guay, D. (2001). *Globalization and 21st century competencies: Challenges for North American higher education.* Western Interstate Commission for Higher Education.

Furnham, A., & Bochner, S. (1982). Social difficulty in a foreign culture: An empirical analysis of culture shock. In S. Bochner (Ed.), *Cultures in Contact: International Series in Experimental Social Psychology* (s. 161–198). Pergamon.

Gök, E., & Gümüş, S. (2018). International student recruitment efforts of Turkish universities: Rationales and strategies. In: A. W. Wiseman (Ed.), *Annual Review of Comparative and International Education 2017* (s. 231–255). Emerald Publishing Limited.

Gonzales, H. (2017). The intercultural effectiveness of university students. *Psychology, 8,* 2017–2030. https://doi.org/10.4236/psych.2017.812129

Griffith, R. L., Wolfeld, L., Armon, B. K., & Liu, O. L. (2016). *Assessing intercultural competence in higher education: Existing research and future directions.* ETS Research Report Series. http://www.mccc.edu/~lyncha/documents/Assessinginterculturalcompetence-ets212112.pdf

Gudykunst, W. B., Wiseman, R. L., & Hammer, M. R. (1977). Determinants of a sojourner's attitudinal satisfaction: A path model. In B. Ruben (Ed.), *Communication Yearbook I.* Transaction.

Hammer, M. R., Gudykust, W.B., & Wiseman, R.L. (1978). Dimensions of intercultural effectiveness: An exploratory study. *International Journal of Intercultural Relations,* 2(4), 382–393. https://doi.org/10.1016/0147-1767(78)90036-6

Hannigan, T. P. (1990). Traits, attitudes, and skills that are related to intercultural effectiveness and their implications for cross-cultural training: A review of the literature. *International Journal of Intercultural Relations, 14,* 89–111. https://doi.org/10.1016/0147-1767(90)90049-3

Harrison, P. (2002). Educational exchange for international understanding. *International Educator, 11*(4), 2–4.

Hawes, F., & Kealey, D. J. (1979). *Canadians in development: An empirical study of adaptation and effectiveness on overseas assignment.* Communication Branch Briefing Center, Canadian International Development Agency, September.

Hawes, F., & Kealey, D. J. (1981). An empirical study of Canadian technical assistance. *International Journal of Intercultural Relations, 5,* 239–258. https://doi.org/10.1016/0147-1767(81)90028-6

Lantz-Deaton, C. (2017). Internationalisation and the development of students' intercultural competence. *Teaching in Higher Education, 22*(5), 532–550. https://doi.org/10.1080/13562517.2016.1273209

Lee, J., & Çiftçi, A. (2014). Asian international students' socio-cultural adaptation: Influence of multicultural personality, assertiveness, academic self-efficacy, and social support. *International Journal of Intercultural Relations, 38,* 97–105. https://doi.org/10.1016/j.ijintrel.2013.08.009

Mamman, A. (1995). Expatriates' intercultural effectiveness: Relevant variables and implications. *Asia Pacific Journal of Human Resources, 33*(1), 40–59. https://doi.org/10.1177/103841119503300103

Margarethe, U., Hannes, H., & Wiesinger, S. (2012). An analysis of the differences in business students' intercultural sensitivity in two degree programmes. *Literacy Information and Computer Education Journal, 3*(3), 667–674. https://doi.org/10.20533/licej.2040.2589.2012.0100

Mcginty, S. A. (2011). Intercultural effectiveness and personality as predictors of performance in multicultural workers. (Unpublished master's thesis). San Diego State University, San Diego, US.

McMurray, A. (2007). Measuring intercultural sensitivity of international and domestic college students: The impact of international travel. (Unpublished master's thesis), University of Florida, Florida, US.

Morales, A. (2017). Intercultural sensitivity, gender, and nationality of third culture kids attending an international high school. *Journal of International Education Research, 13*(1), 35–44. https://doi.org/10.19030/jier.v13i1.9969

Onur Sezer, G., & Bağçeli Kahraman, P. (2016). Evaluating personal qualifications of teacher candidates in terms of intercultural sensitivity levels. *Universal Journal of Educational Research, 4*(12), 1–6. https://doi.org/10.13189/ujer.2016.041301

Paige, R. M. (1993). *Education for the intercultural experience*. Intercultural Press.

Pascarella, E.T., & Terenzini, P.T. (1991). *How college affects students*. Jossey-Bass.

Pedersen, P. J. (2010). Assessing intercultural effectiveness outcomes in a year-long study abroad program. *International Journal of Intercultural Relations, 34*, 70–80. https://doi.org/10.1016/j.ijintrel.2009.09.003

Penbek, Ş., Yurdakul, D. & Cerit, A. (2009). Intercultural communication competence: A study about the intercultural sensitivity of university students based on their education and international experiences. Paper Presented at the European and Mediterranean Conference on Information Systems (EMCIS2009), İzmir, Turkey.

Portalla, T., & Chen, G.M. (2010). The development and validation of the intercultural effectiveness scale. *Intercultural Communication Studies, 19*(3), 21–37.

Pritchard, R. M. O., & Skinner, B. (2002). Cross-cultural partnerships between home and international students. *Journal of Studies in International Education, 6*(4), 323–354. https://doi.org/10.1177/102831502237639

Ruben, B. D. (1976). Assessing communication competency for intercultural adaptation. *Group & Organization Studies, 1*(3), 334–354. https://doi.org/10.1177/105960117600100308

Ruiz-Bernardo, P., Ferrandez-Berrueco, R., & Sales-Ciges, M. (2012). Application of the CIPP model in the study of factors that promote intercultural sensitivity. *Relieve, 18*(2), 1–14. DOI: 10.7203/relieve.18.2.1993

Simkhovych, D. (2009). The relationship between intercultural effectiveness and perceived project team performance in the context of international development. *International Journal of Intercultural Relations, 33*, 383–390. https://doi.org/10.1016/j.ijintrel.2009.06.005

Stone, N. (2006). Conceptualising intercultural effectiveness for university teaching. *Journal of Studies in International Education, 10*(4), 334–356. https://doi.org/10.1177/1028315306287634

Tanaka, T., Takai, J., Kohyama, T., Fujihara, T., & Minami, H. (1997). Effects of social networks on cross-cultural adjustment. *Japanese Psychological Research, 39*(1), 12–24. https://doi.org/10.1111/1468-5884.00032

Thomas, D. C., Brannen, M. Y., & Garcia, D. (2010). Bicultural individuals and intercultural effectiveness. *European Journal of Cross-Cultural Competence and Management, 1*(4), 315–333. DOI:10.1504/EJCCM.2010.037640

Vande Berg, M. (2007). Intervening in the learning of US students abroad. *Journal of Studies in International Education, 11*(3–4), 392–399. https://doi.org/10.1177/1028315307303924

Wang, W., & Ching, G. S. (2015). The role of personality and intercultural effectiveness towards study abroad academic and social activities. *International Journal of Research Studies in Psychology, 4*(4), 13–27. https://doi.org/10.5861/ijrsp.2015.774

Williams, T. (2005). Exploring the impact of the study abroad on students' intercultural communication skills: Adaptability and sensitivity. *Journal of Studies in International Education, 9*(4), 356–371. https://doi.org/10.1177/1028315305277681

Wu, H. (2009). *Intercultural sensitivity of students from departments of nursing and healthcare administration.* Paper presented at the International Conference on Applied Linguistics Department of Applied English, Southern Taiwan University, Taiwan.

Yılmaz, F., & Göçen, S. (2013). Sınıf öğretmeni adaylarının kültürlerarası duyarlılık hakkındaki görüşlerinin farklı değişkenlere göre incelenmesi. *Adıyaman Üniversitesi Sosyal Bilimler Enstitüsü Dergisi, 6*(15), 374–392. https://doi.org/10.14520/adyusbd.649

YOK (2020). Yükseköğretim Bilgi Yönetim Sistemi. Retrieved July 29, 2020, from https://istatistik.yok.gov.tr/

AHSEN AVCILAR has an MSc in Educational Sciences from Recep Tayyip Erdogan University where she serves as an instructor. She is currently a PhD student in Educational Management at Gazi University. Email: ahsen.avcilar@erdogan.edu.tr

ENES GÖK is an associate professor in the department of educational sciences at Karamanoglu Mehmetbey University. He is also currently serving as a consultant at the Higher education Quality Council of Turkey. He holds an MEd (2010) and EdD (2013) in higher education management from the University of Pittsburgh. During his education, he also served as the project associate and program coordinator at the University of Pittsburgh's Institute for International Studies in Education, participating in national and international projects and events. His research interests include higher education administration, internationalization of higher education, comparative education, and quality in higher education. Email: enesgok@gmail.com

Cross-Border Narratives

© *Journal of International Students*
Volume 12, Issue 2 (2022), pp. 550-555
ISSN: 2162-3104 (Print), 2166-3750 (Online)
doi: 10.32674/jis.v12i2.3274
ojed.org/jis

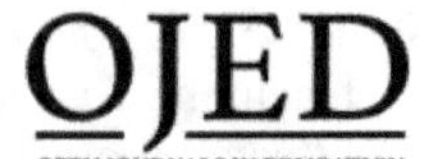

Surviving Impostor Syndrome: Navigating Through the Mental Roller Coaster of a Doctoral Sojourn

Siti Masrifatul Fitriyah
University of Jember

ABSTRACT

Studying overseas may offer myriad riches of extraordinary experiences, especially due to the opportunities to immerse into a different academic culture. However, for some, the difference may be a hurdle that brings them into a mental roller coaster along with their academic career. In this reflective paper, against the backdrop of my overseas studies experiences, I recount my bumpy journey of battling the so-called impostor syndrome which prevented me from being productive until I found the lights at the end of the tunnel and finally found a way to move on with my journey and earned my degree. Self-appreciation and community support seemed to be the most important influences that may have led me to be free from the syndrome and to finally achieve my main objectives.

Keywords: community support, impostor syndrome, mental health, reflection, self-appreciation

Studying in an overseas university, of which academic and social culture may be different from where the students come from, can often carry along with them challenges during the adjustment process in the early stages or in the later phases of their study. Sharing her experiences of such a journey, Palmer (2015) pinpointed how her original academic and social culture differed dramatically from what her overseas university experience offered, which then led her to feel like an outsider. What I experienced during my overseas studies may reflect Palmer's experiences. I pursued my doctoral study in the same overseas university where I obtained my Master's degree. Hence, when starting my doctoral study, I have known most of my lecturers and some of my colleagues and was already familiar with the atmosphere and most of the places in the university. However, being an international student, I also often experienced the feeling of being an outsider and of whether I could be on par with those coming from all different countries.

I wrote this piece of reflective article against the backdrop of my experiences of studying for my doctoral degree in one of the universities in the Midwest of England. Originating from Indonesia, a country in Southeast Asia where English is a foreign language (Kachru, 1990), I often wondered if I could express myself either in writing or in oral presentations in high-quality academic English. The fear of presenting a piece of academic work in unusual or eccentric English to my supervisors, members of audience in conferences, or even my fellow doctoral students in my university kept emerging from time to time. In addition, my perceived differences in the academic culture of the university from that of in my country could have exacerbated the situation. Along my study journey, I battled with a lot of feelings of insecurity, especially the feeling that I was behind everybody else and that everybody else seemed to have better knowledge, better English, better academic writing skills, and better progress in their studies than I did.

My first year ran somewhat more smoothly, as I probably was still in the honeymoon period (Black & Mendenhall, 1991; Schartner & Young, 2015), a phase in my doctoral study when I enjoyed my return to the university immensely. The feeling of becoming an impostor started to show up in my second year, where I felt that everybody seemed to progress much better in their research, draft writing, and their studies than I did. For instance, I knew a couple of colleagues who had published their papers in reputable journals in the early phase of their doctoral study. Being able to publish in a reputable journal is a great achievement in my home country, where the 'publish or perish' culture is getting stronger over these recent years, especially for members of academia like me. Even at that time, my government offered a generous amount of reward for those who can publish their articles in reputable journals. Another example was when I knew that one of my colleagues had finished analyzing his data while I was still struggling with recruiting my participants for my research. This made me worried and kept thinking whether I was on track or was left far behind. These feelings made me struggle to continue with my research and to write my draft. There were times when I was even unable to write a single line despite spending the whole day in front of the computer trying to focus and be productive. This happened for about one term, the whole four months, until one of my colleagues shared her apparently similar feelings with me. That was when I realized that I needed help to cope with these potentially unhealthy feelings.

IMPOSTOR SYNDROME: DO NOT SUFFER IN SILENCE

After some time searching, my colleague and I found a workshop session on mental well-being offered by the students' training center in my university. One of the speakers in the workshop brought up a topic about 'impostor syndrome,' and I was in a state of awe when I heard about this term, and I knew instantly that it was probably what my colleague and I were suffering from. Herrmann (2016) defined impostor syndrome as a feeling that one is not on par with their colleagues in terms of their achievements, intelligence, and that they do not deserve to be in their current position. Those with impostor syndrome often consider that they achieve 'an esteemed position' mainly due to some 'stroke of luck' and not due to their competencies (Feenstra et al., 2020). They often fail to acknowledge their achievements and often think that these are due to 'a lowering of standards, timing of opportunities, or personal charm' (Sverdlik et al., 2018), or due to the help of others, or merely coincidental; meanwhile, they would easily acknowledge their failure as a sign of their perceived 'professional inadequacy' (Bravata et al., 2020).

Wang et al. (2019) believed that this syndrome relates to perfectionism and 'fully mediated the link between perfectionism and anxiety.' These were what could have happened to me. I remember that I was almost always reluctant to submit my assignments or other works before giving them extra-careful repeated checks, as I was worried that there could be errors in my work. I would usually wait until the last minute to submit my work when I thought that nothing else I could do with them to make them more 'perfect'. When the first time I encountered the term impostor syndrome, I was a little relieved, because I then knew what actually may have happened to me. My colleague jokingly said to me that 'if it has a scientific name and many people suffer from it then we should be just "fine".' However, we knew exactly that we were far from being fine. With that realization, I decided that I needed to seek help to free me from the snare of the syndrome.

THE LIGHTS BY THE END OF THE TUNNEL

Self-appreciation

After the realization, I started to reflect on what might be the cause of my impostor syndrome. The first thing that I realized was that I did not give myself sufficient appreciation that I should have deserved. I did not take into account my progress and often compared my achievements with those of my colleagues. I remember how I was intimidated when a colleague finished his data analysis when I, and apparently majority of my colleagues, were still on the data generation stage or when a colleague got their works published. I forgot to put into account how I succeeded to pass my first-year viva without a lot of revisions, or how I got positive responses when I presented my works at conferences. The first-year viva can be a daunting experience for all doctoral students in the United Kingdom as this is the first hurdle that the students have to go through in order to be allowed to continue their studies. In this oral examination, doctoral students are required to present their research proposal to a group of panel examiners who will then decide whether the students need to make some minor changes in their proposal, to rewrite their proposal, or to be considered incompetent to continue the study. The viva is a crucial milestone for the students as this is the first 'break or make' moment and the gate to the actual doctoral student status. Therefore, passing this exam can be an achievement that merits a celebration.

On reflection, I started to realize that everybody had their own pace and also their own challenges. Pursuing a degree is not a race against anyone; it is a race against myself. Hence, I needed to focus on my own goals. As the old saying in my culture, I needed to put on horse winkers and stay focused when working. In my culture, horses are adorned with winkers to prevent them from getting distracted and to ensure that they move straight forward. Therefore, when deciding to wear the figurative horse winkers, I decided to focus on what I aimed to achieve and to avoid comparing myself with others which could be a distraction for me. I also decided to allow myself to be more grateful with every single even so little progress that I make which apparently helped me feel more relieved. This realization helped me immensely to bring my thinking back to work and reduce the level of exhaustion, especially the emotional exhaustion and cynicism which Villwock et al. (2016) mentioned as the impacts of impostor syndrome. Being more self-appreciative allowed me to have better 'positive appraisal of' my values which has protected me against negative influences, to think more positively (Mann et al., 2004) and to eventually improve my mental well-being.

Community Support

We could easily assume that a doctorate study could be a lonely journey, as every other student was busy with thinking about their own research. However, that is not always true. I remember in one of my supervision meetings, my supervisor reminded me not to suffer in silence and that I needed to immediately seek help if I needed one. With that in mind, I started to return to the postgraduate research student network meetings, which I avoided to attend for some time, as I was afraid that I might be discouraged when knowing my colleagues progressed better than I did. Then, I realized how supportive my colleagues were and how everyone had their own problems and battles. It was not that I was happy that everyone may have challenges, I sympathized my colleagues for the problems that they might have, and I believe that my colleagues shared mutual feelings with me. However, people with impostor syndrome, like myself, often over-estimate what others are capable of doing, and underestimate the relentless endeavors of those other people to gain their achievements (Parkman, 2016). I often focused more on what my colleagues had achieved and took little notice of the painstaking efforts they may have done for those achievements.

Our forums always served as a safe zone for us to share our academic work and to seek help for our problems, either academic, social, or psychological. A supportive environment is crucial to help those with impostor syndrome usually linked to low self-esteem; thus, providing constructive feedback instead of criticism will be helpful in this regard (Wang et al., 2019). That was what I felt the doctoral network forum offered: a supportive and comforting environment. With that being said, I ended up co-writing and co-publishing an article with some of my colleagues from the network and when writing this paper, I was on the way to submit another manuscript that I worked with another group of colleagues, also from the network. I remember what Forsdale (1981) highlighted that everyone is 'an island' separated from others, and 'forever physically separated after the umbilical cord is cut'; however, the feelings of anxiousness and desolation urge us to 'create bridges between our islands' so that we can connect with others. Being part of the supportive community helped me immensely and was one of the comforting remedies that helped me reduce my feelings of insecurity. This has helped me feel 'valued, involved' and being an 'integral part' of the academic community which then helped me feel that I am part of the academia (Sverdlik et al., 2020).

After all those realizations, from time to time, the impostor syndrome seemed to reoccur and I felt down again. However, I knew what to do then, i.e., to be thankful for every single progress that I made and also to be thankful for being part of the supportive community. With self-care and appreciation and ample support from my community, finally I found the lights by the end of the tunnel, which eventually led me to finish my doctoral study and to earn my degree.

ETHICAL CONSIDERATIONS

This work has not been reviewed by the Institutional Review Board (IRB) of my home university as it does not involve any other participants other than myself. However, to ensure ethicality, I anonymize the names and places that come up in this reflective account.

REFERENCES

Black, J. S., & Mendenhall, M. (1991). The U-curve adjustment hypothesis revisited: A review and theoretical framework. *Journal of International Business Studies,* *22*(2), 225–247. https://doi.org/10.1057/palgrave. jibs.8490301

Bravata, D. M., Watts, S. A., Keefer, A. L., Madhusudhan, D. K., Taylor, K. T., Clark, D. M., Nelson, R. S., Cokley, K. O., & Hagg, H. K. (2020). Prevalence, predictors, and treatment of impostor syndrome: A systematic review. In *Journal of General Internal Medicine* (Vol. 35, Issue 4, pp. 1252–1275). Springer. https://doi.org/10.1007/s11606-019-05364-1

Feenstra, S., Begeny, C. T., Ryan, M. K., Rink, F. A., Stoker, J. I., & Jordan, J. (2020). Contextualizing the impostor "syndrome." *Frontiers in Psychology,* *11*(November), 1–6. https://doi.org/10.3389/fpsyg.2020.575024

Forsdale, L. (1981). *Perspectives on Communication*. Reading, Massachusetts: Addison-Wesley.

Herrmann, R. (2016). *Impostor syndrome is definitely a thing*. The Chronicle of Higher Education.

Kachru, B. (1990). World Englishes and linguistic landscapes. *World Englishes,* *9*(1), 3–20. https://doi.org/10.1111/j.1467-971X.2011.01748.x

Mann, M., Hosman, C. M. H., Schaalma, H. P., & De Vries, N. K. (2004). Self-esteem in a broad-spectrum approach for mental health promotion. In *Health*

Education Research (Vol. 19, Issue 4, pp. 357–372). Oxford Academic. https://doi.org/10.1093/her/cyg041

Palmer, Y. (2015). The not-so-easy road of overseas study: Life like an outsider. *Journal of International Students, 5*(4), 541–544. http://jistudents.org

Parkman, A. (2016). The imposter phenomenon in higher education: Incidence and impact. *Journal of Higher Education Theory and Practice, 16*(1), 51. https://articlegateway.com/index.php/JHETP/article/view/1936

Schartner, A., & Young, T. (2015). Culture shock or love at first sight? Exploring the "honeymoon" stage of the international student sojourn. In *Transcultural interaction and linguistic diversity in higher education: The student experience* (pp. 12–33). Palgrave Macmillan. https://doi.org/ 10.1057/9781137397478_2

Sverdlik, A., Hall, N. C., & McAlpine, L. (2020). PhD imposter syndrome: Exploring antecedents, consequences, and implications for doctoral well-being. *International Journal of Doctoral Studies, 15,* 737–758. https://doi.org/10.28945/4670

Sverdlik, A., Hall, N. C., McAlpine, L., & Hubbard, K. (2018). The PhD experience: A review of the factors influencing doctoral students' completion, achievement, and well-being. *International Journal of Doctoral Studies, 13,* 361–388. https://doi.org/10.28945/4113

Villwock, J. A., Sobin, L. B., Koester, L. A., & Harris, T. M. (2016). Impostor syndrome and burnout among American medical students: A pilot study. *International Journal of Medical Education, 7,* 364–369. https://doi.org/ 10.5116/ijme.5801.eac4

Wang, K. T., Sheveleva, M. S., & Permyakova, T. M. (2019). Imposter syndrome among Russian students: The link between perfectionism and psychological distress. *Personality and Individual Differences, 143*(September 2018), 1–6. https://doi.org/10.1016/j.paid.2019.02.005

SITI MASRIFATUL FITRIYAH, PhD is a lecturer in Education at the Department of Language and Arts Education, Jember University, Indonesia. Her major research interests include narrative inquiry, language policy, teacher education, bilingual education, and researching multilingually. Email: s.fitriyah@unej.ac.id/ fitrikurn77@gmail.com.

Book Review

© *Journal of International Students*
Volume 12, Issue 2 (2022), pp. 556-559
ISSN: 2162-3104 (Print), 2166-3750 (Online)
doi: 10.32674/jis.v12i2.4722
ojed.org/jis

Review of Building Internationalized Spaces: Second Language Perspectives on Developing Language and Cultural Exchange Programs in Higher Education

Marisa Lally
Lynch School of Education and Human Development, Boston College

Building Internationalized Spaces: Second Language Perspectives *on Developing Language and Cultural Exchange Programs in Higher Education* (Allen et al., 2022) offers case studies of higher education contexts, where the intersection of English language education and internationalization of curriculum at colleges and universities is in evidence. The central argument of the book is that educators should cultivate international/global pers-pectives among all students, but should simultaneously dedicate attention to the specific needs of unique student populations and learning contexts. By exploring various cases that offer practical insights into expanding the boundaries of "traditional" second-language education, this volume aims to "refine internationalization in terms of praxis and indicate how to coordinate curricular and pedagogical efforts to achieve meaningful learning outcomes for all students" (p. 10).

Scholars and practitioners of second-language acquisition and internationalization of curriculum in higher education will benefit from accessing the successes and challenges associated with the innovative practices presented in this book by the educators. The cases represent not only intervention strategies for internationalizing formal classroom curricula but also for the informal curriculum (Leask, 2015), including a university's support services and extracurricular activities that facilitate learning.

The book is divided into two parts: Part I: Revising the Curriculum and Part II: Internationalizing Composition. The first part consists of case studies of various interventions to support English language learners, either international students at American universities or participants in a virtual exchange between American and international universities. The second part explores challenges faced by administrators and educators working with L2 writing and cross-cultural composition programs.

The introduction of the book confronts the evergreen challenge of acknowledging problems with the positioning of English as the dominant language across internationalized higher education systems, while also highlighting its centrality to the process of internationalization given the expectation that university students be proficient in the English language. The editors of the volume argue that scholars have paid little attention to the crucial role that English language professionals and training programs play in the process of internationalization. This theme remains present throughout subsequent chapters, in which contributors to this book (both practitioners and the researchers of relevant programs) explore successes, challenges, and emerging best practices.

Of the nine chapters included in this volume, six focus on programs housed at U.S. universities, one at a Canadian university, one at a Sino-US institution based in China, and one of them at a Colombian university. Although the editors aim to have an intentionally global focus in the volume at hand, readers will find that the book has an explicitly American focus in that the programs highlighted often explore international students' experiences with L2 curriculum in the United States, and with an emphasis on cross-cultural engagement between international and domestic students in extracurricular programs and student support services, both on campus and virtually.

The editors' decision to include chapters that explore the successes and challenges of English language education in virtual spaces is timely, given the dependence on virtual education during the COVID-19 pandemic. The focus on digital education also underscores opportunities for institutions that may be limited in resources such as classroom space and/or travel budgets. The two contributions regarding virtual exchange explore programs that encompass vlogs, digital storytelling, and video conferencing between exchange students. The chapters found that students experienced gains in both cultural understanding such as pragmatic communication strategies in English as well as confidence in their

English language abilities. These pieces not only support the argument that English language instruction is essential to internationalization of higher education but they also demonstrate the efficacy of Internationalization at Home (IaH) strategies through gains in students' self-efficacy in cultural understanding and greater engagement in internationalization from stakeholders across campuses.

The chapters that comprise Part II make a strong case that there should be a scholarly and practical conversation between the areas of internationalization of higher education and English writing and composition. The courses analyzed in these studies often featured "distinct pedagogical features" (p. 158) from their non-internationally focused course counterparts, such as an explicit focus on culture in assignments, applying a multicultural lens to content and grading, and interdisciplinary and "multi-local" engagement for graduate students. Students in these studies expressed that there was a diversity of perspectives present in the classroom and that the course assignments helped them consider cultural values outside of their own in a new way. These findings support Leask's (2015) argument that internationalization efforts have educational benefits to all students and therefore university stakeholders should consider a local implementation of an internationalized curriculum.

While the researchers highlighted the various positive outcomes of interventions in their writing curricula, such as students' increased confidence in their writing skills and expressed gains in various cultural competencies, they also provided potential practical implications for their work. To synthesize the practical implications of the studies in Part II, the scholars argue that practitioners supporting English composition programs should engage stakeholders such as students, academic advisors, and the institution's registrar in participatory curriculum building activities. For example, these stakeholders can provide input on the specific needs of the student population at the HEI, including ESL pedagogical concepts in cross-cultural composition classrooms, and intentionally providing appropriate support services to students like the ones explored in Part I of the book.

Readers of this collection can expect to learn about internationalization in degree and non-degree English language education and cross-cultural engagement among university students in *"contact zones,"* or "social spaces where cultures meet, clash, and grapple with each other, often in contexts of highly asymmetrical relations of power, such as colonialism, slavery, or other aftermaths as they are lived out in many parts of the world today" (Pratt in Gerwash, 2022, p. 171). This book will be particularly useful for higher education professionals who engage with issues of internationalization and cross-cultural pedagogy, especially in the context of the United States. Its primary contribution is highlighting the crucial connection between English language education and internationalization of higher education.

REFERENCES

Allen, M., Ene, E., & McIntosh, K. (2022). *Building internationalized spaces: Second language perspectives on developing language and cultural exchange programs in higher education.* University of Michigan Press. [Global].

Gerwash, G. (2022). Reaching across the aisle: Internationalization through cross-cultural composition courses. In M. Allen, E. Ene, & K. McIntosh (Eds.), *Building internationalized spaces: Second language perspectives on developing language and cultural exchange programs in higher education* (pp. 165–185). University of Michigan Press. [Global].

Leask, B. (2015). *Internationalizing the curriculum.* Routledge.

MARISA LALLY, M.A., is a doctoral student at the Lynch School of Education and Human Development at Boston College. Her research interests include national identity, educational diplomacy, and the internationalization of higher education. Email lallyml@bc.edu

Book Review

© *Journal of International Students*
Volume 12, Issue 2 (2022), pp. 560-563
ISSN: 2162-3104 (Print), 2166-3750 (Online)
doi: 10.32674/jis.v12i2.4729
ojed.org/jis

Humanizing Methodologies in Educational Research: Centering Non-Dominant Communities

By C. C. Reyes, S. J. Haines, & K. Clark. (2021). Teachers College Press, US. ISBN 13 978-0807765548

Reviewed by Xinyue Zuo, *University of Massachusetts, Amherst, US*

Amid the COVID-19 pandemic and continued instances of systemic racism, societies of trauma unfold before us. The impact of these and other events on school children, especially those from non-dominant families, compels a growing number of scholars and educators to act and render care and support. In this context, the book *Humanizing Methodologies in Educational Research: Centering Non-Dominant Communities* written by Reyes et al. was born. These authors apply Ishimaru et al.'s (2016) definition of *non-dominant groups*, which are groups comprising low-income, immigrants/refugees, and other groups of color, marginalized by dominant institutions. They reflect on ethical concerns and methodological challenges associated with leading a community-based research project, *Centering Connections*, which explored the relationship between refugee families and schools. Engaging in critical reflexivity, the authors examine the complex dynamics of power relations in research relationships, particularly between researchers and refugee participants and detail how a humanizing approach is a powerful tool for fostering mutually beneficial researcher-participant relationships. The book challenges the conventional stance of researchers remaining impersonal and neutral, an elitist view of researchers as all-knowing experts, and deficit-based stereotypes of refugee communities.

The book provides practical strategies for research alongside marginalized communities and insightful thoughts on applying humanizing approaches in future qualitative research.

In Chapter 1, the authors delve into relationship building with non-dominant communities, focusing on researchers' commitment to participants. The authors argue that the humanizing approach, based on decolonizing self-reflection within the Filipino concept of *Kapawa* and critical, postcolonial, and feminist theoretical frameworks, helped them cope with the relational tensions encountered in *Centering Connections*. The approach is mainly composed of three key elements: critical reflexivity, humility, and reciprocity. Critical reflexivity requires intentional listening (Paris, 2011) to understand others' ways of knowing, and examining one's own epistemology to develop an awareness of the unequal power dynamics in research relationships. Humility calls for respecting and centering others' ways of knowing and generating learning through dialogic engagement. Reciprocity involves a transactional "give and take" (Harrison et al., 2001) and researchers' initiative to interpret, represent, and center participants' voices. These concepts guide humanizing research relationships, as explained in the chapters to follow.

Chapter 2 examines tensions arising in navigating the Institutional Review Board (IRB) process and following IRB standards regarding research on non-dominant communities, especially with respect to recruiting, obtaining informed consent, and interviews. It discusses the limitations of IRB protocols and questions the term "vulnerable population," which fails to acknowledge participants' strengths and assets. The authors advise researchers to critically examine the language of consent forms and interview protocols and build relationships with participants while maintaining full consideration of the cultural, linguistic, and historical differences to ensure meaningful and respectful engagement.

In Chapter 3, the authors reflect on their experiences working with student researchers (students with refugee backgrounds and their U.S.-born peers), particularly around the dynamics of relationships. The authors emphasize that principal investigators should position themselves as learners and teachers and construct a comfortable, personal, and growing space for the team to thrive. Humanizing the relationship within the team would enable co-construction of knowledge, negotiating meaning from the lenses of cultural insiders and outsiders. Recommended practices for working with students are also put forward.

As principal investigators and the refugee families did not share the same language, partnership with interpreters was essential across the research project in focus here. In Chapter 4, the authors discuss their experiences in working with interpreters through a decolonizing lens. The salient roles different types of interpreters (home-school liaisons, student researchers, and other community members) played are highlighted, including, yet not limited to, participant recruitment, data collection, and data interpretation. The authors also elucidate how interpreters might filter data, thus underscoring the importance of understanding interpreters' connections with the community, seeking interpreters' understanding of the project, and building trust with them.

Chapter 5 further elucidates what "reciprocity" means for both researchers and participants, expanding the notion to encompass "relational reciprocating actions like processing, advocating, and amplifying voices" (p. 129). The authors posit that to make the research mutually beneficial, researchers should approach a project with decent care of relationship-building, creating a space not only for participants to recount their stories but also for researchers themselves to listen intentionally to gain knowledge and establish friendships. Participants' voices as insiders and "co-thinkers" (p. 129) should be respected and augmented through researchers' probing, writing, and disseminating research results.

The authors devoted Chapter 6 to the methodological reflections of guest researchers on their work with "vulnerable" groups. Two guest authors describe a five-step research model they developed for researching individuals with disabilities that stresses focusing on participants' needs and including them throughout the research process. They suggest including reflexivity at every stage, positioning participants as co-researchers and co-constructors of knowledge, and committing to them. Another guest author presents research with undocumented students, demonstrating the importance of transparency, rapport, trustworthiness, and confidentiality in maintaining a connected relationship. The consensus among guest authors is the need for culturally responsive research designs.

The authors conclude the book by summarizing significant insights from each chapter and offering implications to inform future research. The authors recommend (1) creating an inclusive, transparent research space by critically self-reflecting on preconceptions and analytic foci and by simultaneously helping mentees establish such mindset; (2) conducting follow-up participant interviews to co-construct knowledge; (3) engaging multiple embedded case studies; and (4) building dynamic relationships to ensure iterative community responses.

From interrogating the language used in IRB protocols through data analysis, the authors expound on tensions, challenges, and ambiguities researchers experience when performing research with non-dominant populations. This book heightens our awareness of dilemmas researchers frequently encounter by detailing researchers' experiences and presenting relevant examples substantiating the authors' proposed process for pursuing a humanizing approach to research.

Centering Connections describes the intricacies of employing the humanizing approach while critically reflecting on the process. The authors offer insightful, practical strategies for employing this approach, based on the authors' and guest authors' experiences. Interwoven throughout and heavily emphasized is the necessity for researchers to gain participants' trust and build dynamic, respectful, and reciprocal relationships with non-dominant participants, teachers, schools, and interpreters. Through vivid descriptive stories, the authors solidify their case for humanizing research by citing the impossibility of producing iterative community responses yielding substantial change and/or supportive resources for refugee children without it.

The book encourages self-reflexivity and reiterates how researchers should assume the role of a learner. As argued by Nieto in the foreword, researchers should be "more vulnerable, more human, and less certain of our own expertise and knowledge" (p. 12). The authors of *Centering Connections* do a remarkable job of deconstructing deficit perspectives toward refugee families in educational literature. Further, the book makes a valuable contribution to the dearth of literature regarding the ethics of performing research with non-dominant populations.

School administrators, teachers, liaisons, researchers, and members of non-dominant communities can benefit from the ideas this book presents. Policymakers in universities can also derive lessons concerning policies and practices for researching non-dominant populations. While the book reported on a study situated within the educational context, the publication's insights may be generalized and applied across disciplines. Readers may note that the language used to define concepts like "humility" and "reciprocity" distracts from some salient points. Simplifying the verbiage used to describe essential concepts would enhance reader engagement and connectivity with concepts and their applications. However, this does not detract from the overall quality of publication.

REFERENCES

Harrison, J., MacGibbon, L., & Morton, M. (2001). Regimes of trustworthiness in qualitative research: The rigors of reciprocity. *Qualitative Inquiry, 7*(3), 323–345. https://doi.org/10.1177800401100700305

Ishimaru, A. M., Torres, K. E., Salvador, J. E., Lott, J. II, Williams, D. M. C., & Tran, C. (2016). Reinforcing deficit, journeying toward equity: Cultural brokering in family engagement initiatives. *American Educational Research Journal, 53*(4), 850–822. https://doi.org/10.3102/0002831216657178

Paris, D. (2011). "A friend who understand fully:" Notes on humanizing research on a multiethnic youth community. *International Journal of Qualitative Studies in Education, 24*(2), 137–149. https://doi.org/10.1080/09518398.2010.495091

XINYUE ZUO, MAT-TESOL, is a doctoral candidate in Teacher Education and Curriculum Studies at the University of Massachusetts Amherst. Her research focuses on language and literacy development of English language learners, second-language acquisition, and educational bilingual interpreting. Email: xzuo@umass.edu